CW01082560

Operational Risk

FT Prentice Hall
FINANCIAL TIMES

In an increasingly competitive world, we believe it's quality of thinking that will give you the edge – an idea that opens new doors, a technique that solves a problem, or an insight that simply makes sense of it all. The more you know, the smarter and faster you can go.

That's why we work with the best minds in business and finance to bring cutting-edge thinking and best learning practice to a global market.

Under a range of leading imprints, including Financial Times Prentice Hall, we create world-class print publications and electronic products bringing our readers knowledge, skills and understanding which can be applied whether studying or at work.

To find out more about our business publications, or tell us about the books you'd like to find, you can visit us at
www.business-minds.com

For other Pearson Education publications, visit
www.pearsoned-ema.com

PEARSON
Education

Operational Risk

Regulation, Analysis and Management

edited by

CAROL ALEXANDER

 Prentice Hall
FINANCIAL TIMES

An imprint of Pearson Education

London · New York · Toronto · Sydney · Tokyo · Singapore · Hong Kong · Cape Town
New Delhi · Madrid · Paris · Amsterdam · Munich · Milan · Stockholm

PEARSON EDUCATION LIMITED

Head Office:
Edinburgh Gate
Harlow CM20 2JE
Tel: +44 (0)1279 623623
Fax: +44 (0)1279 431059

London Office:
128 Long Acre
London WC2E 9AN
Tel: +44 (0)20 7447 2000
Fax: +44 (0)20 7447 2170
Website: www.business-minds.com

First published in Great Britain in 2003

© Pearson Education Limited 2003

The right of Carol Alexander to be identified as Author of this Work has been
asserted by her in accordance with the Copyright, Designs and Patents Act 1988.

ISBN 0 273 65966 9

British Library Cataloguing in Publication Data
A CIP catalogue record for this book can be obtained from the British Library

This publication is designed to provide accurate and authoritative information in regard
to the subject matter covered. It is sold with the understanding that neither the authors
nor the publisher is engaged in rendering legal, investing, or any other professional service.
If legal advice or other expert assistance is required, the service of a competent
professional person should be sought.

The publisher and contributors make no representation, express or implied, with regard
to the accuracy of the information contained in this book and cannot accept any
responsibility or liability for any errors or omissions that it may contain.

10 9 8 7 6 5 4 3 2 1

Typeset by Pantek Arts Ltd, Maidstone, Kent
Printed and bound in Great Britain by Bookcraft Ltd, Midsomer Norton

The Publishers' policy is to use paper manufactured from sustainable forests.

To Julian Walmsley, a much valued colleague at the ISMA Centre,
who died before completing his chapter on
Operational Risks in Transactions Processing

About the authors

Carol Alexander has written and edited 14 books on mathematics and finance. She consults on the design, development and testing of software for risk management and investment analysis including new models for: GARCH, index tracking, statistical arbitrage, volatility trading, VaR and arbitrage trading. Her recent software designs include a high frequency pricing model for actively managed exchange traded funds and operational risk capital models.

Current research interests are in quantitative hedge fund strategies, orthogonal factor models, calibration of multi-factor pricing models, local volatilities, new GARCH models and lognormal mixture densities.

She was educated at the University of Sussex and the London School of Economics, obtaining a PhD in Algebraic Number Theory and an MSc in Mathematical Economics and Econometrics. In 1996 she became the (part-time) Academic Director of Algorithmics Inc. and in 1998, after 13 years at the University of Sussex mathematics department, she joined Nikko Global Holdings as a Director and Head of Market Risk Modelling. Since 1999 she has been Chair of Risk Management and Director of Research at the ISMA Centre, Reading University, UK. She is also Chair of the Academic Advisory Council of PRMIA.

Dr. Ulrich Anders is Head of Operational Risk in Dresdner Bank Group. He is responsible for the introduction of a comprehensive operational risk process that allows for a pro-active and prudent management of operational risks as well as for the fulfilment of the Basel II operational risk regulatory requirements.

Previously Dr. Anders was employed at Deutsche Bank for market and operational risk and at ZEW for financial market analysis as well as press related activities. Besides his activities in operational risk Dr. Anders has in the past seven years intensively worked on risk management issues such as Raroc and Eva, integration of market and credit risk, e-risks etc.

Dr. Anders is Master of Business Engineering, holds a PhD in the subject of Statistics and Finance as well as an MBA in General Management.

Tony Blunden is Director of operational risk in Ernst & Young's Financial Services Risk Management practice. Tony's areas of focus are the identification and advancement of clients' needs, the development of Ernst & Young's risk product set and internal development. Tony's skill set also includes in-depth knowledge of OTC derivatives and structured products, and financial services compliance.

His recent assignments have included assisting and advising clients on modelling risks and controls particularly using a Scorecard approach, developing and implementing a board risk policy, dimensioning operational risk including risk appetite, investigating and monitoring key indicators, sourcing and using loss events and validating the Basel II operational risk process.

He has worked for a variety of leading City of London firms including banks, full service houses, exchange brokers, an insurance broker, commodity companies, LME companies and consultancies. Tony is a member of the Securities Institute, GARP and ORRF and a Fellow of the Institute of Chartered Secretaries and Administrators.

Victor Dowd is a policy advisor within the UK Financial Services Authority. He is responsible for operational risk policy development and has been heavily engaged with the development of the new Accord through representation on the Basel Risk Management Group and Quantitative Impact Study Group. In addition he is a member of FSA's Operational Risk Implementation Advisory Group. Beyond the FSA, Victor is a member of the Centre for Risk and Insurance Studies advisory board at Nottingham University Business School as well as being a founding member and active participant of the Operational Risk Research Forum. Prior to joining the FSA, he held a number of academic positions, including posts at the University of Cambridge and London University during which time he published papers on mathematical modelling within an engineering context. Victor has a Ph.D. and B.Sc. in Chemistry and an MBA from the University of Kent.

Christos Hadjiemmanuil is a Senior Lecturer in Law at the London School of Economics and a partner in Law Office E. Stratigis, Athens, Greece. He studied law at Athens University (LL.B.) and University College, London (LL.M. and Ph.D.). Prior to joining the LSE, he taught at the Centre for Commercial Law Studies, Queen Mary & Westfield College, and at SMU School of Law, Dallas, Texas. He is the author of the monograph *Banking Regulation and the Bank of England* (LLP, 1996) and a co-editor of a collected volume on EMU. He has also written many articles in the fields of European financial services law, EMU and financial law reform. He teaches postgraduate (LL.M.) courses on European and UK Banking Law, Regulation of Financial Markets, Securities Regulation, EU Law: Economic and Monetary Union, and International Trade Law.

 **Lloyd Hardin** is a Managing Director of OpVantage and leads the product management group and the operational risk consulting division. He has managed consulting assignments that designed and implemented numerous operational risk quantification programmes at major North American, European and Asian financial institutions. Previously, he was a Principal Consultant in the Financial Risk Management practice at PricewaterhouseCoopers in New York where he specialized in developing and implementing models to quantify operational risk for financial institutions and conducted workshops in the collection and categorization of a firm's internal loss data. Prior to this, he worked for Farrell-Wako Global Investment Management, Inc., where he designed an automated trading and allocation system using Excel and Advent to manage client portfolios. He has also worked for Merrill Lynch and Company, as a Project Manager. He holds a BA in Economics from the University of Notre Dame and an MBA in Finance from the Columbia Business School.

 **Michael Haubenstock** is Director of Risk Management at Capital One, a leading consumer finance company. He is responsible for operational risk management and building an enterprise risk management function. Throughout 2001, he was a Partner in the Financial Risk Management practice at PricewaterhouseCoopers where he led the practice for operational risk management for financial institutions. He has worked with leading domestic and international banks in diverse areas including building operational risk policies and methodologies, quantifying operational risk capital, establishing corporate risk functions, assessing risk measurement models, and developing economic capital measurement techniques to support capital allocation.

Michael holds a Bachelor of Science degree from the University of Pennsylvania, a Master of Science degree from Washington University and an MBA from New York University.

Thomas Michael Leddy lives in Zurich and works in a marketing function with Fox Pitt-Kelton (a subsidiary of Swiss Re and part of the Financial Services Business Group) in the Convergence Unit within the Corporate Finance department. He has special responsibility for liaison with the 'Basel Committee' and the European Union on Operational Risks issues.

He has worked for Swiss Re's Legal and Claims department advising on contentious and non-contentious issues for the Engineering, Banking and Credit special lines departments, and from 1997, he worked for leading firms of solicitors specializing in commercial insurance and, in particular, reinsurance, after this he transferred to the global banking practice of Swiss Re New Markets to take up an underwriting role.

Thomas graduated in Political Theories and Institutions from Sheffield University and a post-graduate Diploma in Law from City University in London. He was called to the Bar in 1985 and subsequently admitted as a solicitor in 1990.

Ralph Andrew Nash was a member of the Secretariat of the Basel Committee on Banking Supervision, based at the Bank for International Settlements in Basel, Switzerland when he wrote this chapter. There he was deeply involved in the development of the new Basel Capital Accord. He was Secretary of the Risk Management Group (RMG) and Transparency Group (TG) of the Committee. Prior to Switzerland, Ralph was an analyst in the Financial Stability Area of the Bank of England, focusing on Regulatory Policy where he reviewed the development of the Financial Services and Markets Act and analyzed the impact of regulatory policy in specific areas (deposit protection, market abuse). Immediately prior to working at the Bank of England, Ralph was a Specialist Assistant to the House of Commons Treasury Select Committee, where he worked on enquiries into the collapse of Baring's Bank, Financial Services Regulation, regulation of Lloyd's of London and the regulation and governance of the London Stock Exchange. Ralph holds an M.A. in Geography from Girton College, Cambridge. He is currently the Basel II Operational Risk co-ordinator in the Group Risk function of Royal Bank of Scotland Group in London. Away from work Ralph enjoys football (watching Arsenal, playing for Old Finchleians) and discovering new restaurants (with wife Rose).

 **Anthony Peccia** is a Vice President at the Bank of Montreal (BMO). He is responsible for developing best practice operational risk policies, methodologies and infrastructures as well as developing and implementing treasury market risk management policies and monitoring systems. He is currently the BMO representative and chair of the Operational Management Committee of the Canadian Bankers Association. He chairs the Industry Technical Working Group on Operational Risk, which regularly advises the Risk Management Group of the Basel Committee on Banking Supervision.

Anthony has 20 years' experience in Treasury and Market Risk Management. Prior to joining BMO in 2002, he was with the Canadian Imperial Bank of Commerce in various senior risk management roles. Prior to CIBC he was the Assistant Treasurer of Royal Bank of Canada. Anthony Peccia has an MBA from McGill University and an MSc in Mathematical Physics.

 **Jacques Pézier** worked in the City of London for 20 years, most recently as General Manager at Credit Agricole Lazard Financial Products Bank (CAL FP). Previously, he was Executive Director with Mitsubishi Finance International plc (MFIL, now TMI) in charge of Research and Product Development as well as Risk Management, and Director with Barclays, de Zoete, Wedd (BZW) in the Risk Management Unit of the Equity Division.

He began his career in academia as a lecturer at the Thayer School of Engineering, Dartmouth College, USA and then as assistant professor, HEC and ISA, Paris – before moving into consulting for Stanford Research Institute and Investment Intelligence Systems Corporation, a consulting firm he founded with colleagues and which specializes in decision systems in finance.

He graduated from Ecole Centrale (Paris) and holds a DEA in mathematical physics and a PhD in decision theory. He is currently Visiting Professor at the ISMA Centre, Reading University where he will help create a centre for financial risk management. He also holds titles of Visiting Professor at the Academy of Economic Studies, Bucharest, and Honorary Professor of the University of Warwick.

Diane Reynolds is Senior Financial Engineer and Product Manager for Algorithmics in London. Her primary responsibilities are in marketing, research and product design specification, and she has contributed significantly to the development and launch of Algo OpRisk. Before joining the Algo OpRisk team she was responsible for design, implementation and support of Algorithmics' scenario solution for market and credit risk. She has extensive knowledge and experience of risk technology development and project implementation at major financial institutions. Diane holds a masters degree in computing and mathematics from the University of Waterloo, Canada.

Kenneth Swenson is a senior examiner operational risk on the Federal Reserve Bank of Chicago and is responsible for organizing and leading regulatory operational risk examinations of large, complex banking organizations (LCBOs), many with an international presence as well as capital markets activities. He has been a banking regulator since 1990 and was selected to assist the International Monetary Fund and National Bank of Ukraine in an on-site diagnostic examination of the eight largest banks in Kiev, Ukraine during the Russian debt crisis.

In addition to his undergraduate degree in Economics from the University of Iowa and an MSc in Financial Markets and Trading from the Illinois Institute of Technology, Ken has earned the Bank Administration Institute Certified Bank Auditor designation and is a Certified Risk Professional. He can be contacted by email: usken1@attbi.com

David Syer is Director of Operational Risk at Algorithmics in London, and an expert in operational risk analytics. He is responsible for all aspects of operational risk at Algorithmics, including business strategy, business development, research, technical design, software architecture, product development and marketing. He holds a doctorate degree in Astrophysics from Cambridge University.

Contents

PART II

Analysis

PART III

Management

Foreword

Operational risk is an important and live issue for banks, and indeed for financial institutions generally. The decision by the Basel Committee on Banking Supervision – which develops standards for the minimum capital to be held by internationally active banks in the G10 – to establish a charge for operational risk as part of the new Basel Accord has led to a wide-spread debate. That debate has however, highlighted the range of views on the importance of operational risk, on how it should be measured and on whether it should give rise to a regulatory capital charge – all questions tackled in this volume.

Fraud and other operational-type risks have caused large losses and even the failure of a significant number of large firms – for example, Drexels and Barings[1]. There are, however, serious challenges for any firm in quantifying its operational risk exposure. Major operational risk events are infrequent. Data within individual firms tend to relate to higher frequency and smaller events, so that access to cross-industry data is one important element in exploring the assessment of operational risk. Another consideration is that, unlike credit and market risk where the shock is exogenous to the firm, operational risk is endogenous. It depends upon the structure and effectiveness of the systems and controls within the firm. The first line of defence therefore has to lie in the design of the systems and the incentive structures within the firms. Capital requirements can only be a second-line defence.

But should capital requirements be used at all in the regulatory response to this risk? Banks taking significant operational risks (custodians, payment system banks) may have little credit or market risk, so that relying on capital requirements derived from credit and market exposures may be inappropriate. Also, even for firms with substantial credit and market risk, it cannot be assumed that operational risk is uncorrelated with those risks. The original operational event may be uncorrelated, but the loss may be more likely to be exposed when there is stress on the firm – when it becomes more difficult to hide a fraud for example. Other operational risks may be directly related to the wider problems a firm is experiencing. For example, a firm suffering widespread problem loans may find that its processes for handling the sale of collateral become overloaded, leaving scope for fraud. The firm therefore may have to cover the loss at the worst possible moment in terms of its overall profitability and capitalization.

---

[1] Controlling Securities Fraud, Jacvkson P and W Perraudin, Bank of England Financial Stability Review, Autumn 1997.

Another complex issue highlighted by these examples relates to the boundaries between different types of risk. For example, when is a large loss given default related to inadequate processes within a firm, e.g. the failure to maximise the value of collateral or security sold by the bank when the borrower has defaulted, an operational rather than a credit event? It is important that the quality of the credit risk data should not be undermined now by changing the definition of credit loss in an attempt to strip out operational risk.

Going forward, another important consideration is that regulation of operational risk provides the right incentives to encourage the design of better systems to control and measure the risk within the banks. Therefore any change in regulation needs to be reviewed in this light as well. One very live debate relates to the extent to which risk mitigation through insurance should be recognized in the capital requirements and the incentive effects.

The firms too need to give careful thought to the internal incentives for operational risk to be controlled and problems dealt with. With some of the past cases of major loss, the systems had been in place but had not been fully or effectively implemented. In other cases, systems and controls deficiencies had been spotted but no action had been taken to address them. In effect the controls had been over-ridden.

With the Basel Committee introducing explicit capital requirements for operational risk in 2006 as part of the proposed new Accord many of these questions need to be discussed. This book will provide an important contribution to that debate.

Patricia Jackson
Head of the Financial Industry and Regulation Division
Bank of England

Preface

This book was published towards the end of the long consultative period for Basel II that began in 1999. The possibility of capital charges for operational risks first alarmed the banking industry, then spurred its members into action. There have been seemingly endless debates on whether such capital charges are indeed appropriate. At the same time, numerous methods for quantifying operational risks have been developed and tested, many of which have now been discarded. Is it even possible to 'measure' operational risks, given the paucity of 'hard' data of the type we have grown accustomed to with market and, to a lesser extent, credit risk?

While opinions diverge on all these issues, at least one general consensus seems to have emerged, and that is that the management of operational risks – whatever that means – is a 'good thing'. The financial industry is peculiar in that its compensation structure can reward some dubious management (and accounting) practices. If Pillar 1 charges for operational risks are not, in the end, imposed – and even now after all this costly debate, this is not certain – at least the debate has helped to raise awareness of the need to improve operational risk management in banks.

There are three parts to this book: Regulation, Analysis and Management. On the one hand, the contributions have been chosen to reflect the accepted views that have emerged after much industry debate. Thus, for example, you will find no chapters on some of the advanced quantitative approaches that have fallen by the wayside in our quest to find a suitable operational risk capital model. Instead it will become evident as you read the book that a unified framework for measuring and managing operational risks is now being developed. On the other hand, the proposed regulation of operational risk, and Pillar 1 in particular, continues to divide the industry. So, when choosing the chapters for this book, I have attempted to represent all sides of this debate and several chapters contain disparate views of the same issue.

Are operational risks negligible in comparison to market and credit risks? How should data be used to quantify very low-frequency operational risks with scorecards or external data? Is it meaningful to even attempt to 'measure' these? Are the Basel Committee's Pillar 2 recommendations in its *Sound Practices* documents actually helpful or could they be counterproductive? And what *is* operational risk management, anyway? These are just some of the issues that will be debated in the pages to come.

Part I: Regulation opens with a personal view from a member of the Secretariat of the Basel Committee on the three pillars of operational risk regulation. Its stance on the Pillar 1 capital charge appears to remain firm, although the optimistic amongst us might perceive some signs of a path being laid for a gracious acceptance of defeat. Chapter 2 continues the supervisory theme, discussing some of the guidance on *Sound Practices* from Basel and the 'Risk-Focused Manual' from the US Federal Reserve. The aim of the chapter is to help management to identify, monitor and control all types of operational risks. It also provides an overview of managerial and corporate governance structures and how these relate to the reporting and management of operational risks.

In Chapter 3, the Financial Services Authority in London make their case for the supervision of operational risks under the new Basel Accord. The Basic Indicator and Standardized Approaches for quantifying the operational risk capital charge are explained and justified in some detail. The chapter ends with a discussion of how banks can identify their operational risk exposures and assess their potential impact; monitor and report operational risks on an ongoing basis; and create proper incentives by factoring operational risk into their overall business strategy.

Having heard the views from the regulators, the next three chapters provide an independent and more critical view of the Basel proposals. The constructive review of the Basel proposals in Chapter 4 maintains that Pillar 1 charges are impossible to calibrate so that they reflect the operational risks actually facing an institution. In any case they are inappropriate, since most operational risks should be negligible compared to business, credit and market risks. It is argued that Pillars 2 and 3 are more appropriate than Pillar 1 for the supervision of operational risks and there is the danger that the new Basel Accord will deflect management attention from more important risks, such as business risks.

Why are some types of risk – such as systemic, business and reputational risks – excluded from the Basel definition of operational risks, while other types of risk, such as legal risk and fraud, are included? The opening discussion of Chapter 5 shows that the exact place of legal risks in the broader province of 'operational' risk is extremely difficult to define. Then, several mitigation methods for both legal risks and fraud are discussed, including: internal controls, the evolution of industry-wide practices, and risk transfer techniques. Of these, insurance is viewed as one of the least attractive methods, being tainted by liquidity, legal and credit risks which can limit its mitigation effect.

Quite a different view of insurance as a mitigant of operational risks is presented in Chapter 6, where it is viewed as a cost-efficient and very flexible hedging instrument. The insurance industry is poised to play a niche role providing new products covering certain low-frequency, high-impact operational risks. In contrast to most current insurance instruments, these new instruments will need to become truly demand-driven. Certain necessary modifications are highlighted to bring these products into line with the new regulations, to avoid doubling up on insurance if banks are required to hold operational risk capital, and to address compliance with Basel II. The chapter examines many issues, such as difficulties with the definitions of insurable operational risks, the mechanics of new insurance contracts, legal risk associated with disputes over insurance claims, reinsurance and the evolving role of insurance in the financial industry. Throughout this discussion, great emphasis is put on the need for interaction between insurers, supervisors and banks.

Part II: Analysis introduces statistical models of operational loss distributions and develops their applications to the estimation of regulatory and economic capital. All the chapters in this part of the book focus on the statistical/actuarial approach to modelling operational risks. In this approach, loss frequency and loss severity are regarded as random variables. For a single type of operational risk – external fraud in retail banking, say – the annual loss distribution is the compound of the frequency and severity distributions. The total annual loss distribution is then the sum of all the individual annual loss distributions, and the total 'unexpected loss' is defined as the difference between some upper percentile – such as the 99th or 99.9th – and the mean of the total annual loss distribution. Operational risk capital is defined as the unexpected total annual loss, and under some simplifying assumptions about the severity distribution this can be approximated by an analytic formula – this is what Basel II calls the Internal Measurement Approach (IMA).

Chapter 7 provides a theoretical but didactic introduction to operational risk measurement, including a number of interesting new developments. Data on the operational risks that really matter from the point of view of risk capital (the low-frequency, high-impact risks) – whether derived from scorecards or from external data consortia – are bound to be subjective. For these risks, and their loss distribution parameters, Bayesian rather than classical estimation methods are advocated. The dependencies between operational risks are captured by different copulas, and the consequent aggregation algorithm for the total loss distribution is illustrated with spreadsheet examples. Useful tables of the Basel 'gamma' factor in the IMA formula are provided, and this formula is shown to be an analytic approximation to the unexpected loss, which could also be approximated by simulation. An example is provided showing that the results are about the same when certain assumptions are made about the severity distribution.

Chapters 8, 9 and 10 provide complementary interpretations and different applications of the simulation approach to estimating the unexpected loss in annual loss distributions. The Basel Committee calls this the 'Loss Distribution Approach' (LDA), and Chapter 8 focuses exclusively on compliance with the regulators' views. It begins with a discussion of the likely costs (and the Basel quantitative requirements in particular) and perceived benefits for banks wishing to adopt this approach. The comprehensive coverage in this chapter includes all the steps to building, validating and applying the LDA model, and these are illustrated with an informative real-world case study, where the 'relative relationship' is introduced as a method for combining internal and external data.

Chapter 9 is perhaps the most theoretically advanced chapter in the book. It emphasizes the scenario analysis capabilities of an advanced approach to simulating operational loss distributions. A model in which dependencies between operational risks are contained by the frequency of losses but not their severities is discussed in some detail, and some very useful technical appendices on actuarial loss models are provided. Chapter 10 develops the statistical/actuarial approach into an important economic capital allocation tool, where the percentile can be specified according to the internal requirements as well as external requirements imposed by Basel II. To be compliant with internal and external needs requires an approach that is flexible enough to combine the regulatory and the economic world but that is also stable and robust over time in order to allow for risk analyses over time and across business units. For this purpose a model is suggested that compounds severity and frequency for the essential risk factors of the organization. The parameters of these distributions can probably be estimated most effectively by experts, based on a business anaylsis, loss data, Key Risk Indicators, and industry experience. Such estimates also have the advantage of being forward looking.

Part III: Management opens with the 'scorecard approach' in Chapter 11. It focuses on the management and shareholder benefits that can be derived by using a scorecard approach to quantify a risk inventory. The design of risk and control self-assessments to identify, monitor and control the organization's key risk indicators is discussed. It is also shown how scorecard models can be used to measure the firm's 'risk appetite' and in stress-testing of the risks and controls. Chapter 12 reviews the implementation of a risk management framework that will be mandatory, under Pillar 2, for banks wishing to use advanced approaches for estimating the regulatory capital charge. The main part of this chapter describes the development of a dynamic risk management process, with the identification of risks and controls, and their assessment, measurement, monitoring and reporting. It argues that the operational risk strategy, process, infrastructure and environment should be reinforced by a risk culture and language common to all the business areas in the organization. Key factors for success include senior management support, incentive schemes and 'ownership' of risks.

Chapter 13 describes the risk management applications of an operational risk model based on the actuarial approach. It begins by reviewing the risk management framework, including the identification of key risk drivers, and risk and control self-assessment techniques. Subsequently, the measurement of operational risks is discussed, following closely the Basel recommendations, but also considering how risk measurement can be related to the key risk drivers. The result is an integrated 'bottom-up' operational risk framework that links risk management to capital allocation and regulatory capital. Chapter 14 continues the 'bottom-up' theme, describing how Bayesian networks can be used to relate key risk drivers or other 'causal' factors, to key risk indicators – or indeed directly to the operational loss distribution. The framework is very useful for scenario analysis and, if the network is augmented with decision nodes and utilities, the cost–benefit analysis of management decisions can also be extended to a scenario framework.

Finally, we take a new and more sceptical view of operational risk management in Chapter 15. Here operational risks are classified into nominal, ordinary and exceptional operational risks. It is shown that, for everything other than the exceptional operational risks, there are other aspects of risk management – such as business, credit or market risks – that are far more important than operational risks. A case study of an exceptional operational risk is discussed in detail, where the 'risk attitude' of the firm is shown to be the key factor for risk management decision-making.

I have thoroughly enjoyed editing this collected work. Although at times it has been a challenge to bring together some divergent views under the same cover, all of the authors are acknowledged experts in their fields, and are highly respected for the lucidity of their insights to operational risk. The contributions have come from regulators, supervisors, risk managers, management and software consultants, insurance consultants and academics. If the book receives some acclaim, this will be due to the authors, each a pioneer in the development of operational risk measurement, management and control for financial institutions, and I would like to conclude by expressing my gratitude and appreciation to them all.

Carol Alexander

PART I

Regulation

CHAPTER 1

The three pillars of operational risk

Ralph Nash

1.1 Introduction

Operational risk hit the headlines again in February 2002 when it emerged that alleged fraudulent trading at a US subsidiary of Allied Irish Banks had led to losses of around $750 million. This case, following on the heels of other high-profile losses, showed the big-ticket potential of operational risk, and served as a timely reminder that regulatory interest in the subject is warranted. Not that any such reminder should be needed. In the UK, two large operational risk losses – BCCI and Baring's – had generated the political impetus for the transfer of banking supervision from the Bank of England to a newly created unitary regulator, the Financial Services Authority. To lose one bank was unfortunate, but to lose two appeared to the politicians as carelessness, and the role of these losses in shaping the UK regulatory regime – now seen as something of a role model for other jurisdictions – should not be underestimated.

But the UK case is by no means unique: indeed, operational risk has struck across jurisdiction, culture and financial sector. This need occasion no surprise. Operational risk is a fundamental part of doing business and, as such, cannot be fully eliminated: the common interest of banks and supervisors is that such risk is identified, measured, monitored and controlled. Under the existing Basel Accord, banks are required to hold capital, based on a crude assessment of their credit risk exposure, including a 'buffer' for other risks. In light of the spate of high-profile operational risk losses it is not surprising that the Basel Committee on Banking Supervision ('the Committee' or BCBS) took the view that such a crude approach to operational risk should be refined, with the aim of generating an environment in which improvements in risk management are rewarded.

Accordingly, the proposed new Basel Capital Accord introduces an overt treatment of operational risk. For the first time, banks will be expected to hold separately identified regulatory capital for operational risk (Pillar 1), will face additional supervisory scrutiny of their risk management (Pillar 2) and will be expected to disclose the size of the capital charge for operational risk, as well as the technique used to calculate it (Pillar 3). This chapter provides a commentary of the proposed three pillars of the new Basel Capital Accord.

1.2 Pillar 1

Pillar 1 is the name given to the minimum regulatory capital requirements in the new Basel Capital Accord. In the case of operational risk, the first issue facing the Committee was to define the scope of the capital charge. In early work, the Committee resorted to a negative definition of 'other risks' – all risks except credit, market and interest rate risk in the banking book – but, as the industry rightly pointed out, this provided no real basis for the measurement of risk and assessment of capital. The Committee's latest operational risk definition – 'the risk of loss resulting from inadequate or failed internal processes, people and systems or from external events' (BCBS 2001a, p. 2; 2001b, p. 8) – has achieved fairly general acceptance, particularly with the additional clarification that, for the purposes of minimum regulatory capital, strategic, business and systemic risk are excluded.

Once defined, there remains the question of how to calibrate the regulatory capital charge – put more simply, how big is operational risk? Not surprisingly, there is no convincing answer to this question, although the evidence suggests that – for those few banks that are able to provide data – an allocation of around 15 percent of internal economic capital for operational risk is common. For the purposes of calibrating the charge, the Committee has equated this economic capital figure with 12 percent of existing minimum regulatory capital across the system as a whole (or, if you prefer, current risk weighted assets × 8 percent × 12 percent). This extrapolation from a small sample of banks' internal capital allocations – based on different definitions of operational risk and different confidence intervals – to the banking sector as a whole suggests that the figures are rough and ready, but it is not hotly disputed that the numbers are at least directionally correct.

The next task facing the Committee was to design a mechanism to assess a regulatory capital charge. In the case of operational risk this is no mean feat. There is no handy metric agreed by the industry that the Committee can simply pick up and run with. Indeed, a number of banks argue that operational risk cannot, at this stage, be measured with any degree of certainty. This has left the Committee in a dilemma. It could build a crude mechanism that simply generates a capital charge, but this provides no incentive for banks to better manage operational risk, is inconsistent with the overriding idea that the new Basel Capital Accord should be risk-sensitive, and serves to bolster those who argue that the Committee is not serious about operational risk and is simply seeking to plug the probable gap in capital – at the aggregate level – that results from the more sensitive treatment of credit risk. Alternatively, the Committee could seek to develop a more risk-sensitive and sophisticated approach, but in the absence of a wide industry consensus on a suitable metric and technique for the assessment of operational risk, this potentially puts the supervisory cart before the industry horse, thus inhibiting the development of credible approaches to operational risk.

The Committee has addressed these issues by developing a spectrum of approaches – of increasing sophistication – and leaving the door open for the development of a range of advanced approaches. Therefore, we are faced with three different categories of approach to assessing regulatory capital for operational risk: a Basic Indicator Approach, a Standardized Approach and the Advanced Measurement Approaches (AMA).

1.2.1 The Basic Indicator Approach

The Basic Indicator Approach bases the capital charge upon a fixed percentage (termed 'alpha') of an indicator of operational risk exposure, currently proposed as 15 percent of gross income. The extent to which this is a true indicator of operational risk is debatable, but there appear to be few alternatives: asset-based indicators duplicate the credit risk charge and other indicators are difficult to define. While it is difficult to argue that gross income bears any real resemblance to the true operational risk exposure of a particular bank, it appears that gross income is the least worst option, and, despite numerous consultations, credible alternatives are thin on the ground.

1.2.2 The Standardized Approach

The Standardized Approach also bases the regulatory capital charge on gross income, but seeks to set different percentages (termed 'betas') for different predefined business lines, based on an assessment of the relative riskiness of the different businesses (per unit of gross income). The Committee currently proposes eight business lines – corporate finance; trading and sales; retail banking; commercial banking; payment and settlement; agency services and custody; asset management; and retail brokerage – and banks would be expected to map their own activities and associated gross income to this structure.

In its previous format, the approach used different indicators for different business lines, which were intended to provide a closer link to real operational risk exposure and so increase risk sensitivity, but difficulties in definition and calibration led the Committee to move to a single indicator. Moreover, the Committee's September 2001 working paper (BCBS 2001b) showed the difficulty in setting different percentages of the same indicator – gross income – for different business lines with any degree of confidence. But what benefits arise from having two simple approaches based on the same indicator? We shall address this question below.

1.2.3 The Advanced Measurement Approaches

Advanced Measurement Approaches are designed to allow a range of credible approaches to the measurement of operational risk to flourish, and a single approach has not been prescribed. Rather, the intention is to provide a framework in which banks' own internal assessments of operational risk may be verified and accepted for supervisory purposes. The framework provides banks and supervisors with a set of criteria which must be met in order to qualify for recognition of an advanced treatment.

As an incentive to move to an advanced approach, a bank will be able to hold less capital than indicated by the simpler approaches based on its internal capital assessment. At one stage the Committee had suggested that this internal assessment would be subject to a floor based on one of the simpler approaches, but its latest thinking indicates that this has been dropped (in favour of a floor on overall capital). The intellectual arguments for the abolition of the operational risk floor are indisputable. It is bizarre for supervisors to require banks to collect and model internal data, use scenario analysis and expert opinion on events and internal systems and build this into decision-making, but then place more belief in a crude number based on a single financial indicator for regulatory capital requirements.

As currently structured, the AMA provide for a 'laboratory' in which banks can test and develop approaches to operational risk quantification. It is not a single approach that banks can take and adopt, and it has been suggested that 'a thousand flowers' might bloom in this laboratory. While it is certainly less prescriptive than earlier incarnations of the 'advanced approach' – namely the Internal Measurement Approach that the Committee set out previously (BCBS 2001a) – there are various key ingredients that all approaches will use. The exact mix of these ingredients will be determined by each bank. So, while a thousand flowers might bloom, it seems that they will all be roses, but of different sizes, shape, fragrance and colour.

The lack of prescription in AMA brings certain benefits and challenges. On the plus side, it should allow a range of approaches to operational risk quantification to develop and banks may make different, but equally valid, assumptions about the nature of risk in their particular institution. It avoids the significant criticism that the Committee risked jeopardizing the development of credible approaches by being too prescriptive too early. The downside of this flexibility is that it places a great burden on supervisors to verify and accept banks' internal approaches to operational risk. While the qualifying criteria provide a framework for this supervisory analysis, they do not give rise to a supervisory approach that can be easily codified and will require significant judgement and knowledge on the part of supervisors. Whether supervisory authorities within the Basel Group, let alone those elsewhere, have the resource and expertise available, or can afford to obtain it in time for the launch of the new Basel Capital Accord, is far from clear.

Data requirements

The proposed framework for the AMA is necessarily flexible, but a key component that warrants further discussion is the data requirement. The Committee has proposed a series of business lines (the same eight as for the Standardized Approach) and seven loss event categories (internal fraud; external fraud; employment practices and workplace safety; clients, products and business practices; damage to physical assets; business disruptions and system failures; and execution, delivery, and process management) as a means by which banks may collect the full scope of operational risk loss event data. Internally, banks would be free to use alternative structures, although the ability to map to this framework (with some degree of flexibility and supervisory judgement) is needed to allow supervisory verification and acceptance, as well as data sharing. Mapping to the business lines seems the more questionable requirement, since it is not clear exactly how this will help supervisory validation.

This framework is significant because it demonstrates the range of operational risk events encompassed by the charge – more than just 'operating' risk, a term sometimes wrongly used interchangeably with operational risk. Furthermore, evidence suggests that unless banks import some external data to supplement their own loss information, be it 'public' externally reported data or shared 'internal' data from other banks, perhaps via consortia, then they are unlikely to adequately capture the 'tail' of the operational risk distribution, and would fail to convince supervisors that their approach is suitable for acceptance.

This 'judgement' by supervisors will be crucial to the implementation of the AMA concept, although banks will rightly be concerned about the comparison of treatment across jurisdictions. While some degree of supervisory judgement and flexibility is in the very nature of the AMA framework, the Committee will owe it to itself and to the industry to see that minimum standards are met on an initial and ongoing basis if the credibility of the framework is to be established and maintained.

The issue of data also raises the extent to which 'operational losses' are lurking in the credit and market risk databases of large institutions. There can be no doubt that certain approaches to risk management encourage the classification of operational losses as credit or market risk losses: these losses might be seen as bad luck, whereas operational risk, even by its definition, attaches some kind of blame or failure. As a result, there must be 'operational risk' losses recorded by staff as credit and market risk losses, impacting both the individual institution's assessment of operational risk and, consequently, the Committee's assessment of the calibration and distribution of capital charges. There is no easy way round this and banks cannot be expected to reconstruct long runs of data, not least as the calibration of the credit risk capital charge in the new Basel Capital Accord is based, necessarily, on existing data. At present the Committee is encouraging banks to clearly define and earmark operational losses for management purposes, without disrupting credit loss data history. However, this issue is likely to continue to raise questions throughout the implementation process.

1.2.4 Why three approaches?

While there remain questions over the feasibility of implementing a credible AMA framework – and if it is offered in the new Basel Capital Accord a core of banks will expect their supervisors to be able to accept approaches from $T+1$, i.e. a year of testing in 2006 and acceptance of AMA on 1 January 2007 – a second key issue must be the need for three regulatory approaches to operational risk. More specifically, what benefit arises from having two simple approaches based on the same indicator?

In its original conception, the Standardized Approach used different indicators – gross income, assets and throughput indicators – for different business lines in an attempt to reflect the underlying operational risk in the business. For valid definition and calibration reasons, the Committee found it too difficult to develop a 'simple' approach based on a range of indicators. At this point it could have chosen to drop one of the simple approaches, but instead kept both, with the Standardized Approach adopting the same indicator – gross income – as the most basic approach. This leaves us with two similar approaches and saddles the Committee with the difficult task – at this stage – of setting different multiples of gross income across business lines, while maintaining the overall level of capital. So far the Committee has found it impossible to be prescriptive about the levels of the multiples (alpha and betas) in either of the simpler approaches, and a lack of evidence on the relative riskiness of business lines per unit of gross income implies that in any case the dispersion of betas, and hence the supposed risk sensitivity, of the Standardized Approach will be limited. Indicative levels of alpha and beta were published in August 2002, but are likely to be subject to future revision.

As an alternative to a quasi-intermediate approach that adds nothing in terms of risk sensitivity, but simply adds pages to an already voluminous accord, the Committee has a number of options. One would be to abolish the Basic Indicator Approach, and to keep the Standardized Approach in place with temporary betas (multiples) all set at the same level. Once better evidence of the relative riskiness of business lines becomes available, then the Committee could adjust the betas, and could further consider whether different indicators could be used. A second alternative would be to abolish the Standardized Approach and simply have a Basic Indicator Approach and the AMA options. If banks were unwilling or unable to move all of their business simultaneously to an advanced approach, then the Basic Indicator Approach could apply to that portion of gross income arising in business lines or entities not covered in the advanced approach.

Despite these options, three approaches remain, and there are a number of political and, in some cases, very practical reasons why banks and supervisors might support the retention of an intermediate approach, despite its limited theoretical merit. A number of banks may not be ready to implement an advanced approach at the outset of the new Basel Capital Accord. The existence of a quasi-sophisticated intermediate approach prevents them from looking so much the poor relation when compared to their competitors using an advanced approach. Further, some banks with business focused in 'low-risk business lines' will have estimated that the existence of an intermediate approach, with lower multiples of gross income, will save them capital compared to the Basic Indicator Approach, where the same multiple applies to all gross income wherever generated in the bank.

Perhaps most importantly, within the EU context, non-banks, particularly asset managers, have argued that their operational risk is low and that the Basel proposals could be penal. The Standardized Approach would allow the future EU Directive on Capital to address this problem to some extent, since the low-risk business lines tend to be asset management, retail banking and retail brokerage, and so beta for these business lines could be set below the level of alpha.

From the supervisory perspective, some authorities see the Standardized Approach as a useful lever to encourage better risk management in banks, by attaching qualifying criteria to the use of the approach. With a single simple approach this potential is lost since there can be no barriers at the point of entry for the capital charge. If there were numerous qualifying criteria banks might – accidentally on purpose – find themselves unable to fulfil the criteria and would save themselves any capital charge for operational risk! However, Pillar 2 exists as a means to encourage better risk identification, measurement, monitoring and control. Developing qualifying criteria that have no direct link to the approach itself (i.e. banks can assess gross income by business line in the absence of an operational risk management or measurement framework!) is dubious practice.

1.3 Pillar 2

The implementation of Pillar 2 – the supervisory review process – will raise resource and competitive issues, not just for the Basel Committee constituents and not just in the area of operational risk. The Pillar 2 framework is based around four key principles. In essence, these are: that banks should have mechanisms to assess their risk (and hence capital adequacy); that supervisors should review banks' internal capital adequacy assessments and should take appropriate supervisory action if they are not satisfied with the result of this process; that supervisors should expect banks to operate above the minimum regulatory capital ratios and should seek to intervene at an early stage to prevent capital from falling below the minimum levels required to support the risk characteristics of a particular bank; and that supervisors should require rapid remedial action if capital is not maintained or restored.

1.3.1 *Sound Practices*

In the area of operational risk, the Committee has added further flesh to these bones by setting out, for consultation, *Sound Practices for the Management and Supervision of Operational Risk*. This paper was originally published in December 2001 (BCBS 2001c), and a revised draft issued in July 2002 (BCBS 2002b). The paper follows a series of studies by the Committee, now subsumed under the Pillar 2 umbrella, providing guidance on the management – that is, identification, assessment, monitoring and control – of key banking risks. The paper recommends key elements of a framework for the management of operational risk that supervisors would expect to see in place at banks. These include the development of an appropriate risk management environment, through the role of the board and senior management, information flows across the organization, and techniques for risk management. The paper also considers the role of supervisors and disclosure.

1.3.2 Additional Pillar 2 charges

While leading banks are already compliant with much of what is set out in *Sound Practices*, there remain the questions of what, in practice, supervisors will do under Pillar 2 with regard to operational risk and, as a result, the nature of the interaction between Pillar 1 capital requirements and Pillar 2 recommendations. Given the range of supervisory styles and powers, and the range of institutions and circumstances, Pillar 2 cannot be designed for fully predictable and formulaic responses: there can be no 'if X, then Y', but rather 'if X, then maybe Y, Z or nothing'. Indeed, if such predictable supervisory responses (i.e. if X, then a capital charge of Y) were possible, then a Pillar 2 treatment would not be necessary – it could be dealt with through 'rules' in Pillar 1.

Rather, Pillar 2 exists to bolster and deepen the relationship between supervisor and bank. While this may be anathema to compliance purists – and indeed there must be concerns about inequality of treatments within jurisdictions, let alone between them – it seems likely that Pillar 2, in the area of operational risk, will remain a qualitative approach, hopefully with some degree of similarity of treatment within a common framework.

One key question in this regard is whether the Pillar 2 process for operational risk will result in additional regulatory capital charges. On first impressions the answer is yes, given the nature of the Pillar 2 framework, where additional capital is identified as a potential supervisory response. However, in view of the proposed Pillar 1 framework for operational risk, the question becomes rather more complex. For banks using the simpler approaches – the Basic Indicator and Standardized Approach – the capital charge will be calculated on the basis of an accounting figure (gross income) without any specific reference to the real size of operational risk within the individual bank. In the absence of any quantification of operational risk, how will the supervisor justify additional capital, and how much? While supervisors may well, through the Pillar 2 process, identify risk management weaknesses in banks using simpler approaches, how will they justify increased capital, if the size of operational risk within the bank is not measured in the first place?

Furthermore, it is difficult to see that increased capital, other than as a threat or punishment, serves to address the root issue of an identified risk management weakness. Surely it is better to address the control weakness itself than to hold extra capital and wait for the losses to arise. In response, supervisors can argue that the requirements in Pillar 1 represent *minimum* capital requirements for well-managed banks, so additional capital could be appropriate for banks using simpler approaches, even if the risk is not measured directly. This still leaves open the question of how much additional capital should be required for particular weaknesses or breaches. The Committee will never be in a position to set a menu for supervisors – 'lack of segregation of duties = +10 percent; failure to report losses = +20 percent; ...' – so any additional capital charges will necessarily be arbitrary and banks will rightly squeal at the prospect of different Pillar 2 treatments for the same 'offence'.

While banks using AMA are clearly attempting to measure operational risk, and hence some of the issues mentioned above are solved, different problems arise for the functioning of an operational risk Pillar 2 framework, and the requirement for additional capital. A quick review of the qualifying entry criteria, as set out in the Committee's Working Paper on Operational Risk (BCBS 2001b) shows that the Pillar 1 requirements are at least as rigorous as the Pillar 2 recommendations (BCBS 2001c, 2002b). While this balance is fine in itself, it begs the question of how a supervisor would justify additional capital for a bank using an advanced approach. If a bank breaches qualifying criteria for AMA, then the supervisory response would reasonably be that the bank must address the breach immediately, or have acceptance of its advanced approach rescinded and face relegation to one of the simpler capital approaches. Perhaps additional capital might be used to jog the bank along the way, but it cannot be seen as a long-term substitute for meeting the advanced criteria. As with banks using the simpler approaches, additional capital does not address the root of the issue.

Certainly, in the short term additional capital can be a useful tool in the Pillar 2 framework for operational risk but, in this analysis, it seems unlikely that the spectre feared by banks of permanently holding additional capital for ill-defined operational risk issues under Pillar 2 will appear. Where Pillar 2 can add real value is in giving supervisors a lever to encourage improvements in risk management at banks. Furthermore, the increasing and well-founded demands for supervisory transparency under the new Basel Capital Accord, if fulfilled, will serve to encourage the justification of particular Pillar 2 treatments for both individual banks and in particular jurisdictions.

1.4 Pillar 3

In terms of quantity of pages, Pillar 3 is certainly the most succinct element of the new operational risk framework. Indeed, the current requirements for public disclosure by banks may be summed up in just a few sentences. A bank must disclose: its strategies and processes for managing operational risk, the structure and organization of the risk management function, the scope and nature of risk reporting and/or measurement systems, and its policies for hedging and/or mitigating risk, strategies and processes for monitoring the continuing effectiveness of hedges and/or mitigants. A bank should also disclose the approach(es) to regulatory capital assessment that it qualifies for, a description of the advanced measurement approach (if used by the bank), and the operational risk capital charge (per business line if available).

Despite its brevity, this is not to say that Pillar 3 will lack bite. Perhaps the two most significant of these disclosures are the size of the capital charge and the technique used to calculate it. The capital charge is the only comparable measure of exposure available, while the technique used gives an indication of the sophistication of the institution's risk management and, to some extent, the emphasis accorded to the issue by the bank. This proposed disclosure also helps explain the desire of some banks to retain three approaches, since disclosing that a bank is using the Basic Indicator Approach may not be in its best interests.

It remains to be seen how the market will respond to the disclosures. Some banks may choose to remain on the simpler approaches, disclose the fact and add qualifying discussion on why they have not moved to an advanced approach – perhaps on the basis of costs and benefits, or perhaps because their internal approach has not achieved supervisory acceptance. Perhaps rating agencies and counterparties will be content with this, but it seems likely that once a critical mass of significant banks have achieved acceptance of their Advanced Measurement Approach, their peers will soon wish to follow suit and a momentum towards the enhanced risk management inherent in AMA will be achieved. An interesting by-product of the disclosure will be the number of banks in different jurisdictions achieving AMA status. Such information could be indicative of a concentration of sophisticated banks in a particular jurisdiction, but could also indicate regulatory forbearance – something that both rival banks and fellow supervisors might be concerned about.

The later versions of Pillar 3 have responded directly to some vehement, perhaps venomous, criticisms of earlier proposals. In particular, the industry was almost hysterical about a proposal to disclose large individual losses, citing legal and competitive considerations as major financial impediments. While some doubts remain over the real threat from such disclosures – indeed, in time it is possible that banks will make such disclosures of their own volition – the Committee has responded positively by dropping the requirement. Responses from the industry have generally accepted that the revised Pillar 3 proposals on operational risk are a step in the right direction, which is hardly surprising as there is a reduced level of disclosure. Clearly the Pillar 3 framework will evolve as the Pillar 1 world is finalized, but it seems that disclosure of key features of risk management will form an important part of the treatment of operational risk in the new Basel Capital Accord.

1.5 Insurance

Many aspects of operational risk are covered, at least in part, by conventional and increasingly innovative insurance products. With the proposed operational risk capital charge in the pipeline, banks and insurers have argued that the regulatory regime should recognize the existence of such policies and, to some extent, provide relief from capital as a result.

The Committee has accepted the argument in principle, but has limited relief to those banks that use an advanced measurement approach. In such an approach, policies can be hypothecated to particular business lines and risk types and loss data amended accordingly. However, insurers, banks and some supervisors have argued that insurance should also be recognized in the simpler approaches. While conceptually this may be valid, it is difficult to envisage how insurance coverage can be equated to a reduction in a crude capital charge (based on gross income) in anything but a vague and rather spurious way, and the Committee has so far resisted such calls. If a bank cannot measure its operational risk exposure it is difficult to see how the impact of mitigation of that exposure can be measured.

The Committee is still in the process of working with the industry to develop criteria for the recognition of insurance, along with other aspects of the regulatory regime, and will need to produce more rigorous and detailed criteria for insurance to form part of the Accord. For banks using simpler approaches, supervisors could use Pillar 2 to encourage (or punish) the (lack of) prudent insurance purchasing, but as indicated above this is most likely to happen at the discretion of the national supervisor.

1.6 Conclusion

This chapter has reviewed some issues surrounding the development of a regulatory capital charge for operational risk. There is still a fair way to go on this subject, and final proposals (Consultation Paper 3) are expected in May 2003, with a final Accord text in the fourth quarter of 2003.

A number of banks and some supervisors still question the merit of building a minimum regulatory capital charge for operational risk, citing difficulty in calibration and measurement and the nascent state of risk management practices and techniques in many banks. While there is some truth in these criticisms, the Committee has so far remained firm on a Pillar 1 capital charge for operational risk. There is, no doubt, a slim chance that, once the final new Basel Capital Accord poker game is over, the risk will be dealt with purely under Pillar 2, or perhaps with a single simple approach in Pillar 1 and additional guidance in Pillar 2. Indeed, the AMA concept nods in the direction of a Pillar 2 treatment, given the degree of supervisory flexibility and judgement inherent in the approach.

However, the Committee would need to consider carefully the impact of such a change. There can be no doubt that the threat/promise of a minimum capital charge has focused banks on this topic, and ensured that it receives attention at board level. A somewhat more vague threat of a Pillar 2 treatment would surely not have had the same effect: it would be instructive to know the amount of time the boards of internationally active banks have devoted to interest rate risk in the banking book – a Pillar 2 risk – compared to operational risk! In any event, there can be no doubt that the Committee has galvanized work on operational risk that will not be lost, whatever happens in the future.

Indeed, the role of the Committee as a promoter of change should not be overstated. The real impetus for work on operational risk must ultimately come from the banks themselves. The catalogue of large operational risk events shows that for reasons of sound governance, maintenance of shareholder value and internal risk management – regardless of what happens in the Basel Committee room – bank management ignores the issue at its peril. Raising capital is the easy part of this process, and if the Committee was only interested in that it could do so simply by adding a 'tax' for operational risk on the credit risk capital charge. The more difficult part is improving risk management in the business lines of individual banks and changing the collective mindset from an *ex post* 'blame'-based approach to operational risk, to one where the risk is *ex ante* actively managed. In this regard the Committee's work must surely have already made an impact.

Ultimately, the key question is not whether the operational risk charge is calibrated at this or that percentage, nor even whether it is dealt with in Pillar 1 or Pillar 2, but rather whether banks see the management of operational risk as an additional regulatory intrusion or as an opportunity to assess and price their business in a new, more coherent fashion. We must hope it is the latter.

CHAPTER 2

A qualitative operational risk framework: guidance, structure and reporting

Kenneth Swenson[1]

2.1 Introduction

In this chapter the supervisory treatment of operational risk will be discussed. An overview of selected Basel guidance, implementation issues and US Federal Reserve System supervision will be provided. The chapter will seek to establish a happy medium so that firms can utilize sound and emerging operational risk management practices in a cost-effective manner in anticipation of management's expectations. Background is provided in the next two sections on guidance and management structure. Section 2.4, on management reporting, addresses tools and deliverables.

This chapter will help business unit management, senior management and the boards of directors to identify, assess, monitor and control/mitigate enterprise operational risk. It will be based on sound and emerging practices utilized by large, complex banking organizations (LCBOs) and supervisory expectations. We will examine risk-focused principles, the use of a three-pronged operational risk management-reporting tool set, and deliverables. Our goal is to assist firms to balance the trade-off between operational efficiency and infrastructure expenditure. This is *not* an exhaustive listing of operational risk supervisory guidance. The purpose is to highlight a sampling of emerging practices. Overlap exists between LCBO and regional bank risk management practices. However, community banks do not directly lend themselves to these practices. They generally operate as a single business activity. Also, they may lack internal audit and centralized risk management functions.

Table 2.1 summarizes the ten concepts that will be discussed along the continuum towards mature operational risk management.

---

[1] The views expressed in this chapter are those of the author, and not necessarily those of the Federal Reserve Bank of Chicago or the Federal Reserve System.

TABLE 2.1 ■ Status of operational risk management practices

Common practice	Emerging practice
1. Siloed business unit risk management	Integrated corporate risk management
2. 'Business line managers own the risk'	Corporate risk management does *not* supplant business line risk ownership; it supplements and reinforces it
3. '*Ad-hoc*' or no risk self-assessment	Uniform risk self-assessment across business units, facilitated by corporate risk management
4. Voluminous performance indicators	Core set of key risk and performance metrics/escalation triggers
5. Too much or too little information, inconsistent business unit reporting	Concise, uniform reporting to senior management and the board of directors
6. Track accounting loss	Track economic loss through root cause and effect
7. Internal data only	Internal and external data
8. Blunt capital indicator	Increasingly 'risk-sensitive' capital assessment
9. Heuristic 8% minimum regulatory capital framework	Capital relief for well-managed institutions
10. Basel is an '*end* to a means'	Basel is a '*means* to an end'

2.2 Guidance

This section addresses the status of the supervisory playing field. It outlines the methodologies that supervisors use to assess how firms identify, assess, monitor and control/mitigate operational risk. An overview of selected Federal Reserve System and Basel II guidance is provided.

The Basel Committee on Banking Supervision (BCBS) has helped to pave the way for explicit supervisory review of LCBO operational risk. It expands upon the traditional assessments conducted by supervisors who focus on operational risk from more of a business line and/or back office context. The operational risk supervisory mandate is in part predicated upon Principle 9 in BCBS (2001c):

> Supervisors should conduct, directly or indirectly, regular independent evaluation of a bank's strategies, policies, procedures and practices related to operational risks. Supervisors should ensure that there are effective reporting mechanisms in place which allow them to remain apprised of developments at banks.

Operational risk guidance for banks has been issued by the Federal Reserve System in the form of the *Framework for Risk-Focused Supervision of Large Complex Institutions* ('Risk-Focused Manual') and by the BCBS (2001a, 2001b, 2001c, 2002b).

2.2.1 Risk rating methodology

The Federal Reserve System (1997) advocates a threefold risk-rating scheme. The scheme includes measures for inherent risk and risk management to arrive at a holistic view of composite risk. Many supervisors, including the Federal Reserve System, utilize a risk-rating lens that looks at three risk components:[2]

- inherent risk;
- risk management;
- composite risk.

These are augmented with a directional component, that is, a trend which is rated as increasing, stable or decreasing.

Inherent risk may be viewed as the level of risk without consideration of risk-mitigating controls. Inherent risk resides, principally, at the business unit level, and is supervised through a review of significant activities. These activities are evaluated to arrive at the firm-wide inherent risk rating. Inherent risk is based upon various factors, among which are:

- level of activity or positions relative to the firm's resources or peer group;
- number of transactions;
- complexity of activity; and
- potential loss to the organization.

Although inherent risk principally resides at the business unit level, it can be evaluated solely on a firm-wide basis. However, it is incumbent upon the reviewer to take into account the robustness of such an assessment.

Some risk management functions reside at the business activity level. Other control points operate across the organization as part of the corporate risk management infrastructure. Supervisors place primary consideration on the following risk management components:

- board and senior management oversight;
- policies, procedures and limits;
- risk management, monitoring and management information systems; and
- internal controls.

Notably, the emergence of enterprise risk management should further integrate these often disparate and decentralized processes. It should also help to fulfil the role of keeper of firm-wide corporate governance responsibilities.

---

[2] Inherent risk and composite risk are rated high, moderate or low. Risk management is rated strong, acceptable or weak.

Composite risk is essentially the net risk after accounting for inherent risk and risk mitigating controls. In other words, after considering both inherent risk and risk management, the resultant risk is known as composite risk. Mathematically:

Inherent risk – Risk management = Composite risk.

The Risk-Focused Manual (Federal Reserve System 1997) contains a matrix that maps the relationship of inherent risk, risk management and composite risk (see Table 2.2). The matrix provides structural guidance for inherent risk, risk management and composite risk ratings. In other words, one could not assign, for example, high inherent risk, weak risk management and low composite risk.

Risk assessment should apply to the entire spectrum of risks facing an institution, including:

- credit risk;
- market risk;
- liquidity risk;
- operational risk;
- legal risk;
- reputational risk.

For Basel purposes, operational risk includes legal risk but excludes reputational risk, and to a certain extent market risk includes liquidity risk. For purposes of discussion within this chapter, then, the Federal Reserve System's six risk types can be folded into four: credit, market, operational and reputational. Further, since many consider reputational risk *not* susceptible to quantification, we arrive at the risk trinity of credit, market and operational.

The Risk-Focused Manual also specifies that a risk matrix is used to identify significant activities, the type and level of inherent risks in these activities, and the adequacy of risk management over these activities, as well as to determine composite risk assessments for each of these activities and the overall institution. A simplified, illustrative example of such a matrix is given in Table 2.3.

TABLE 2.2 ■ Relationship between inherent risk, risk management and composite risk

Risk management systems	Inherent risk of the activity		
	Low	Moderate	High
	Composite risk assessment		
Weak	Low or Moderate	Moderate or High	High
Acceptable	Low	Moderate	High
Strong	Low	Low or Moderate	Moderate or High

Source: Federal Reserve System (1997, p. 24).

TABLE 2.3 ■ Firm-wide risk matrix

Functional activities	Inherent risks			Risk management systems	Composite
	Credit	Market	Operational		
Business Unit 1: Investment Banking	Moderate	High	Moderate	Acceptable	Moderate
Business Unit 2: Banking	High	Moderate	High	Acceptable	High
Business Unit 3: Others	Moderate	Low	Moderate	Strong	Low
Overall composite risk					Moderate

2.2.2 Comments on Basel II

BCBS (2001b) states: 'The New Basel Capital Accord is based on three complementary pillars – minimum capital requirements (Pillar 1), the supervisory review process (Pillar 2) and the enhancement of market discipline through disclosure (Pillar 3).' This chapter focuses primarily on Pillar 1 implementation implications for minimum regulatory capital requirements. Nevertheless, Pillar 2 and Pillar 3 will be addressed periodically throughout this section.

Operational risk Basel II guidance suggests the following hypothesis: assuming an institution has appropriate risk management, the use of increasingly sophisticated capital approaches should result in lower operational risk minimum regulatory capital. In other words, lower capital induces firms to have sophisticated risk management practices. In increasing order of risk sensitivity, the continuum of approaches includes: the Basic Indicator Approach; the Standardized Approach; and the Advanced Measurement Approaches (AMA).[3] For a firm to utilize the more sophisticated approaches (Standardized and AMA), the institution will be expected to demonstrate compliance with eligibility requirements stipulated and validated by supervisors. BCBS (2001a) states that, while the Basic Indicator Approach might be suitable for smaller banks with a simple range of business activities, the Committee expects internationally active banks and banks with significant operational risk to use a more sophisticated approach within the overall framework.

The Basel paradox is that supervisors and the financial industry alike may be subject to a dilemma. The dilemma is that 'internationally active' and/or 'significant operational risk' organizations may be expected to use more sophisticated approaches while the eligibility requirements to use such approaches may not have been met. The resulting ramifications are unknown at this juncture. Regulators may be saddled with the scenario of imposing sanctions without the wherewithal to enforce them. They may hold a carrot but lack a stick.[4] Time will tell.

---

[3] Annex 4 of BCBS (2001b) mentions three Advanced Measurement Approaches: Internal Measurement Approaches; Loss Distribution Approaches and scorecard approaches.
[4] The 'stick' could possibly be Pillar 2 (the supervisory review process), and a higher minimum regulatory capital requirement.

BCBS (20001b, pp. 11–12) proposes seven qualifying criteria for the Standardized Approach. The criteria include four qualitative 'effective risk management and control' standards and three quantitative 'measurement and validation' standards:

(i) Effective risk management and control

- The bank must have a wall-documented, independent operational risk management and control process, which includes firm-level policies and procedures concerning operational risk and strategies for mitigating operational risk.

- There must be regular reporting of relevant operational risk data to business unit management, senior management and the board of directors.

- Internal auditors must regularly review the operational risk management processes. This review should include both the activities of the business units and the operational risk management and control process.

(ii) Measurement and validation

- The bank must have both appropriate risk reporting systems to generate data used in the calculation of a capital charge and the ability to construct management reporting based on the results.

- The bank must begin to systematically track relevant operational risk data, including internal loss data, by business line.

- The bank must develop specific, documented criteria for mapping current business lines and activities into the standardized framework. The criteria must be reviewed and adjusted for new or changing business activities and risks as appropriate.

Each criterion will be discussed in more detail throughout the remainder of this chapter.

The Standardized Approach is the second of three approaches. Therefore, in addition to further criteria, *all* the above factors apply to the most risk-sensitive approach, the AMA. No eligibility criteria apply to the initial approach, the Basic Indicator Approach.

An emerging theme expressed by a number of large firms in reaction to the Basel proposals centres around the desire for operational risk to receive Pillar 2 (the supervisory review process) treatment. Under this treatment, institutions could be allowed to develop their own systems and risk management practices. Only thereafter could a supervisor impose operational risk minimum regulatory capital requirements.

Much discussion is also based on the dichotomy between institutions that believe they are AMA-ready and institutions that know they are not. Optimists believe that by the end of 2006 most data issues should largely be resolved. According to the Basel Consultative Document (BCBS 2001a):

> At present, it appears that few banks could avail themselves of an internal methodology for regulatory capital allocation. However, given the anticipated progress and high degree of senior management commitment on this issue, the period until implementation of the new Basel Capital Accord may allow a number of banks to develop viable internal approaches.

It appears the Basel Committee may provide capital incentives to large institutions to integrate operational risk management across the enterprise. Some large institutions are vehemently opposed to such a structure. However, the launching of Pillar 3 (the enhancement of market discipline through disclosure) may offer capital incentives to reconsider a corporate control framework. The alternative is for firms to remain relegated to the siloed approach at their own peril. Less than certain is whether the alternatives offered by stockholders, and the market, will be as forgiving.

2.3 Management structure

This section provides an overview of managerial and corporate governance structures. We will review siloed business line risk management and the role of internal audit. In addition, business line-resident and corporate risk management structures will be discussed.

2.3.1 Siloed business line risk management

Operational risk has existed since the first institution opened its doors. In response, operational risk management naturally cropped up. The initial period of operational risk management lingered for some time through siloed business unit risk management. In some circles, management remains in this phase. Many supervisors are familiar with the 'business line managers own the risk' axiom. The response to how line managers manage the risk goes something like 'The CEO manages the risk. For validation the supervisor need look no further than the financial results and the stock price!' – a compelling answer. However, one should consider whether such performance was the beneficiary of a strong economy. How do we know that financial performance would not have been better given robust operational risk management?

Senior management may acknowledge the usefulness of operational risk management, but likewise may suggest that the internal audit department fills this vacuum. An effective audit department is independent, provides cross-checks, identifies the risk universe, performs risk assessments, identifies material risks and gaps, etc. So ... is this the zenith of operational risk management? Of course not! In light of emerging risk management practices, not to mention Basel II eligibility requirements, what department is responsible for auditing corporate risk management? It cannot be the business line, which, by definition, lacks independence. It cannot be internal audit, because audit cannot audit itself. Perhaps the answer is that internal audit must audit a separate and distinct corporate risk management department. This is the starting point to understanding a need for explicit operational risk management, independent of both the business unit and internal audit.

2.3.2 Internal audit

BCBS (2001b) states the following as one of the qualifying criteria for the Standardized Approach: 'Effective risk management and control ... Internal auditors must regularly review the operational risk management processes. This review should include both the activities of the business units and the operational risk management and control process.'[5]

LCBOs are encouraged to establish independent internal audit and corporate risk management groups in the structural hierarchy. A challenge lies in the fact that some firms initially place operational risk management within audit. Moreover, some institutions assert that audit *is* the operational risk management department. However, the Basel II rollout scheduled for the end of 2006 suggests that, for institutions expecting (and maybe required) to use the higher approaches (Standardized and AMA), traditional decentralized business line management should be complemented by both independent internal audit and corporate risk management. In this way, business unit management will be reinforced by firm-wide controls that are subject to periodic validation by internal audit. The fallout is that larger firms will be encouraged to keep pace with Basel's eligibility requirements for more sophisticated and, ostensibly, lower operational risk minimum regulatory capital requirements. Non-compliance with the requirements might compromise stock price as a result of Pillar 3.[6] In sum, under Basel II, if you are not moving forward, you are losing ground.

Traditionally, internal audit has alternatively served as the first line of defence against operational risk and the last bastion of operational risk control (in addition to the business unit, although more independent). In this context internal audit, not unlike supervisors, has typically looked at *operations* risk, not *operational* risk. The distinction lies in the fact that the former is limited to back office reconciling, processing and the like. The latter permeates from the front via the middle to the back office platform. In the latter approach, *operational risk* includes loss due to inadequate or failed internal processes, people and systems, or from external events – sound familiar?[7] At any rate, under Basel II, internal audit's traditional role as the only independent operational risk guardian may change.

The Organization for Economic Cooperation and Development has defined corporate governance as follows: corporate governance involves a set of relationships between a company's management, its board, its shareholders and other stakeholders. It also provides the structure through which the objectives of the company are set, and the means of attaining those objectives and monitoring performance are determined. In short, it is the system by

---

[5] This criterion correlates with the inherent risk and risk management concepts addressed in Section 2.2. In effect, Basel is advising internal audit to look at both inherent risk within business lines and risk management across the corporation.

[6] The caveat to this hypothesis is an institution with less than satisfactory risk management practices. In such a case, it is possible that when moving from the Standardization Approach to the AMA, given the introduction of institution-specific data, risk sensitive captial would be higher, not lower.

[7] This is the core definition that has been established by the industry and Basel II.

which businesses are directed and controls are implemented. Qualitative factors to develop a robust operational risk management-reporting framework include, but are not limited to: the establishment and documentation of a firm-wide framework; the carrying out of risk and control self-assessments; and the prioritization of a core set of key risk/performance indicators. Notably, various approaches are used to establish and document the firm-wide framework. The traditional approach is jointly sponsored by the business unit and internal audit, and results in siloed business line risk ownership.

2.3.3 Business line-resident and corporate risk management

BCBS (2001b) states the following as one of the qualifying criteria for the Standardized Approach: 'Effective risk management and control ... The bank must have a well-documented, independent operational risk management and control process, which includes firm-level policies and procedures concerning operational risk and strategies for mitigating operational risk.'

A well-crafted corporate operational risk policy should, as a minimum, strive to:

- define operational risk and the sub-components therein;
- adequately identify the roles, responsibilities and interrelationships between the business unit, internal audit, business line-resident risk management and firm-wide risk management;
- provide guidance commensurate with the size, complexity and risk profile of the firm;
- document the process by which risk self-assessments shall be completed;
- establish templates for a risk-focused operational risk reporting package that includes, at a minimum, risk and control self-assessment, key indicators and loss tracking;
- address and/or cross-reference corporate and business activity guidance in selected areas (e.g. loss escalation, separation of duties, conflicts of interest).

Two forms of integrated operational risk management have emerged. Some firms opt for a mix of the traditional siloed approach along with a touch of enterprise-wide oversight. While business line managers are closest to the risks to be managed, at the same time they lack independence. Business unit risk management is a good starting point. However, the explicit inclusion of audit, business line-resident risk management and some centralized risk management further refines governance. Under this framework the familiar 'business line managers own the risk' credo reigns. Risk managers are aligned alongside business line management, and report directly thereto. There is a small corporate risk management department that may be mainly administrative in terms of facilitating the initial self-assessment rollout. Thereafter, business line staff is responsible for self-assessments. Ultimately, corporate risk management focuses on training and warehousing self-assessments in a corporate database. However, enterprise risk management oversight may be largely absent. Most corporate governance is based on business line-resident risk management reporting to business unit management. Little or no top-down firm-wide oversight may exist.

A number of international organizations utilize a more centralized risk management approach. Here there is an established operational risk management group. In addition to setting policies and facilitating development of operational risk reporting, the team may internally handle much responsibility and accountability for enterprise risk management (e.g. independent monitoring). This includes establishment of business unit and enterprise key indicators and bottom-up empirical capital allocation. In this approach, centralized risk management, not the business line, assumes increased responsibility for standardizing the risk and control environment self-attestation. Separate and distinct risk management departments are established for the risk trio of credit, market and operational risk. All three departments report to the chief risk officer.

Admittedly few, if any, empirical cost efficiency studies favour any of the above three approaches. But for LCBOs, the latter two approaches may afford more effective risk management. They may also be more desirable from a Basel II minimum regulatory capital perspective. It is important to note that, even in the absence of Basel II, investment in risk management practices should make sense both from a cost–benefit and competition standpoint.

2.4 Reporting

BCBS (2001b) states that in order to qualify for the Standardized Approach, 'There must be regular reporting of relevant operational risk data to business unit management, senior management and the board of directors' and that 'The board of directors and senior management must be actively involved in the oversight of the operational risk management process'.

This last section consists of two parts. The first part introduces a concise operational risk reporting package. The package aims to help alert senior management and the board to the risk profile of the firm through streamlined reporting. The second part addresses firm-wide deliverables. The point here is *not* that operational risk tool set and/or firm-wide deliverable implementation will single-handedly satisfy Standardized Approach eligibility requirements. Rather, the implication is that the absence of these tools and/or deliverables *may* preclude eligibility for the higher approaches.

2.4.1 The operational risk tool set

The operational risk discipline is in an embryonic state. As evidence, one need only look at a discipline such as loss tracking. The Risk-Focused Manual guidance on risk classes makes clear distinctions between market, credit and operational risk. Basel's operational risk definition, however, suggests that a breakdown or inadequacy in, for example, credit risk reporting may be operational risk. The distinction is cause and effect. To illustrate, a breakdown in credit risk monitoring could be due to an underlying operational risk cause, but might be manifested as a 'credit' loss.[8] To truly identify the root cause of a problem, the

---

[8] For example, failure to perfect a lien on property that secures a loan is an operational failure. However, this failure is, typically, counted as a credit loss if the debt is not repaid in full. Currently, counting this in a comprehensive and non-overlapping manner (as credit) is a sound practice. The emerging practice is to attribute it, from a root cause analysis perspective, to operational risk.

analysis should identify both cause and effect. This method can more acutely track loss (effect) and may help to rectify the cause (in this simplified case, operational risk). To come full circle, operational risk management does not always reside in a binary, readily attributable, clean-cut risk world. It requires more than perfunctory review and arbitrary cause attribution. With this caveat in mind, we now describe the operational risk tool set under three headings: risk assessment; key indicators/triggers; and loss reporting.

Risk assessment

BCBS (2002b, p. 8) defines risk assessment as when '*a bank assesses its operations and activities against a menu of potential operational risk vulnerabilities. This process is internally driven and often incorporates checklists and/or workshops to identify the strengths and weaknesses of the operational risk environment*'.

One method of risk and control self-assessment is a small, central corporate risk management department that sets policies and procedures. Internal audit is charged with compliance validation. Alternatively, a business unit resident 'self-assessment champion' can facilitate the process. This individual knows the business activity and establishes working relationships with unit personnel. This segregation of responsibility frees up corporate risk management to focus on standardizing and monitoring the process. Self-assessment emerging practices include, but are not limited to:

- corporate risk management reporting control gaps to senior management and the board;
- reinforcing business unit risk ownership by requiring management to self-attest to risk levels through senior management and board reporting;
- tiering the self-assessment cycle after successful iterations span the corporation;
- including an inventory of outsourced relationships in each risk self-assessment;
- promoting transparency and accountability, for example, requiring business unit managers to present a summary of the risk self-assessment to the board and risk committee.

Siloed and disparate risk and control self-assessment processes may be adequate for firms beginning to integrate risk management across the firm. But, as institutions improve their firm-wide self-assessment process, increased automation may become necessary to promote corporate usefulness and accessibility. Some firms are adopting the emerging practice of an internally developed or vendor-based database package. A database can afford efficiencies and support the risk control process.

What are the advantages of risk and control self-assessment by a business unit over audit risk assessment? Given the premise that 'business line managers own the risk', is it not best for such business managers to assess the risk themselves? Thus, the onus for risk identification resides in the self-assessment, not audit's risk assessment. At the same time, the role of internal audit migrates to self-assessment validation. Also, line management has first-hand knowledge of activities. Thus, the self-assessment framework is more efficient in terms of risk identification, assessment, monitoring and control/mitigation.

Risk indicators and escalation triggers

Now let us consider the 'key' risk indicators and escalation triggers, the second of the three essential ingredients of the operational risk tool set. BCBS (2002b) defines 'key risk indicators' as:

> statistics and/or metrics, often financial, which can provide insight into a bank's risk position. These indicators tend to be reviewed on a periodic basis (such as monthly or quarterly) to alert banks to changes that may be indicative of risk concerns. Such indicators may include the number of failed trades, staff turnover rates and the frequency and/or severity of errors and omissions.

In the same paper, thresholds/limits are described as follows: 'typically tied to risk indicators, threshold levels (or changes) in key risk indicators, when exceeded, alert management to areas of potential problems'. Given the credit and market risk management paradigm, escalation triggers are simply the limit that has been placed on the indicator (e.g. the position). A threshold breach is not unlike limit excess. A two-tiered escalation process starts with an initial internal threshold breach prompting business unit management reporting. A more material breach triggers senior management and board reporting. Emerging practice institutions have embraced the concept of establishing centralized monitoring and reporting of business line key indicators/triggers and associated loss indicators.

The opaque and institution-specific nature of operational risk calls for business unit metrics for both inherent risk and risk management. Currently, we lack readily identifiable markers for operational risk severity, frequency and volatility. A few institutions are on the brink of leveraging risk self-assessment data to generate useful risk and performance indicators. This information may help to satisfy qualitative eligibility requirements. The information can also support risk management effectiveness and a forward-looking perspective. Operational risk key indicators include key performance indicators (KPIs) and key risk indicators (KRIs). Three meaningful distinctions are shown in Table 2.4.

So, poor performance may lead to an increase in material risk, but not all poor performance percolates to material risk increase. As others have said, the importance of indicators is not that we get the metrics just right, but that we don't get them just wrong, and we shouldn't let perfection preclude progress. For example, often key indicator[9] 'islands' exist across

TABLE 2.4 ■ Key indicator comparison: risk versus performance

KPIs	KRIs
Shorter-term, profit/loss and income statement related	Longer-term, balance sheet and capital related
Bottom-up, used by business unit management	Top-down, used by senior management and the board of directors
More metrics more useful to more people	Less metrics more useful to fewer people

[9] For purposes of simplicity, the indicators will be generically referred to as *key indicators* in the remainder of this chapter.

firms through various policies and directives. However, typically, centralized key indicator reporting and escalation are not formalized. We need to build consensus both across and within business lines. In conjunction with other tools (i.e. loss database and self-assessment), key indicators should provide the appropriate incentive and flexibility for risk management and capital allocation. Indicators are more prospective than retrospective. However, looking forward alone is not sufficient. Thus, there has been a proliferation of experimental loss tracking methodologies and database efforts.

Loss reporting

BCBS (2001b) states the following qualifying criteria for the Standardized Approach: 'Measurement and validation ... The bank must have both appropriate risk reporting systems to generate data used in the calculation of a capital charge and the ability to construct management reporting based on the results.'

Loss tracking is the final leg of the operational risk tool set. Firms have traditionally tracked losses – in particular, fraud – through subsidiary ledgers and general ledger accounts. However, such loss tracking is generally based upon fiscal year (i.e. when loss occurred). For Basel II, loss tracking through economic based root cause analysis is also suggested. In this way, firms identify cause and effect, and also earmark loss attribution.

Some firms use blunt top-down indicators to establish economic capital levels. An example is the percentage of non-interest expense (NIX). The NIX dilemma is that, as a firm invests in internal controls (thereby presumably lowering composite risk), the NIX-generated minimum economic capital amount increases. More risk-sensitive, bottom-up and, at the least, directionally correct indicators are required. Shifting away from only tracking accounting loss from an effect standpoint encourages more sophisticated loss tracking. It is also useful to track economic loss to identify root cause analysis. Attaching the loss type to the business line where loss occurred further enhances risk identification, measurement, monitoring and control. Selected loss tracking emerging practices include establishment of:

■ a 'de minimis' loss reporting threshold (e.g. $10,000 equivalent per loss event) commensurate with the size, complexity and risk profile of the institution;

■ a loss escalation policy;

■ appropriate security provisions to safeguard input to the loss database system;

■ an appropriate time for loss record retention (at a minimum, five years).

2.4.2 Deliverables

From a 'top-down' perspective, quarterly reporting of the operational risk tool set to senior management and the board is the aggregate emerging practice deliverable. Subsequent to a successful launch and maturation of the tool set elements, the key challenge is *linkage*. For example, how can one integrate risk self-assessments, key indicators and audit scoring? To truly have robust operational risk reporting, it is necessary to establish all three reporting types, and then successfully wed them together. Therefore the deliverables should include: integrated risk assessment; Basel's key indicator metrics; and Basel's loss database format.

Integrated risk assessment

Integrated risk assessment is a 'top-down' LCBO emerging practice that can be used to track composite risk at the Basel business line level 1, as discussed later in this chapter.[10] The tool colour-codes the high composite risk level as red, moderate as yellow and low as green (colours not shown in the example in Table 2.5). The basis for business line risk ratings can be derived from internal audit reports, risk self-assessments and supervisory reviews.

This tool can allow business unit management, senior management and the board to look at a single piece of paper and pinpoint the firm's high-risk areas. This may be looked at by risk, business activity, in aggregate, or a combination thereof. It is also a useful tool to trend risk levels over time for a given unit, business line and enterprise-wide. The use of integrated risk assessment by regulators and the industry encourages, for a given change in risk, a corresponding shift in the firm's risk management and supervisory programme. This promotes closer linkage between the enterprise's risk profile, risk management and risk-focused supervision.

Basel's key indicator metrics

BCBS (2001b) states the following qualifying criteria for the Standardized Approach: 'Measurement and validation ... The bank must develop specific, documented criteria for mapping current business lines and activities into the standardized framework. The criteria must be reviewed and adjusted for new or changing business activities and risks as appropriate.'

Many firms are challenged to find appropriate indicators to track operational risk. Fortunately, Basel has established an introductory emerging practice roadmap to track

TABLE 2.5 Integrated risk assessment: simplified example for illustrative purposes

Business unit	Business line	Credit	Market	Operational
Investment banking	Corporate finance	Moderate	High	Low
	Trading and sales	Moderate	Moderate	High
Banking	Retail banking	Moderate	Low	Moderate
	Commercial banking	High	High	Moderate
	Payment/settlement	Moderate	Low	Low
Others	Retail brokerage	Moderate	Moderate	Moderate
	Asset management	Low	Moderate	Low
	Composite	Moderate	Moderate/High	Moderate/Low

[10] Typically, auditable entities reside at the more granular Basel level 2 business line. Alternatively, 'standardized' risk assessment can drill down to that level.

operational risk. Basel's approach encompasses three business units (investment banking, banking and others) that collectively span eight business lines. As part of the Standardized Approach, an indicator is used in conjunction with the business line *beta factor*.[11] The product is the amount of operational risk minimum regulatory capital allocated for that business. This approach uses industry data and does not take into account firm-specific risk mitigating controls (e.g. loss experience in addition to various qualitative factors such as key indicators and self-assessments). These factors are only included in the AMA.

BCBS (2001b, p. 6) also states: 'Within each business line, there is a broad indicator specified that reflects the size or volume of banks' activities in that area. The indicator serves as a proxy for the scale of business operations and the likely scale of operational risk exposure within each of these business lines.'

BCBS (2001a, p. 7) originally stipulated the matrix of business lines in relation to indicator shown in Table 2.6). It is noteworthy that BCBS (2001b) later specified gross income as the indicator across *all* business lines. There are four lines where alternative indicators were stipulated in BCBS (2001a), specifically retail banking, commercial banking, payment and settlement, and asset management. For these lines, the specified secondary indicators may be used with gross income to achieve a more focused evaluation of the operational risk trend. As such, a more cohesive explanation of operational risk fluctuation is signalled. The point is *not* that gross income is a panacea. Rather, it is that tracking financial performance at the business line level can provide a gateway to more granularity so that firms can generate improved bottom-up business line specific metrics. Further, this is where the firm

TABLE 2.6 ■ Business units, business lines and size/volume indicators of the Standardized Approach

Business unit	Business lines*	Indicator
Investment banking	Corporate finance	Gross income[†]
	Trading and sales	Gross Income
Banking	Retail banking	Annual average assets
	Commercial banking	Annual average assets
	Payment and settlement	Annual settlement throughput
Others	Retail brokerage	Gross income
	Asset management	Total funds under management

* An eighth business line, agency services and custody, was added in BCBS (2001b) as part of the banking business unit.

† BCBS (2001b, p. 7, note 5) defines gross income as follows: 'Gross Income = Net Interest Income + Net Non-Interest Income (comprising (i) fees and commissions receivable less fees and commissions payable, (ii) the net result on financial operations and (iii) other gross income. This excludes extraordinary or irregular items). It is intended that this measure should reflect income *before* deduction of operational losses.'

[11] BCBS (2001a) states: 'The *beta factor* serves as a rough proxy for the relationship between the industry's operational risk loss experience for a given business line and the broad financial indicator representing the bank's activity in that business line, calibrated to a desired supervisory soundness standard.'

bridges the gap from tracking loss origin ('the collateral that is in the vault'), to leveraging a cost-effective corporate framework. As such, this practice is not only a regulatory exercise, but can also enhance organizational efficiency and stakeholder value.

Given quarterly tracking, once sufficient data are accumulated, meaningful trend information can be obtained. A firm may chart each business line's inherent operational risk level. Significant information can be tracked at the business line level by the finance department. This approach does not provide a high level of depth and does not incorporate firm-specific risk management. However, trend information at the line level would be useful in establishing guidelines for the necessary investment in risk management, number of employees, audit staff, etc. In cross-analyzing the latter risk management types against the former risk proxies, one would expect to observe a correlation. Thereby, noted risk increases would be accompanied by increased risk management expenditures. In contrast, divergences could be back-tested against business line loss history. BCBS (2001b) suggests that using an average figure (e.g. three-year average) could be preferable, given certain circumstances.

Basel's loss database format

BCBS (2001b) states the following qualifying criterion for the Standardized Approach: 'Measurement and validation ... The bank must begin to systematically track relevant operational risk data, including internal loss data, by business line.' However, under the current proposals, detailed loss data by risk type are only relevant to those banks using the AMA.

For firms endeavouring to move towards the advanced approaches, implementation of a disciplined database is encouraged to help improve risk management. BCBS (2001b) includes a methodology for loss tracking using a matrix of business lines against event types. The eight business lines are complemented by loss event type classification to identify the risk management activity. The matrix changed from its inception as Annex 4 of BCBS (2001a) to Annex 2 of BCBS (2001b). The current version of the matrix is shown in Table 7.2 on page 132. The matrix will probably continue to evolve as the definitions of event types are refined further.

2.5 Conclusion

As recently as the late 1990s, establishing a corporate risk management function to explicitly manage operational risk seemed a far-fetched proposition. Conversely, in the Basel II arena, some firms plan by 2007 to have an operational risk management department on the same level as credit and market risk – in other words, mostly completed, or at a fairly mature and independent stage. Reality lies between these polarities.

Business lines traditionally manage operational risk on a largely intuitive basis. The result ranges from the typical organization that has had a couple of bumps along the road to corporate governance breakdowns such as Baring's. Historically, operational risk management has been conducted under the axiom 'if it ain't broke, don't fix it'.

Industry guidance, not the least of which is Basel II, follows the concept that operational risk management is a reiterative and non-linear process. Unlike other 'building block' approaches (e.g. a value-at-risk model) the unique and idiosyncratic nature of operational risk precludes such a disciplined, straightforward and direct problem-solving approach.[12] To illustrate, some institutional cultures favour quantitative risk management at the outset. Such firms focus on tracking losses to build operational risk value-at-risk engines that produce a measurable outcome. Other institutions initially prefer qualitative risk management and conduct risk self-assessments and track gaps.

The point of this chapter is *not* to endorse a given approach or framework, but to highlight the appropriate discipline and managerial expectations for risk management and corporate governance. While the process should improve over time, the key to a successful operational risk management programme is that 'it's not about the destination, it's about the journey'.

Users expecting a quick fix from this programme would be well advised to look elsewhere, or be content with the pedestrian Basic Indicator Approach and conventional 8 percent regulatory capital charge. Little to no industry literature has empirically validated the economic benefit of having such a programme in place. But to quote the view of most experienced operational risk managers: 'There is not only Basel, but also risk management and process improvement. Capital calculation is of less interest, it will happen whether we want it to or not. The name of the game is cost-effective process improvement.'

---

[12] For credit and market risk, loss is due to empirical and observable market factors, such as inability of an obligor to pay. For operational risk, the problem often resides within firm-specific breakdowns such as inadequate underwriting and/or suitability standards, and improper oversight.

CHAPTER 3

Measurement of operational risk: the Basel approach

Victor Dowd

3.1 Introduction

Operational risk and its measurement are among the most topical issues in the current debate on risk management. Regulators have played an important part in this. The work of the Basel Committee on Banking Supervision ('the Committee' or BCBS) on a regulatory regime for operational risk contributed enormously to the width and depth of the debate. This and other books and articles on the subject would probably not have been written without the Committee's initiative.

More importantly, despite much controversy and initially strong opposition by many industry professionals to the Committee's proposals, this debate has been immensely productive. Industry and academia have made enormous progress in understanding operational risk and developing techniques for its assessment and measurement. Over the past few years banks in the forefront of the development have started implementing firm-wide systems for collecting information on operational losses and other relevant quantitative and qualitative data. A variety of techniques are being developed for the analysis of this information and the generation of aggregate and disaggregate measures of operational risk.

The initiative of regulators would surely have been much less influential had they only considered requirements for the proper management of operational risk. It was the prospect of a Pillar 1 capital charge, the commitment of regulators to formulate measurement approaches to the quantification of operational risk regulatory capital, that spurred the debate and the progress that has been made over the past few years. This chapter aims to set out the basic framework of the Committee's proposals for the operational risk capital charge. Its focus is on the definition of operational risk and its quantification under the proposed Basic Indicator Approach (BIA) and Standardized Approach (STA).

However, measurement of risk is not an end in itself. It is part of the wider risk management process and informs the monitoring, control and mitigation of risks. As such measurement of risk and the increasing sophistication of measurement techniques have played a pivotal role in the history of the Accord and the wider regulatory developments in particular since the beginning of the 1990s. At the same time and partly as a result of advances in the understanding and measurement of market and credit risk, the significance and perception of operational risk in today's financial markets have changed. An outline of both these developments will enable an understanding of the rationale and basic design of the Basel approach and why regulators believe that a regulatory framework for operational risks is now needed.

3.2 Development of the Basel Accord

3.2.1 'The Accord is dead – long live the Accord'

That is how Howard Davies, chairman of the Financial Services Authority, commented on the launch of the review of the Accord some four years ago. It is probably safe to assume that the banking industry does not cheer the rule of the Accord with quite the same enthusiasm. However, the overhaul of the current Accord is something the banking industry has been asking for as a matter of urgency and for very good reasons.

The deficiencies in the measurement of credit risk underlying the current capital requirements and the arbitrage opportunities it provided became increasingly intolarable and created significant distortions. These deficiencies have been the driving force behind the launch of the Capital Review, as the Committee's work on the revision of the Accord is commonly known. The regime enshrined in the 1988 Accord, with its crude bucketing of risk asset classes, is far from generating risk-sensitive capital requirements. Even worse, the uniform risk weightings of, for instance, 100 percent for corporates, whether AAA or investment grade, give perverse incentives. In terms of capital requirements and related costs, high-risk, high-return lending in too many instances is 'cheaper' than low-risk, low-return lending. And recent experience has demonstrated that the sovereign risk associated with lending to OECD countries is not as risk-free as the Accord's 0 percent risk weighting suggests.

The Committee has not been blind to the shortcomings of the regime. Already in the 1988 Accord it reckoned that the framework of risk weightings had been kept as simple as possible, with some inevitable 'broad-brush judgements' as to the risk weights applicable to different types of assets (BCBS 1988, p. 8). Despite these shortcomings, the Committee felt that the proposed approach was best suited to furthering the primary objective of the Accord: to 'strengthen the soundness and stability of the international banking system' by introducing a regime that has a 'high degree of consistency in its application to banks in different countries', thus 'diminishing a source of competitive inequality among international banks' (BCBS 1988, p. 1). That has been achieved, and the Accord's recommendations and their translation into European banking legislation proved immensely successful in triggering the convergence of regulatory concepts well beyond the participating G10 countries and the European Union.

The Accord's focus was on credit risk as the most prominent risk category at the time. However, the Accord explicitly acknowledged that 'other risks .... need to be taken into account by supervisors in assessing overall capital adequacy' (BCBS 1988, p. 1). The primary objective was to provide an approach to a rough and ready quantification of regulatory capital, with some built-in conservatism to ensure some additional buffer against other risks. Over time the adverse effects of the overly crude risk measurement on the risk-taking behaviour of banks became only too apparent. Among the risks that were not, or not adequately, captured market risk was the most prominent.

3.2.2 From quantity to quality

The shortcomings of the Accord in capturing market risk resulted in the first major amendment to the Accord. The advances of the industry in the measurement of market risk determined much of its design. The 1996 Market Risk Amendment was the first stepping stone in the move of regulators towards more risk-sensitive capital requirements. As such it marked a change of paradigm for banking regulation. It is striking that this change of paradigm, though driven by the increasing sophistication of the techniques for measuring risk, was referred to as the move 'from quantity to quality'. Despite increasingly complex rulebooks specifying how to quantify regulatory capital, quality of the management of risk is still the ultimate objective of regulators and the 1996 Amendment has delivered on this objective.

The Amendment introduced a regulatory framework for market risk based upon a choice between simple standardized risk measurement approaches and the use of sophisticated internal risk modelling techniques combined with the prospect of benefiting from a more risk-sensitive and significantly reduced capital charge. The advantage of a reduced capital charge comes at a cost. The use of internal risk modelling for the quantification of regulatory capital was made subject to explicit supervisory approval and review to ensure adherence to high standards for managing market risk and a sound control environment surrounding the internal risk model. Thus, the Market Risk Amendment introduced a direct regulatory link between internal, more risk-sensitive techniques for the quantification of regulatory capital on the one hand, and the quality of the management processes and controls surrounding the measurement system on the other. For the first time regulators did not simply take the stick but offered a carrot. They provided a capital incentive to encourage firms to migrate from standardized approaches to more sophisticated internal techniques of measuring risk and, more importantly, the much improved risk management that goes along with the refined measurement.

It is noteworthy that at the same time the Committee, together with the Technical Committee of the International Organization of Securities Commissions, launched a series of annual surveys on banks' disclosure of information on their trading and derivatives activities.[1] The explicit objective of these surveys was to foster market discipline as a supplement

---

[1] BCBS and Technical Committee on the International Organisation of Securities Commissions (1995). This first report, which was accompanied by recommendations on appropriate public disclosure of information, was followed by a series of annual surveys. The Committee's increasing interest in fostering market discipline by public disclosure resulted in the setting up of the Transparency Sub-Group and the publication of a number of papers on the issue (BCBS 1998, 1999, 2000).

to supervisory discipline. Thus, the basic elements of the revised Accord, in current jargon, the three pillars of regulation – minimum capital requirements, supervisory review and disclosure requirements – were already in place by the mid-1990s. That is the essence of the new regulatory paradigm and it did not require much prophetic vision to foresee that credit risk and ultimately operational risk could not escape this paradigm. The underlying concept and basic elements of the proposed regulatory framework for operational risk follow closely the logic of the 1996 Market Risk Amendment. The framework consists of:

- a spectrum of increasingly sophisticated measurement approaches, the Basic Indicator (BIA), the Standardized (STA) and the Advanced Measurement Approaches (AMA);

- a calibration of the charge generated by the BIA and the STA such as to create a capital incentive to move to the more risk-sensitive AMA; and

- rigorous qualitative and quantitative entry requirements for the AMA and to a lesser extent for the STA.

Supervisory review and approval of the STA and the AMA as well as disclosure requirements to foster market discipline complement the framework.

3.2.3 'Like matter, risk cannot be destroyed'[2]

Instead it rather changes form and operational risk seems to be an increasingly prominent form risk takes.

The move of regulators towards incorporating operational risk in the regulatory capital as a distinct risk category does not blindly follow the logic of the new paradigm. It responds to the increasing significance of operational risk, the need to reflect this risk category in banks' assessment of their full risk profile, and the concurrent shift in its perception and the risk-taking attitude of banks and other financial institutions towards operational risk.

Risks are compounded. Credit and market risks, the raw material of the business of banks and other financial institutions, do not exist in a pure form. The handling of these risks is based upon transactions that presuppose an operational infrastructure comprising people, systems and processes within and outside the organization. There are many examples that highlight the increasing significance of operational risks in today's financial markets. To name just a few:

- The growing e-commerce brings with it operational risks including exposure to external fraud and system security risks of unprecedented scale and impact.

- Large-scale mergers, demergers and consolidations test the viability of new or newly integrated systems.

- The use of more highly automated technology transforms risks from manual processing errors to high-impact system failure risks, as greater reliance is placed on globally integrated systems.

[2] From Clarke and Varma (1999).

- Growing use of outsourcing arrangements and the participation in clearing and settlement systems mitigate some risks but can also present significant other risks to banks.
- Conversely, banks are increasingly acting as very large-volume service providers insourcing back and middle office functions to capitalize on their expertise and comparative advantage in handling operational risks.

The rise of operational risk is not driven solely by its role as an undesired by-product of increasingly complex business activities and operations. As the trend towards insourcing demonstrates, operational risk is becoming a risk that banks and other financial institutions are taking deliberately for hoped-for returns.

More generally, in today's increasingly complex domestic and global markets with squeezing margins, a cost-effective operational infrastructure and economies of increased scale are key drivers of profitability. Risk cannot be destroyed and yesterday's credit and market risks, at least some of them, are the operational risks of today and tomorrow. Sophisticated measurement and management of risk, the decomposition of risks into risk components, and the design of products with ever more complex risk features resulted in a more and more widespread use of complex products and strategies for taking and mitigating market and credit risks. This increasing sophistication allows for much improved management and control of these risks, but the concurrent complexity exposes firms to increasing operational risks that are incurred deliberately instead of the mitigated credit or market risks. Examples of common ways of taking operational risk are as follows:

- The use of sophisticated techniques for mitigating credit and market risk (e.g. collateralization, netting, credit derivatives, asset securitization) transforms these risks into operational risks.
- Trading activities in increasingly complex products or based upon complex arbitrage strategies may leave banks with limited or no market risk but significant exposure to operational risks.
- Any form of disintermediation implies that those acting in the capacity of agents take operational risks instead of the mediated credit or market risks.

As a result of these developments operational risk is becoming an increasingly significant element of banks' and other financial institutions' risk profile. It may affect different business lines in different ways and to different degrees, but, whatever the exposure, operational risk can no longer be conceived as a risk that is solely associated with the cost dimension of doing business. Instead it has to be viewed as an integral part of the bundle of risks that are taken with a view to generating profits. The more accurate the measurement of market and credit risk becomes, the more obvious it is that operational risk impacts upon the profit margin and has to be analyzed in terms of the income stream that a business generates.

Banks and other financial institutions increasingly acknowledge the importance of operational risk and that proper risk measurement and allocation of commensurate economic capital are a necessary prerequisite for identifying which businesses are truly profitable and therefore increase shareholder value. In the Committee's Quantitative Impact Study of 2001, 41 banks reported economic capital for operational risk. On average, these banks allocated 16 percent of economic capital to operational risk. The techniques of the majority of these banks for measuring operational risk were probably still rather crude. But the need to assess operational risks properly and to reflect these risks in the economic capital allocation across the different businesses is now widely accepted.

The Basel approach to operational risk responds to this need. As for market and credit risk, the underlying logic of the proposed regulatory framework is that of a move from quantity to quality. The spectrum of approaches for the quantification of regulatory capital aims to provide capital incentives for banks to migrate to the most sophisticated techniques for measuring operational risk, and, more importantly, the much improved risk management that goes along with them. The Committee's recent decision not to impose a minimum floor requirement for AMA re-emphasizes this logic and encourages the industry to speed up further its efforts to achieve credible and robust industry-wide standards for advanced measurement of operational risk in time for the implementation of the revised Accord.

3.3 Definition of operational risk

Measurement has to start with a clear understanding of what is to be measured. By the time of the launch of the Capital Review there was no commonly accepted definition of operational risk. After a lengthy debate between regulators and the industry, views converged towards a definition of operational risk as 'the risk of loss resulting from inadequate or failed internal processes, people and systems or from external events'. Some of the problems with the measurement of operational risk have been addressed by excluding from this definition certain aspects which are particularly difficult to measure. BCBS (2001b, p. 2) specifies that for the purpose of the Pillar 1 capital charge the definition of operational risk includes legal but excludes business and reputational risks. The paper also clarifies that the Pillar 1 capital charge is not meant to capture or reflect systemic risks.

It is important to note that this definition is based on the underlying causes of operational risk. It seeks to delineate operational risks from other risks by referring to key internal and external aspects of the business operation that, alone or in combination, can cause operational losses. The focus on causes is imperative for the management of operational risk. However, for the purpose of measuring operational risks and assessing their potential impact in terms of both the frequency and severity of operational risk events the analysis of causes is arguably of little assistance.

Therefore regulators, together with the industry, developed a more complex concept of operational risk, which is based upon the distinction between causes, actual risk or loss events, and the related profit and loss effects, that is, the operational losses (see Figure 3.1). Operational risk can be analyzed at each of these levels.

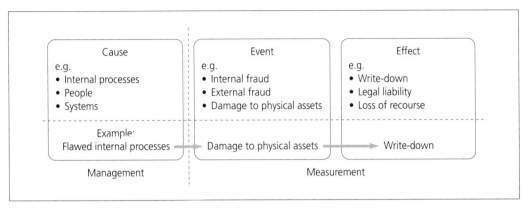

FIGURE 3.1 ▥ Analysis of operational risk by causes, events and effects

The concept allows for a granular mapping of operational risk based upon identified risk or loss events. With the help of the industry the BCBS (2001b, Annex 2) developed a matrix with seven broad categories of loss events that are further broken down into sub-categories and related activity examples (see Table 3.1). This classification of loss events is very similar to the typology of 'hazards' used by the insurance industry.

TABLE 3.1 ▥ Detailed loss event type classification

Event-type category (Level 1)	Definition	Categories (Level 2)	Activity examples (Level 3)
Internal fraud	Losses due to acts of a type intended to defraud, misappropriate property or circumvent regulations, the law or company policy, excluding diversity/ discrimination events, which involves at least one internal party	Unauthorized activity	Transactions not reported (intentional) Transaction type unauthorized (with monetary loss) Mismarking of position (intentional)
		Theft and fraud	Fraud/credit fraud/worthless deposits Theft/extortion/embezzlement/ robbery Misappropriation of assets Malicious destruction of assets Forgery Check kiting Smuggling Account take-over/impersonation Tax non-compliance/evasion (wilful) Bribes/kickbacks Insider trading (not on firm's account)

TABLE 3.1 ■ *Continued*

Event-type category (Level 1)	Definition	Categories (Level 2)	Activity examples (Level 3)
External fraud	Losses due to acts of a type intended to defraud, misappropriate property or circumvent the law, by a third party	Theft and fraud	Theft/robbery Forgery Check kiting
		Systems security	Hacking damage Theft of information (with monetary loss)
Employment practices and workplace safety	Losses arising from acts inconsistent with employment, health or safety laws or agreements, from payment of personal injury claims, or from diversity/discrimination events	Employee relations	Compensation, benefit, termination issues Organized labour activity
		Safe environment	General liability (slip and fall, etc.) Employee health and safety rules events Workers' compensation
		Diversity and discrimination	All discrimination types
Clients, products and business practices	Losses arising from an unintentional or negligent failure to meet a professional obligation to specific clients (including fiduciary and suitability requirements), or from the nature or design of a product	Suitability, disclosure and fiduciary	Fiduciary breaches/guideline violations Suitability/disclosure issues (KYC, etc.) Retail consumer disclosure violations Breach of privacy Aggressive sales Account churning Misuse of confidential information Lender liability
		Improper business or market practices	Antitrust Improper trade/market practices Market manipulation Insider trading (on firm's account) Unlicensed activity Money laundering
		Product flaws	Product defects (unauthorised, etc.) Model errors
		Selection, sponsorship and exposure	Failure to investigate client per guidelines Exceeding client exposure limits
		Advisory activities	Disputes over performance of advisory activities
Damage to physical assets	Losses arising from loss or damage to physical assets from natural disaster or other events	Disasters and other events	Natural disaster losses Human losses from external sources (terrorism, vandalism)

TABLE 3.1 ▦ *Continued*

Event-type category (Level 1)	Definition	Categories (Level 2)	Activity examples (Level 3)
Business disruption and system failures	Losses arising from disruption of business or system failures	Systems	Hardware Software Telecommunications Utility outage/disruptions
Execution, delivery and process management	Losses from failed transaction processing or process management, from relations with trade counterparties and vendors	Transaction capture, execution and maintenance	Miscommunication Data entry, maintenance or loading error Missed deadline or responsibility Model/system misoperation Accounting error/entity attribution error Other task misperformance Delivery failure Collateral management failure Reference data maintenance
		Monitoring and reporting	Failed mandatory reporting obligation Inaccurate external report (loss incurred)
		Customer intake and documentation	Client permissions/disclaimers missing Legal documents missing/incomplete
		Customer/client account management	Unapproved access given to accounts Incorrect client records (loss incurred) Negligent loss or damage of client assets
		Trade counterparties	Non-client counterparty misperformance Miscellaneous non-client counterparty disputes
		Vendors and suppliers	Outsourcing Vendor disputes

The importance of the definition of operational risk and the suggested loss event typology can hardly be overestimated. Both have helped pave the way for an understanding of operational risk and an operational risk terminology that is now widely shared among industry professionals and academia. This emerging operational risk language, like any other, will have to evolve over time in order to live up to a changing and increasingly complex world of operational risk and to reflect the evolving understanding of this world. 'Dialects' that are likely to emerge, in particular in the course of ongoing work on different types of advanced measurement approaches or components thereof, ranging from loss distribution approaches to Bayesian networks and scorecard-based methodologies, will enrich rather than threaten this language. The fact that regulators, by drawing on existing knowledge and industry expertise, have significantly assisted and indeed triggered this language-building process is probably not a particular merit but it could prove their most important and lasting achievement. Whatever changes we will see over time, the understanding and analysis of operational risk in terms of loss event types as they cut across business lines is very likely to be here to stay.

The Committee reckons that analysis of operational risk on the basis of loss event types and their potential impact across different business lines is demanding and cannot be achieved easily even by many of the large internationally active banks within the Accord's remit. Accordingly, collection and analysis of operational loss data and other more qualitative risk information in the suggested or some other customized format are required only under AMA. As an alternative to these advanced approaches the Committee has developed the much simpler Basic Indicator and the intermediate Standardized Approach which we will be discussing in more detail in the next two sections.

3.4 The Basic Indicator Approach

The Basic Indicator Approach is the default position and as such no conditions, other than those required for market entry, are prescribed. Given that the Basel proposals are specifically designed with sophisticated large internationally active and diverse banks in mind, why has such an approach been included? The answer is simple. As mentioned earlier, Basel has developed a spectrum of increasingly sophisticated approaches and the BIA is the starting point in this evolutionary framework. The BIA will be used not only by large internationally active and diverse banks but also by smaller domestic institutions. For example, the EU will translate the Accord into a directive on capital adequacy. This directive, referred to as CAD3, will be much more extensive in scope than just large internationally active and diverse banks considered under Basel. CAD3 will be applied to credit institutions which include the Basel banks, investment firms, building societies and asset managers. Secondly, the 1988 Accord has been implemented in over 100 countries worldwide, and there is no reason to believe that the new Accord will not be likewise implemented.

As the BIA is the default option, the only requirement on institutions using the BIA is to be able to measure the indicator used in the capital calculation, which under the BIA is gross income. The formula used for calculating the capital charge under the BIA is

$$K_{BIA} = \alpha\, GI,$$

where K_{BIA} is the capital charge under the Basic Indicator Approach, α is the predefined scaling factor set by the Committee[3] and GI is the gross income used for regulatory capital purposes, which is the average of gross income over the past three years.[4]

However, before considering what gross income is, a more apt question ought to be considered: why gross income?

Application of an indicator for use in a measurement system, which is evolving and has no entry criteria, presupposes that the indicator is not only uncomplicated and basic but already in use, or at least that the components which make up the indicator are already in use. As the BIA would be universally applied, the indicator, gross income, needs to be comparable across the different jurisdictions. Consistent use in different jurisdictions also implies some degree of validation by a third party or independent source such as an external auditor. Although numerous possible indicators were put forward by industry representatives and discussed with regulators, no perfect indicator was found. However, what did become apparent was that in virtually all cases, gross income was the least worst option available. It is the least worst option as:

- income is no measure of operational risk but a reasonably reliable indicator for size of activities;
- it is readily available;
- it is verifiable;
- it is reasonably consistent and comparable across jurisdictions; and
- it has the advantage of being counter-cyclical.

For the purposes of minimum regulatory capital requirements, the Basel Committee has defined gross income as the sum of net interest income, net non-interest income, net trading income and other income. It is gross of provisions, exclusive of extraordinary or irregular items. This is not an accountancy definition, not least as four of the elements of gross income, three are explicitly netted figures and the other has an implicit reference to a netted figure. That said, the definition has its origin in the OECD, and has been in use for some time. The proposals in the Basel Accord are to be applied to banks at the highest level of consolidation, and at this consolidated level many large, internationally active and diverse institutions will have non-banking subsidiaries such as insurance companies. It is worth noting that the Basel proposals explicitly exclude insurance companies from this framework

---

[3] At the time of writing, the Committee has set α at 0.15. However, this value may change as a result of the QIS3 survey.

[4] A three-year average is used as a smoothing mechanism. The results from previous surveys from Basel have indicated that gross income can be a volatile metric.

as they are subject to a different regulatory regime. How do the individual elements of gross income map into the current regulatory requirements and in particular the Banking Accounts Directive within a European Union context? Taking the four components of the Basel definition in turn, net interest income equals interest receivable and similar income minus interest payable and similar charges; net non-interest income equals commissions receivable minus commissions payable; net trading income equals net profit or net loss on financial operations; and other income equals income from securities[5] plus other operating income.

3.5 The Standardized Approach

Moving along the spectrum of increasing sophistication from the BIA, we find the STA. As in the BIA, the capital charge is levied on the basis of gross income. In this respect gross income is still the 'measure' of operational risk. However, entry to the STA is conditional upon the fulfilment of specific criteria. These criteria are aimed at measuring a bank's operational risk management and as such many of the conditions do not readily lend themselves to quantification, let alone quantification in a consistent manner across the various G10 jurisdictions. Therefore, the operational risk measurement paradigm under the STA is more assessment than quantification.

What are the differences between the two approaches? Unlike the BIA, the use of the STA presupposes that operational risk is explicitly recognized and managed as a distinct and separate risk category – distinct and separate from risks such as credit, market, interest rate and liquidity, for example. This explicit recognition would be demonstrated via management treatment of operational risk, especially management's view of the potential threats to the bank's safety and soundness. Under this stipulation, the measurement requirement may be considered as a simple binary function: either the bank does or does not meet the demand. Operational risk is present in virtually all bank transactions and activities, which means that in the absence of strong, clear, concise and dynamic guidance from senior management, including the board of directors, there is a likelihood that some operational risks will go unmanaged.

A second difference is in the use of the business lines. Under the BIA the bank is treated as a single entity, whereas under the STA it is subdivided into smaller units, namely the eight business lines shown in Table 3.2.

In terms of operational risk measurement, under the Standardized Approach, a bank is expected to be able to map its gross income into these business lines, and in this respect the principles required for determining gross income under the BIA are equally applicable. The principles for business line mapping are as follows:

(a) All activities must be mapped into the eight level 1 business lines in a mutually exclusive and jointly exhaustive manner.

(b) Any banking or non-banking activity which cannot be readily mapped into the business line framework, but which represents an ancillary function to an activity included in the

---

[5] Income from securities is placed within other income for reasons of consistency with the EU proposals on capital adequacy and operational risk.

TABLE 3.2 ■ Mapping of business lines

Level 1	Level 2	Activity groups
Corporate finance	Corporate finance Municipal/government finance Merchant banking Advisory services	Mergers and acquisitions, underwriting, privatizations, securitization, research, debt (government, high yield), equity, syndications, IPO, secondary private placements
Trading and sales	Sales Market making Proprietary positions Treasury	Fixed Income, equity, foreign exchanges, commodities, credit, funding, own position securities, lending and repos, brokerage, debt, prime brokerage
Retail banking	Retail banking	Retail lending and deposits, banking services, trust and estates
	Private banking	Private lending and deposits, banking services, trust and estates, investment advice
	Card services	Merchant/commercial/corporate cards, private labels and retail
Commercial banking	Commercial banking	Project finance, real estate, export finance, trade finance, factoring, leasing, lends, guarantees, bills of exchange
Payment and settlement*	External clients	Payments and collections, funds transfer, clearing and settlement
Agency services	Custody	Escrow, depository receipts, securities lending (customers), corporate actions
	Corporate agency Corporate trust	Issuer and paying agents
Asset management	Discretionary fund management	Pooled, segregated, retail, institutional, closed, open, private equity
	Non-discretionary fund management	Pooled, segregated, retail, institutional, closed, open
Retail brokerage	Retail brokerage	Execution and full service

* Payment and settlement losses related to a bank's own activities would be incorporated in the loss experience of the affected business line.

framework, must be allocated to the business line it supports. If more than one business line is supported through the ancillary activity, an objective mapping criterion must be used (such as proportional allocation of the indicators).

(c) When mapping gross income, if an activity cannot be mapped into a particular business line then the business line yielding the highest charge must be used. The same business line equally applies to any associated ancillary activity.

(d) The mapping of activities into business lines for operational risk capital purposes must be consistent with the definitions of business lines used for regulatory capital calculations in other risk categories, i.e. credit and market risk. Any deviations from this principle must be clearly motivated and documented.

(e) The mapping process used must be clearly documented. In particular, written business line definitions must be clear and detailed enough to allow third parties to replicate the business line mapping. Documentation must, among other things, clearly motivate any exceptions or overrides and be kept on record.

(f) Processes must be in place to define the mapping of any new activities or products.

(g) Senior management is responsible for the mapping process (which is subject to the approval by the board of directors).

(h) The mapping process to business lines must be subject to independent review.

The capital charge under the STA for operational risk is equal to the sum of the capital charge for each business line:

$$K_{STA} = \sum_{i=1}^{8} \beta_i \, GI_i$$

where K_{STA} is the capital charge under the Standardized Approach, GI_i represents the average annual level of gross income over the past three years, as defined above in the Basic Indicator Approach, for each of the eight business lines, and β_i are the beta values for each of the business lines, as given in Table 3.3.

TABLE 3.3 ■ Beta factors for the eight business lines

Business lines	Beta factors
Corporate finance (β_1)	[18%]
Trading and sales (β_2)	[18%]
Retail banking (β_3)	[12%]
Commercial banking (β_4)	[15%]
Payment and settlement (β_5)	[18%]
Agency services (β_6)	[15%]
Asset management (β_7)	[12%]
Retail brokerage (β_8)	[12%]

At the time of writing the Committee has set the beta values given above. However, these numbers may change as a result of the QIS3 survey.

3.6 Quantification of management quality

A major difference between the BIA and STA is the expectation of regulators that, under the STA, a well-run and well-managed institution will be able to:

- identify its operational risk exposures and assess its potential impact;

- monitor and report its operational risk on an ongoing basis; and

- create proper incentives by factoring operational risk into its overall business strategy.

A well-run and well-managed institution would be expected to be able to identify and understand its operational risks. It is expected to be able to aggregate these risks, and so develop its risk profile. The risk profile for each institution is unique and will reflect the size, scope and culture of the organization. The scope of operational risk events, as given above, is wide-ranging and covers events such as simple processing errors like fat finger syndrome through to unauthorized activities like rogue trading. Through the activities of the likes of John Rusnick (estimated cost to Allied Irish/All First of roughly $640 million) and Nick Leeson (which proved fatal to the long-term survival of Baring's) rogue trading has become widely publicized.

These two examples provide an assessment, albeit after the event, of the operational risk through the impact on bank solvency when operational risks crystallize. However, it should be noted that operational risk is more than just rogue trading, and the impact on bank solvency is not the sole measure of an operational risk event. As no demand is placed on a bank to collect operational risk losses (except where material), other measures or benchmarks should be employed as necessary.

Assessment of the identified risk will be largely dependent upon the judicious selection of an appropriate indicator, or other metric. In turn this will be reliant on many other factors such as the nature of business activity, geographic location, scale and complexity of the operation, and intended use within an organization, whether within a department, division, strategic business unit or at board level. Irrespective of the indicator selected, it should be an easily identified, clearly understood metric which is relevant to the needs of the business environment.

It follows that an assessment of operational risk must use a well-reasoned and well-defined set of objective criteria providing important information concerning the bank's risk profile. On the basis of this assessment, the bank has a measure of its risk exposure, both on an aggregated and individual risk basis. Armed with this information, the bank may decide to adjust its risk exposure either on an individual risk-by-risk basis or on a more aggregated basis.

The risk assessment exercise may yield a risk profile which is larger, or smaller, than that desired by the bank. In either case, the bank is likely to seek a realignment of its risk profile to fit more closely with its risk appetite. It is worth remembering that a bank is not required to eliminate, minimize or reduce its operational risk but rather to understand its risk exposure and accept an operational risk exposure it considers manageable.

In addition to identifying and assessing the risks inherent in existing products and within current activities, banks would be expected to be proactive and identify risks in new products and activities.

The result of the identification and assessment process is likely to generate a number of indicators, or metrics, through which operational risk may be monitored on an ongoing basis. This raises the questions of when and how to monitor. If operational risk is to become embedded within the culture of the organization, then monitoring should be conducted on a frequent and regular basis; in some cases this may mean monitoring in real time, in other circumstances daily, weekly or even monthly monitoring may be more appropriate. In addition, supplementary risk monitoring may also be deemed necessary, especially in the light of unusual or irregular events.

The organization must implement a system of internal reporting of operational risk with the reporting mechanism geared to the needs of the end user. This is essential if the bank's operational risk policy is to be established and evaluated. In general, the board of directors should receive higher-level information that is more focused than that needed by senior management. That is to say, the board of directors should receive enough information to understand the bank's overall operational risk profile and its material operational risks. Reporting to senior management should be from both business units and the internal audit function concerning operational risk. It is expected that such reports would cover the results of the monitoring activities including, for example, trend analysis and compliance reviews. The latter may result from internal audit but may also be derived from externally generated reports such as Section 166 reports prepared for supervisory authorities, in this case the UK FSA.

Reporting should not be viewed as a one-way street, with information only being passed upwards. Equally important is downward dissemination or feedback. An impression may be given here that only vertical information flows between a business unit and a corporate centre are to be encouraged. Vertical information flows within strategic business units are also important. As operational risk often cuts across business units, horizontal information flows across strategic business units and through the wider organization are not to be ignored.

Under the Standardized Approach, a bank is required to have an incentive structure which promotes sound operational risk practices. While nobody disagrees with the sentiment expressed, the question remains how such incentives might be measured. As stated above, many of the measurements used under the Standardized Approach are 'soft' assessment measures rather than 'hard', more traditional quantiles. Though soft, the wide range of key risk indicators are suitable for setting business-specific targets and thus providing incentives to individuals and business units to improve their performance in controlling and mitigating operational risk. It is perfectly conceivable to set a target in terms of, for example, the number of settlement errors, or the number of complaints, or the speed of error resolution, and so forth. Although many of these metrics will be unique to each bank, this does not prevent them from being used to provide incentives for the business. That said, senior management within the bank can utilize the income and expense streams which constitute gross income. For example, within a trading environment, profits from traders, either individual traders or trading teams, could be regularly reviewed and benchmarked to minimize the possibility of fraud through unauthorized trading and/or trading above set limits. In terms of the individual employee, his trading target is continually being revised which should mean, all other factors being equal, that a good end-of-year bonus may be received.

An alternative approach considers how a bank treats its own internal capital, or more specifically its internal capital allocated to operational risk. As capital is an expensive form of finance, it could have valuable uses as an operational risk management tool. The obvious way internal capital could be used is through its allocation, not only to the individual business units but also through the redistribution within the business units themselves. Not only do institutions allocate capital internally, they also set an expected return on this capital.

Allocation of economic capital reflecting operational risks means that the performance in controlling and mitigating operational risk – as measured by key risk indicators, etc. – does have an immediate impact upon return on capital. If economic capital commensurate with risk, including operational risk, is disaggregated and allocated across the bank's businesses, individuals and business units would get a strong incentive to manage operational risk in such a manner as to optimize their return on capital ratio.

Very simply, the allocation process itself becomes an operational risk management incentive, with riskier business units and/or activities attracting higher capital allocations either in absolute or proportionate terms. Over time, as the risk profile alters through a better understanding of activities, improved systems and controls, and introduction of new products, this capital allocation process would be adjusted to reflect this new profile.

3.7 Conclusion

The Basel approach, with the proposed continuum of increasingly sophisticated and risk-sensitive methodologies for quantifying the capital charge, conceives measurement of operational risk in the wider context of its proper management. Measurement is nothing more and nothing less than an integral, yet pivotal, element of the risk management cycle. It is addressed under the Basel approach much in the spirit of what Lord Kelvin (1824–1907) said already more than a century ago:

> I often say when you can measure what you are speaking about, and express it in numbers, you know something about it; but when you cannot measure it, when you cannot express it in numbers, your knowledge is of a meagre and unsatisfactory kind.
>
> (*King 2001*)

Of course, Lord Kelvin's remarks relate to science and an accuracy of measurement which for operational risk will never be achieved. In relation to operational risk the use of the word 'measure' reflects challenge and ambitious aspiration more than reality (in fact what 'measure' means for operational risk is probably closer to 'assess' or 'estimate', as will be explained in the next chapter). However, like measurement in a scientific context, assessing operational risk and, to the extent possible, expressing it in numerical terms is crucial in order to develop the understanding and knowledge necessary for its proper management.

The BIA and the STA can help to provide a reliable estimate of operational risk only where the gross income-based 'measurement' is complemented by a risk management framework that incorporates additional quantitative and qualitative assessment techniques including the analysis of key risk indicators. They are, however, necessary stepping stones in a regulatory framework that is aimed at providing incentives to the industry to further the impressive progress that has been made over the past two or three years. The ultimate objective is to promote the emergence of widely accepted standards for the proper management of operational risk, including its measurement. High standards in measuring and, more importantly, managing operational risk will provide a safer marketplace for both banks and their customers.

CHAPTER 4

A constructive review of the Basel proposals on operational risk

Jacques Pézier

4.1 Introduction

Risk and *loss* are common words that need to be clearly defined when embarking on the task of assessing operational risks. Financial institutions may rush into implementing the methodologies proposed by the Basel Committee on Banking Supervision (BCBS) in the hope of achieving better risk management – or simply to satisfy a regulatory request – but without giving enough thought to this enterprise. We show that the methodologies proposed by Basel to assess risks and calculate capital requirements are indeed poorly defined and, as far as they can be understood, misconceived. When restricting our attention to operational risks we find that their impact in the vast majority of cases is negligible compared to other risks, be they credit, market or general business risks. A few truly exceptional operational risks may, of course, lead to catastrophic consequences, but then the answer does not lie in an extra capital buffer that would have to be enormous to be of any use. An attempt to aggregate purely operational risks, as proposed by Basel in the so-called Advanced Measurement Approaches, is as futile as it is difficult. What matters in risk management is balancing all risks, whatever they are, against costs and revenues. And risks do not add up; it is the interaction between operational risks and other risks as well as the risk–reward trade-off that are of interest. Basel recognizes this broader aspect of operational risk management in its guidance notes for the development of an operational risk management framework and the supervision of risk management. Recent redrafting of these notes suggest a change of emphasis from loss data collection towards more forward-looking risk assessment and comprehensive risk management.

4.2 Critical examination of the Basel proposals

4.2.1 The importance of definitions

Contrary to popular opinion, risks cannot be measured. A risk is not like a length of hosepipe that can be checked by anyone with a measuring tape and which can be connected to other lengths of hosepipe to reach the back of the garden. A risk is about the future; it can only be assessed by using some model, some hypothetical representation of possible future realizations. A model is necessarily subjective. At best a group of reasonable people may agree to settle on the use of a particular model for a particular purpose, but a model is never valid in any objective or absolute sense. It may be accepted as good enough in a particular environment until a better model is put forward.

Strictly speaking, one cannot even measure losses without making some subjective judgements or without following some agreed conventions. What we measure in the financial world and add and subtract at will are cash flows. Accountants are very good at that. Whether a particular cash flow should be labelled as a loss rather than viewed as a normal expense depends on what we choose to identify as being abnormal: perhaps someone is to blame for incompetence or fraud, or an unexpected event or accident has happened, or the expense appears to have no real purpose.[1]

What I am leading up to with these rather philosophical statements is that the definition and the assessment of operational risks are not trivial matters. We need to develop a better understanding of operational risks before launching into the calculation of capital charges. There is nothing wrong in principle with requesting a capital buffer for any sort of risk, but if the calculation method is poor, the resulting capital charge will only create unsound incentives, and I have grave doubts that charges, either imposed indiscriminately or based solely on operational loss experience, can do anything to improve operational risk management.

I hope to show that my concerns are pertinent, not pedantic. It is true that we would be hard pressed to give exact definitions of most things, be they as simple as a 'chair' or a 'table', yet we know where to sit and where to put our plate. But risks are trickier – they are perceived in the mind, they are a reflection of our ability to imagine and weigh possible future consequences, good and bad, of our actions; they may offset each other rather than add up. Poor definitions will distort risk assessments and lead to bad decisions.

Casual assessments of risks may indeed lead to the opposite of the desired effects with potentially disastrous consequences. The supervisor who 'prudently' does not recognize a certain risk mitigation tool because it is imperfect may lead a bank not to use that tool to save costs, and thereby leave it exposed to greater risks. The reluctance to accept 'fair value' accounting because the future cannot be assessed accurately throws a veil over critical risks. Developing more risk-sensitive capital charges without a mechanism to use the capital as a

---

[1] 'A distinction is often made between an *expense*, which is made to benefit the operations of a period, and a *loss*, which is an expenditure that does not benefit anything ... there is no great need to draw a fine line between them' (Anthony 1960, p. 134).

buffer in critical times may turn a minor crisis into a major crash. Making detailed risk monitoring and reporting demands in a format that is one-sided (looking at losses only) and
drowns major losses in a sea of minor ones, may confuse rather than enlighten and will
detract management's attention from its primary task of managing crucial risks.

4.2.2 Conflicting goals

With its CP2.5 consultative paper on operational risk, so called because it comes between
CP2 and the promised but many times delayed third Basel II consultative paper, the BCBS
(2001b) has relaxed and made more flexible its original proposals for an operational risk
capital charge under the new Accord.

The date for implementing the new Accord has also been postponed twice in view of the
many industry comments, on credit risks as well as on operational risks, pointing to the
need for further reviews and quantitative impact studies. The proposals are now said to be
on track for implementation, at least among the G10 countries, by the end of 2006.

In the meantime, the Basel Committee has released (BCBS 2001c) and recently updated
(BCBS 2002b) a draft statement of sound practices for operational risk management and
supervision which, taken with CP2.5, indicates how Basel intends to apply its 'three pillars'
philosophy to the newly defined field of operational risks.

From these documents, one perceives that the Basel Committee strives to reconcile multiple objectives and constraints. First and apparently foremost, the Committee wants to
leave the overall level of capital requirements in the banking system more or less unchanged
while introducing more comprehensive and risk-sensitive methods for calculating these
requirements. But there is also a need to remedy accounting inadequacies; so, some future
expected losses that are not recognized under current accounting standards are added to
risk-weighted assets in the denominator of the capital ratio rather than taken away from eligible capital in the numerator. Third, there is an overwhelming desire to rely on objective
inputs and methods in order, one presumes, to facilitate the role of the supervisors, those
impartial empires of the legendary level playing field; that may be over-ambitious when dealing with rare events. Fourth, there is a need to provide methodologies that are accessible to
a wide range of financial institutions with different types of activities, sizes and degrees of
sophistication, hence the idea of providing a menu of methodologies, subject to some eligibility criteria. Fifth, there is a desire to provide incentives for better risk management, which
translates into reduced capital charges (everything else being equal) for those institutions
that qualify for and use more advanced risk assessment methodologies.

The list could go on and on; many difficult trade-offs have to be struck in designing regulations suitable for a wide range of banks with varied financial activities. The old reflexes of
dividing to conquer in the face of complexity and prudence in the face of doubt need to be
checked. Breaking down and analyzing risks into more and more components allows for the
development of specific methodologies adapted to each of these components but creates
difficulties in aggregating the results. Apparently safe assumptions, such as ignoring offsets
that are imperfect or adding capital charges – unless there is *empirical* evidence of a lack of

correlation (BCBS 2001b, p. 19) – create a distorted and misleading picture of the relative importance of risks.

So, what is achieved by the current operational risk 'measurement' proposals? Will advanced approaches assist better operational risk management? Should, therefore, all banks aim to put into place an advanced methodology? Or is the imposition of capital charges largely irrelevant to the task of managing operational risks? At the time of writing this chapter, the Basel Committee is still considering evidence on the relative importance of operational risks in banking as well as on the impact of the new proposals for credit risk capital charges. The Committee should be commended for starting this debate and for listening to the industry. Recent postponements may be read as an indication that the Committee is more interested in 'getting it right' than in rushing through untested innovations in banking regulation. There is still time, many hope, for some fundamental rethinking.

4.2.3 Capital charges guesswork

It was initially feared that the Basel II proposals would reduce the capital requirements for credit and market risks by an average of 20 percent. Simultaneously, there was the realization, often brutal and embarrassing, that some risks, neither clearly market nor credit (i.e. positions-related or 'warehousing' risks) but generally operations-related, such as fraud, terrorism, technology failures and trade settlement errors, were escaping the regulatory net. Indeed, the trend towards greater dependence on technology, greater competition among banks and globalization may leave the banking industry more exposed to operational risks than ever before. These circumstances led the Basel Committee to propose a new tranche of capital charges for operational risk equal to 20 percent of purely credit and market risk minimum capital requirements.

Then came evidence from the second Quantitative Impact Study (QIS2 Tranche 1: BCBS 2001e) conducted by the Risk Management Group (RMG) of the Basel Committee, which revealed that, on average, the responding banks allocate about 15 percent of their overall economic capital to operational risk. That turned out to be equivalent to about 12 percent of the minimum regulatory capital (MRC) of the reporting banks calculated according to the current Basel I Accord with an 8 percent minimum capital asset ratio.[2]

The evidence was weak. Only 41 banks responded to the questions on operational risk in the first tranche of QIS2; they were given neither standard definitions of economic capital nor guidelines for the allocation of economic capital to operational risk. Nonetheless, on this basis, and perhaps in response to some other industry concerns, the Basel Committee proposed to reduce the operational risk minimum regulatory capital figure from 20 percent to 12 percent of MRC.

This reduction gave a new meaning to the so-called 'top-down' approach! It was all the more welcome to the industry that QIS2 also revealed that the new credit risk proposals are not bringing nearly as much reduction to credit risk capital charges as was first expected. In

---

[2] We shall use this specific definition of MRC throughout this chapter. Note that, curiously, if on average 15 percent of economic capital equates to 12 percent of MRC, economic capital calculated by banks would be only 80 percent of MRC.

fact, in most cases credit risk capital requirements would increase under the new proposals or would remain unchanged,[3] thus leaving no room for a new operational risk capital charge unless other capital charges are revised down to keep the total roughly unchanged. In fact, this is what may well happen: capital charges for both credit risks under the Internal Ratings Based approach and operational risks may still be reduced.

Interestingly, QIS2 also collated operational loss experience from 30 Group 1 banks (capital larger than €3 billion) over three years (1998–2000). We analyze these results later when we examine the calibration of capital charges for the so-called Advanced Measurement Approaches that are based on loss experience.

4.2.4 A critique of the Basic Indicator Approach

Setting the overall size of the new operational risk capital requirement at a certain percentage of existing requirements can be done in one stroke; devising a method to allocate this new requirement to various financial institutions is more challenging. The allocation should be related, one would hope, to some indicator of operational risk, otherwise the regulator might as well reset the current minimum capital ratio to whatever new level he views as sufficiently prudent.

In the spirit of flexibility, the Basel Committee proposes a menu of three approaches, from crude but simple to more refined but also more demanding. At the crude end, presumably for small domestic banks, it proposes the Basic Indicator Approach as a straightforward way to relate the operational risk capital charge to an operational risk indicator. The operational risk capital charge is simply calculated as a fixed percentage, alpha, of gross income, whatever the range of activities conducted by the regulated institution.

Why gross income? Possibly because it is readily available, it reflects business volume and thereby may be related to operational risk exposure. But the connection is loose. Gross income is about the past; risks are about the future. Gross income does not reflect the quality of operational risk management. Between two institutions with similar earnings, why penalize the one with the largest gross income, that is, with the smallest profit margin? With this choice of indicator, would banks not have an incentive to increase profits by reducing operating expenses rather than by increasing gross income, thus possibly cutting down on risk controls and mitigation tools? That has been known to happen in difficult times.

It is somewhat surprising that the Basel Committee has not found other indicators that could be more relevant and less liable to perverse consequences. To explore just one alternative, why not choose a few months of operating expenses? That was used and is still being used in some countries as a base capital requirement. Compared to gross income, it may be rather more related to operational risks than to credit or market risks. There would be no disincentive to increase gross income. Capital requirements could be immediately adjusted down in case of rationalization. If a bank were in terminal difficulties, the capital charge

---

[3] Only G10 Group 1, that is, large banks in the most developed countries, may benefit from reduced credit risk capital charges if they opt for the Advanced Internal Ratings Based approach according to QIS2.

would be strongly related to expenses during liquidation. On average, three months of operating expenses as base capital requirement might not be much different from the target of 12 percent of current MRC for the new operational risk tranche; if it were different, one could adjust the time period to reach the desired level.

And why should there be a linear relationship with a volume indicator? Would we not expect the larger institutions to have more sophisticated operational risk management in place and to experience less operational loss volatility than the smaller ones?[4] Indeed, it seems intuitive that large institutions with diversified activities would be less likely than small, specialist institutions to be brought down by, say, fraudulent activities or systems failures.

Undeterred by the potential difficulties of using gross income as the operational risk indicator, and apparently without testing the linearity assumption, the Basel Committee proceeded to estimate alpha for each reporting bank as the ratio of 12 percent of MRC over gross income per year. This led to a provisional recommendation for 'alpha' in the range of 17–20 percent. Not surprisingly, ratios for individual banks in the survey were widely dispersed. The latest word from Basel representatives at the time of writing is that alpha could be down to 15 percent of average annual gross income[5] over the previous three years.

What the Basic Indicator Approach achieves, compared to imposing a flat operational risk capital charge equal to 12 percent of credit and market risk capital, is that businesses with little or no credit or market risks according to current Basel rules, such as advisory services, agency services and asset management, will now face operational risk capital charges as long as they generate gross income. Conversely, businesses such as trading, which attract large capital charges for market risks but might generate low income at times, will be relatively spared.

What it certainly does not achieve are incentives for better operational risk management. In fact, the Basel Committee, recognizing the limitations of the Basic Indicator Approach, very much hopes (or may even demand?) that internationally active financial institutions with significant operational risk exposures move up at least to the next level of model sophistication, the Standardized Approach.[6]

4.2.5 A critique of the Standardized Approach

The Standardized Approach will be available to banks meeting some minimum standards of operational risk management and control as well as having in place measurement methods to track and report operational risk by business lines as defined by the regulator.[7]

---

[4] See, for example, Shih *et al.* (2000) and International Swaps and Derivatives Association (2002) claiming that a square-root function of size, or even a lower power, is supported by empirical evidence.

[5] The definition of gross income proposed by Basel is not a standard accounting definition. It includes (i) net interest income, (ii) net non-interest income and (iii) net trading income and other income. It is gross of provisions. It excludes (i) extraordinary or irregular items, (ii) gains/losses on positions in the banking book and (iii) income from insurance. Obviously it excludes operating expenses.

[6] The possibility has been raised (BCBS 2002b, p. 11) that supervisors could impose additional capital charges on sophisticated banks that would opt for the Basic Indicator Approach.

[7] The European Commission may stop short of imposing this last condition.

Accepting that some financial activities are more exposed than others to operational risk, at least in relation to gross income, the RMG proposes to differentiate the capital charge according to eight business lines. For each line the operational risk charge is defined as a percentage, the beta factor, of a relevant exposure indicator.

The RMG proceeds to make the somewhat unimaginative assumption that the best exposure indicator is still gross income for each business line.[8] Furthermore it assumes that operational risks still vary proportionally to gross income for each business line (what would happen if gross income in, say, trading is negative?) Finally, it states that the total charge will be the sum of the charges for individual business lines as if the risks were closely related across business lines. Of course, it is very hard to imagine that low frequency risks in one business line, such as corporate finance, could be closely related to high frequency risks in another, such as retail banking, but never mind.

All this seems very gratuitous but difficult to debate without a better definition of what Basel means by risk. As we mentioned at the start, we believe that this is a far from trivial matter. The Committee begins its definition of operational risk with 'The risk of', thus presuming that 'risk' is a basic concept that does not warrant clarification. We might as well accept that whatever Basel has decided to measure is what it means by risk. We would remark, however, that the Basel measure, which is additive and proportional to volume, would be consistent with an interpretation of risk as a sum of cash flows (presumably those classified as losses?). It could not have anything to do with uncertainties since generally uncertainties are neither additive nor proportional to a number of chance events or to a business volume indicator.

Will the Standardized Approach be more risk sensitive than the Basic Indicator Approach? In theory it might, but QIS2 shows no clear evidence that different business lines should have different betas (see Figure 4.1[9]). Basel wants to base the betas on industry-wide experience, but stops short of making specific recommendations at this stage; BCBS (2001b, p. 4) simply states that the beta estimates 'fall in a range around the alpha level'. Therefore banks should not hope for any reduction in capital charges under the Standardized Approach as a reward for meeting the qualifying risk management standards, nor will the quality of their risk management affect the capital charge.

In brief, in its current form, the Standardized Approach is subject to eligibility criteria but does not appear to be markedly more risk-sensitive than the Basic Indicator Approach. It offers neither any hope of a reduction in capital charges compared to the Basic Indicator, nor any incentive for better risk management. As such, it is hard to believe that banks would adopt it willingly; it might as well be scrapped.

However, it leaves flexibility in the future for Basel to modulate the betas or the choice of exposure indicators according to business lines. Indeed, there are now proposals to set the betas between a low of 12 percent (retail banking, retail brokerage, asset management) and a

[8] Basel will provide criteria for the mapping of gross income for each business line.
[9] In the left-hand column of Figure 4.1 are the eight business lines defined by Basel. For each business line, the interquartile range is the range that contains half the responses in QIS2, with a quarter of the responses falling below the lower end (the first quartile) and a quarter falling above the upper end (the third quartile).

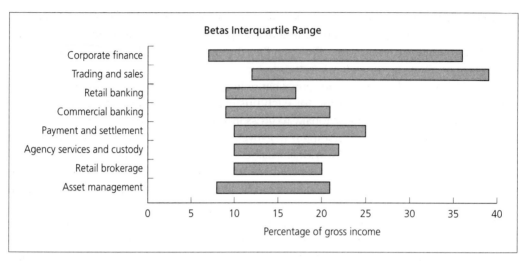

FIGURE 4.1 ■ Dispersion of betas from QIS2 survey

high of 18 percent (corporate finance, trading and sales, payment and settlement) of the business line gross income (the commercial banking and agency services lines would be left at 15 percent), subject to periodic reviews of these factors.[10] No doubt there will be hard political negotiations around these issues. There will also be an incentive for 'cherry picking', i.e. to use the Standardized Approach only for those business lines with betas smaller than alpha, and the Basic Indicator Approach for the others. Supervisors will have to impose rules for allowing or disallowing the use of the Basic Indicator and the Standardized Approaches.

Finally, one ironic consequence of the two simple approaches is that banks may retain more operational risks than before the imposition of capital charges. Indeed, managers may reason that the new capital buffer makes it possible and more economical to self-insure some operational risks that they formerly covered with traditional insurance products (e.g. damage to physical assets, key person insurance, etc.). Why should a bank contribute to the profits of an insurance company if it has new capacity to self-insure and if insurance cover does not reduce the capital charge?

4.2.6 A critique of the Advanced Measurement Approaches

The carrot of lower operational risk capital charges is promised only to those banks that will use an advanced measurement approach for calculating these charges. Basel announced in CP2.5 (BCBS 2001b) that it does not want to impose a single such approach at this stage but would rather see the industry develop its own ideas: 'Let one hundred flowers bloom', as Mao Zedong famously said. But a bank will have to be able to demonstrate to its supervisor that its chosen approach captures potentially severe 'tail' loss events. By that Basel means

---

[10] ISDA (2002) has strongly recommended that Basel should commit to review the charges (alpha and beta factors) and their impact within two years of implementation and with further periodic reviews.

operational loss levels that have not less than a 0.1 percent probability of being exceeded over a one-year horizon. How one can reliably estimate operational loss levels over one year at a 99.9 percent confidence level, as it were, is a bit of a mystery. Estimating this level within a factor of 2 to 5 would already be quite an achievement and that is only one source of uncertainty in the determination of operational risk capital charges that supervisors will be facing with AMA. As floors have now been removed, the other sources of uncertainty will be the amount of cover that banks will be able to claim because of their provisioning of pricing policies and the freedom of banks to design their own models and use their own estimates.[11]

So Basel has stepped back from imposing the Internal Measurement Approach (IMA) it had put forward earlier. Nonetheless, it has kept some basic features of the IMA as minimum quantitative qualifying requirements, among them the following:

(i)   Any advanced approach must be 'bottom-up', that is, rooted in loss experience, as opposed to the two simpler 'top-down' approaches which apply industry-wide parameters.

(ii) Each bank will have to monitor its loss experience and make use of the loss experience of other banks according to 56 categories of losses corresponding to all combinations of the eight business lines defined in the Standardized Approach and seven loss event types defined in BCBS (2001b).

(iii) The risk 'measure', that is, the 99.9 percent confidence level estimate or the capital charge must be supported by loss data and appropriate analytics.

(iv) The regulatory capital requirement will be calculated 'as the sum of expected loss (EL) and unexpected loss (UL), unless the bank can demonstrate that it is adequately capturing EL in its internal business practices' (BCBS 2002c, p. 122).

(v)   The total operational risk capital charge should be calculated as the sum of charges for individual risks in the absence of 'specific, valid, correlation estimates'.[12]

(vi) There must be regular 'validation' of parameter estimates and results based on subsequent loss experience or other techniques.

More details and specifications (such as the requirement to use a minimum of five years of loss experience) have been released. To these requests Basel adds a few strong recommendations such as: to quantify risks as multiples of expected losses; and to calculate capital requirements as the sum of expected loss and unexpected loss unless the bank can demonstrate that it is

---

[11] Basel seems prepared to accept 'cherry picking' of methodologies according to business lines; i.e. a bank could select the Basic Indicator Approach for some marginal business lines, the Standardized Approach for other lines and perhaps the AMA for some core activities, thus implicitly accepting that banks could choose the least onerous methodology. On the other hand, Basel is unlikely to accept reversions to simpler approaches once the advanced approach has been approved. The issue of a floor for AMA is more contentious; an initial demand by Basel to set a floor at 75 percent of the Standardized Approach has caused much criticism and has been replaced by a floor on total Basel II requirements for IRB credit and AMA operational risk capital changes equal to 90 percent of credit risk capital changes under Basel I for the first year and 80 percent for the second year (BCBS 2002c, p.6).

[12] 'In the absence of specific, valid correlation estimates, risk measures for different business lines and/or event types must be added for purposes of calculating the regulatory minimum capital requirement' (BCBS 2001b, p. 20). How correlations (the wrong measure anyway) between rare events can be 'measured' with any degree of accuracy would need to be explained.

making adequate reserves for expected loss or is pricing expected losses into its products and services. Regrettably, we think that some of these requests and recommendations work against the objectives of greater risk sensitivity of operational risk capital charges and make it nearly impossible to achieve a coherent calibration with other capital charges

Problems with identifying relevant losses

All Advanced Measurement Approaches will be based on operational loss experience. BCBS (2001b, p. 2) defines an operational loss as a 'loss resulting from inadequate or failed internal processes, people and systems or from external events'. We are assumed to be able to identify a loss and to decide whether it should be categorized as 'operational' according to its cause.

What is a loss? It is, of course, extremely difficult to define precisely anything that pertains to the real world (the world of mathematics is far simpler). Most of the time approximate definitions suffice, but that is not the case here. Those who have tried to construct operational loss databases know the difficulties.

A loss is defined by accounting standards and other conventions that may vary from activity to activity (e.g. accrual accounting in a banking book or fair value accounting in a trading book) and country to country. Generally speaking, a loss, as opposed to a profit, is a negative net result over an accounting period. But for the purpose of Basel we need to label as losses specific negative cash flows resulting from some types of causal events.

Is that sufficiently clear? Perhaps it is in very rare, high-impact cases. Take a rogue trader, a major systems failure, an act of terrorism or other rare situations with potentially disastrous consequences. No doubt the damage they may cause should qualify as losses, although it may still be difficult to decide upon the extent of the losses to be reported. Some of the largest consequences could be regarded by Basel as indirect or difficult to measure (e.g. reputational effects) and therefore not reportable under the operational loss label. There may also be positive consequences such as insurance payments, indemnifications or other recoveries: should they be taken into consideration?

That was the extreme case; consider now more common examples, say, fraudulent use of credit cards, transaction settlement errors, or complaints from clients or staff. Should the consequences be recorded as losses? These are, no doubt, undesirable incidents but they are usually regarded as par for the course. One would not stop a profitable business purely because of such problems unless they really got out of control. As such, why should they be reported as losses and justify capital charges rather than be budgeted as expenses?

The issue here is twofold: how to assess expected results and measure deviations from them (positive as well as negative) to gauge uncertainty,[13] and how to account for both the

---

[13] In common parlance *expected* (*unexpected*) is an expression similar to *regarded as highly probable* (*unlikely*). In mathematics, the *expected value* of an uncertain quantity has a very specific and different meaning; it is defined as the sum of all possible values weighted by the respective probabilities we attach to them. It is a value that is not necessarily likely; indeed, it may be an impossible value to achieve. In the operational risk management literature, the expression *unexpected loss* is sometimes used but it may be ambiguous for the reasons explained above. Should it be interpreted as an improbable outcome (common sense) or as a measure of deviation from the (mathematically) expected? We shall use *expected* in its mathematical sense and refrain from using *unexpected* for fear of causing confusion.

expected and the unexpected. In an extreme high-impact, low-probability case, the expected loss is small compared to the possible losses and might therefore be ignored. In the more common low- to high-frequency cases, say, for loss events that have more than one chance in ten of occurring per year, expected losses are sufficiently large not to be ignored. They should be budgeted.

If an activity is under fair value accounting there is no problem. All relevant future cash flows (positive and negative) are supposed to be included in the accounts on an expected value basis; this is what market values, if they exist, do automatically. The fair value of an activity will, of course, evolve over time. Some values become realized, some unrealized values change with new information, others are added with new business; those variations in value reflect the volatility or 'riskiness' of the activity.

If, on the other hand, an activity is under accrual accounting (and most banking activities still are!), there is no ready basis to assess risks. I do not see any alternative other than to overlay fair valuation for the purpose of risk assessment. Some may argue that in accrual accounting there are provisioning and reserve mechanisms to account for probable losses. But provisioning rules are restrictive and one-sided as accounting standards seek to maintain objectivity as well as prudence. For example, according to International Accounting Standards 37, specific provisions for operational losses should be made when and only when there is a reliable estimate of a present obligation resulting from past events. In other words, specific provisions are restricted to highly probable future losses and have nothing to do with mathematically expected losses and gains. Even after adjustment for specific provisions,[14] therefore, it remains a matter of judgement to determine what the expected net results (i.e. margin of gains over losses) are.

In brief, there is little point in trying to assess operational risks separately from other risks to which they are associated, and even this limited objective would require a great deal more than the recording of certain negative cash flows labelled 'operational losses'. All major costs and revenues attached to a particular activity and their variability should be assessed. Otherwise there cannot be any sensible risk management.

Problems with distinguishing operational losses from other losses

By comparison, deciding whether the causes of a loss event are operational rather than, say, credit or market related should be relatively easy and, at any rate, inconsequential for calculating capital requirements, as long as there is no double counting. In theory, capital requirements should be consistently calibrated and it should not matter greatly whether a risk is categorized as credit, market or operational; in practice, of course, it may make a difference. It is also informative to understand the source of a risk in order to improve risk

[14] General provisions should not be taken into account, as they are included in Upper Tier 2 capital – and are therefore available as a buffer for credit, market and operational risks. The treatment of general provisions is a clear example of the inability of accrual accounting principles to cope with probabilities and therefore with any form of risk assessment.

management; many a bank that has conducted an operational risk review will have discovered that losses that were casually attributed to market or credit actually had their roots in operational risks.

Of greater importance is the distinction between reportable operational risks, on the one hand, and business and reputational risks, which are not recognized in the current proposals, on the other. Casual observation suggests that these unaccounted risks, as well as the consequential damage from operational risks, may be more significant than the direct operational losses the industry has been asked to monitor. It looks as if these other risks are left out not because they are small but because they are difficult to assess; it is the reasoning of the man looking for his keys under the lamppost, not because he lost them there, but because it is the only place where he has enough light to see clearly.

Consider, for example, the losses of Jo Jett at Kidder Peabody. In 1994 he was accused of having recorded $350 million of fictitious profits (and of having collected an $8 million bonus in the process); Kidder went bankrupt. By Thanksgiving 1997 Jett was cleared of the major charges against him (although he was fined $200 000 for 'books-and-records violations' and ordered to return his bonus). It turned out that he had been asked to close down rapidly a huge bond portfolio; profits had evaporated in the process. So, had it been a liquidity risk or business risks or an operational risk, and if the latter, how much would have been reportable? Look at NatWest Markets; in 1997 the Financial Services Authority (FSA), the UK regulator, imposed a fine for their failure to notice an overvaluation of some interest rate options to the tune of £77 million. Few will remember the name of the trader; a loss of £77 million should not have been a fatal blow for a bank recording profits in billions. But the situation had been concealed, heads had to roll, the market lost confidence in the ability of NatWest to manage derivatives portfolios, and eventually, the bank was sold.

One could give several more examples where loss of reputation and consequential loss of business far exceeded any direct loss and where the initial cause was a combination of circumstances where poor business judgement as well as perhaps a dose of human incompetence and even downright deception played a role. Should these events be ignored because they do not fall neatly into the codified categories of credit, market and operational risks?

4.3 Analysis of reported operational loss data

4.3.1 Operational losses reported in the second Quantitative Impact Study

Mindful of the difficulties in identifying and assessing operational losses, we now review the evidence gathered so far about their relative importance. Industry associations and commercial enterprises have been busy constructing operational loss databases for several years. But following the specification in BCBS (2001b) of the type of operational losses that should be recorded and of the matrix of 56 loss categories into which they must be catalogued, some early data gathering exercises have become largely obsolete. Many of the remaining publicly available data sets, either from commercial sources or from co-operative ventures, are suspected to be severely biased and cannot claim to represent an industry average (Haubenstock 2000). So, rather than venture into a discussion about the possible merits and shortcomings of various databases, we shall limit our attention to the data collected by the Basel Committee in their own second Quantitative Impact Study.

In a review of QIS2 Tranche 2 data published in January 2002, the RMG of the Basel Committee reminds us that it is 'necessary to be cautious in using these data to draw any conclusions about the extent of operational risk exposures' (BCBS 2002a). However, after carrying out their own clean-up and standardization, the RMG claims to be 'reasonably certain that the data … do not have significant reporting errors or inconsistencies'. At any rate, these are the main data that have been used by the RMG to conduct calibration exercises.

Thirty banks reported individual operational loss events exceeding €10 000 and quarterly aggregates over a three year period (1998–2000) as well as quarterly information on a wider range of potential exposure indicators related to specific business lines. The banks are spread across 11 countries in Europe, North America, Asia and Africa, but the sample may not be representative of the banking industry as a whole. In particular, all respondents but one are Group 1 banks, that is, they are international and diversified banks with Tier 1 capital in excess of €3 billion. Furthermore, the data may not even be very representative of the sample as 19 banks were unable to make any representation about the comprehensiveness of their reports.

With all these caveats in mind, let us look at the data. They are best represented on decimal logarithmic scales because of the wide range of reported frequencies and severities. Figure 4.2 shows the reported losses in each of the 56 regulatory categories with frequencies vertically and severities horizontally. The frequency scale runs from –3, meaning one event in a thousand years, to +3, meaning one thousand events per year. The severity scale runs from –6, or one-millionth of the current MRC, to 0, meaning the total MRC of an average bank in the sample. Scaling to MRC is essential to gain an appreciation of the relative importance of the recorded loss events.

Loss frequencies per annum for an average bank in the sample were obtained by dividing the total number of reported losses by 90 (3 years × 30 banks). Scaling loss severities to the MRC of an average bank in the sample required some guesswork: the RMG is unwilling to reveal the regulatory capital of the respondents, even as a group total. On the basis of some back-of-an-envelope calculations, it seems safe to assume that the average MRC (calculated at the minimum 8 percent solvency ratio, as we have done previously) for banks in the sample is well in excess of €3 billion;[15] an average two or three times larger would not be surprising, but to avoid understating the losses as a percentage of MRC, we assumed the

---

[15] We know that 29 out of the 30 banks in the sample have Tier 1 capital in excess of €3 billion. We also know that a majority of banks have the cheaper eligible Tier 2 capital up to the level of Tier 1. Finally, we know that most of the large, internationally active banks have a solvency ratio above the 8 percent minimum, but not greatly so. Therefore, it is likely that for the average bank in the sample, MRC is well above €3 billion.

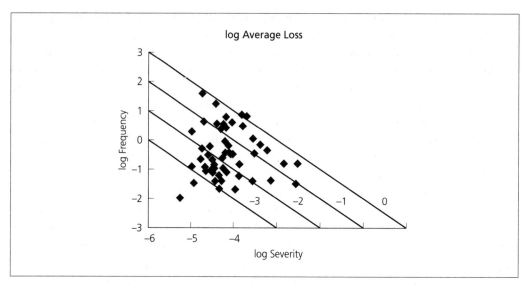

FIGURE 4.2 ■ Average operational losses per year reported in QIS2

average bank had an MRC of just €3 billion.[16] It should also be noted that the data in Figure 4.2 are for gross losses before insurance and other recoveries. Although answers to the questionnaire were difficult to interpret on this topic, it appears that there was a recovery rate of about two-thirds on one-third of the significant losses.[17] Net losses after recovery would therefore be only about 78 percent of the reported figures.

4.3.2 Estimation of average losses

In Figure 4.2, categories of equal average losses lie along straight lines running diagonally from top left to bottom right. The diagonal marked '–3' represents an average loss equal to one-thousandth (0.1 percent) of MRC per year. Only three categories in QIS2 contribute average gross losses in excess of 0.1 percent.[18] Total gross losses amount to $2613 million for the 30 banks over three years, or, at a maximum, 1 percent of their MRC per year.

Of course, any loss event that has less than a 1 percent probability of occurring per year is unlikely to appear in this collection of 90 bank-years of data. But we shall explain in a moment that the contribution of these rare events to average losses is small, perhaps of the

[16] Note that, consequently, the €10 000 reporting cut-off in QIS2 corresponds to about – 5.5 on the relative severity scale, and we will have no observations below this level.

[17] Interestingly, only 15–20 percent of recoveries came from insurance; other recoveries must have been obtained from counterparties (i.e. reported losses were not irreversible) or from various indemnifications.

[18] These are: (i) clients, products and business services in retail banking; (ii) execution delivery and process management in trading and sales; and (iii) internal fraud in commercial banking.

order of another 1 percent or 2 percent per year. On the other hand, it is likely that the reported losses were more than covered by expected profits in the corresponding business lines. As we have also neglected recoveries and underestimated the average capitalization of the banks in the sample, it seems fair to conclude that the reported average operational losses are negligible compared to capital.

We have been careful to speak about the 'average' when reviewing historical observations. Turning to the future, we shall speak instead about expected losses. Now it may well be that, despite our low 'average' findings, for a particular bank at a particular time, management could 'expect' significant operational losses over the following year. In fair value accounting, any material expected loss that is not covered by an expected future profit should be deducted from regulatory capital. If this is not possible, whether for regulatory, accounting or other reasons, an alternative with similar effect on the solvency ratio should be sought, for example, adding 12.5 times (or 1 over the minimum solvency ratio) the excess expected loss (i.e. not covered by an expected profit) to the risk-weighted assets in the denominator of the solvency ratio, but that is not what Basel proposes (see Section 4.3.5).[19]

4.3.3 Estimation of loss variability

Quite rightly, the authors of the review of QIS2 Tranche 2 findings on operational losses point out that:

> To assess the extent of risk, it would be necessary to assess the extent of variability of both number and value of loss events around their expected, or mean values …
> Simple tabulation of the data … does not supply significant insight in this regard. To gain insight, it would be necessary to model this variation, an exercise that is beyond the scope of this paper (BCBS 2002a, p. 6).

Possibly! But someone could have attempted this exercise before suggesting capital charges. So let us try.

Suppose that all we know about each loss category is (i) the frequency of arrival of loss events and (ii) the average loss severity. The minimally prejudiced inference[20] we can make is that the loss event process is Poisson (i.e. the arrival time of the next loss event is independent of the arrival time of any previous loss event) and that the distribution of loss severities is exponential. These assumptions can be modified as soon as further information becomes available. For example, we might become aware of some pattern in the arrivals of loss events (either bunched up during some periods or, on the contrary, regularly spaced)

---

[19] The effect is similar only if the excess expected loss is still small compared to the regulatory capital (say less than 10 percent) and the target ratio is 8 percent. More generally, one could add $y = x/r(1-x/N)$ to the denominator rather than subtracting the expected excess loss x from the numerator N when the target solvency ratio is r.

[20] We qualify as *minimally prejudiced* the inference that is compatible with the information at hand without making additional assumptions. Formally, it is the maximum entropy probability distribution that matches the available information (where entropy is a general measure of uncertainty in information theory). See, for example, Tribus (1969, p. 121).

or that the dispersion (standard deviation) of loss severities is larger than their average. Whichever model is used, model parameters can be tested against historical data, but management will have to use its judgement to select the model in the first place and then to choose parameter values to forecast future losses.

A general property of a process with a random number of loss events, N, over a certain period and an independent distribution for the loss severity, L, per event, is that the uncertainty of total losses over the period, X, as expressed by its variance, is

$$\mathrm{Var}(X) = \mathrm{E}(N)\mathrm{Var}(L) + \mathrm{Var}(N)\mathrm{E}(L)^2, \tag{4.1}$$

where $\mathrm{E}(\cdot)$ stands for the expected value and $\mathrm{Var}(\cdot)$ the variance of a random variable. In particular, if N is Poisson-distributed and L exponentially distributed, then $\mathrm{Var}(N) = \mathrm{E}(N)$ and $\mathrm{Var}(L) = \mathrm{E}(L)^2$, and therefore (4.1) reduces to

$$\mathrm{Var}(X) = 2\mathrm{E}(N)\mathrm{E}(L)^2.$$

Of course, no model is absolutely right, and this one is no exception. We should hasten to test our hypotheses. No doubt information will flood in with operational risk managers, consultants, information vendors and regulators actively analyzing data and building up models. Already, there is some evidence that the dispersion of loss severities per risk category (at least for some important categories) could be wider than that of an exponential distribution,[21] so, to avoid understating risks, we double the variance of the severity to $\mathrm{Var}(L) = 2\mathrm{E}(L)^2$ and, consequently, use $\mathrm{Var}(X) = 3\mathrm{E}(N)\mathrm{E}(L)^2$.

The last step is to relate the variance of total losses over the period to the capital requirements suggested by Basel, that is, capital sufficient to cover losses over one year at a 99.9 percent confidence level.[22] If annual losses were normally distributed, the 99.9 percent confidence level would be about 3 standard deviations from the mean. That would be the case if annual losses were the sum of many similar losses, say, for risk categories where the frequency of occurrence of losses is greater than ten per year. For lower frequencies it is not possible to equate the 99.9 percent quantile to a set number of standard deviations; it matters how many loss events register at that confidence level. For example, the 99.9 percent quantile for an arrival rate of one loss event per year would correspond to four loss events, but for an arrival rate of 3 percent per year only one loss event would register, and for an arrival rate of 0.1 percent or below none would register, that is, the capital requirement would suddenly disappear.

So, for risk categories with a loss occurrence rate of ten or more per year, we assume a normal distribution for total annual loss and calculate the capital charge as three standard deviations, or

$$\text{Capital charge} = 3(3\mathrm{E}(N))^{1/2}\,\mathrm{E}(L). \tag{4.2}$$

---

[21] The distribution of loss severities across loss categories would, of course, be far broader, the loss categories being themselves important indicators of loss severities.

[22] Total losses over the period are henceforth referred to as annual losses. Further, we assume here that expected losses are, in the words of Basel, 'adequately captured' and we base capital requirements on loss variability (unexpected losses) only. This assumption is discussed further in section 4.3.5.

Categories with equal capital charges would again line up on our graph of log frequency versus log severity, but this time the lines would have a slope of –2.[23] This is what Figure 4.3 shows in the top section where the frequency of loss is greater than 10 per year; equal capital requirements lines run down from left to right twice as steeply as the lines of equal expected losses. The line marked '–3' corresponds to a capital requirement equal to one-thousandth of the current MRC.

As the frequency falls below ten per year, the equal capital charges lines start to fall more steeply and then flatten out to approach the horizontal line at a frequency of one in a thousand years. The exact shape depends on the precise distribution we select for loss severity. Here, for a distribution with variance equal to twice the mean, we have chosen a chi-square distribution with degree one, that is, the distribution of the square of a standard normal variate.

To calculate a total capital requirement at the 99.9 percent level for all operational risks, an additional factor must be taken into account, namely, the extent to which various categories of operational risks may be mutually dependent. Intuition strongly suggests that risks from different operational causes and in different business lines should have little to do with each other; they would not share common factors. In other words, they should be largely independent of each other. In that case, a simple summation of individual variances would yield the total variance. Under the normality assumption for the total of all losses, the QIS2 data would then show a total capital requirement for operational risks of about 1 percent of

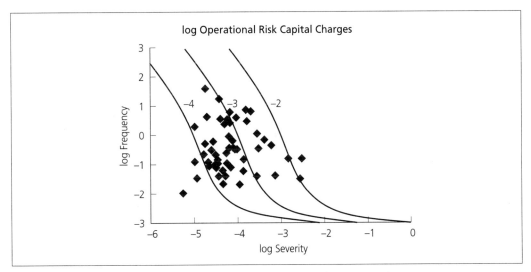

FIGURE 4.3 ■ Operational risk capital charges inferred from QIS2 data

[23] Taking the logarithm of (4.2) and rearranging the terms gives:

$$\log(E(N)) = -2 \log(E(L)) + 2 \log(\text{Capital charge}) - 3 \log (3).$$

[24] The distribution for the total of all operational losses across the 56 categories is much less skewed than the distribution for losses within each category. Taking the skewness into account would push up the capital charge but it would not exceed 2 percent of MRC.

current MRC.[24] If, in addition, we assume that operational risks are largely independent of credit and market risks, the relative importance of operational risks compared to credit and market risks would be only five in one hundred thousand.[25]

On the other hand, if we were to accept the rather ridiculous assumption that losses with about 0.1 percent chance of occurrence per year in each of the 56 loss categories would all happen together if they happened at all, then we should add up capital requirements across all loss categories, as Basel suggests.[26] Total operational risk capital charges would then reach around 7 percent of current MRC requirements. Yet, if we still held the view that operational losses are largely independent of credit and market risks, we would conclude that, on the basis of observations from QIS2, the marginal influence of operational risks on total capital requirements should be less than half a percent of MRC;[27] again, a negligible effect.

What may not be negligible is the interaction between operational risks and uncertainties in costs and revenues in the corresponding activities, uncertainties that Basel has chosen to ignore so far. Financial institutions seek to achieve a balance between risks and returns; operational losses are a small part of this equation. Basel has chosen to raise the level of awareness about these losses. But by concentrating exclusively on operational losses and requiring an aggregation of purely operational risks, banks have to engage in an exercise that is as difficult as it is futile. The possible dependencies between various types of operational risks, whether it is between frequencies or severities or both, are bound to be less important than the dependencies between operational and other risks. We show this further in Chapter 15. We even find common situations where operational risks may reduce rather then increase global risks!

4.3.4 Beyond QIS2 data – high-impact rare events

Let us now address the issue posed by the very low-probability but possibly very large-impact events that are absent from QIS2. It is easy to imagine disasters that would have between one chance in a thousand and one chance in a hundred of occurring per year and that would therefore enter into the scope defined by Basel for capital requirements although, thankfully, most banks would not have incurred such losses in the past. Losses caused by a skilful rogue trader, an act of terrorism, a crippling lawsuit or a major security breakdown have been observed in the banking industry and are recorded in several industry-wide databases. How would they affect expected results and uncertainties for a single firm? Industry-wide data may be useful as a checklist to help us imagine what disasters could possibly befall a particular firm, but firm-specific estimates should take into account the particular business profile, organization, quality of controls, etc., that characterize the firm.

---

[25] The total standard deviation and therefore the total capital requirements should be increased by $(1 + (0.01)^2)^{1/2} - 1 = 0.00005$.

[26] BCBS (2001b, p. 19) states that a bank would be allowed to 'recognize empirical correlations ... provided that it can demonstrate that its systems for measuring correlations are sound and implemented with integrity'. Note that empirical correlations of rare events are almost impossible to obtain and that correlation would not be a meaningful measure of dependency anyway.

[27] The total capital requirement would be the square root of the sum of the squares of requirements for credit and market risks, on the one hand, and operational risks on the other, that is, $(1 + 0.07^2)^{1/2} = 1.0049$, compared to a requirement of 1 without operational risks.

Without entering into specific considerations, we shall try to guestimate the impact of exceptional losses. Our first judgement is that events absent from QIS2 data would still have a low impact on expected losses. The missing events would have probabilities below a few per-cent per year. If we were so pessimistic as to assume exceptional losses as large as 30 percent of MRC with total probability of 3 percent, their contribution to expected losses would still be only 1 percent; add a few one-chance-in-a-thousand catastrophes where the entire capital could be wiped out, and we would have an additional contribution to expected losses of per-haps another 1 percent. Since the expected return on capital of a bank is typically 5 percent to 15 percent per year, the expected loss due to the missing rare events should still be small compared to expected profits.

Our second guess is that exceptional losses could indeed be large compared to the capital of a bank. Basel demands a buffer against operational losses at the one-chance-in-a-thousand confidence level. Now suppose one bank in a thousand per year could be fatally hit by some operational loss (perhaps a slightly pessimistic view compared to historical records, but not unreasonable if vulnerability to operational risks is on the increase). Does it not follow that banks would need to increase their capital significantly, perhaps doubling it up, as a protection against these extreme risks? Of course, that would be inconsistent with the other view from Basel that the current global level of capital in the banking industry is sufficiently safe and should not be changed. In other words, the level of confidence required to determine operational risk capital charges is a very sensitive number: a 99 percent level could mean an insignificant increase in capital charges for operational risks, whereas a 99.9 percent level could mean a doubling up of capital charges. What should it be?

Setting a satisfactory confidence level is about as challenging as tweaking an old manual shower to find that elusive comfort zone between freezing cold and boiling hot. In fact there may not be any satisfactory level. One that would lead to a capital charge of the order of 10 percent of existing capital charges (Basel's wish) would be simultaneously too onerous for operational losses as reported in QIS2 and useless as a buffer against catastrophic losses. To continue our watery analogies, it would be rather like carrying a tiny umbrella when the probability of rain is small.

4.3.5 The arbitrariness of operational risk capital charges

The banking industry is keenly aware of the advantages of maintaining a high credit rating and therefore of maintaining capital commensurate with the risks undertaken. Most banks, at least among G10 countries, would find it unacceptable to be rated below A; the cost of funds would increase materially, credit lines would be restricted, business would tarry unless more prom-ises were made to clients and therefore greater risks were undertaken, thus possibly leading to a downward spiral. There is little argument, therefore, with Basel's plan to expand the role of capital charges as a buffer against a wide range of risks, to make the capital calculations more risk-sensitive and to set the minimum standards in the vicinity of the A rating level.

But for operational risks as we understand them today, the Basel top-down approaches are arbitrary and the bottom-up approaches, even if left entirely to the design of the industry, will be almost impossible to calibrate. Medium- to high-frequency risks should require only negligible capital whereas high-impact, low-frequency risks might require a huge amount of extra capital to meet the confidence level targeted by Basel. Fortunately, there are better ways to cope with the latter risks than by increasing capital (see Part III of this book, Chapter 15 in particular).

The degree to which insurance can be taken into account and expected losses (why expected only?) can be demonstrated as adequately captured introduces two additional sources of uncertainty in the calculation of the operational risk capital charge using advanced measurement methods. On the one hand, it seems natural to recognize insurance cover and anticipated profits; on the other hand, Basel falls into a logical trap: what is the point of measuring losses at a 99 percent confidence level if profits and other compensations are not themselves assessed at the same confidence level? Why assess some uncertainties with great care when others with which they combine are overlooked?

Thus Pillar 1 for operational risks is inconsistent and ineffectual. The data Basel wants to be collected is arbitrarily defined, one-sided, incomplete and therefore incapable of being assembled into a meaningful whole. It is obviously very weak for rare events even when external databases are taken into consideration. Surveys (e.g. RAFT International 2002) have shown that only a minority of banks collect internal loss data in a systematic way, and although one-third of banks may subscribe to external loss data, only a third of that third find any interest in it other than complying with Basel quantitative standards for using an advanced measurement approach.

Operational risk capital charges, as currently defined, are even dangerous because they produce a distorted picture of risks by concentrating on losses rather than considering the whole range of uncertainties in earnings, and using untested linearity and additivity assumptions, unless such assumptions are contradicted by empirical evidence. These calculations divert resources and detract management and supervisory attention from more important problems. There are still blind spots in the regulator's field of vision, such as business risks and the banking book black hole for market risks, both on assets and liabilities. There are still calibration problems to be resolved with credit risks and aggregation problems between various kinds of risks, in particular between market and credit risks.

There are also dangers lurking in embracing ready-made solutions to the assessment of capital requirements. The recent focus on operational risk has been a godsend for many consulting firms: they are pleased to offer solutions at a price, and banks are willing to pay for the aura of objectivity and credibility a consultant brings to the exercise. Consultants come equipped with operational loss data pooled from various external sources. Such data are somehow filtered and scaled and combined with the client's internal data to form the basis on which extreme losses, at the 99.9 percent confidence level, are estimated. Whichever specific method is used, suffice to say that it requires substantial extrapolations. It is fundamentally difficult to assess probabilities and severities of future extreme events that are essentially firm-specific as they depend on unique combinations of persons, organizations, activities, markets, locations,

---

[28] If a large industry-wide database contains comprehensive operational loss data from 1000 banks over ten years it will still show only about ten extreme events at the one-chance-in-a-thousand confidence level.

[29] In March 1995, following the Baring's debacle, practically all bank chief executives in the UK were asked by their board 'Could this happen to us?' (the Bank of England also raised the same question); I surmise that the answers were generally 'no' and were supported with good arguments.

systems, etc. Industry-wide databases showing a few[28] examples of very large operational losses will stimulate management's imagination about potential dangers, but it is unlikely that any of the observed extremes could translate immediately into an assessment of probability and severity for a specific institution.[29] No amount of simulation can make up for the lack of a proper assessment of probabilities.

In short, at this stage, it would be wise to pursue the discussions on operational risk capital charges but to delay the erection of Pillar 1 until better plans are produced.

4.4 Other supervisory proposals and conclusions

In the Basel scheme, Pillar 1 – capital charges – is part of a group of three pillars that are expected to reinforce each other. Pillar 2 – supervision – is designed to ensure that an operational risk management framework has been developed within each institution and that the process of operational risk management is adequately audited and supervised. Pillar 3 – public disclosures – is expected to bring market pressure for good operational risk management through the disclosure of operational risk management methods and exposures.

The roles that supervision and public disclosures are expected to play have been substantially revised in Basel's latest draft of *Sound Practices* (BCBS 2002b). The first draft (BCBS 2001c) attracted a number of comments from the industry as well as supervisory authorities. It is particularly interesting to note the main alterations to the first draft.

4.4.1 Pillar 2: increased reliance on supervision

The operational risk management framework

Pillar 2 reaches beyond the qualitative and quantitative requirements stipulated for the calculation of operational risk capital charges. It requires that 'all banks, regardless of size, have an effective framework in place to identify, assess, monitor and control or mitigate material operational risks as part of an overall approach to risk management' (BCBS 2002b, p. 5). I quote here Principle 8 of the revised draft of the *Sound Practices* document because, I am sure, all the words have been carefully chosen and are, as one says, operative:

(i)   It is addressed to 'all banks, regardless of size', whereas the previous draft (BCBS 2001c, p. 5) simply mentioned 'banks'. I would not be surprised if, in fact, the implementation of this principle is spread beyond banks to other financial institutions in the spirit of harmonization of supervision across financial services.

(ii)   'An effective framework' (a better word than the former 'system') is defined by what it is supposed to do, namely, 'identify, assess, monitor and control or mitigate material operational risks'. Elsewhere (BCBS 2001c, p. 4, para. 10) these activities altogether are used to define what Basel means by the 'management' of operational risks. Therefore, Basel is concerned that all banks should have an effective framework (or structure, or environment) for the management of material operational risks.

(iii) Note also how the definition of management has evolved from the previous draft: 'assess' replaces 'measure' (very wisely, in my view!) and 'mitigate' is added to 'control' (again very wisely) and how 'material' sets the focus.

(iv) Finally, this framework should be 'part of an overall approach to risk management'. That is not new, but is clearly restated and reinforced in other places.

It is a common frailty of human nature to read in a text what one would like to see, but I cannot help but believe that the Basel Committee has expressed concern for the *quality* of the risk management process in all financial institutions, which, to be effective, must be *adapted* to the characteristics of each institution. It has stressed that operational risks are part of *all* risks, that attention should be concentrated on the *most significant* risks, and that these risks should be *managed*, that is, not just 'measured and controlled' (an accounting, backward-looking view) but identified, assessed and mitigated (a forward-looking, proactive view). What a difference compared to the technical guidelines for calculating operational risk capital changes! One could wonder whether the over-enthusiastic statisticians who wrote the *Technical Guidelines* have read *Sound Practices*.

All this is grist – and water! – to my mill (see Chapter 15 for illustrations of operational risk management problems) but it makes the task of supervision all the more demanding because more subjective and all embracing than before.

The *Sound Practices* document puts flesh on the concepts outlined above. It spells out what the framework should consist of, what should be the roles and responsibilities of various parties, the reporting flows, the need for qualified staff, independent audit, etc. So, supervisors can conduct objective checks as for a compulsory car inspection: has it got brakes, lights, etc., do they function adequately... so, is the car road-worthy? But unlike car mechanics, supervisors must also check the quality of the drivers: whether they are qualified, fit, of good character, not under undue pressure, etc.

The analogy, like any analogy, can help illustrate a point, namely that there is something objective about a risk management framework that can be inspected, but like any analogy, it fails when pushed too far. In this case, the inspection or supervision of a bank's risk management process is much more complex and subjective than checking the roadworthiness of a car or even the fitness of its driver. The problems faced in risk management are highly complex and the goals largely subjective and so will be the task of the supervisors.

Challenges for supervisors

Banking supervision faces several dilemmas that would merit discussion.

Costs/benefits. There is no hiding the fact that the implementation of Basel II proposals will be very costly. A survey of 3000 banks has indicated an estimated cost of €23 billion just for gearing up to the new rules, that is, excluding the cost of running the new system and, in the case of operational risks, the cost of remunerating whatever additional capital charges are imposed. Supervisors, in particular, will have to increase their staff and ensure that they are properly trained and paid.

Can we expect commensurate benefits in return? If the global effect of the new rules were simply that 'approved' banks would be recognized as having at most a 0.1 percent probability of default, that is, their ratings would be confirmed as A or better, whereas banks that failed to meet Basel's criteria would be, as it were, blacklisted and therefore pushed further down into a limbo, would consumers and society as a whole benefit? It could be argued that rating agencies and financial analysts, that is, the market in general, already do a decent job and that Basel's criteria, sophisticated as they are or will be, are still crude (e.g. ignoring as they do wide fields of business and reputational risks).

One must therefore believe that the Basel rules are contributing additional benefits such as a better understanding of risks and, consequently, more efficient use of capital and other resources. Basel could be viewed as a forum for the promotion of better risk management in the banking industry. But then, one could also argue that banks have natural incentives to improve the quality of their risk management and that there are already many institutions such as universities and professional bodies whose main role is to carry out research, disseminate information and promote knowledge. Is Basel in a privileged position to carry out this educational role? Probably not in general, but there may be some areas, such as systemic risks, where the concerns and perhaps the knowledge of regulators and supervisors go beyond those of individual banks. Perhaps regulators should focus their attention on these areas.

Dialogue/penalties. The documents from Basel stress the importance of maintaining a close dialogue between regulators and the industry. That is all very well, but regulators make rules that bind and punish; industry representatives could be excused for feeling a bit nervous. If they are to design a rod for their own back and ropes for their feet, may the rod be gentle and the ropes not too tight.

The dilemma is the same at the enforcement level. 'We are looking for a frank and open discussion', says the supervisor, perhaps forgetting to add 'but remember that we make half of our revenues from imposing fines'.

The policeman cannot be the confessor, indeed the confessor vows not to speak to the policeman. Both play useful but separate roles; supervisors should not delude themselves into thinking that they can do both. Should there be two types of supervisors, or should there be simply a clearer distinction between the various types of information to be exchanged, from statutory, public disclosures to confidential 'off-the-record' discussions?

Understanding/responsibilities. Basel claims in various places to have a 'good understanding' of risk management; we can only be thankful for that. Supervisors, likewise, would like to know and understand as much as possible about the firms they examine. What could be wrong with that?

The nub is that supervisors could get too close to their banks. If a patient closely attended by his/her doctor falls gravely ill or, God forbid, dies, the doctor feels at least some moral responsibility. If a supervisor has a good understanding of a bank and, as it were, gives it a clean bill of health, or dispenses the correct medicine, what happens if the bank subsequently falls into deep trouble?

There seems to be no escaping the chain of logic: understanding the bank, enforcing appropriate corrective measures, sharing in the responsibilities for failure. What is needed are clearly defined legal powers and legal protection for supervisors. These may not be sufficiently well defined in many countries.

Legal matters will be concerned with the fine line between supervising a risk management framework and being perceived as approving specific decisions. A methodology or the fitness of an individual is part of the framework. Supervisors can 'recognize', that is, accept the use of a methodology or the presence of an individual in a given function at a given time (which recognition should be subject to regular reviews) but should stop short of 'approving' of people or methodologies which could be interpreted as expressing backing or even a warranty. In the same line of thought, supervisors should not necessarily be made aware of some decisions less they be perceived as condoning these decisions.

4.4.2 Pillar 3: public disclosures and market discipline

Operational risk is the risk that dare not speak its name. There is a stigma attached to it; no one likes to own up to a mistake. It is therefore very difficult to trace causes internally, and perhaps even more difficult to explain to the public how an operational loss took place.

There is also a danger in revealing too much about operational losses (as well as about near misses, which could be more numerous and more instructive). Vulnerabilities should not be divulged for fear of increasing exposure. Reasons for failures could destroy confidence and thereby cause consequential damage that could far exceed direct losses. Revelations could interfere with the process of recovering damages.

Basel is well aware of the need for discretion in certain areas. Sources of information collected in surveys are kept confidential as well as much raw data. Supervisors are also keen to maintain confidentiality in their own assessments of risks for fear of causing damage to the banks they inspect. For example, it is well known that the UK supervisor, the FSA, carries out its own risk assessments of all banks it inspects. It is used to determine a profile for each bank according to its intrinsic business risks and the quality of its controls. On that basis, the FSA makes free use of its authority to set solvency ratios for the more 'risky' banks well above the minimum 8 percent ratio set by Basel. Both the ratings of the FSA and the trigger ratios are given in confidence.

It is somewhat comforting, therefore, to note that Basel has stepped back from earlier intentions to request a comprehensive public disclosure of operational risk loss data and exposures as well as management methods. Inasmuch as the definitions of losses and 'measurements' requested under Pillar 1 are still unclear and arbitrary, it would be rather premature and not very illuminating to request their public disclosure now. Even in the long term, it does not appear to be wise to force banks to reveal operational loss data and exposures, for the reasons mentioned above.

On the other hand, banks would see no harm in disclosing operational risk capital requirements and calculation methods *provided that* a measure of capital requirement that makes sense has been generally agreed – still a tall order!

Disclosing the operational risk assessment approaches that a bank has put in place appears to be the most beneficial type of disclosure. To have real value, it should be part of statutory documents subject to independent auditing.

4.4.3 Summary

To paraphrase, 'It's the management, not the measurement, stupid!'. The Basel Committee has been very busy trying to improve risk management in banking but has been tied up in measurement problems. There are several reasons for that state of affairs (desire for objectivity, prudence, level playing field, menu of solutions, capital incentives, etc.) but the great culprit is certainly the lack of a proper basis for risk assessment in accrual accounting. The current trend towards fair value accounting will facilitate the work of regulators. In the meantime they have to make various compromises, trying to alleviate the inadequacies of the accounting system with strange calculations of capital requirements.

The strange calculations include assumptions of linearity of risks with size of bank or business activity, additivity of capital charges across widely different types of risks, estimations of 'unexpected losses' as multiples of 'expected losses' and, perhaps most importantly, setting as an ultimate goal the estimation of the extreme tail of a purely operational loss distribution. As we explained, such assumptions and methods are baseless, and the estimation of a total operational loss distribution is as difficult as it is futile. Other risks, costs and rewards matter. We think that such calculations are even dangerous because they create a distorted picture of risks and divert management's attention from critical issues. If carried out as requested in the most 'advanced' approaches, the calculations would justify only negligible capital requirements for common risks but possibly enormous capital requirements for exceptional risks. In other words, the results are arbitrary and one might as well do away with capital charges for operational risks, at least for the next few years.

What is important is to improve the quality of risk management and the *Sound Practices* draft document produced by Basel is helpful in that respect. It demands that an effective operational risk management framework be put in place in all banks. 'Effective' could be understood as meaning adapted to the bank, concentrating on the most significant risks, their identification, assessment and control or mitigation. This framework should be an integral part of general risk management and, indeed, of good management.

Of course, it is a tall order for supervisors to examine, discuss, evaluate and even promote such risk management frameworks. At the same time, supervisors should be careful not to become involved in the management of banks; they would have to share responsibility for any failure. Several related issues would merit a more public debate: a cost–benefit analysis of the new Basel proposals; the extent of the legal rights and the legal protections to be given to supervisors; the benefits and drawbacks of various types of public disclosures. There is still much work to be done!

CHAPTER 5

Legal risks and fraud: capital charges, control and insurance

Christos Hadjiemmanuil

5.1 The Basel definitions of operational risk and legal risk

The consultative package on a new Capital Accord, issued by the Basel Committee on Banking Supervision (BCBS) in January 2001, contained a detailed paper on operational risk (BCBS 2001a), against which banks will be required to hold adequate capital, once the planned reforms are implemented. Operational risk is defined in the paper as 'the risk of direct or indirect loss resulting from inadequate or failed internal processes, people and systems or from external events'. The origins of this definition can be traced to an industry-commissioned report entitled *Operational Risk: The Next Frontier* (Robert Morris Associates *et al.* 1999).

In response to industry-led criticism, the Committee has since eliminated the perplexing reference to 'direct or indirect' losses. It has also produced a more precise analysis of the various types of loss events which are considered relevant for the determination of bank regulatory capital requirements and which should, accordingly, be captured by banks' internal loss data. Nonetheless, the tenor of the definition has been retained unaltered. In this regulatory context, operational risk is specifically stated to include 'legal' risk, but to exclude 'systemic', 'strategic' and 'reputational' risks – whatever all these terms may mean.

5.1.1 Definition of operational risk

In the opinion of many commentators, the Committee's attempt to define operational risk is deeply flawed. It is not based on some generally accepted understanding of operational risk, since there is no consensus on this issue in the banking industry. It is also opaque and open-ended, failing to specify the component factors of operational risk or its relationship to other forms of risk. Thus it leaves unanswered many questions concerning the exact range of loss events that can be attributed to operational failures. Moreover, the conceptual heterogeneity of the definition permits alternative, equally plausible but non-coexistive, categorizations of the identifiable instances of operational risk.

More specifically, the classification of operational losses can be approached from three alternative angles: the putative causes of operational failure; the resulting loss events; and the legal and accounting forms of consequential losses. In each case, however, the comprehensive classification of losses under contiguous but non-overlapping sub-categories remains elusive. Moreover, the causal relationships between the three levels (causes, events and effects) are complex and even indeterminate.

At first sight, the Committee's definition espouses the first alternative: it purports to identify the ultimate sources of operational losses by pointing to four broad categories of causes (people, internal processes, systems and external events). Nonetheless, these generic sources of operational risk cannot be straightforwardly linked, in one-to-one causal relations, either to the general types of loss identified in Annex 4 of BCBS's January 2001 document on operational risk (BCBS 2001a)[1] or to the classes of loss events suggested in Annex 2 of the September follow-up paper (BCBS 2001b).[2]

The explicit reference to 'legal risk' in the margin of the Committee's definition of operational risk clearly establishes that this is one of the types of risk against which the regulatory capital requirements are intended to provide cover. Nonetheless, the abrupt manner in which the concept is brought into the discussion, but then left undeveloped, begs many questions. What is the exact meaning of the term? Does it refer to a separate source of risk, existing in parallel to the four sources of operational risk identified in the main part of the Committee's definition? Or does it simply denote a particular class of loss events, which present, of course, certain distinctively 'legal' characteristics but are otherwise ultimately attributable, in causal terms, to one of the four general underlying sources? In other words, is legal risk something distinct from human faults, breakdowns in internal processes or systems and external disruptions, or only a particular way or form in which such failures crystallize and exercise their effects? What is the relationship of legal risk to the risk of fraud? To what extent can legal risk provide credible justification for the Committee's actual proposals for operational-risk-related capital charges?

5.1.2 Legal risk: a subset of operational risk?

Significantly, the Committee takes it for granted that legal risk is part of the broader notion of operational risk. This is neither self-evident nor universally accepted. For instance, in May 2000 the IFCI Financial Risk Institute, a not-for-profit foundation established by derivatives exchanges, market participants and regulators, issued descriptions of the 'princip[al] sources of risks which concern regulators' in derivatives and commodities markets. These are stated to include market, credit, settlement and 'other' risks. On this account, the residual 'other' category covers, in particular, liquidity, legal and operational risks. Operational

---

[1] That is, (a) write-downs, (b) loss of recourse, (c) restitution, (d) legal liability, (e) regulatory and compliance, and (f) loss of or damage to assets.

[2] That is, (a) internal fraud, (b) external fraud, (c) employment practices and workplace safety, (d) clients, products and business practices, (e) damage to physical assets, (f) business disruption and system failures, and (g) execution, delivery and process management.

risk is defined as 'the risk of unexpected losses arising from deficiencies in a firm's management information, support and control systems and procedures', while legal risk is analyzed separately as 'the risk that a transaction proves unenforceable in law or ... has been inadequately documented'. Typical examples of legal risk are also given. These include legal uncertainties surrounding the legal capacity of banks' contractual counterparties to enter into binding transactions, the legality of derivatives transactions and/or the recognition and effectiveness of netting arrangements in particular jurisdictions, or the effectiveness of collateral arrangements in bankruptcy (IFCI Financial Risk Institute 2000).

Such an approach to the classification of risks is not unreasonable. Drawing a distinction between operational risk, on the one hand, and legal risk, on the other, might potentially contribute to a more precise identification of the pathology of banking operations. It would appear that, despite the lack of agreement on the exact scope of the term 'operational risk', its core meaning refers to failures in a bank's information systems and operational and control procedures. There is little doubt that the risks of human error and fraud are closely associated with such failures, since the perpetuation of negligent acts and/or frauds critically depends on the existence of blind spots within the banking organization and an inability of control systems to detect wrongdoing. In this sense, they can be usefully analyzed as aspects, extensions or effects of operational risk.

The Basel definition, however, goes beyond losses directly or indirectly attributable to internal defects of a banking organization (especially flaws in its systems and controls) to cover under the same rubric 'external events' and 'legal risk'. However, the former are, by definition, an outside source of risk; occasionally, the same is true of legal risks, since these coincide only in certain cases with internal organizational defects and breakdowns.

One bad reason why many people associate legal risk with operational risk is that they consider fraud to be both (a) the most significant category of operational loss event and (b) a 'legal issue'. Fraud is indeed a matter of legal relevance, in the sense that it consists in behaviour of which the legal system explicitly disapproves and which triggers significant legal liabilities – whether civil, criminal or even administrative – for the perpetrator. For the victim bank, however, legal risk, in the sense of some uncertainty regarding the true legal position or the rights and duties of the parties involved, is rarely an active question in cases of fraud; what is more important is its practical inability to recover assets lost as a result. For this reason, legal risk and fraud should be analyzed separately, as independent types of risk.

5.2 The varied meanings of 'legal risk'

What is legal risk? Understanding the concept is necessary for the evaluation of its regulatory implications. This is not, however, an easy task. Occasional attempts towards a definition are not particularly satisfactory and have yielded only partial and mutually inconsistent results. As for the Basel Committee, it simply ignores the issue.

In one sense, even credit risk may include a legal aspect. Consider the commencement of insolvency or reorganization proceedings in relation to a bank's borrower. In this case, the subsequent inability of the debtor bank to enforce its claim may not be due to a total unavailability of assets in the hands of the borrower. It may, instead, be the consequence of a law-mandated protection of such assets or a moratorium on insolvent persons' existing debts. This is a legal event. In most jurisdictions, the declaration and legal effects of insolvency do not follow automatically once a financial threshold has been crossed. Instead, the commencement and operation of insolvency proceedings are placed under the control of the courts, and they depend to a significant extent on the exercise of judicial discretion. In such cases, insolvency, in addition to being a legal event, is also an event that is not totally predictable or determinate. In other words, it is not the direct and unavoidable legal consequence of certain factual circumstances, but a risk superimposed on the risk of occurrence of such circumstances.

One could go even further. All financial events affecting a bank can be expressed as legal events. Whether the bank has property over certain assets is a legal, not a purely factual question. The same applies to the existence of liabilities towards, and claims against, other parties, as well as to the allocation of the risk for particular types of losses. A change in the legal norms would immediately transform, for better or worse, the economic situation. For instance, as far as the recognition of bank failure is concerned, it would make all the difference in the world if the state assumed an ultimate legal duty to compensate banks for non-performing assets. Thus, all banking risks could be redescribed as legal risks, because they are borne by the bank, and the resulting losses are ascribed to it, only as a result of the operation of the law.

Of course, this over-expansive notion of legal risk is not consistent with the ways in which the term is used in practice. Legal risk is almost universally understood in narrower terms. It is typically distinguished from direct economic risks, such as credit or market risks. For the estimation of the latter, the legal environment is taken for granted and the question turns to the potential loss implications for a bank's transactions and investments of its counterparties' ability to perform or of the behaviour of the market at large, respectively.

Nonetheless, this still leaves us very far from possessing a working concept of legal risk or being able to distinguish it clearly from other forms of risk. The fact that the term is commonly taken to exclude certain sources of loss does not mean that it is used with any degree of uniformity. Its meanings vary, depending on the specific context and the practical concerns of the persons employing it. In relation to litigation or liability insurance, the term may refer primarily to civil liabilities, including duties to compensate the victims of torts and to make contractual payments or provide indemnities in certain contingencies. In derivatives markets, much emphasis is placed on uncertainties regarding the legal recognition of novel contractual arrangements, which have not been tested in the courts. In international lending or project finance, a major concern is the relative risk of doing business in different countries; to a significant extent, this depends on differences between their legal and judicial systems – in particular, their effectiveness in enforcing creditors' rights.

These examples point to three very different ways in which loss may arise, all of which are often (although not uniformly) classified under the rubric 'legal risk'. Thus, the loss may be attributable to: (a) legally flawed actions of the bank or its employees and agents; (b) uncertainties regarding the requirements and effects of the law itself; or (c) the relative inefficiency of a country's legal system.

5.2.1 Liabilities and losses attributable to legally flawed actions

In the first place, the loss can be attributed to legally flawed actions of the bank or its servants and agents, as a result of which the bank either incurs direct liabilities or becomes unable to ascertain in law certain rights in order to protect its interests. This result may, indeed, come about for a variety of legal reasons. Occasionally, the persons concerned simply ignore the relevant norms or act upon false assumptions and misunderstandings about their content. More often, non-compliance is due to a negligent or wilful disregard for well-known requirements.

Probably the best way of classifying the cases is by reference to the area of the law which creates liability for the bank or leaves it without an effective remedy. The various branches of private law may be of particular significance in this context, especially in so far as they require compliance with transactional formalities or impose liabilities for the actions of certain parties.

Evidently, issues of contract law are of utmost importance for the fate of commercial transactions. The transactions may be inadequately documented. Or they may be illegal and unenforceable. A counterparty may lack the legal capacity to enter into contracts of the particular description. The drafting of contracts may be less than fully competent, resulting in stipulations which misrepresent the true intention of the parties, allocate risks in a manner that was not within their contemplation or fail to make provision for eventualities that should have been specifically covered. Appropriate binding commitments and warranties may not be taken from the counterparty. Formalities on which the valid formation of contracts depends may be disregarded. For instance, an oral agreement may be unenforceable, even though both parties originally intended to be bound by it, simply because the law recognizes contracts of the relevant description only if they are in writing.

The preservation of assets also depends on taking correct procedural steps. For example, a failure to observe registration requirements may thwart the perfection and priority of a bank's interests in collateral or the protection of its real or intellectual property rights. More generally, losses may be suffered whenever third parties successfully assert property rights over assets that the bank assumed to be under its proprietary control.

Where a bank enters into transactions with another company, the operation of various norms of company and insolvency law or of that company's own constitutional documents may create additional difficulties. Potential problems include the legal capacity and valid representation of companies, the powers of their board of directors, the possibility of invalidation of transactions entered into once a company approaches insolvency, etc. Similar considerations apply to transactions with public bodies.

Company law, including norms regulating corporate finance and governance, also constrains the internal management of banks. Breach of such norms by the management or the majority shareholders may result in liability. Alternatively, groups of shareholders may be able to rely on their procedural or substantive rights to block the implementation of a bank's senior management strategy. However, costs already incurred in relation to the aborted action plans may be non-recoverable.

At the same time, banks' internal organization and business activities are affected by an array of rules that could be collectively characterized as social legislation. The violation of labour laws, anti-discrimination provisions, community reinvestment obligations, etc. – all these can be grounds of liability for a bank. Complying with the relevant norms, of course, may also entail substantial costs. Such compliance costs, however, are predictable operating costs and cannot be attributed to legal risk, except in the third, broader sense, which will be discussed later on.

More generally, liabilities may accrue as a result of any act of the bank – or, to be more precise, of individuals within the banking organization – which breaches legal rights of third parties or entails the commission of other wrongful acts. Directors, managers or other employees may negligently or intentionally contravene regulatory or other legal duties, and this may generate for the bank unforeseen liabilities. This is a consequence of the attribution in law to the bank of the acts of those individuals who carry on its affairs or, to use a different formulation, of the bank's vicarious liability, or responsibility for the actions of its servants and agents. One could include under this heading not only the commission of civil wrongs (or torts) but also the failure to comply with administrative and regulatory requirements or the infraction of criminal laws. In the former instance, the bank will have to compensate the victims of the wrongful acts; in the latter, it will be subject to administrative enforcement or even criminal penalties (provided, of course, that a particular legal system imposes criminal liabilities on legal persons as well).

In this context, it should not be forgotten that, in cases of very serious misconduct, the response of the supervisory authorities could be extremely severe and their administrative sanctions could even encompass the withdrawal of the bank's licence. Moreover, indirect reputational costs may ensue as a result of negative publicity. Some people use a special name for this: 'regulatory risk'.

The risk of loss as a result of wrongdoing by the bank or by insiders for whose actions the bank bears responsibility is closely related to, but should not be confused with, the risk of fraud where the bank itself is the victim. The latter will be examined in Section 5.3. However, the two types of risk can overlap: a single event of fraud may be the cause of both direct losses and legal liability. Specifically, where the perpetrator of a fraud is its employee, the bank may suffer direct losses as a victim and at the same time be held responsible in civil or regulatory proceedings for its failure to manage effectively its internal affairs and to control the actions of its staff.

There are many more situations where a bank's lack of compliance with rules of law regulating some aspect of its activities – from an inadvertent failure to comply with seemingly pointless formalities to the most serious breach of public duties – becomes the source of loss. In cases of this type, the true legal position may be relatively clear and easy to determine, at least with the benefit of competent legal advice. If so, due care and diligence on the part of the bank – including the taking of legal advice, where this appears appropriate – would be sufficient for the avoidance of losses.

5.2.2 Legal uncertainty

This does not apply to a second category of legal risk cases, where the source of loss is legal uncertainty, pure and simple. Since this is an external parameter, which does not depend on any fault of the bank itself, it affects even the most diligently and prudently run institutions.

The law is commonly imagined to be settled and knowable. In fact, however, it is often impossible to establish unambiguously the true position on a legal issue. In all areas of the law anomalies abound as a result of the complexity and/or obscurity of the norms, but also because future events may impinge on the legal position in irregular and unexpected ways. A legal system may never have addressed a particular issue by way of authoritative legislative or judicial decisions. Alternatively, there may be general agreement that certain sources of law govern the matter at hand, but their substantive content may be in dispute and their interpretation contested. The sources may not provide sufficiently clear and comprehensible guidance for action, or may be in conflict with one another. Problems of interpretation often accompany the introduction of novel statutory provisions. Under such conditions, the operation of the law can appear uncertain and indeterminate and nobody can predict with a high degree of confidence how the courts or other authoritative decision-makers, such as arbitrators or regulators, will eventually resolve potential disputes.

Sometimes, the law is intentionally expressed in general and abstract terms. Of course, the importance of legal certainty and predictability is universally recognized. In practice, however, it is frequently counterbalanced by the demand for flexibility and open-endedness. Because of informational constraints, as well as limited legislative time and resources, it is impossible to draft complete rules, making special provision for each and every eventuality. On the other hand, where a rule is intended to regulate a wide range of cases, a concrete and precise formulation may be deemed undesirable: an exact and technical rule can lead to situations where compliance with its letter will be incompatible with the true legislative aim, and vice versa. In order to avoid the problem of imperfect fit between formal rules and their underlying purpose, legal systems often resort to legislation by general principles or standards. Indefinable and ambiguous concepts, such as 'good faith', 'fairness', 'reasonableness', 'abuse of right' or 'due diligence', fill the legal landscape. They figure prominently both in statutes and in judicial precedents. But what exactly do they mean? Rather than providing objective *ex ante* guidance for market participants, the various standards and principles may simply disguise the subjective – and sometimes unpredictable – *ex post* evaluation of their actions by administrative and judicial decision-makers.

Where the meaning of legal rules is unclear, a bank may try to protect itself by procuring legal opinions. Even the best legal advice that money can buy, however, may be inconclusive and leave the bank in the dark. To make things worse, legal risks may be latent. Market participants may fail to realize that a transaction could turn sour for legal reasons. They may even act on the basis of reasonable and stable expectations regarding the general state of the law and the implications of provisions in statutes and contracts. Nonetheless, such expectations may be upset *ex post facto*, by reason of a contrary judicial, administrative or, more rarely, legislative interpretation. For those adversely affected by unanticipated rulings, the applicable rules are essentially rewritten with retrospective effect, even if officially they remain the same: in short, the law proves to be a treacherous guide for commercial behaviour.

In general, then, the second category includes cases where the law is up for grabs. This is the stuff of which the landmark cases of commercial and banking law are made. The decisions in such cases increase legal certainty for the future, because they provide pointers that banks can rely upon. As far as past activities are concerned, however, the results can sometimes verge on the catastrophic.

The decision of the highest English court, the House of Lords, in *Hazell* v. *Hammersmith and Fulham LBC* [1992] 2 AC 1, provides a classic illustration of precisely this type of legal risk. The question for the court was whether local authorities had the legal capacity to enter into interest rate swap transactions. The court decided that they did not. Many high-value contracts entered into over a number of years between local councils and banking institutions were thereby invalidated. As a consequence, the unsuspecting banking institutions might be unable to recover moneys owed to them under the terms of the contracts, thus sustaining very substantial losses. Eventually, this precipitated a change in the law, in the form of a subsequent judicial ruling in *Kleinwort Benson Ltd* v. *Lincoln City Council* [1999] 2 AC 349 (HL). It should be noted that in *Hazell* the court dealt with the issue at the instigation of the auditors of the 'defendant' authority and based its decision on the interpretation of statutory powers of the latter. The financial implications of the declaration of the transactions' unenforceability did not constitute a relevant consideration, and the judges did not even have a clear idea of the identity, number or size of the transactions indirectly affected by their pronouncement.

One could point to many other examples of uncertainty relating to the content of legal norms. In some jurisdictions there are doubts about the enforceability of certain derivatives transactions, set-off and netting agreements in the event of bankruptcy, index clauses, compound interest provisions, etc. Only recently, the legal questions regarding the continuity of contractual obligations denominated in the precursor currencies following the introduction of the euro were the cause of much anxiety across the European Union.

Even where the current state of the law is known with absolute certainty, there is always a residual risk that the law will change, or that regulatory discretions will be exercised, in a way that will render certain banking activities uneconomic. This can occur, for example, in the event of an increase in the tax burden of certain transactions; a regulatory change which does not directly affect the bank, but undermines the financial prospects and creditworthiness of its borrowers; or the imposition, perhaps for consumer-protection or law-enforcement reasons, of new conduct-of-business rules, with which the bank can comply only at considerable additional cost.

Some governmental decisions may even make the continuation of certain activities or the collection of assets legally impossible. Thus, an enactment could suddenly introduce exchange controls, create moratoria, or freeze the financial assets of the government and nationals of countries subject to international trade sanctions. (Note, however, that the effect of financially repressive or confiscatory decisions may be beneficial, not detrimental, to the banks concerned. An example is the 'Corralito', a scheme restricting withdrawals of deposits in cash, which was imposed by the Argentine government in late 2001, in an attempt to prevent a run on the banks and a wholesale shift from deposits to currency.)

Not only the substance of legal rules, however, but also their enforcement may be subject to uncertainty. A bank may be unable to collect an asset not because it does not have a good claim, but because the latter cannot be enforced in practice. An intransigent counterparty may refuse to perform some obligation, or seek to delay performance, in which case litigation may be the only way forward. Nonetheless, this form of collection may prove costly or futile for procedural and evidentiary reasons. Witnesses may die; certain facts may become impossible to prove; otherwise good claims may be impossible to validate due to failures in the records and systems of custodians and other third parties; litigation may have to be conducted abroad, giving rise to special difficulties and excessive costs; and so on. Many enforcement problems will, of course, be attributable to defects in the documentation of transactions or to other legally flawed actions occurring at an earlier stage, which should be classified under the first heading of legal risk. Procedural constraints and delays on enforcement may, however, combine with a deteriorating financial situation of the counterparty, or of the market at large, to preclude full and effective recovery without any fault of the bank itself. Thus, the way in which the legal system processes claims may heighten the credit and liquidity risk of transactions.

5.2.3 Legal uncertainty and financial innovation

The role of financial innovation must be emphasized in relation to legal uncertainty. Since the 1960s the financial sector has been undergoing continuing and accelerating structural transformation. The Basel Committee has repeatedly observed that the ongoing changes involve substantial and growing amounts of operational risk for banking institutions. Examples include the information-technology-based automation of banking operations, the related sharp increase in the volume and turnover of transactions processed, or the adoption of innovative transactional techniques, which may help reduce traditional credit and market risks but at the same time create additional operational risk. All these make banks particularly vulnerable to computer breakdowns, other system failures or, in cases of outsourcing of certain functions or reliance on outside infrastructures, third-party defaults. Technical innovation also provides new opportunities for fraudsters. In particular, some forms of fraud can become prevalent in an information-technology-dependent environment, especially when banking services are provided electronically from a distance, as in the case of Internet-based e-commerce.

Innovation, however, is a significant contributor to legal risk as well. The adoption of new and complex transactional techniques, in particular, is often surrounded by significant legal uncertainty and can expose banks to potentially catastrophic risks.

Most traditional types of banking transactions (paper-based payment transactions, overdrafts, secured loans, letters of credit, etc.) have a long legal history. They have been tested repeatedly in the courts. The relevant law is more or less settled and the contractual documentation reflects the accumulated experience. Less time-honoured transactional techniques, however, may be subject to unforeseen – even unforeseeable – legal challenges. The novel, untested contracts may not only be inadequately documented, they may also cut across traditional legal categories in ambiguous ways. Technical problems of legal characterization arise as a consequence. The existing rules and principles of contract law may be inappropriate for the clarification of the situation, because they take as typical situations which, in the new environment, are of merely marginal importance and rely on conceptual distinctions which may be difficult to apply to hybrid financial instruments. For instance, in jurisdictions where the law disapproves of gaming contracts, certain derivatives contracts may sit uncomfortably between the class of 'legitimate' hedging transactions and that of 'illegitimate' gaming or speculative ones; as a result, their enforceability may be put in question.

Another problem concerns the exportation of successful transactional innovations. Financial techniques developed in one country tend to be adopted by business people everywhere, if they appear to work. However, the contractual provisions supporting the new transactions do not work in isolation; they operate against a fully-fledged legal system, they are adaptations to a concrete legal environment. For this reason, they do not always travel well from one legal system to another. Once transplanted, they may interact with their new habitat in perverse ways.

Analogous difficulties can arise from legal innovations and the proliferation of multilevel systems of norms. For example, norms originally promulgated by the Basel Committee may be incorporated into European law in the form of directives, and then transposed into the national legal systems of EU member states. However, the technical reformulation of the provisions at the various levels will frequently generate inconsistencies and implementation failures, defeating expectations and increasing legal uncertainty.

Of course, while legal transplants may sometimes increase complexity and uncertainty, the absence of harmonization and the continuing fragmentation of legal systems are a perennial source of problems. For institutions engaging in cross-border business, the great disparity in the way in which different jurisdictions treat similar issues entails acute risks. The competing claims of the various legal systems connected to a transaction raise questions of conflict of laws, often of a highly complex nature. In practice, the answers to such questions can only be conclusively given *ex post facto*, because much depends on whose courts will eventually determine a dispute. This is a cause of legal uncertainty for the transacting parties, which is complemented by the difficulty of knowing the law of foreign countries – something necessary for understanding the exact implications of contractual arrangements and predicting the outcome of potential litigation.

The emergence of e-commerce in financial services, in particular, is affected by very significant risks of legal uncertainty, of all types described above. The enforcement of contracts entered into through the Internet, the identification of customers, the protection of privacy and the application of mandatory consumer-protection-related provisions of contract law or regulatory rules affecting the promotion of investments and the conduct of financial business – these and other issues raise difficult questions of national law. In a growing number of cases with cross-border connections, however, the electronic provision of services is further plagued by complex jurisdictional considerations.

5.2.4 Country-specific legal perils and costs

In addition to legally flawed actions of the bank and legal uncertainty, the term 'legal risk' sometimes refers to a third consideration: the relative risk of doing business in different countries, as a function of the quality of their legal systems. Jurisdictions can be compared by reference to the effects of their laws and judicial systems in terms of increasing or attenuating the risk (as well as the direct costs) of otherwise identical banking activities. From this perspective, legal riskiness is primarily an attribute of the legal systems, not of the banking organizations or of their activities. This approach may be useful in relation to international lending or project-finance activities, where the evaluation of a country's relative legal risk can have significant pricing and risk management implications.

Relative legal risk depends, of course, on a country's overall level of legal risk in the second sense, that is, of legal uncertainty, because the predictability of legal outcomes will be a significant parameter in comparing jurisdictions. But the overlap is only partial. A jurisdiction may represent a significant risk for market participants even if its legal rules are clear as well as stable. In particular, the substantive legal norms may be misconceived or ill-drafted, imposing undue burdens on transactions. In other words, the law may be the source of well-understood but unnecessary costs and inefficiencies.

Many legal systems are unfavourable to creditors. They lack orderly, fast and effective insolvency procedures, give wide discretion to the insolvency court, are biased in favour of the continuation of failed enterprises and create impediments to the foreclosure and realization of collateral security. Generally speaking, legal systems belonging to the Anglo-American or common law family may tend to provide stricter enforcement of creditor rights than those of civil law European countries or of emerging economies. The willingness of courts to go beyond the strict terms of contracts, to allow the avoidance of transactions or to adjust the obligations of the parties on grounds of fairness or equity or of changes in the underlying circumstances may also be more pronounced in civil law than in common law jurisdictions. The degree of creditor-friendliness and insistence on the strict enforcement of property and contractual rights is, accordingly, an evident criterion for ranking jurisdictions in terms of legal risk.

The quality and reliability of a country's political system, public administration and judiciary are also critical. A relative absence of red tape and delays facilitates the enforcement of rights and the realization of assets. Conversely, where administrative and judicial incompetence or corruption are prevalent, legal risk increases dramatically. The ideological outlook of official decision-makers or, more precisely, their socio-economic beliefs, values and attitudes are also significant: such factors do not influence only the adoption of legal rules, but also the ways in which they are interpreted and implemented. Equally important is the degree of expertise of judges and regulators and their familiarity with various types of financial activities carried on by banks.

Even amongst economically advanced countries with sophisticated, creditor-friendly systems of commercial law and a solid tradition of rule of law, however, the degree of legal risk faced by banks will not be the same. For example, while the basic principles of liability of the

English and the American common law of torts may appear to be the same, an English court may be more circumspect than an American jury in deciding cases of alleged corporate wrongdoing. Moreover, as a result of the system of contingency fees, the aggressive role played by tort lawyers in the initiation of law suits and the greater likelihood of remedies of a very high financial order, including hefty compensatory and punitive damages, the dynamics of litigation in the USA are very different than in England. Accordingly, a bank operating in the USA may be more exposed to litigation risks than one active in the UK. For analogous reasons, the risk of regulatory activism, leading to unpredictable or particularly harsh enforcement costs, may be much pronounced in the USA.

5.3 Banks and the risk of fraud

The term 'fraud' does not have an exact legal or regulatory meaning. It is used as a generic term, to designate a variety of forms of non-violent economic wrongdoing, whose commission constitutes a criminal offence and/or a civil wrong (either the tort of deceit, giving rise to an action for damages, or a fraudulent misrepresentation, rendering contracts entered into under its influence voidable); see, for example, Kirk (2000). Theft, conversion, unauthorized withdrawal of money from ATMs, forgery of instruments, false accounting, fraudulent conveyance and unauthorized trading are only some of the types of behaviour that fall under the rubric. The forms are diverse and do not always share many elements in common. Some common threads, however, can be identified. These include the dishonesty of the perpetrator and the economic objectives of his acts. In particular, the fraudster does not pursue his objectives by exercising or threatening violence, but seeks to deceive others through false representations or misleading conduct. Generally, his intention is to confer some economic benefit on himself or a third party or simply to cause loss to the victim. However, deceptive behaviour that takes place with reckless indifference as to the potential loss implications for the victim could be equated with fraud.

Since frauds are designed to go undetected, at least at the time when they are committed and perhaps for some time thereafter, the detrimental effect may only be discovered a long period after the act. This characteristic makes an exact estimation of the incidence and impact of fraud particularly difficult. The problem is compounded by a failure of many victims to report events of fraud.

There is no doubt, however, that fraud is a perennial problem for the banking system and its users. One should distinguish here between three different roles that a bank can play in a fraud: those of perpetrator, vehicle or victim of the fraud.

Tax fraud and money-laundering offences are common examples of economic crimes committed by banks. But frauds can also be committed by banks or their individual managers and employees against clients and counterparties. In this context, it would be misleading to describe fraud as a risk faced by the bank. If anything, the bank itself is the source of the risk, which is borne by outside parties! From the bank's perspective, the potential risk in this context is a legal risk in the first sense analyzed above (i.e. the risk of legal liability for failure to prevent staff frauds or regulatory risk). For regulators, the primary question here would not be how to back up internal risk management or enhance the bank's capacity to withstand losses, but how to assist the detection of irregularities and penalize criminal misconduct. Capital adequacy requirements, however calculated, would not alter the situation.

In the second case too (that is, where banking transactions are the vehicle or form of frauds against clients or third parties), the bank is not subject to direct risk of loss. The residual risk is primarily reputational. However, there may be cases where the law reallo-cates the financial risk, forcing the bank to bear the loss and compensate the immediate victims. This may happen on grounds of contributory negligence or some breach of con-duct-of-business standards, but in certain conditions even a diligent bank may bear the risk of fraudulent transactions involving its clients' accounts, say, in a payments context. Moreover, a bank's failure to detect fraud by third-party perpetrators and with third-party victims, which nonetheless takes place through its systems, may bring to light organizational shortcomings and security failures, which are penalized by way of regulatory enforcement.

In contrast, where the bank is the victim, it can incur potentially critical losses. Although in theory the perpetrators will be civilly liable to compensate the bank, in practice it may be impossible to obtain satisfaction, because they may be unknown or have concealed or dissi-pated the proceeds of their fraud. The likelihood of asset recovery depends on the timeliness of identifying wrongdoing and the diligence displayed in stopping further dissipa-tion and discovering and attaching assets already in the hands of the perpetrators, their accomplices or people holding on their behalf.

Cases where a bank is the victim or the vehicle of fraud can further be distinguished on the basis of the perpetrator's identity. Some frauds are internal, in the sense that they are committed by, or with the help of, insiders such as managers or employees, while others are the acts of individuals outside the banking organization.

Huge numbers of fraudulent transactions take place daily at the retail level, especially in relation to cheques, payment cards, cash withdrawals from ATMs and, more recently, Internet-based banking transactions. The fraudulent acts often involve the assumption of individual clients' identity, the unauthorized use of their cards, personal identification num-bers or other data, and the execution of payments or deposit withdrawals which are charged to their accounts. However, the risk is not always borne by the affected clients, who are often protected by law. Instead, at least part of the losses may be allocated to the payment intermediaries and credit-card issuers. The cumulative cost can be staggering. One source estimates the annual losses from cheque-related fraud in the USA at approximately $10 bil-lion. In 1994, an ABA survey found that, during the previous year, the vast majority of large and medium-sized banks and more than half of community banks had sustained losses of this nature, amounting in total to $815 million and 1 276 000 cheques!

Despite their great aggregate significance, frauds relating to payment services tend to result in only limited losses per event and institution. Taken on their own, they are unlikely to cause a bank's failure. Moreover, due to the high volume and low average impact of rele-vant loss events, predicted losses can be evaluated with some degree of confidence, making possible the effective management of risk and its pricing, which is reflected in the margin of transactions. There would appear to be little basis for regulatory intervention in the form of capital charges.

Nonetheless, it should be noted that in certain idiosyncratic cases the losses due to payment fraud have been both unexpected and very substantial. Recent technological developments increase the risk that pseudonymous or unauthorized transactions will result in major losses and call for heightened awareness of the problem. The adoption of powerful informational technology permits the centralized, wholesale management of retail transactions, but at the same time creates unprecedented possibilities for instantaneous execution of fraudulent transactions on a massive scale, sometimes on a cross-border basis. The risk is compounded by an environment of open, or partially interconnected, communication networks, which include the Internet, intranets and various special-purpose limited-access communication systems. These heighten the possibility of unauthorized remote access to a bank's computer systems and outside interference with data. For example, in 1994 Citibank suffered a cross-border electronic breach of security in relation to certain institutional customers' accounts which were accessible on-line, resulting to the transfer of some $12 million to overseas accounts controlled by the perpetrators.[3] Generally, the penalization of this type of breach of security and resulting fraud is hampered by unavailability of robust evidence of guilt, meeting the criminal standard of proof ('beyond reasonable doubt') and the difficulty of pursuing fraudsters in foreign, often exotic, jurisdictions. This increases the importance of computer security, encrypting technologies and verification systems.

It is the possibility of idiosyncratic large-scale frauds by bank insiders that poses the most serious risk to banks, however. Catastrophic losses due to internal fraud have always been a primary cause of bank failure.[4] In some cases, events of fraud and other misconduct are widespread and a culture of wrongdoing permeates the highest echelons of the bank's managerial hierarchy. Amongst the most notorious examples, one could mention the collapses of Banco Ambrosiano in 1983 and, most notably, BCCI in 1991. BCCI is an extreme example of an institution that, until its spectacular collapse, was run by its owners and senior management in a deeply corrupt way, as an instrument for a complex set of illegal activities. Operating the bank was the essential form of the fraud. In one sense, this is a mixed example of bank involvement: BCCI was both a perpetrator of illegal acts that could benefit it financially (e.g. money laundering) and the victim of various crimes (fraudulent lending, theft and other practices of its management aimed at the misappropriation of its assets, as

---

[3] Note, however, that the bank itself allowed the transfer of the bulk of this amount (approximately $11.6 million) after the detection of the breach, in order to enable the identification of the perpetrators. (See Walden 2000, pp. 396–397.)

[4] On the other hand, sometimes the significance of fraud as a cause of bank failure is exaggerated and technical regulatory breaches are equated, following a bank's insolvency, with calculated criminal misconduct. As observed by Olson (2000, p. 313): 'The pervasive characterisation of bank insolvency as the result of fraud or other criminal activity has been reflected historically in America by a search for scapegoats to bear the responsibility and burden of bank losses.'

well as false accounting and falsification of records for the purpose of concealment of the crimes and resulting losses). In the end, the failure caused enormous losses to depositors and other third parties.

In other cases, however, the undetected wrongful acts of a single trader or manager may be sufficient to bring down a bank. In recent years, many instances have come to light of large-scale unauthorized trading by a few securities, commodities and derivatives 'rogue traders' within large banking groups, leading to very substantial losses and even to the relevant bank's insolvency. Examples include the Baring's collapse in 1995, then the Daiwa Bank and Sumitomo Corp. cases and, only recently, the AIB debacle. Invariably, in order to conceal from their superiors their excessive trading and losses, which often continue for months or even years, the unauthorized traders also engage in falsification of records and documents and accounting frauds. In its turn, the circumvention of internal procedures is made possible only because of gaps and inefficiencies in the affected banks' organizational environment, including faults in their record-keeping systems and controls, mismanagement, perverse incentives and conflicts of interest, absence of strict separation between front and back office functions and ineffective internal and external audits.

5.4 Implications for the proposed capital charges for operational risk

5.4.1 Role of legal risks and fraud in the calculation of capital charges

The exact scope of notions such as legal risk and bank fraud may be of limited relevance to the determination of the capital charge for operational risk. Two of the three proposed methods for calculating the charge do not depend on the characterization and classification of exposures by reference to particular categories of operational losses.

The simplest Basic Indicator Approach is essentially little more than a flat scale-of-activity-related charge, and is technically calculated as a specified percentage (so-called 'alpha') of gross income.

The somewhat more 'advanced' Standardized Approach will be used by banks meeting certain qualitative standards of effective risk management and control, including procedures for the reporting, measurement and monitoring of operational risks faced by their various business units. It will be based on a division of a bank's activities (excluding its insurance-related business) in a limited number of standard business lines (probably: corporate finance; trading and sales; retail banking; commercial banking; payment and settlement; agency services and custody; asset management; and retail brokerage). For each business line, a single financial indicator of total activity volume will serve as a proxy for the level of operational risk exposure assumed by the bank in the course of engaging in related activities. The Basel Committee's revised proposals of September 2001 (BCBS 2001b), envisage that gross income will be used as the initial exposure indicator for all business lines. Using a common exposure indicator across business lines is a means of ensuring simplicity, comparability and the avoidance of regulatory arbitrage between different forms of banking intermediation. On the other hand, the operational-risk-related capital charge will be calculated under the Standardized Approach separately for each business line, as a specified fraction of the indicator. This will be achieved by applying to the indicator a business-line-specific factor ('beta'), to be set by the supervisors at a level which is supposed to reflect the industry-wide relationship between aggregate levels of activity and loss experience for each category of activity. The total capital requirement to cover operational risk will be the simple sum of the capital charges for the various business lines.

It is clear that in the case of both the Basic Indicator Approach and the Standardized Approach the basis for calculating operational-risk-related capital charges is a bank's volume of activities.[5] The analysis of specific types of risk and the estimation of their prevalence in each institution do not affect the regulatory outcome. Of course, one might contend that regulators must implicitly take into account the significance of various sources of risk, including legal risks and the risk of fraud, in the context of assigning a specific value to the alpha and beta factors. In truth, however, these factors are likely to depend not on detailed risk classifications and risk measurement, but mostly on the overall calibration of the capital charge, whose essential aim is to ensure that, as a total sum, the new credit and operational-risk-related charges will rise to current average capital levels. In other words, the operational-risk-related charge will function in practice as an arbitrary add-on to the credit-risk-related capital requirements.

The situation is somewhat different only as far as the third and most complex method of calculation, the Advanced Measurement Approaches (AMA), is concerned. Only banks meeting very demanding standards relating to the quality of their risk management and control processes and the robustness of their loss data and internal risk measurements will be allowed to use AMA. The method is based on the identification of seven general types of operational-risk-related 'loss events'. Applied to the eight standard business lines of the Standardized Approach, the seven classes of loss events produce a matrix of 56 line–event combinations. Eligible banks will calculate their own capital requirements against operational risk, based on internally generated expected loss estimates for each line–event combination (subject, however, to an overall floor of 75 percent or so of the capital charge estimation under the Standardized Approach). For this purpose, they will need to calculate the scale of their exposure for each business line, the probability of loss events of the relevant class, as

[5] Large banks have objected to the Committee's adoption of gross income as exposure indicator, on the ground that operational risk is non-linear with respect to regulated institutions' size or activity level, tending to decline as scale grows. In fact, as exposure indicators go, gross income can appear perverse even if one does not object to otherwise linear indicators. Some operational risks may be especially pronounced in business lines characterized by automation, very high numbers of transactions and low margins – for example, in the payment and settlements or agency and custody areas. For such business lines, gross income may fail to reflect the underlying risk exposure. More generally, gross income penalizes high-margin activities and businesses indiscriminately, whether the additional income is the result of superior performance or the recompense of increased risk-taking.

well as the average level of loss if an event occurs, using internal and, where appropriate, industry-wide loss data. In this context, internal and external frauds form two of the seven classes of relevant loss events. Of the remaining five classes, two (damage to physical assets; and business disruption and system failures) appear to relate to physical events, internal human errors and crimes of violence, but in some instances the loss may be attributable, at least in part, to legal risks or fraud.[6] The final three classes (employment practices and work-place safety; clients, products and business practices; and execution, delivery and process management) comprise an array of loss events that could be attributed to legal risk – but not exclusively nor exhaustively. Some forms of legal risk – essentially, of the first type described above, that is, risks of liability and losses due to legally flawed actions of the bank and its employees – are included, albeit in a haphazard way, while others are completely excluded.

To assist the classification of loss events, the Committee can only offer lists of indicative examples of relevant activities. For instance, the 'employment practices and workplace safety' class is subdivided into the 'employee relations', 'safe environment' and 'diversity and discrimination' categories. Examples of activities leading to loss are given for each of them. Under the 'employee relations' rubric one can find the following examples: 'compensation, benefit, termination issues' and 'organized labour activity'. The first example involves primarily legal risks, the second not (except if one considers that the exercise by employees of collective labour rights is a legal risk, perhaps in the third sense described above). This approach makes it impossible (but also practically unnecessary) to determine whether a loss event is due to legal risk or some other source of risk, or is a joint effect of a combination of perils.

In short, the exact place of legal risks in the broader province of 'operational' risk remains ambiguous. This is not surprising, considering the general conceptual confusion surrounding the issue of operational risk. On the other hand, this definitional vagueness is hardly compatible with the Basel Committee's insistence that banks should systematically collect and analyze operational-risk-related loss data. The problems relating to the measurement of operational risk are well known. The lack of good historical loss databases is a major barrier to more accurate estimations of expected losses – especially from low-frequency, high-severity events.[7] But the compilation of robust series of data critically depends on a robust approach to the identification and classification of loss events and resulting losses. Precisely this is lacking in the measurement of operational risk. The scope of relevant events is not coherently defined, while the resulting losses may be subject to double counting, since operational and legal failures often concur with credit or market risks and the same losses can be recorded under both headings.

---

[6] Thus, it is not evident whether accidents involving cars that belong to a bank should be interpreted as human error, physical damage or legal risks.

[7] However, the main problem in relation to rare catastrophic losses may not be the insufficiency of historical data, but the lack of stable relationships between the relevant risk factors and their effects in terms of the frequency and size of losses.

5.4.2 Fraud, other operational losses and the regulation of bank capital adequacy

A separate issue is whether operational risk should ever be subject to capital charges. Capital adequacy standards are intended to exclude the possibility that, until the next reporting period, a bank may become insolvent because of excessive losses on its loan portfolio or from trading activities. The basic assumption is that no single loss event can deplete the bank's total capital base. For this reason, capital charges are combined with restrictions on large exposure. Another assumption is that the bank's financial position is accurately reflected in its accounts. Both assumptions may be inapplicable to operational losses and, in particular, to fraud.

Many operational or fraud losses are small and occur with a high degree of regularity. The risks are well understood and reflected in the margins of banking transactions. As such, they do not justify regulation. At the other extreme, certain rare but catastrophic loss events can wipe out a bank's full net worth in one go. In the area of operational risk, there is nothing equivalent to large-exposure regulation that could prevent this type of event. At the same time, the loss may not be immediately apparent or accounted for.

For instance, fraud-induced losses are a common cause of bank failures. Whether they should be of particular concern to regulators is another question. Almost without exception, such failures are correctly perceived by the market to be institution-specific, and there is little evidence that they can cause contagion or have systemic implications.

Assuming that this is an appropriate area for regulatory interventions, however, it is doubtful whether capital requirements are the best instrument. It is not clear how regulators can estimate the risk of large-scale idiosyncratic fraud and capture it in their capital standards. As explained above, common payments-related frauds by outsiders, as well as some types of small-value insider frauds, such as 'phantom withdrawals' from ATMs, can be captured with relative ease in historical loss databases and their future value can be estimated and priced. This is not generally possible, however, for rare incidents of high-value unauthorized trading and other insider fraud or outside security breaches – all typical outlier events. Due to leveraging, losses from unauthorized trading can increase dramatically within a very limited period, as in the Baring's case. Even where this is not the case, the recognition of accumulated losses is likely to hit the bank suddenly and with great force. As a result, the bank's supposed capital buffer may be already depleted at the time of reporting!

Finally, the identification of major losses from fraud is bound to trigger significant organizational corrections within the bank. Accordingly, the historical loss data, even if they exist, may be a bad indicator of present risk. For these reasons, a capital charge may be superfluous for small-value frauds, which are already priced in the margin of banking transactions, and inappropriate for idiosyncratic large-scale frauds. For the latter, the appropriate remedies are more likely to be found in improved internal systems and controls and in better incentive structures for managers and supervisors, including effective *ex post facto* penalties following the detection of wrongdoing within their lines of responsibility.

5.5 Containing and managing legal risks and fraud

Although legal risks and the risk of fraud are ubiquitous, banks do not lack all means for containing and managing their exposure. The first line of defence, of course, is a bank's control environment. An effective system of internal controls can play, in particular, a primary role in containing the risk of fraud. The banking industry can also take collective steps to improve legal predictability and safety, sometimes in areas where individual institutions, acting alone, cannot contain risks. Finally, legal and fraud risk transfer techniques, especially in the form of liability insurance and insurance products providing cover against losses from fraud, are available – and are widely used by banks. Still, the level of residual legal risks is bound to remain significant, while the possibility of fraud always lurks on the horizon, calling for perpetual vigilance.

5.5.1 Risk management by individual banking institutions and the significance of the internal control environment

The level of operational risk faced by a banking institution depends to a great extent on the quality of its internal control systems. A major factor is the distribution of incentives for risk control and the allocation within the banking organization of managerial responsibility for particular loss events. Business line managers are generally considered to be in the best position to detect and control operational risk. Accordingly, many banks incorporate data on operational risk in their business line evaluation methodologies, charge operational losses to particular business areas and make business line managers accountable to senior management for such losses. In addition, they emphasize compliance with proper operating procedures and control requirements and seek to identify problems through their supervisory and internal audit mechanisms.

Similar considerations apply – but only up to a point – to legal risks and the risk of fraud. An effective internal control environment is, undoubtedly, of utmost importance for the prevention of fraud. By ensuring that any signs of wrongdoing will be spotted at the earliest possible opportunity, it not only minimizes the financial consequences, but also dissuades potential offenders. Appropriate control mechanisms can also reduce the incidence of certain losses due to legal risks – especially those of the first type described above, that is, losses due to non-compliance with the requirements of civil, regulatory and criminal law. Transactional losses can be minimized if a set of internal legal due-diligence procedures is adopted, with the aim of ensuring the proper documentation and legality of transactions and the perfection of collateral security. More generally, the implementation of operating procedures, computer and physical security measures and internal verification mechanisms able to detect errors, breaches of legal rules and fraudulent acts at the level of individual transactions may be more important in this context than the estimation of the incidence of loss events and the aggregate ensuing losses.

On the other hand, even the most sophisticated internal control systems may yield mixed results in terms of avoiding risks arising from the indeterminacy of the law or costs associated with inherently inefficient and/or unpredictable legal systems. The identification of potential problems is probably more important in this context than the effort to provide solutions, since this may be largely outside a bank's hands. Even this, however, may be difficult to achieve in practice. External legal advice and opinions may be the best means of assessing the situation, but they are costly and should be used sparingly. Moreover, the decision whether to procure a legal opinion depends on a preliminary internal assessment of the risk, which must also be accurate. It should also be noted that legal opinions are often inconclusive. They oscillate between the generic and the transaction-specific, but rarely span all levels of specificity or identify both the potential problems of legal interpretation and the practical difficulties arising in the context of enforcement of claims. Occasionally, they stress theoretical doubts about the operation of legal rules, which are unlikely to cause problems in real life. The converse can also happen. Thus, legal opinions may set out what their authors consider to be the 'correct' or standard view of the law, but fail to identify viable alternative interpretations or to predict 'anomalous' judicial decisions. This can be a particular problem when a bank seeks to establish the true state of the legal environment in a foreign jurisdiction.

5.5.2 Penalization of fraud and incentive structures

The BCCI case indicates not only the potential size of the problem of banking fraud, but also the limited effectiveness of criminal enforcement. Although evidence of criminal wrongdoing was plentiful, so that this would appear to have been an open-and-shut case, it proved exceptionally difficult to apprehend some of the main culprits, who resided in Pakistan and the Gulf states. Moreover, even where sentences were passed on individuals, these were merely of a few years' length. It is questionable whether relatively short sentences, applied with a relatively low degree of probability, can have a sufficient deterrent effect when the upside for the fraudster can be enormous. A related issue is what proportion of a nominal sentence's length is actually served. In other words, the incentive effects of the criminalization of financial wrongdoing depend on the degree of cross-national co-operation in securing evidence and prosecuting or extraditing criminals, as well as on the harshness of individual countries' systems of criminal justice. The latter can be measured by reference to the rates of detection, severity of nominal penalties and extent of actual enforcement of sentences. US law stands out for its uncompromising stance, both in terms of characterizing below-standard behaviour, including breaches of technical rules, as fraudulent and criminal and for the harshness of its penalties, compared to which the treatment of white-collar crimes in European countries may appear exceptionally lenient.

An additional factor in relation to internal fraud is whether, beyond the immediate culprits, other people in the organization or its professional advisers can be subjected to penalties. This includes, in particular, those responsible for managerial supervision, record-keeping, legal advice and internal and external audit, who might also be penalized, following the detection of fraud, for technical crimes or for violations of regulatory rules and standards. For such persons, the incentive implications of penalization will be more pronounced, because they internalize only the downside of the wrongful activities but cannot participate in the upside, which is usually appropriated by the fraudsters alone. Moreover, it is likely that such persons can actually make a difference in terms of the prevention or early detection of fraud. Line managers and those responsible for back office activities can make fraud much more difficult to commit, through strict recording and verification of transactions.[8]

For their part, lawyers and accountants, who become involved at the stage when illegal schemes are disguised as legitimate transactions, can play a critical role in identifying suspect dealings. On the other hand, a balance has to be drawn. In particular, attempts to expand the responsibility of the accountancy and legal professions for the detection and reporting of suspected fraud are bound to meet strong resistance, especially if the new liabilities are not civil but regulatory or criminal in nature. Such expansions of liability conflict with long-established notions of professional confidentiality – although apparently in the post-BCCI era bank auditors have not found it particularly hard to combine their loyalties to their client with new duties to report perceived misconduct to regulators. More substantially, the potential imposition of penalties places professionals under extreme risk if they have acted subjectively in good faith but have been objectively ineffectual. In the wake of the Enron crisis, it may not be politic for the professions to openly defend their turf, but in the longer run they do not lack means for keeping public demands on them under control.

5.5.3 Market initiatives and dedicated law-reform agencies

In relation to the second and third types of legal risk, the ability of individual market participants and collective industry-based organizations to resolve problems of legal uncertainty and inefficiency is limited. Nonetheless, in many cases, the stance of trade associations and the uniform transactional behaviour of their members can influence the interpretation of norms of state law. This can happen where compliance with an abstract standard – say, of usual, reasonable or good commercial conduct – can only be determined by reference to what sort of practices are commonly considered appropriate, or at least acceptable, in the market in question. More substantially, private initiatives can be very useful in terms of drawing attention to common problems, designing effective contractual solutions, facilitating the avoidance of risky transactions and shaping the public reform agenda.

In particular, dedicated organizations, such as industry-based trade associations or specialist institutes, but also state-based law-reform commissions, can play a major role in the improvement of the legal environment for banking transactions. Their initiatives can take a broad range of forms: from the promulgation of standard terms and documentation for

---

[8] In a similar spirit, Instefjord et al. (1998, p. 587) argue that imposing more severe penalties on wrongdoers may not reduce the incidence of financial fraud, because it can lead to an offsetting relaxation of internal monitoring and control of subordinates by their managers. Instead, regulators should focus on an appropriate incentive structure for monitors at different levels in financial institutions' managerial hierarchies. Ex post penalties should be imposed on managers who have failed to detect wrongdoing by their subordinates, while financial institutions should provide rewards for managers who discover frauds and avoid a close alignment between the level of compensation of managers and the profits reported by the persons for whom they are responsible.

financial contracts, through an identification of inefficient or perverse legal norms and procedures and residual areas of legal uncertainty, to the preparation and promotion of legislative proposals. Even though such institutions cannot on their own adopt changes in national legal systems, their influence in terms of bringing perceived problems to public attention and lobbying for legislation can be a formidable tool for law reform and harmonization.

To give just one example, in the UK, a concerted effort to minimize legal risk in the financial sector was initiated under the auspices of the Bank of England in 1991, with the establishment of an *ad hoc* study group, the Legal Risk Review Committee. This committee published two reports (Legal Risk Review Committee 1992a, 1992b) recommending the creation of a permanent body, the Financial Law Panel. This should act as a primary forum for the identification of areas of legal uncertainty affecting UK financial markets, the dissemination to the industry of information on legal risk and advice on best market practice, the encouragement of the formulation and use of standard documentation and procedures, the elaboration of proposals for law reform and the review of proposed legislation, the monitoring of relevant developments in European law and the encouragement of consistent approaches to financial law in all major jurisdictions. Over the next decade and until its dissolution in March 2002, the Financial Law Panel performed these tasks by exploring a broad range of issues, sometimes of a narrow and technical nature but often relating to uncertainties in the operation of general principles of the law of money, agency, electronic commerce in financial services, etc.

5.6 Insurance and the mitigation of losses from legal risks and fraud[9]

A wide variety of insurance contracts are available to banks for the purpose of transferring risks. The extent of protection offered by an insurance policy is defined by way of a maximum amount of cover (in the aggregate, but often also for any one loss event) and a deductible or excess; the latter is a relatively modest amount of loss that cannot be recovered under the policy and which the insured party must accept before claiming payment for the rest of its loss.

As things currently stand, no single instrument provides protection against all operational, legal and fraud risks. Nonetheless, many sub-categories are covered by existing peril-specific insurance policies. Such policies address losses attributable to a particular cause or set of causes. Taken together, the existing policies offer high levels of protection for banks willing to pay the requisite premia.

Various common liability insurance policies provide direct cover against legal risks (civil liability, directors' liability, employment practices, general and other liability). Policies mitigating the risk of fraud include the so-called 'bankers' blanket bonds' (or 'fidelity' insurance policies) and policies offering cover for unauthorized trading and computer crime. Many of these instruments are long-established and their effectiveness is proven. The same or other policies can also provide protection against various types of physical risks, computer failures and violent crime, etc.

[9] The author extends his thanks to Jeremy and Normi Wall for valuable information, on which this section is largely based.

5.6.1 Liability insurance

Civil liability and professional indemnity policies cover particular forms of legal risk. In such contracts, the insurance company undertakes to indemnify the insured bank whenever the latter is under a legal obligation to compensate a third party on some non-contractual ground relating to the provision of financial services. Relevant sources of liability include the commission of torts, breaches of statutory duties and breaches of trust, as well as obligations of a restitutionary nature. The cover does not include as a matter of course civil liability incurred as a result of intentional misconduct, fraudulent acts, or criminal wrongdoing committed by the bank's employees; however, some versions include intentional wrongdoing by staff (but not deliberate breach of the law by the bank itself or its directors). Civil liability policies do not protect against 'regulatory risk' in the form of fines, penalties, punitive damages, etc. imposed by reason of the bank's transactional misconduct; but they may sometimes include 'civil' liability for compensation or damages for misconduct, even where the relevant amounts of 'damages' or 'compensation' are owed to the regulatory authorities, rather than the immediate customers and counterparties of the bank. The cover is generally limited to liabilities for economic loss; accordingly, property or environmental damage, bodily harm and the like are excluded. Finally, this type of policy covers legal costs incurred by the bank in defending civil claims; as in most other policies, however, the insurance company must authorize the proceedings (but also, conversely, any admission of liability on the bank's part) and retains some control over their conduct.

It is noteworthy that civil liability policies specifically exclude claims litigated in the courts of particular jurisdictions or according to their law, and even claims merely relating to acts or omissions which took place in these jurisdictions. In Lloyd's policies, the USA and Canada usually figure prominently among the excluded jurisdictions. Indeed, the USA does not have to be named in the optional schedule of the policies, but is automatically excluded by the standardized contractual conditions. The evident explanation is that insurers perceive the US legal system as involving a different – in fact, much higher – level of liability risks than, say, the UK, necessitating separate pricing. This confirms the view, expressed earlier on, that even countries at comparable levels of economic development and legal sophistication can present very different characteristics in terms of legal risk, in the third sense of the term.

Claims by shareholders or bondholders in relation to the bank's corporate governance, or by employees in relation to its employment practices, as well as claims relating to corporate events such as mergers and acquisitions or insolvency proceedings involving the bank, are excluded from the cover of civil liability policies. However, special employment practices policies can provide cover against work-related claims by employees – for instance, for unfair dismissal, discrimination or sexual harassment. In addition, directors' and officers' liability policies indemnify specified individuals for potential legal claims against them personally in relation to the performance of their functions as directors and officers of a bank. In this respect, the policies benefit the individuals primarily concerned, even though their bank may pay the premia. Nonetheless, they may also provide cover to the bank itself against losses from indemnities that it has provided in their favour.

5.6.2 Insurance against fraud

Turning to the risk of fraud, a bankers' blanket bond provides protection for losses due to a range of causes, many of which involve internal or external fraud, but also certain crimes of violence. Specifically, the perils covered include the 'infidelity' of managers and other staff; this is generally defined as dishonest or fraudulent behaviour committed by an employee, acting alone or in collusion with other persons, with intent to cause loss to the bank or to ensure for himself a financial gain (but only by way of theft, embezzlement, conversion of property, etc., and not through increases in salary, commissions or other performance-related benefits). The policy also covers loss of, or damage to, property if this takes place within the bank's premises or in transit while in the possession of the bank; significantly, loss of property is covered whether this is the result of fraud or of violent crime or even of unexplainable disappearance. Other insured perils typically include losses due to the forgery or alteration of cheques, bills of exchange and other banking instruments, as well as equities, bonds and government securities, and the counterfeiting of currency. Variations of the bankers' blanket bond cover legal costs incurred in relation to defending claims which, if accepted, would constitute losses covered by the policy, possible liability for the contents of safe-deposit boxes, etc.

A bankers' blanket bond will often exclude losses due to computer frauds, breaches of electronic security and the alteration or destruction of electronic data. It will also exclude losses attributable to unauthorized trading by employees on account of the insured bank or its client, and losses from credit or debit cards. Protection against such losses can be purchased separately under special forms of insurance policy.

Thus, recently developed electronic and computer crime policies cover various forms of 'new economy' frauds. These include misappropriations of funds or property through the fraudulent input of data in the insured bank's computer system, or in interbank or bank–client communication systems, the fraudulent destruction or alteration of programs or data belonging to the bank, or for whose corruption the bank is liable, inputs of viruses, interference with electronic communications and transmissions, tampering with the electronic securities account kept by the bank with a central depository, and frauds involving voice-initiated instructions.

While computer frauds can be either internal or external, the primary risk of fraud by insiders concerns unauthorized trading by employees trading on behalf of the bank. Special policies have been devised to provide protection against this risk. Typically, such policies cover unauthorized trading activities meeting certain criteria with regard to the types of trading (securities, commodities, currencies, derivatives, etc.), the absence of authorization (determined by reference to the financial limits, permitted products and permitted counterparties, as set out in the bank's written trading policy) and the presence of elements of deception (concealment or false recording of the relevant transactions).

5.6.3 Limited hedging effect of insurance and potential recognition of insurance as an operational risk mitigant in the new Accord

In all cases, the policies include contractual covenants and conditions, which are designed to neutralize the moral hazard inherent in the availability of insurance protection and to induce banks to take effective steps against avoidable risks. The deductible is only one means by which insurers seek to achieve these objectives. Other conditions often require banks to take reasonable precautions for the avoidance of relevant losses, to maintain written rulebooks for various activities and functions and to police compliance with their rules, to ensure that transactions are not initiated and recorded by a single employee, to undertake internal audits and examinations at regular intervals, and to report to the insurer certain critical corporate events, which may have potential implications for the quality of management.

Other contractual provisions are aimed at controlling the cost to the insurer. Generally, the cover provided by insurance policies is confined to direct losses, and does not include loss or deprivation of potential income or other indirect or consequential losses. Moreover, the costs incurred by a bank in its attempt to establish the occurrence of a loss event and the extent of resulting loss are non-recoverable. The policies impose procedural requirements, including time limits, for the notification of loss events, the making of claims and the proof of losses. They also transfer to the insurer significant elements of control over the conduct of related legal proceedings and the ability of the insured to waive rights or acknowledge liability. They impose on the insured bank the obligation to take reasonable steps for the mitigation of its loss, and exclude claims for events for which the bank can claim alternative insurance cover.

There is no doubt that the conventional insurance products are effective in providing protection against a broad range of losses. Nonetheless, their characteristics are such that they cannot fully hedge operational risks, as defined by the Basel Committee. The insured perils are narrowly defined and exclude many relevant loss events, while the size of cover and the period for which it is available are limited. Even where a loss is covered, the need to comply with burdensome rules concerning the making and verification of claims and the existence of strict conditions and other restrictions reduce the certainty of payment, in exactly inverse proportion to the protection that they afford to insurers. Verification requirements, sometimes in conjunction with disputes about the facts of the case and the obligations of the parties, can also result in payment delays. A substantial amount of time may thus lapse between the occurrence of loss and its indemnification by the insurer, but this involves additional costs and, more significantly, creates liquidity risks for the insured bank. Finally, while insurance is generally effective for high-frequency small claims, it may not be as dependable for very large idiosyncratic claims. Since the track record for such claims is patchy and the amounts at stake colossal, there is a heightened possibility of legal disputes. In addition, such claims can even put the insurer's own solvency in jeopardy. Thus, exactly in the context of substantial losses from a single source, when it could act as a buffer against the threat of bank insolvency, insurance can prove unreliable and tainted by liquidity, legal and credit risks.

For these reasons, regulators are particularly reluctant to take into account insurance cover as a mitigating factor in the calculation of operational risk exposures. On the other hand, the pressure by the banking industry to recognize risk-transfer techniques, including insurance, is strong. In response to intensive lobbying, the Basel Committee announced in September 2001 that its proposed capital charges for operational risk would be calibrated at around 12 percent of overall bank capital requirements (BCBS 2001b, p. 4), and not at the 20 percent level originally suggested in the January 2001 consultative package. One explanation for the lower new figure is that banks purchase insurance in order to hedge, at least in part, operational risks. Significantly, however, the Committee did not endorse calls for the explicit incorporation of insurance in the calculation of exposures.

Potentially, the incorporation of insurance in the quantitative formulae could be made to depend on several qualitative criteria, subject to regulatory assessment. The contractual characteristics of policies could be taken into account, especially in order to ensure that they guarantee wide scope of cover, a long period of coverage and easy renewal, a relative lack of conditions reducing the certainty of recovery, and the timely indemnification of losses.[10] But such contractual terms shift significant liquidity and credit risks to the insurers, and are unlikely to be offered to all banks. The criteria could further include the creditworthiness of the insurer (who may need to show a high credit rating and satisfactory supervisory control, in order to preclude the substitution of counterparty risk for the operational risks covered by the policies) and his transactional record (for instance, his claims payment rates). Other issues that need to be resolved before insurance is recognized concern the quantification of the mitigation effect, the possibility of reinsurance arrangements, etc. Early indications suggest that the Basel Committee might choose to confine the recognition of insurance only to the small number of global banks that will be eligible to use the most sophisticated approaches (AMA) for the calculation of their operational-risk-related capital charges. As the effectiveness of the insurance hedge depends primarily on the insurer and the terms of the insurance contract, not on the sophistication of the insured, this would appear completely unjustifiable and discriminatory.

5.6.4 Possible emergence of 'basket' policies providing cover for operational risks

In any event, the new Accord proposals have provided insurance companies with a specific incentive to develop new, widely framed 'basket' policies, roughly covering the risks classified by the Basel Committee as operational for regulatory purposes. The evident rationale for such basket policies, explicitly aimed at operational risk, is that, if they gain sufficient

---

[10] The latter can be achieved by agreeing that claims will be paid up-front, without need to wait for the insurance company to conduct a review.

favour with the banking market, the pressure on regulators to recognize them as effective mitigants for capital-adequacy purposes will be irresistible; in its turn, regulatory recognition will further increase demand.

Ideally, by providing comprehensive cover, basket operational risk policies can avoid the gaps or overlaps of existing insurance products. As the latter uniformly disallow recovery of losses for which the bank could claim under other insurance contracts, an additional benefit of basket policies is the elimination of disputes regarding responsibility in situations of double cover.

Basket policies can be created by bundling together relevant insuring clauses from existing peril-specific contracts. Two insurance companies in particular, Aon and Swiss Re, have jointly developed a policy called Financial Institutions Operational Risk Insurance (FIORI), which is supposed to cover 66 percent of operational risk exposures. The policy includes five main headings: 'physical asset risk', for example, the risk that fire will cause damage to buildings; 'technology risk', that is, the risk of loss from computer breakdowns, software faults, systems unavailability or corrupt data; 'relationship risk', that is, the risk of loss as a result of problems in relationships with clients and counterparties, including liability for the marketing of inappropriate investments to clients; 'people risk', that is, the risk of internal fraud and other misconduct by personnel, such as sexual harassment, causing losses or creating liability for the bank; and, last but not least, 'external fraud'. Apparently, the policy will be available with a maximum amount of cover of at least $1 billion. Upon making a claim, insured banks will not need to wait for full verification, but will be entitled to receive within seven days up-front payments, which the insurance companies will be able to reclaim if the payment proves on review to be unjustified.

A more complex, but possibly more robust, approach would be to insure particular types of 'operational' loss effects, regardless of their exact cause. Designing products of this form can raise especially thorny questions, both definitional and actuarial. Similar problems, however, make the accurate pricing of all basket policies especially difficult. Wide and heterogeneous definitions of the insured perils or effects may lead to the transferral to insurers of unknown or hidden risks, while the absence of reliable databases, capturing banks' historical loss experiences, impedes a reasonably precise estimation of expected losses. At the same time, the market for basket products is still very thin. The number of insurers is not large enough to permit reinsurance arrangements, while the pool of insured banks is very narrow for risk-spreading purposes.

Whether such problems can be resolved or not, it is unlikely that a basket product could be developed with the specific aim of providing cover against all forms of legal (as distinct from operational) risk. The various legal risks could hardly be defined as a single insurable risk, and their actuarial quantification on a comprehensive basis is probably impossible. Accordingly, the most that may happen is the emergence of policies that would provide cover for particular legal risks (especially civil liability) under the heading of 'operational risk'.

CHAPTER 6

Operational risk and insurance

Thomas Michael Leddy[1]

6.1 Introduction

'One growing risk mitigation technique is the use of insurance to cover certain operational risk exposures .... Specifically, insurance could be used to externalise the risk of potentially "low frequency, high severity" losses.' With these words, the Risk Management Group of the Basel Committee for Banking Supervision (BCBS 2001a, p. 15) put the future of insurance for financial institutions under the spotlight of what has become a wide-ranging, though at times half-hearted, debate.

The background to or context of this chapter is, therefore, the ongoing debate among banking regulators. This debate surrounds the overhaul of the current Basel Accord and issues surrounding regulatory recognition of instruments of insurance to reduce capital held against operational risk. This recognition, either in its implicit or explicit forms, notwithstanding the constraints that may be imposed by regulators, is a manifestation of extraordinary developments in the interconnection between two very different 'industries'. Whether this may also be the precursor of, or excuse for, further regulatory changes will not be addressed here.

To understand how and within what limitations insurance instruments may operate and the way in which the industry can and should play a niche role in the modern financial system, it is necessary to analyze the essence and nature of such instruments (here 'essence' relates to the relationship between parties and 'nature' to the purpose and uses of these instruments). In so doing we examine the current forms of instruments and outline the likely issues and problems that regulators must address. Management and supervision of these instruments is likely to be through the establishment of criteria against which current and perhaps new products will have to be assayed. This is to ensure that they are fit for the purpose, and up to the standards, required.

---

[1] The views expressed are those of the writer alone and not necessarily of his employer.

There are arguments – and these have been expounded in previous chapters – for and against the holding of capital under some form of supervisory directive. The overwhelming political orthodoxy accepts the premise that regulatory prescribed capital levels is one of the core 'pillars' of the Accord and the most tangible or, perhaps more loosely, objective buttresses for the financial system. Regulatory capital is therefore the bedrock for the stability of the banking industry. Notwithstanding this, it is universally accepted that the use of capital can never act as a substitute for rigorous risk management. Capital is not a means to avoid catastrophes in the first place, and it offers no assistance in learning lessons from events.

The 'new' Basel Accord is, at the time of writing, still under discussion and may not even take effect in a form recognizable from the current draft. That said, most, if not all, of the points made here remain valid in the context of economic capital management. Leading banks are increasingly focused on developing and implementing systems and models to allocate economic capital against all risks. While these are still (relatively) underdeveloped, strides are being made in understanding and handling operational risk. This work by risk management departments foreshadows or apes the anticipated regulatory regime. It is also clear that some national regulators recognize the parallels and are already liasing closely with their leading constituent banks. The goal of a risk-sensitive Accord will demand from banks and their regulators co-operation to explore and resolve many of the practical issues that dog implementation and execution of any revised Accord.

This chapter will begin by discussing the definitions of insurance and operational risk. Then the mechanics (and nature) of insurance contracts will be explained, and the final focus will be on the present and future role of insurance in the financial industry. Here and throughout the chapter, the word 'insurance' will be used in a very wide sense and so is not necessarily limited to policies commonly found in the market today. A large number of issues need to be covered to show how insurance may play its role, and some specific themes merit particular mention and crop up throughout:

- the partial analogy that may be drawn between capital and insurance;
- parallels between the roles of bank supervisors and insurers as well as their comity of interest with banks and, perhaps, with the banks' own risk management departments;
- the metamorphosis of an essentially bilateral contractual relationship into a tripartite matrix by the imposition of a supervisory risk-based system;
- the challenges to the current forms of insurance policies and practices that must change so as to satisfy appropriate capital market standards.

6.2 Definition of insurance: a working draft

To try and define 'insurance' or describe it can easily lead to confusion. The language used may be a bar to clarity, particularly when great efforts are made to achieve precision or with too much reliance on the crutch of jargon. The results can never be entirely satisfactory. To begin, we will strip down and analyze the essence of the contract basis and the purported object of an instrument of insurance. The definition of insurance we shall therefore use is of our own: 'Insurance is a promise to alleviate part or all of the financial consequences of an undesired but foreseeable event that causes tangible harm to the insured.'[2]

In recent years insurance has been often linked with the term 'risk transfer', and this is certainly a useful tag. It is important, however, to bear in mind that 'insurance' *per se* does not *transfer* any risk. A sword swallower does not avoid the risks he undertakes by purchasing medical (or life) insurance – he transfers the risks by getting his apprentice to go on to the stage in his stead. It is only the financial consequences of an untimely sneezing fit that can be mitigated through a suitable insurance policy. What, then, is the benefit of insurance? It is the mitigation of the threat of financial ruin.

In the case of the homeowner we see, in its simplest form, the practical expression of insurance's role as capital. The homeowner commonly purchases life, property and car insurance. Using the example of the homeowner, we can make the following statements:

- To be without a roof over one's head is unthinkable.

- The most secure protection is to hold enough funds to replace the building and contents from the date of ownership. This, however, is likely to be impractical and impose an extraordinary financial burden, limiting both current and future action.

- One option is to build up, through the homeowner's own efforts, enough funds to replace the building, etc. over a number of years.

- Another option is to hold enough funds from income to enable alternative accommodation to be taken (renting) so as to enable the homeowner to ultimately refinance the building of a new house, i.e. hold no capital and not have to build up a capital buffer.

- The homeowner may use an insurer to fund the replacement of the destroyed property in return for a premium.

The issues that face the homeowner and indeed a bank's risk managers (both internal and supervisory) are quite similar. However, banks and regulators have not yet embraced the use of insurance.

While not wishing to overstate the case, we shall discuss in a later section the way in which the requirements imposed contractually by insurers promote and reward proactive risk management and thereby indirectly reduce either the likelihood of an accident or mitigate its severity.

---

[2] Some phrases and words that help fix the terms of reference are:

'a promise'	a contractual relationship;
'alleviate'	a remedy, not a prophylactic;
'financial consequences'	there is a money valuation;
'undesired ... event'	'fortuity' a prerequisite;
'tangible harm'	the damage must be real.

6.3 Definition of operational risk

In the context of the financial industry, much of the thinking in recent years has flitted around the musings and writings of the Basel Committee or, more accurately, the Risk Management Group. Operational risk concepts have begun to be addressed more or less deliberately and systematically by a number of banks over the past decade or so. What is often overlooked is that the original Basel Accord fixed on the '8 percent rule' to cover all banks' risks. It is only in recent years that explicit reference has come to be made to the constituent elements of the regulatory charge. We need to bear in mind two general points first, that operational risk is not the same as 'operations risk'; and second, that a bank's definition of operational risk may not match that of the regulators (and it may well be wider).

Those banks that pioneered the allocation of risk capital against, *inter alia*, operational risk effectively did so in a regulatory vacuum. As has been pointed out, while the original Basel Accord encompassed risks such as operational risk, it did so tacitly. No (systematic) guidance has ever been given, and the banks had to define, capture and quantify this most difficult and nebulous of risk categories from first principles of their own devising.[3]

Looking forward, however, it is clear that the pre-eminent determinant of the minimum scope of operational risk will be that laid down by regulators. We shall focus our attention on this, though it will be appropriate to bear in mind the diversity of (broader) approaches that are likely to continue and subsist under the new Accord.

Operational risk's first definition was the 'other risks' non-definition. This was the catch-all for risk that was not market or credit risk. Unsurprisingly, this was felt to be unassailable but rather opaque and less than useful. Its uselessness derives from its reliance solely on, in effect, a top-down calculation of the size of operational risk and its inability to advance systematic risk management of operational risk. We shall return later to the issue of top-down and bottom-up calculations.

A further criticism must be that there is an implicit assumption that the definition of market and, in particular, credit risk is sufficiently certain to enable a clear line to be drawn between them. That there are in fact varying practices among banks over what falls into credit risk as opposed to operational risk shows that this is certainly not the case. Indeed, as will be apparent from the nature of operational risk, with its multiplicity of direct and indirect causes, no such line can be drawn nor can a definitive taxonomy (a collation of risk event types) be drawn up such that the danger of an ambiguous event is completely eliminated.

The Risk Management Group of the Basel Committee came up with a definition of operational risk in January 2001 (BCBS 2001a). It has been amended and given riders culminating in the so-called CP2.5 of September 2001 (BCBS 2001b). While it is a definition

---

[3] It is outside the scope of this chapter to discuss the issue, but there is a mismatch between banks holding capital (for economic or regulatory purposes) and the hypothecated – rather than composite – capital charges proposed under the new Accord's structure. The powers of Pillar 2, the supervisory discretion element of the Accord, may paper over or remedy the flaw but, given the likely disparity in approaches across national supervisors, the aspiration to achieve consistency is unlikely to be realized.

for the purposes of Pillar 1, its application will overshadow the supervisory discretion regularized under Pillar 2 as well. It is as interesting for what has been excluded as much as for what has been included. As currently formulated and explained, the definition is as follows: 'The risk of loss resulting from inadequate or failed internal processes, people and systems or from external events' (BCBS 2001b, p. 2). There is a rider to this definition: 'for the purposes of a Pillar 1 capital charge, strategic and reputational risks are not included ... [nor are] all indirect losses or opportunity costs' (BCBS 2001b, p. 2).

The first part of the definition seeks, in very general terms, to stake out the common ground of what broadly constitutes operational risk. Any close inspection reveals ambiguities (an early clarification was that legal risk – an aspect which we shall consider further – is included). Others no doubt may offer improvements with greater attention to nuances and the conditionality required distinguishing market, credit and business risk. If ever there was a case where 'less is more', it is here. We are, however, of the view that any debate on the definition is to a large degree irrelevant. The whole accord is a self-justified artificial construct (and not necessarily the worse for being so). The aim of this construct is to 'capture', perhaps clumsily, risks in a charge using a quasi-quantitative multi-stepped process. This is not to say that any old phrase would do, rather that for Pillar 1 purposes a reasonably comprehensive and comprehensible fixed definition suffices.

One important point to be borne in mind throughout is that the definition has two equally important purposes which need to be briefly examined: first, to create a common framework from which the size of the charge can be calculated (ignoring the fact that the aggregate sum of all component parts ought to give the old 8 percent as the answer); and second, to frame the search for data and provide the cornerstone for any risk management culture and system. This framing of the operational risk landscape through a taxonomy (see below) also sets the cornerstone for bank's operational risk management and will be a theme to which we shall return.

Absent a regulatory framework, many banks have undertaken projects to assess their individual exposures to 'other' risks only tacitly covered under the current Accord. In this vacuum the banks' motivation to do this is difficult to categorize since bank's cultures are very individual. It is, however, fairly clear that, while not necessarily consonant with the Pillar 1 definition, the use of the taxonomy to tease out the elements that comprise the aggregate Pillars 1 and 2 exposures will prove to be of great use to regulators when seeking to work on implementation issues.

'Business risks', also known as 'strategic risks', are those that are undertaken lawfully by the institution to further the profitability of the institution. These risks are potentially huge yet fall outside the regulatory definition of operational risk, the reason being that banks as banks (as opposed to employees and officers of the banks) deliberately take business, credit and market risks with a profit motivation. Operational risks, on the other hand, while frequently driven by personal or collective greed, stupidity or criminality, are never, or only rarely, confused with a bank's own proper commercial objectives.

The nature of operational risk is so complex in its causes, sources and manifestations that it is impossible to agree on any single golden thread of common understanding as to its limits. Even *ad hoc* assessments will not always find mutual understanding. This leads to the inevitability of any decision being on pragmatic – though hopefully rational – grounds. The boundary with credit risk is too difficult to describe (to a much lesser extent, so is the interface to market risk). It is therefore a weakness (rather than a flaw) in the whole edifice, but if this is recognized and accepted, it may be of limited impact and so be 'fudged' satisfactorily through supervisory discretion or judgement.

Why have a capital accord? Irrespective of the intellectual justifications for relying on pure market forces to manage the banking system, it is manifest that the interventionist system expressed by the Basel Accord is here to stay. It is the purpose of the capital rules to focus on consumer and systemic protection. A run on a bank causing private depositors to be out of pocket is politically unacceptable. It is assumed, furthermore, that such a run could destroy the confidence held in the financial system upon which the last 250 years of capitalist growth has been based.

Clearly the regime has in mind the wider concept of protecting the banking system as a whole. But protecting against what? This is less clear, but it would seem to be against losses of sudden and unmanageable proportions that could bring down a bank almost overnight. 'Unmanageable', that is, by either the bank's own officers or the national supervisor. Expected or 'attritional' losses are not likely to be covered by the charge – these losses should be priced in the ordinary course of business (arguably therefore a business risk?). The high-severity, low-frequency risks *are* specifically covered by the proposed capital charge. However, it must be noted that at the very end of the scale beyond the high-severity, low-frequency risks – the catastrophic losses – no capital is held and the risks will still be left with the equity stakeholders.

We should mention that the exclusion of indirect and opportunity costs as well as reputational risks demonstrates that 'sudden' shocks are of much greater concern to regulators than a 'wounded' bank, which, like a stag, will be brought to bay. These forms of incidents, where the bank haemorrhages, are those capable of being handled by the market or by governors' eyebrows in a calm and efficient way.

6.3.1 'An elephant in the mist': regulatory taxonomy and the problem of form and substance

The next question must be to determine as precisely as possible the components of operational risk. The vogue word for a landscape or list of categories of operational risk is 'taxonomy'. The crucial reason for setting up a taxonomy is the necessity for the sizing of the charge and is one of the principal aids in establishing a comprehensive risk management architecture in a bank. Various forms of taxonomy have been put forward, all with their merits and flaws. Ultimately, within the necessarily artificial regulatory construct of the Accord, there is no right or wrong answer to the composition of the taxonomy or allocation of event types to specific subgroups beyond certain core event types (from the insurance perspective the 'proper' or at least logical allocation is of some significance). The result is that either banks' risk management teams have already determined the scope of operational risk for their bank or it is to be decided for them by national or supranational regulators. Under the new Accord it is unlikely that some guiding or even prescribed taxonomy will be set, but regulators should be encouraged to establish a reasonably consistent minimum benchmark.

During the consultative period the taxonomy has been developed down to the third layer of granularity. In the Appendix to BCBS (2001b) is a draft taxonomy of operational risks: it is little more than a list of all the categories of events that may be encompassed by a given definition. The benefits to supervisors, banks and insurers however are almost incalculable because while risk management and supervisory setting of the charge do give 'numbers', the sea-change in the perception of operational risk management is far greater in its qualitative impact. The cornerstones described by the taxonomy's contents enable a common understanding of the composition of operational risk for the purposes of the capital regime and, in particular, Pillar 1 thereof. This certainty will aid advances in the understanding of operational risk exposures and, while by no means perfect, constitutes a very useful first stab at a solution to the problems of opacity and ambiguity that are embedded in operational risk.

A taxonomy of risks is an invaluable aid to risk management. Looking, for example, at the taxonomy in BCBS (2001b), the granularity at level 3 can obviously be taken further to a level 4 and so on *ad infinitum*. The value of level 3 and possibly further advances is to a large degree limited to risk management issues rather than the problem of setting the charge. After all, a calculation of the appropriate operational risk charge may be effected from a top-down perspective without the need for any of the granularity shown. Banks and supervisors (insurers too), however, would rather avoid the events themselves than pay out the allocated capital. One must accept as obvious that to prevent the events in the first place one must understand them. Thus the benefits of an established taxonomy may begin to be seen in stark relief.

Ultimately data can only be collected systematically through an established framework. While of itself not a loss prevention system, to have a defined universe means risk managers can create and refine the architecture of their systems to match the individual bank's own operational risk landscape.

At the risk of stating the obvious, bottom-up quantification – that is, the calculation of the risk through the aggregation of its granular components – while not free of the risk of specious accuracy, is of greater and more general value than a top-down approach. It is through study of the individual risk types that risk management departments (and, indirectly, supervisors) are able to apply resources more efficiently to those risks and units within the banks where losses are most likely to arise. Furthermore, the use of such data and the knowledge, experience and wisdom derived from them will be much more effective in securing changes in culture. From this, risk managers will find it easier to apply lessons learned by one business unit to its peers. This is a good thing as the overarching objective is to pre-empt the events that could have a material impact on the financial stability of the institution.

6.4 The mechanics and nature of insurance contracts

6.4.1 Which risks are insurable?

It must be stated at the outset that commercial entities will often conflate three phrases: 'we do not', 'we cannot' and 'we may not'. From the industry's perspective only that which is outside the law (or licence) cannot be insured. In practice, therefore, the absolute limits of insurance lie with the laws or practice of a specific jurisdiction; for example, there may be a requirement of an insurable interest against the occurrence of the insured event. This distinguishes insurance from gaming contracts (though given some of the commercial decisions taken by some insurers, one really must wonder). Finally contracts that offend public policy are readily understood – burglars' 'all risks' policies are generally thin on the ground.

But there are practical limitations that transcend, if not invariably then as a general rule, mere commercial appetite. For a risk to be regarded as insurable it must have to be definable, calculable and without moral hazard. The first two are fairly self-evident if an insurer is to accept and put a price on a risk. The third characteristic requires some further explanation. It means that the insured event is unintended (in a nutshell, you insure *against* the event) either before or during the contractual term. The term 'moral hazard' does not always connote dishonest or disreputable conduct. The insured as the possessor of the risk and, at the same time, the beneficiary of the policy has a potential conflict of interest with his insurer. To put it bluntly, if the insurer will pay for any loss which arises, then why should the insured avoid risks that enjoy protection? Insurers are acutely conscious of the risk that the presence of insurance may have an unintended perverse effect on the insured's behaviour. At its most acute it may be seen in the recently developed 'Unauthorized Trading' insurance protections, whereby it is often stipulated that the existence of a policy must be kept secret from the traders whose unit benefits from it. The fear is that the risk-taking culture would loosen the constraints of prudence once it was known that the bank and the traders' bonuses were protected by an insurance safety net. This consciousness of the perverse impact that insurance might have on behaviour finds its echo in a number of supervisory pronouncements. In this, as with a number of other aspects of risk management issues, there is a clear comity of interest between insurers and supervisors to eliminate the impact of moral hazard.

As will be seen below, there are a number of ways in which insurers seek to protect themselves. Invariably there is the requirement that a deductible is sufficiently large that an insured will suffer real financial pain (and thereby have an incentive to manage the risks away) before a policy responds. The use of mechanisms to secure an alignment of interest between the risk bearer and the risk 'taker' is adduced as further evidence why supervisors should view insurance as an added factor tending to improve risk management.

An additional concern under the overall heading of 'moral hazard' is the prospect of insurers accidentally covering risks that it is more proper for shareholders to carry, namely business risks (we have touched on business risks earlier) – these are usually excluded more by reference to the nature of risks covered than by explicit exclusions.

6.4.2 The relationship between insurer and insured

The insured 'owns' the risk. The insurer offers its balance sheet as a repository of the financial consequences of the risk. The insurer is prepared to put its capital at stake while not being an investor (a point to which we shall return in Section 6.5.2), and so remains outside the insured. The assumption in commercial insurance, and it is largely a reasonable one, is that the insurer knows less about the potential insured's exposure to risk than does the insured. A caveat must be made to this last statement. An insurer may (and should) have a better view of the general exposure (taxonomy) to certain risks of the insured's industry. It will have had a number of years of experience and a mature book of numerous similar risks against which to benchmark the insured and to assess the price of the risks being insured. However, as regards the day-to-day exposure of the specific insured the position is reversed, save where perhaps the insured is about to embark on a new business line.

It has therefore generally been considered that the usual rules of contract under capitalism, namely *caveat emptor* (let the buyer beware), need to be suspended or at least modified. Where the relationship between insured and insurer is exclusive, this creates few problems and those which do arise are limited to the contracting parties. However, as will be discussed in a later section, insurance (or the failure of insurance) often affects a number of other parties who may be disadvantaged through no fault of their own, as a result of a breach of contract that nullifies the benefits of a policy.

Furthermore, insurers may, as a precondition to accepting a risk, impose various terms or set down assumptions upon which cover is granted. In this way, the insurer may indirectly take on a risk management function for the insured; for example, requiring expenditure that otherwise would not have been made (commonly that fire sprinklers are installed and/or maintained throughout the term of the policy). However, failure by the insured to comply with such conditions may also allow the insurer to decline to settle a claim. The significance of these points for financial institutions under the Basel Accord will be covered in the following sections.

In the case of financial institutions, we would draw certain parallels here between the insurers' position and that of the regulators – as we might also between the business units of a bank and the risk management. In short, each (insurer, regulator and risk manager) is an outsider looking in on the business (at bank or unit level). Each sizes the operational risk exposure that the bank or unit is running. The regulator, when verifying the size of the capital charge for operational risk, is effectively performing the same analysis of an institution's risk profile as does the risk manager for the purpose of economic cost allocation and insurers when determining the risk premium.

We see a limited but significant comity of interest between insurers and regulators on the need for risk management (and ongoing commitment thereto), the need for incentives under any regime to manage and mitigate risks as well as the need to create a shared perception of what may constitute operational risks. Where the challenge remains – we shall address this later – is if and how insurance can properly complement the regulator's requirement for hypothecated capital which is hedged with an instrument to substitute that capital.

6.4.3 How is an insurance policy created?

To enter into a contract, an insurer is offered the risk by an applicant. The basic insurance transaction may be encapsulated in the following six-stage process:

1   A risk is identified and protection required.

2   An application for protection is made to the insurer.

3   The insurer is educated as to the risk(s).

4   A form of protection (the policy) is formulated.

5   A 'small' premium is paid.

6   A promise is given to pay in the event of the policy being triggered.

Even a specialist insurer is not a banker or a widget maker – it is only the banker or the widget maker who best knows his business and the risks it faces. Where there is no legal requirement to purchase insurance the applicant will make specific requests as to the size and scope of the protection it needs to address identified exposures according to its risk sensitivity. As different markets in a specific risk class have been formed at different times, insurance has generally been demand-driven and historically never looked at corporate risk, let alone bank risks, in a holistic manner. Therefore the solutions commonly found in the insurance market are quite specific 'rifle shot' solutions.

As described in the previous paragraph, once the risk is identified, the insurer is then educated as to all its facets, and a corpus of data is examined to assess the probability and severity of loss. A policy is then crafted around this specific risk class or, where only partial coverage of the various causes of this form of risk is felt to be prudent, a conditional protection devised. Absent a holistic approach, the cardinal aim for an insurer is precision in respect of the cover being granted. This has some attendant problems.

Insurance is traditionally *cause-based*. At its starkest (and somewhat simplistically) credit risk transfer instruments – which are well established risk hedges – are *effect-based*. In credit risk protections the trigger is more 'has there been a default?' and not 'what has caused the default?' – a much more specific and potentially complex question. As the roots of insurance are in a more bespoke solution approach answering specific demands of clients, it is inevitable that insurers, seeking to understand, measure and price those risks, will focus on the enumeration of the causes that are covered. This is particularly marked in what is sometimes quaintly called the 'non-life' sector.

Since, upon an event, the insurer is only obliged to pay for contracted losses, it is right and proper for an investigation into the causes of the event to take place. As evidence as to the causes of a loss may be obscured through the destruction of evidence, moral turpitude, complexity or even an honest disagreement over the interpretation of the facts. The diagnostic process is therefore often protracted and may sometimes only be resolved by reference to a tribunal (see Section 6.4.5 below).

Related to the previous paragraph, it is worth bearing in mind that the protection under an insurance policy is purchased for a payment of a *small* premium.[4] Contrary to first impressions, this is not a loaded remark by an insurer's employee bemoaning the current state of the market. However, for a set amount of capacity the risk premium may range down to as low as one basis point (i.e. 1 percent of 1 percent of the risk). If a severe loss occurs therefore the pay out will be enormous compared to the premium. As indicated earlier, insurers always prefer to see deductibles carried out by the insurers, to preserve incentives against lax risk management and moral hazard generally. Often insurance may be purchased at relatively low loss levels, namely close to the expected loss. This form of policy is often written to enable an insured to deal in part with the impact of volatility on its profit and loss account. In the main, however, a policy against which a loss has been claimed, even if expected to be renewed after a loss-making year (loss-making for the insurer, that is), is rarely likely to become profitable. An insured may decide that a cheaper alternative insurer is preferable to paying the increased premium sought by the paying insurer. Therefore it is often the case that, in the event of a loss, the payout will vastly exceed the premium. This is particularly the case when the insurance protections attach further and further away from the expect loss levels. It is natural and proper, therefore, that insurers satisfy themselves that the loss event falls within the risk categories for which protection was actually purchased.

6.4.4 Insurance and diversification

Nevertheless, insurance works. The ability of insurers to undertake their business commercially is based on the law of large numbers – the many shall pay for the few – i.e. diversification. Ten thousand homes with identical policies over, say, a ten-year period will suffer a predictable number of fires. The risk pricing of those risks is likely to be straightforward (the pricing of a policy is much more complex than simply the risk price). Volatility in risk pricing comes with smaller numbers, multifaceted risks and where external forces can trigger significant loses. Examples of these external forces are the weather, new technology and, for financial institutions, the behaviour of people.

Diversification comes about when an insurance company is able to manage the risk to its capital through accumulating portfolios of risks in the same classes and then further diversifying them with portfolios of other, preferably non-correlated, risks. This diversification may also be taken to a higher degree. Through reinsurance, the insurer itself taps into a deeper market of other insurance companies to reduce the impact of the losses even further. This sharing of risks manifestly strengthens the ability of the industry to bear even the most cataclysmic of events. Reinsurance is therefore another 'good thing', but there is one caveat;

---

[4] There are finite insurance structures that are effectively self-funding and so transfer only the timing of certain risks – these are not discussed here.

this is that the transparency as to who actually bears the bulk of the financial burden of the loss may be lost (although the legal obligation remains with the original insurer). While the legal obligations may be clear that is of little comfort to the stakeholder in the proceeds of the insurance policy (be it the insured bank or regulator). In a number of commercial settings (see below) this issue is already a frequent topic of concern and addressed often at the request of banks. The use of cut-through clauses and warranties as to the security rating of insurers demonstrate that the 'shadow beneficiaries of policies' ensure that their interest in the payments are secured and the policies enforced. It is to be expected that regulators will take comfort from these examples and will make regulations to secure similar advantages.

Diversification of risks is particularly significant in the case of financial institutions who, in many ways, are past masters of risk management. However, unlike credit risk and market risk, operational risks are very much less susceptible to management through hedging or diversification *within* an institution itself. Simply put, XYZ Bank's dishonest, negligent or lecherous bank managers are their own and losses arising from their conduct are also their own, save through purchasing insurance. Insurers, on the other hand, have thousands of potentially dishonest bank employees on their books through policies and assume that they will not all misbehave at the same time (Christmas parties excepted).

6.4.5 Settlement issues

In practice, insurance companies usually settle claims against their policies in a timely fashion. That this is not always fast enough for the policyholder may simply be a result of a mismatch of interests and expectations. Insurers largely live by their reputation and will rarely be found ever to have abused their position and delayed settlement once the contractual position has become clear. It is right, of course, to examine why the perception is often that 'an insurance policy is an option on a court case'. Several points need to be covered and, as will be seen, these link to other themes outlined in this chapter.

As has been explained above, insurance contracts are usually 'cause-based' and designed to put the insured back into the position, financially at least, in which it would have been had the event not taken place. The obligation is to pay cash and so it is the duty of the insurer to its own shareholders and, to a lesser extent, to others insured, to settle only upon satisfaction that the policy has been properly triggered (see Section 6.4.7).

Insurance policies may be said to cover risk within one of two broad categories of exposure. These two are referred to by various terms, such as 'property and casualty/liability' or 'first and third party'. Again a brief digression is needed to address certain issues which will again impact any role for insurance under the Accord.

First-party policies protect an insured's own property – the car owner's vehicle, for example. Third-party cover meets the obligation to pay the owner of the other car for losses caused by the insured. The loss under the former is a matter of computation once the peril, or causes of loss covered by the policy, are found to apply. The investigation into the cause, and therefore the loss, in traditional first-party policies is crucial. Thereafter, subject to any other policy conditions, the loss may be settled as soon as the value of the loss is known. Often, in practice, as the figures emerge interim payments in advance of final computation are made for sums that are not, or no longer, in dispute.

Third-party policies are creatures of law (in some jurisdictions they are monsters). The existence of a *legal* obligation to pay is the minimum standard. Certainly policies may exclude various types of legal obligation either on the ground that it is illegal to insure (e.g. to insure against payment of criminal fines) or certain events are business risks (e.g. the deliberate breach of contract to supply goods or services). It follows that the insurer's consent to settle a claim must be obtained where no judgement from a competent tribunal has been obtained, but a compromise or out-of-court settlement is possible. However, it should always be borne in mind that while legal disputes may last many years, the obligation of the insured to pay (and therefore for the insurer to settle its share) arises only upon judgement (see below). Apart from where there are disputes between insurer and insurer, it is very rare for any delay to arise in discharging obligations in such circumstances.

The issue of payment may be broken down into two separate issues. The first is how soon the insured is certain that an event is covered by the policy *and* that there is no impediment to a recovery under the contract. The second is the actual discharge of the obligation to pay: this may be either to the insured itself or on the insured's behalf. The second point may be disposed of quickly – where liability under the contract is certain, be it under a first- or a third-party policy, then it is largely a credit risk issue, absent any wilful refusal to pay a claim, as to settlement. On unwarranted denials of a claim or loss, see Section 6.4.9.

It has been shown above, and it will be seen in Section 6.4.9, that there may be a number of potential issues embedded in an insurance policy that could impair recovery, whether partially (because in compromise settlements of coverage disputes, a commercial discount is applied for the risk that the coverage may not apply at all) or *in toto*. *Irrevocable confirmation* of coverage is therefore the key. Once that is obtained then, assuming no credit risk or bad faith from the insurer, the loss will be settled subject only to the limits of the policy (i.e. excess of the deductible and up to the limit of protection).

On occasions this can take some time and, in some cases, tribunals (courts of law or arbitration) are required to resolve disputes. However, it must be remembered that these matters are structural issues that spring from within the contracts themselves and – save where national law forbids – these issues may be addressed by the contracting parties to meet regulatory demands. Disputes over coverage may arise in a number of different forms:

- between insured and insurer over whether the event type is covered;
- between various insurers and the insured over which of a number of policies should respond;
- between insured and insurer about adherence to terms or obligations under the contract;
- between insurer and insured over the amount of the loss suffered;
- between various insurers over the allocation of a loss event to one or more policy years.

The motives for disputes are innumerable and often, though not always, all parties are honestly convinced (often on the advice of their counsel) of the reasonableness of their position. Negotiations will therefore be inevitable and litigation may well ensue. The result in both cases is delay, uncertainty during that delay and, potentially, only a partial settlement to reflect a discount for this uncertainty. At the time of the incident there is only a limited degree of certainty over who pays and how much. Note that the 'how much' question is likely to be unclear anyway, irrespective of the issue of the insurance obligation (what is the value of a claim and of a smoking ruin when the accident happens).

For the regulator, or indeed the insured bank, any delay is an evil. From an insurer's perspective, however, the usual range of insurance products purchased have hitherto never been required to deliver confirmation and/or settlement within short prescribed periods. All reputable insurers are committed to using their best proactive efforts in the investigation, quantification and settlement of a loss. However, where the product purchased requires certainty as to the cause of the event and that no breaches of contract have occurred, it is not surprising that on occasions the insured's expectations (unreasonable though they may be) are not met.

To eliminate structural reasons for each of the listed dispute scenarios is not technically difficult. Is it commercially difficult? Yes, but these issues, as in most commercial matters, can usually be resolved through price and competition.

In the years leading up to the new Accord, risk management departments, using models for allocating capital against operational risk, will begin to demand that current insurance programmes deliver significant capital relief. Generally, policies in their current form are often given no (or merely negligible) credit by banks' risk management departments. Business units, therefore, now question whether insurance protections for which they are internally charged do in fact deliver commensurate reductions in capital charges. As regards their approval (or otherwise) of hedging strategies (i.e. buying insurance) bank risk management departments act rather like their external counterparts, the regulators. Currently no insurance programme (group of policies) is given credit by the 'external' regulators (some jurisdiction require minimum insurance as a prerequisite for a licence). As to both (external and internal regulators), historical ignorance of the use or applicability of insurance, combined with the lack of attention to this subject in the original Accord, has made it difficult to build a case for restructuring programmes and their constituent policies in order to address operational risk holistically. In turn and regrettably, the insurance industry has perhaps been content to respond as it has traditionally done, waiting on demand-led change and reviewing structures in an incremental fashion rather than from a coherent set of principles or criteria.

The omens for the future are, however, encouraging. The discussion initiated by the Risk Management Group has deepened the debate and fuelled extraordinary efforts within banks to look at, *inter alia*, the operational risk capital components of their capital allocation models. We foresee that this work and the co-operation needed to advance further will lead to enhanced interaction between banks and regulators to make the new Accord work. In tandem, insurance solutions will be structured to meet the minimum criteria stipulated by the bank's risk management and regulators.

We have previously touched on the multiplicity of interests that may subsist within an insurance contract, and we examine this in greater detail below.

6.4.6 Insurance as part of a tripartite relationship

The insurance policy is an expression of the contractual nexus between policyholder and insurer. Although designed primarily as a bipartite contract, it is commonly undertaken for the benefit of third parties. We have discussed above the manner in which a policy for a particular risk may be created (Section 6.4.3), and the components of that policy are discussed below.

The reason why a policy is offered and bought is a product of a number of usually consistent though independent motives. Aside from prudence the law (public policy) may require it; in many countries lawyers, doctors, architects and others are required to hold valid policies against liability for professional mistakes before they are allowed to set up in business. The principles underpinning this requirement are threefold:

1 *Consumer protection*. Clients who need to rely on the special skills of the professionals need to be protected from potentially disastrous mistakes (wrong leg amputated, no upstairs bathroom, etc.).

2 *Market development*. The professional must be able to make a living without the constant fear that a single mistake could lead to bankruptcy.

3 *Confidence building*. It is important to maintain the reputation and confidence society feels ought to reside in certain professions.

The new Accord may be said to seek to do the same for the banking industry. This first point needs no further comment.

The second point shows that, absent an insurance policy, the professional would need to build up capital to meet possible claims before prudently embarking on his chosen career. As to the third point, there can be no real argument that the underpinning of the banking industry by capital is driven by the need to maintain confidence in the system. Whereas for professionals insurance (and sound training/practice) provides the capital against unforeseen mistakes, for banks, currently, only regulatory capital (and good risk management) performs this function.

Often, therefore, because of this public policy element in some niches of commercial insurance, limitations on insurers' constructual rights are imposed or accepted as part of good practice or a code of conduct. These generally restrict or annul the right of insurers to deny coverage under the contract where the factual matrix means that the event or loss would otherwise be covered. This occurs where, for example, wrongdoing or errors on the part of the insured in its application for cover could deprive the innocent victims of recourse under the policy.

Looking at the commercial sectors, banks are very familiar with tripartite relationships which may impact on otherwise bilateral insurance contracts. Major projects requiring bank funding will almost invariably require insurance policies, purchased by the projects' principals to secure assets against certain risks. Here we see the 'beneficiary' being the bank – even though it has not paid the premium and is not a party to the contract. Indeed the bank, though in some areas external to the project, often stipulates the minimum credit rating of insurers and that it must have the right to receive loss payments. Perhaps most significantly, it may require some or all of the insurance policy's defences for breaches to be waived. Absent such policy amendments, the funding costs of projects would doubtless be higher, or they simply could not go ahead at all.

We would here draw an analogy with the proposed role of insurance in the Capital Accord. Insurance, if accepted by regulators as an acceptable replacement for capital, would create a form of regulatory 'beneficial interest' in the unimpaired performance of the policy. However, this interest would be at the mercy of the banks' own compliance with the terms of the contract. It is likely, therefore that any system would need to secure for regulators similar protection akin to that enjoyed by members of the public in respect of liability actions against professionals in some jurisdictions.

6.4.7 The building blocks of an insurance policy

The most significant components of an insurance policy are as follows:

Insuring clause(s)

The insuring clause acts as the definition of the field of risk(s) intended to be covered. In many instances it is not possible to easily describe the specific risks, and the language of the draftsman will often need to address both positive and negative issues. These latter often (but not always) take the form of exclusions and are, despite the occasional and unfortunate lapse, intended as an aid to both insurer and insured in setting down the limits of the bilateral contract.

Exclusions

The usual charge levelled at insurers is that by careful use of exclusions (and to a lesser extent special conditions) the bulk of the protection purportedly given under the insuring clause is then retracted. This is unfair; exclusions are valuable to both the prudent insured (i.e. that rare breed which reads the policy carefully before a loss occurs) and the insurer for the following reasons. First, exclusions clarify what neither party expects to be covered (a comprehensive car policy would not be expected to cover burglary at the insured's home). Second, exclusions can clarify the intentions of the parties with regard to certain manifestations of a risk that the insurer has either no intention of offering to the insured or which the insurer cannot assess and therefore price. Third, exclusions can reflect those risks against which an insured chooses not to be protected.

Special conditions

These terms are specially agreed between insured and insurer. Often they will impose separate limits for the maximum payout in the event of certain specified events (often called sub-limits) or added obligations, such as in risk management processes, claims handling procedures or notification processes These are usually inserted after specific consideration of the insured risk profile, either to extend coverage or to impose some additional rubric. Sub-limits may, in ambiguous cases, create an internal tension within the contract where coverage may not be in dispute but there is then some dispute over the exact categorization of a loss event.

Warranties

Insurers, like supervisors and stakeholders, are outsiders and have only a limited degree of access into the inner workings of the insured. Therefore, before accepting a risk, the insurer may require unequivocal confirmation that, for example, sprinkler systems are in place to prevent fire spreading. Breach of such a warranty may result, in some jurisdictions, in the loss being declined or settlement being adjusted for a notional premium that would have been charged.

Disclosure and misrepresentation

Insurers must, for reasons of efficiency and economy, accept risks to a greater or lesser degree on trust. That is to say, information about the insured and the risks it undertakes is almost invariably only really understood by the insured itself. Practicality demands that the insured advises the insurer about all material aspects of the risk. It can therefore be seen quite clearly that the usual rules of contract (let the buyer beware) cannot apply – in a sense it is analogous to much of the consumer protection legislation which recognizes the disparity of expertise and information between that held by the supplier and the purchaser of goods and services. In this case the insurer is the 'buyer of risk' with the intention of absolving the insured of its financial burden in the event of a loss occurring.

Obligations

We have drawn attention to the similarity between the position of regulators and insurers in that both look at a company from the outside in. The manner in which such asymmetry of information is rebalanced has historically been through the imposition, by law or custom, of onerous duties of disclosure on insurers. These duties are, to the inexperienced, essentially 'latent contractual obligations'. This is because these obligations will rarely, if ever, be spelled out in the contract and therefore may be missed by the unwary. Perhaps foremost amongst these obligations is that the insured must describe the material facts of its own risk; truthfulness, 'warts and all'. This is often regarded as a fundamental protection for an insurer against taking unacceptable risks, or alternatively mispricing them.

The consequences of a breach of these obligations will vary according to national practice.

Transparency of risk bearers – reinsurance and syndication

In the simplest expression of an insurance policy, a single insured would conclude a contract with a single insurer. The average homeowner's policy is an example. From the outset of modern insurance, however, larger risks were syndicated, with individual insurers taking a specific share of the risk for their own account. This diversification through syndication protects the insured only in the sense of the credit risk, as each insurer takes a smaller part and any default will only marginally impact the protection enjoyed. It must be remembered that each insurer has a separate contract (albeit in the same terms) and is usually not responsible for making good any default by the other members of the syndicate. As mentioned earlier, diversification by the insurers may also come through the acceptance of a number of risks within a class and further by accepting risks of non-correlated classes.

Where an insured has a number of different insurance policies to cover different aspects of operational risk and there are different insurer interests, syndication may lead to disputes over which policy should respond. A solution to this is discussed in Section 6.5.

Reinsurance is a further enhancement of diversification. The reader is spared a treatise on the subtle nuances of the reinsurance system – to put it simply, reinsurance occurs where part (or in some cases all) of the insurer's share of the risk is in turn passed on to a one or more other insurers in return for a share of the premium. Massive risks are thereby spread across the industry, minimizing the impact on each and thereby eliminating – in respect of a single risk – the credit risk of the insurer. From the insured's perspective there is also the comfort of knowing that, irrespective of the reinsurance arrangements that may be put in place to cope with its risk, the insurer with whom it contracts remains exclusively liable for its share. All in all, therefore, reinsurance is a 'good thing'.

However, two further aspects need to be noted that may impact upon regulators' treatment of insurance, however. Where insurers accept risks that they would not themselves be able to carry on their own balance sheet (because of the size of obligation) they rely on reinsurers to lend their balance sheets to carry the bulk of the risk. It may happen that an insurer insures a large share of a risk but then reinsures out between 90 percent and 100 percent of the risk. Commercially, an insurer doing so would earn a commission and therefore keep back part of the premium. Leaving aside any moral hazard that the reinsurer may face, the crucial point is that while legally the obligation to meet the risk is still carried by the insurer, the financial burden has been 'privately placed' (so far as the bank and regulator are concerned) elsewhere. So it is necessary that either direct contractual links are made between insured and reinsurer, or regulators satisfy themselves that the primary obligors (the insurers) are able to discharge their contractual obligations. We discuss this further in Section 6.5.

A second point to be made concerning reinsurance is increased legal risk. At a minimum, there are two mutually exclusive contractual relationships. The number of potential legal issues in play will certainly be greater. To this must be added the complications that an intermediary is often retained to arrange reinsurance placements and that issues can arise as to their conduct. These issues may imperil the smooth performance of the contracts. Of course if, as is usually the case, the insurer is capable of meeting the primary obligation without awaiting funding from reinsurers, this risk largely falls away. That said, regulators may feel that they need to be informed of reinsurance arrangements to monitor this slight residual risk.

Finally, we would point out that reinsurance is often a cross-border placement, and that law and practice do differ from jurisdiction to jurisdiction. While reinsurance law is relatively uniform, it is by no means consistently so. In the credit risk markets most contracts are subject to a single generally accepted law, and that, together with perhaps a single tribunal applying that law, would reduce inconsistencies down to a minimum. This may be a (perhaps distant) goal for regulators.

6.4.8 Insurance as part of risk management – Pillar 3

Insurers play a role in reducing risk itself. As one of the parties facing loss if a fire strikes a property, the insurer has a strong vested interest in minimizing hazards that give rise to the risk of fire. The insurer's impact on risk management may be both direct and indirect. In the first instance the insurer is likely to try and accept only 'better' risks. Certain minimum standards will therefore be brought to bear on the pool of potential insureds. Insurers will also take into account distinguishing factors in pricing a risk. Hazardous activities will carry a premium that may be considerably abated where risk control and management systems are in place. As discussed above, insurers, through warranties, may stipulate not only that risk management systems exist but also are actively prosecuted and improved upon. While this is more readily seen in property insurance (fire sprinkler systems, for example) similar requirements are also made in liability programmes. Furthermore, an insurer will have a set of more or less coherent criteria by which to judge a good risk. These will often be discussed with the insured and thus the insured will gain some knowledge of wider industry standards against which its own risk profile is to be judged.

The new Accord proposes market disclosure on operational risk through Pillar 3. The wider capital markets which hitherto have rarely priced the embedded operational risk of business are likely to begin to do so. The amount of information available will greatly increase and it may be anticipated that those banks that are in a strong position will be able, through greater degrees of transparency, to apply pressure on less forthcoming competitors and signal to regulators the current standards that best reflect good practice.

6.4.9 Contract legal risk

Legal risk is highlighted as a source of concern by regulators. Legal risk is not confined to operational risk insurance: it is prevalent in any contractual arrangement. There are two forms of legal risk: the exposure to legal liability and the inherent risk of securing compliance under a contract. The former may arise from various sources, such as employees, shareholders, members of the public, business partners (depositors, creditors, debtors and suppliers) and civil authorities (compliance and criminal). These sources of risk and the loss events that they throw up are largely understood and measurable. Liability to third parties is a product of national law, and decisions of courts or tribunals are well publicized. This is not to say that the severity and frequency of these events are completely understood. However, data is likely to be readily available to those who search for it.

Of greater difficulty is the inherent risk in securing execution of promises or obligations that are the subject matter or concomitants of a contract. This issue is not confined to operational risk insurance and is embedded in credit risk management instruments and in the ordinary course of a bank's business. Whenever a third party is under an obligation to perform there is a risk of non-performance. These risks may be described as 'can't pay' (credit risk), 'shouldn't pay' (public policy prohibition) and 'won't pay' (legal risk). This section will only look at 'won't pay'. At its most egregious, a refusal to perform may be an act of bad faith – a wilful refusal to fulfil the contract. Such conduct is very rare, though it must be acknowledged that in contradistinction to the capital market the impact on a company's reputation of such a refusal is unlikely to be as fatal as were a banking institution to 'default' on an obligation. In the insurance industry some companies have been severely criticized, on occasion by courts, for their failure to settle, while continuing to operate successfully.

One of the reasons for this disparity, and the reason why there are far more disputes over claims under insurance policies than in the capital markets, is the inherent nature of 'rifle shot' policies. The 'shots' carry an element of playing the lottery with risk – to carry the metaphor further – where a non-holistic approach to operational risk is taken, risk management departments play Russian roulette, gambling that their systems controls and personnel will not slip up on risk where no protection is purchased. The history of drafting policies to cover only that for which there is demand (and a willingness to pay) means that insurance contracts admit of much more ambiguity than credit hedging instruments. Thus any deliberate 'welching' on a contract is unlikely to be so obvious to disinterested parties and may be explained away with more or less specious excuses. The merits and validity of such arguments will not be determined until after critical or penal judgments are handed down.

Much more common is a dispute over what precisely are the mutual intentions or obligations of the contracting parties. Disputes may be over what is the subject of the contract and/or whether an obligation was contingent on events or preconditions. The problems under any form of contract may arise because:

1 the parties did not fully understand the subject matter;

2 the parties did not understand each other's requirements or obligations;

3 the language used did not accurately reflect the common intentions;

4 the language used was in breach of rules of law or practice;

5 the law court reached an unexpected decision;

6 the law changed during the currency of the contract.

Looking, necessarily briefly, at each in turn in the operational risk context, steps may be taken to mitigate or eliminate the attendant risks:

1   Operational risks can never be fully understood. However, if there is a taxonomy that bounds the subject matter for regulatory purposes contracts may be made consonant with the scope of part or all of that taxonomy.

2   Subject to the applicable law, many (if not all) rights and obligations may be waived. Therefore only explicitly reserved rights may be allowed to subsist and all others waived, thereby minimizing if not eliminating confusion.

3   The more narrow or precise the intentions, the more complex the language needed and, in the case of the English language at least, the greater the scope for ambiguity. If the intentions behind the contract are kept simple then the scope for error may therefore be greatly reduced, if not eliminated.

4   Laws and practice governing the contracts are usually understood by experts and must be properly proofed. Ideally, and perhaps in time, standardized forms of contracts should eliminate much legal risk save in respect of the issues described in the next two paragraphs.

5   All legal tribunals are human agencies and so subject to error. However, professionally trained and commercially/legally experienced triers of fact and law are usually more predictable than otherwise. In the commercial context of operational risk for financial institutions, intellectual integrity, predictability and consistency of application of legal precedents and principles are by far the most important virtues.

6   Future changes of law may impact pre-existing contractual arrangements. Insurers will often be concerned with an additional factor of unpredictability in the risk profile where multi-year contract are proposed. In most jurisdictions we anticipate such changes are 'grandfathered', thereby mitigating the additional exposures to which insurers may be subject. Therefore, though unpredictable in the specifics, the contingency itself may be addressed under the terms of the contract and, where uncertainty in the legislative field does exist, policy terms of a shorter duration may need to be allowed.

6.5 The present and future role of insurance in financial institutions

We have tried to show in the preceding sections why insurance industry practice is as it is:

- Operational risk and its sub-classes are nebulous and difficult to define.
- History and competition have tended to create a diversity of tailored products as opposed to standard forms.
- Diversity of products has militated against predictability and uniformity of coverage and practice.

- Diversity of applicable laws, judicial systems and language has fragmented approaches to interpretation.

- Products are cause-based, creating a need for investigation into the facts behind the events.

- Insurance is usually premised on the need to pay only for actual losses, requiring investigation of the amount of losses.

In this section we cover the ways in which insurance may meet the issues and challenges of justifying replacement of economic and regulatory capital.

Reliance on any legal document to secure the performance of obligations or to provide an injection of funding (capital) is risky. That banks and regulators have countenanced this risk for over a decade now, in the form of credit default swaps and other market instruments that transfer or hedge risks, shows that there is no objection in principle to such structures. The rub is that the operation of the hedge must be understood (it is assumed for the purposes of this chapter that market and credit risk hedges are so understood). The issue for operational risk and insurers is, however, one of credibility – that the risk is understood and that the instruments used transfer the risk satisfactorily.

The burden on the insurance industry is not to justify its current customs and practice *per se*, but rather that, in so far as it wishes to play a role in adjusting bank economic or regulatory capital, it must accept regulatory considerations and market requirements to enforce changes in their practices. An important point to remember here is that the 'market' includes regulators' requirements, as they are representative stakeholders in the capital adequacy regime. Where insurance acts as a 'capital substitute' then one of the likely consequences will be to create new forms of policies, leading towards standard forms of contract, as has been seen in the credit risk transfer markets. Issues of certainty over cover and liquidity will need to be squarely addressed.

We have assumed, for the purposes of this chapter, that regulators and banks wish to obtain access to insurance-type products that are certain as to coverage, and swift in settlement, thereby acting to some considerable degree as capital held contingent on the adverse events occurring. Operational risk is the most difficult to encapsulate and it is impossible to capture all of its manifestations. Fortunately, in an artificial construct such as the new Basel Accord, a definition, and through that definition the taxonomy, means that operational risk for regulatory purposes can be captured.

The ambiguity and nuances of first or sole causes lend themselves to honest disputes over the precise categorization of a risk event. There are two potential solutions for this: an independent unimpeachable arbiter; or elimination of the relevance of causation in the instrument. The arbitration of disputes is well known and widely practised. It is a quasi-judicial approach and therefore may result in unacceptable delay in resolving disputes. The appointment of an arbiter, specified in the contract at inception, with an exclusive and unappealable mandate to determine the cause of loss where it is the only coverage issue in question, would be an advance on current practice. This is hardly innovative but ultimately needs to be uniform practice.

A more radical option is to adopt the approach taken in the credit risk market for hedging instruments: render the causal issue irrelevant. By focusing on effect (i.e. is there a judgement? has there been a fire?) rather than cause (was the fire electrical or arson?), a myriad of issues fall away. Remember, however, that the cause of a loss would always remain important and would still need to be fully investigated. This is because insurers, supervisors and risk managers need this information for reporting, risk control and avoidance, and potentially future pricing/costing of risk (by each of the three interested parties). However, as regards the issue of whether the policy would respond or not, it would be very much quicker if causal issues are out of the way. Such an effect based trigger for the instrument would mean that confirmation of coverage – which, as we have argued earlier, is the most critical issue other than settlement – could be effected very quickly.

This speed of confirmation is of critical importance because at the time of an event *the availability* of the limits of the insurance policy would secure the situation for regulators, risk managers and the equity markets pending the time when settlement was required (as the quantum of loss is revealed or judgment handed down). A bank in this situation would be able to report to the markets and its regulators both that the event had occurred and that the ultimate loss would be capped or reduced by the extent of the policy limits.

In respect of first-party risks (recall that these are the insured's own property losses), the effect-based trigger ought to rely on the fact of the loss, perhaps as defined and calculated according to generally accepted accounting principles, thereby fixing the loss to be settled (subject to deductibles and limits). For third-party policies (liabilities under law to other persons) the test would be a final finding of law against the insured.

6.5.1 Is partial coverage of taxonomy going to work?

History and competition have tended to create diversity of tailored products, as opposed to standard forms. Diversity of products has militated against predictability and uniformity of coverage and practice and increased the likelihood of conflicts. Wherever there is a conflict of interest, uncertainty will exist.

Early in the chapter we discussed the numerous ways in which conflict could arise between insurer and insured, and among insurers themselves. The former is inherent in the relationship of a contract, but may be addressed as discussed. Disputes between insurers may arise when they are covering different parts of the risk, or are liable for different risks at different attachment points (levels of coverage). As already mentioned, issues may arise where certain risks are protected to differing extents (see the 'special conditions' in Section 6.4.7).

The only real solution is to work to eliminate those conflicts – again the most effective way to do this is to render such issues irrelevant. Any insurer participating in a protection programme must cover all the same risks as its co-syndicators. It does not follow that all need take the same share of the risk, merely that the exposure profile across the risks must be the same.

Just as comity of interest requires insurers to co-syndicate on a quasi *pari passu* basis, the issue then arises as to whether a protection of part of the operational risk is viable. It is viable, provided the added risk is acceptable to risk management and, crucially, to regulators who are asked to sanction capital substitution. There is, however, a risk embedded in such partial solutions.

Instruments based on or referenced against a common taxonomy (perhaps approved by the relevant national regulator) certainly mark a significant advance on the current patchwork of policies. Such instruments, being effect-based homogenous coverages per risk class, would reference one or more of the exposures as described in level 1 or 2 of the taxonomy. There would remain, however, a residual uncertainty as to the categorization of a risk event even at this very broad level. Such disputes could arise where numerous events came together at the same time to cause a loss. Where such sources cross over the scope of a contract, potential for dispute would clearly be present. Partial coverage of operational risk through a patchwork of more or less co-ordinated policies will never give the clarity of coverage required. Therefore, we would recommend that comprehensive contracts are the cleanest and least risky solution. We do not say, however, that only blanket policies should be accepted. Ranges of solutions, taking into account market appetite and capacity, are relevant factors, as is the need to be flexible where reservations of coverage are reasonably quantifiable and cleanly removable from the protection.

Within credit risk, a high degree of standardization has been achieved, not through cartels but because the market participants understand the common usages of the market, and each player is as likely to be a buyer as a seller. There is, therefore, no commercial dynamic to tip the balance of advantage in favour of either. This is not the case with insurance. Unfortunately, therefore, it is unlikely that standard forms will emerge quickly. Any imposition of such 'master agreements' could fall foul of anti-competition regulations. We do foresee that, were taxonomies to be the benchmarks for approval on a national level, and disputes to be resolved by arbitration panels specially versed in this area, then in time a similar degree of consistency in approach would be required by banks and their regulators. This demand would then have to be met by the insurance industry.

Diversity of applicable laws, judicial systems and language has fragmented interpretation of contractual instruments. As discussed earlier in the chapter, the insurance contract usually contains both explicit and implicit rights and obligations. In so far as insurance instruments are to play a role in capital management, then such implicit rights and obligations ought to be eliminated. For risk management departments this then secures the added certainty that the policies will respond as anticipated to covered risk events. And for regulators, no added uncertainty outside of the residual credit risk and the scope of the cover need be considered.

The use of brokers as advisers to insureds is well established and secures a high degree of transparency to the market. It balances the scales of expertise between buyer and seller. However, the use of agents as an additional component in the factual matrix, either in the insurance or the reinsurance of operational risk may add to the legal risks. The impact of additional factors within and on the fringes of the contractual matrix is self-evident. The most practical solution is that issues relating to agents, and the associated risks, must be expressly waived as regards the performance of the instruments.

Disputes will arise, and this is not peculiar to operational risk. Courts, while unbiased, are rarely well versed in the relevant laws, customs and practices. Where lay finders of fact are used, a whole range of additional factors may be played upon to influence decisions creating unpredictability. On the subject of insurance for capital, unpredictability and uncertainty are perhaps cardinal vices. An arbitration tribunal as an authoritative court specializing in the relevant area of disputes, reaching decisions impartially according to the settled customs of the market, will be the paradigm. When manned or presided over by experienced persons well versed in the practice and law of the market, these would be able to ensure that, along with predictability and certainty, the decisions could be consistently applied around the world and reflect common usage in the market.

To mitigate or avoid the risk of juridical jealousy, neutrality of the applicable law of the contract between domiciles of insurer and insured may also help create the requisite degree of certainty over the operation of a policy, and thus enable the development of a market. Where numerous insurers each take a share, the policy should stipulate that all insurers must abide by decisions of the tribunal, whose finding are not to be impeached by any court.

Therefore we would argue that the interests of both the insurance and banking industries would benefit from a joint forum to host such a tribunal.

6.5.2 Role of risk financing

This rather short subsection contains perhaps the most revolutionary aspect of the subject. No matter how broad the coverage under an instrument, *vis-à-vis* the taxonomy there will remain a residual area of doubt as to whether the event falls within the regulatory definition/taxonomy or insuring clause at all. Risk financing through the use of contingent capital structures may be the solution, removing disputes over coverage of operational risk events. How so?

Insurance is risky for the insurer, and risk is its business. Insurance that indemnifies a loss usually results in a settlement of money wholly disproportionate to the premium, when looked at from an individual risk viewpoint. It hurts, therefore, to write the cheque. Additionally many insurers may have a traditional antipathy to taking on certain types of risk, thus limiting the market for the broadest of coverages.

As we stated earlier in the chapter, an insurer makes its capital available to an insured but is not an investor. The capital at risk is 'drawn' upon the contingency contracted for, and the payment of money enters the insured's profit and loss account. A supplemental or alternative structure would be that the insurer is committed to purchase, at a pre-agreed price, a limited amount of hybrid capital, provided the loss event is greater than the attachment point specified in the instrument. The trigger for the instrument could be the same as or even broader than the regulatory taxonomy. The difference with the technique of risk financing is that the purchase gives the insurer a valuable asset, and so it becomes an investor. That investment may be held or sold off in the capital market. The insurer therefore may commit to a swifter response time and allow, when the risk financing element overlays (or extends the scope of) the indemnification obligation, an injection of capital to be made pending investigation of the event. Upon determination, the instrument would be cancelled where it was found that the event was under the indemnification coverage (probably the reference taxonomy).

6.6 Conclusion

Insurance is an immensely flexible instrument. It is also very cost-efficient given the exposures against which it offers protection. For financial institutions the current usage of insurance will change radically over the next few years, irrespective of the terms in the new Basel Accord. As risk management departments increase their sophistication in defining and capturing 'other risks' for their own internal purposes, the capping or mitigation of losses will take on an increasingly 'capital' aspect.

This exciting opportunity for the insurance industry to take up a niche position within the core of an institution's management agenda should, frankly, raise the value of the products they wish to sell. Concomitant with this, however, will be an additional burden – that of partnership. The instruments will need to become truly demand-driven, not merely a partial response from the market. Financial institutions will accurately describe their requirements and specify the instrument(s) and structures needed. In so far as this scenario eventuates before the Accord, we see the bank risk management and treasury departments acting as shadow supervisors.

It is the writer's view that the forment caused by the Basel process has made an astonishing impact on risk management and the perception of insurance – while scepticism still abounds, the current situation is already a marked step forward from the hitherto prevalent disinterest. Provided the insurance industry delivers on its potential, that scepticism will fall away.

The degree to which supervision needs to be based on compulsion as opposed to free will and market forces will reflect national or individual prejudices. The author sees no insuperable difficulty in creating a light but comprehensive framework. Such a framework would need to avoid developing unproductive and intrusive minutiae and their concomitant lacunae. Any regime designed to protect society from a harm that is so inherently a mortal danger (whether expressed through system or human agency) needs to be seen as 'organic'. Simply requiring capital to be held is only a small part of the answer. It is worse than useless without the right culture, with risk management measures and loss control systems as the executive expression of that culture. Beyond these two, further refinements may come into play. Supervision, transparency and mitigation all then create a superstructure of overlaying screens to render even more improbable the failure of the financial system.

Finally, when all else has failed and the event has occurred, insurance (in whatever form) will self-evidently act as the final safety net.

PART II

Analysis

CHAPTER 7

Statistical models of operational loss

Carol Alexander

7.1 Introduction

The purpose of this chapter is to give a theoretical but pedagogical introduction to the advanced statistical models that are currently being developed to estimate operational risks, with many examples to illustrate their applications in the financial industry. Section 7.2 begins with a discussion of the definitions of operational risks in finance and banking, and then considers the problems surrounding data collection, the design of scorecards and the use of external data. Section 7.3 describes a well-known statistical method for estimating the loss distribution parameters when the data are subjective and/or are obtained from hetero-geneous sources. Section 7.4 explains why the Advanced Measurement Approaches (AMA) for estimating operational risk capital are, in fact, all rooted in the same 'Loss Distribution Approach' (LDA). The only differences are in the data used to estimate parameters (score-card versus historical loss experience) and that, under certain assumptions, an analytic formula for estimating the unexpected loss may be used in place of simulation. In Section 7.5 various generalizations of this formula are deduced from different assumptions about the loss frequency and severity, and the effect of different parameter estimation methods on the capital charge is discussed. We derive a simple formula for the inclusion of insurance cover, showing that the capital charge should be reduced by a factor of $1 - r$, where r is the expected recovery rate. We also show how the Basel 'gamma' factor should be calibrated and provide some useful reference tables for its values.

Section 7.6 gives a brief account of the simulation algorithm used in the full LDA, but this is discussed in much more detail in the other chapters in this part of the book. An example is given, showing that the regulatory capital requirement estimate based on simulation of the total loss distribution is approximately the same as the regulatory capital requirement estimate based on the analytic approximation. Section 7.7 considers the aggregation of individual unexpected losses – and annual loss distributions – to obtain the total unexpected loss – and the total annual loss distribution – for the bank. The assumption that operational risks are perfectly correlated would imply that all the operational losses in the bank must occur at the same time! We therefore consider how to account for decorrelation between risks, and how to model dependencies that are more general than correlation. The aggregation problem is discussed in some detail, explaining how to use copulas to account for codependence when aggregating the individual annual loss distributions. A useful appendix on copulas is also presented. The section ends by describing how a bank might specify the likely codependence structure, by examining the likely effect of changes in the main risk drivers on different operational losses. Section 7.8 summarizes and concludes.

7.2 Operational risk types

This section begins with some definitions of the operational risks facing financial institutions. These risks may be categorized according to the frequency of occurrence and their impact in terms of financial loss. Following this there is a general discussion of the data that are necessary for measuring these risks. More detailed descriptions of loss history and/or key risk indicator (KRI) data are given in later sections. The focus of this introductory discussion is to highlight the data availability problems with the risks that will have the most impact on the capital charge – the low-frequency, high-impact risks. Internal data on such risks are, by definition, sparse, and will need to be augmented by 'soft' data, such as those from scorecards, expert opinions, publically available data or data from an external consortium. All these 'soft' data have a subjective element and should therefore be distinguished from the more objective or 'hard' data that are obtained directly from the historical loss experiences of the bank. Section 7.3 will introduce Bayesian estimation for loss frequency and severity parameters. This is a standard approach to combine data from different sources to obtain parameter estimates for the loss distribution.

7.2.1 Definitions of operational risks

After much discussion between regulators and the industry, operational risk has been defined in the Basel Committee working paper, also known as Consultative Paper 2.5 (BCBS 2001b), as 'the risk of loss resulting from inadequate or failed internal processes, people and systems or from external events'. It includes legal risk, but not reputational risk (where decline in the firm's value is linked to a damaged reputation) or strategic risk (where, for example, a loss results from a misguided business decision). BCBS (2001b) also defines seven distinct types of operational risk: internal fraud; external fraud; employment practices and workplace safety; clients, products and business practices; damage to physical assets; business disruption and system failures; and execution, delivery and process management. Detailed definitions of each risk type are given in BCBS (2001b, Annex 2).

Historical operational loss experience data have been collected in data consortia such as OpVantage (www.opvantage.com), British Bankers Association (www.bba.org.uk) and ORX (www.orx.org).[1] Figure 7.1, from the OpVantage website, shows the total losses (amounting to $272 billion) recorded over a period of more than ten years on more than 7000 loss events greater than $1 million. In Figure 7.1 they are disaggregated according to risk type.

More than 70 percent of the total losses recorded were due to clients, products and business practices. These are the losses arising from unintentional or negligent failure to meet a professional obligation to specific clients, or from the nature or design of a product. They include the fines and legal losses arising from breach of privacy, aggressive sales, lender liability, improper market practices, money laundering, market manipulation, insider trading, product flaws, exceeding client exposure limits, disputes over performance of advisory activities and so forth. The other two significant loss categories are internal fraud and external fraud, both relatively low-frequency risks for investment banks: normally it is only in the retail banking sector that external fraud (e.g. credit card fraud) occurs with high frequency.

7.2.2 Frequency and severity

The seven types of operational risk may be categorized in terms of frequency (the number of loss events during a certain time period) and severity (the impact of the event in terms of financial loss). Table 7.1, which is based on the results from BCBS (2002a), indicates the frequency and severity of each risk type for a typical bank with investment, commercial and retail operations.

Banks that intend to use the Advanced Measurement Approaches (AMA) proposed by BCBS (2001b) to quantify the operational risk capital requirement (ORR) will be required to

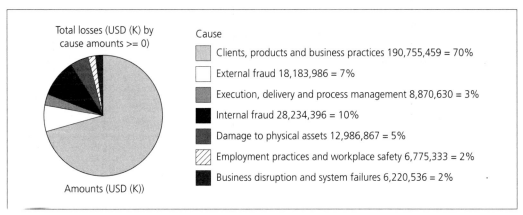

FIGURE 7.1 ■ Total losses by risk type

[1] ORX is a not-for-profit data consortium that is incorporated in Basel as a Swiss Association of major banks. Data collection started in January 2002, building on the expertise of existing commercial data consortia.

TABLE 7.1 ▪ Frequency and severity of operational risk types

Risk	Frequency	Severity
Internal fraud	Low	High
External fraud	High/medium	Low/medium
Employment practices and workplace safety	Low	Low
Clients, products and business practices	Low/medium	High/medium
Damage to physical assets	Low	Low
Business disruption and system failures	Low	Low
Execution, delivery and process management	High	Low

measure the ORR for each risk type in each of the following eight lines of business: investment banking (corporate finance); investment banking (trading and sales); retail banking; commercial banking; payment and settlement; agency services and custody; asset management; and retail brokerage. Depending on the bank's operations, up to 56 separate ORR estimates will be aggregated over the matrix shown in Table 7.2 to obtain a total ORR for the bank.

TABLE 7.2 ▪ Frequency and severity by business line and risk type

	Internal fraud	External fraud	Employment practices and workplace safety	Clients, products and business practices	Damage to physical assets	Business disruption and system failures	Execution, delivery and process management
Corporate finance	L H	L M	L L	L H	L L	L L	L L
Trading and sales	L H	L L	L L	M M	L L	L L	H L
Retail hanking	L M	H L	L L	M M	M L	L L	H L
Commercial banking	L H	M M	L L	M M	L L	L L	M L
Payment and settlement	L M	L L	L L	L L	L L	L L	H L
Agency and custody	L M	L L	L L	L M	L L	L L	M L
Asset management	L H	L L	L L	L H	L L	L L	M L
Retail brokerage	L M	L M	L L	L M	L L	M L	M L

Each cell of Table 7.2 indicates the frequency (top) of the risk as high (H), medium (M) or low (L), and the severity (bottom) also as high, medium or low. The indication of typical frequency and severity given in this table is very general and would not always apply. For example, employment practices and workplace safety, and damage to physical assets are classified in the table as low/medium frequency, low severity – but this would not be appropriate if, for example, a bank has operations in a geographically sensitive location. Also business disruptions and systems failure may not be a low impact risk in e-banking.

Certain cells have been highlighted. The low-frequency, high-severity risks that could jeopardize the whole future of the firm are the risks associated with loss events that will lie in the very upper tail of the total annual loss distribution for the bank. Depending on the bank's direct experience and how these risks are quantified, they may have a huge influence on the total ORR of the bank. Therefore new insurance products, covering such events as internal fraud, or securitization of these risks with operational risk 'catastrophe' bonds are some of the mitigation methods that should be considered by the industry. For further discussion of the insurance of these risks and the likely impact of the Basel II proposals on the insurance industry, see Chapters 5 and 6.

Other highlighted cells indicate the high-frequency, low-severity risks that will have high expected loss but relatively low unexpected loss. These risks, which include credit card fraud and some human risks, should already be covered by the general provisions of the business. Assuming expected loss is provisioned in the proper way, they will have little influence on the ORR. Instead, these are the risks that should be the focus of improving process management to add value to the firm. The other cells in Table 7.2 indicate the operational risk types that are likely to have high unexpected losses – thus these risks will have a substantial impact on the ORR. These medium-frequency, medium-severity risks should be a main focus of the quantitative approaches for measuring operational risk capital.

7.2.3 Risk maps

In the quantitative analysis of operational risks, frequency and severity are regarded as random variables. Expected frequency may be expressed as Np, where N is the number of events susceptible to operational losses, and p is the probability of a loss event. Often the number of events is proxied by a simple volume indicator such as gross income, and/or it could be the focus of management targets for the next year. In this case it is the loss probability rather than loss frequency that will be the focus of operational risk measurement and management, for example in Bayesian estimation (Section 7.3) and in the collection of scorecard data (see Chapter 11).

A probability-impact diagram, a visual representation of different risks, is commonly used for risk impacts that are more general than financial loss, for example time delay, or operational events that can make gains as well as losses. But more common in finance are 'risk maps', such as that shown in Figure 7.2. This is a plot of expected loss frequency against expected severity (impact) for each risk type/line of business. Often the variables are plotted on a logarithmic scale, because of the diversity of frequency and impacts of different types of risk. Other examples of risk maps are given in Sections 4.3 and 12.4.5. This type of diagram is a useful visual aid to identifying which risks should be the main focus of management control, the intention being to reduce either frequency or impact (or both) so that the risk lies within an acceptable region.

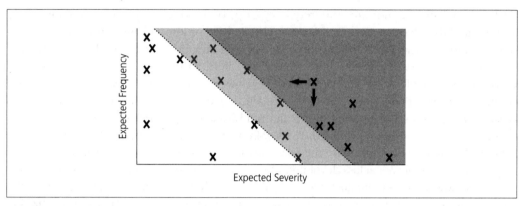

FIGURE 7.2 ■ A risk map

In Figure 7.2 the risks that give rise to the black crosses in the dark shaded region should be the main focus of management control; the reduction of frequency and/or severity, indicated by the arrows in the diagram, may bring these into the acceptable region (with the white background) or the warning region (the light shaded region). Section 4.3 shows how these regions can be defined.

7.2.4 Data considerations

BCBS (2001b) states that banks that wish to quantify their regulatory capital (ORR) using a loss distribution model will need to use historical data based on actual loss experience, covering a period of at least three years (preferably five years), that are relevant to each risk type and line of business. But data on the frequency and severity of historical losses are difficult to obtain. Internal historical data on high-frequency risks such as execution, delivery and process management should be relatively easy to obtain, but since these risks are also normally of low impact, they are not the important ones from the point of view of the ORR. The medium-frequency, medium-impact risks such as clients, products and business practices and the low-frequency, high-impact risks such as internal fraud are the most important risks to measure from the regulatory capital perspective. Thus the important risks are those that, by definition, have little internal data on historical loss experience.

With sparse internal data, the estimates of loss frequency and severity distribution parameters will have large sampling errors if they are based only on these. Economic capital forecasts will therefore vary considerably over time, and risk budgeting will be very difficult. Consequently, the bank will need to consider supplementing its internal data with data from other sources. These could be internal scorecard data based on risk owners or expert opinion or data from an external consortium, or public data.

Scorecards

Chapters 10 and 11 consider an alternative data source that will be acceptable for capital models under the new Basel Accord, and that is scorecard data. For reasons explained in those chapters, even when loss event data are available, they are not necessarily as good an indication of future loss experience as scorecard data. However, scorecard data are very subjective:

- As yet we have not developed the industry standards for the key risk indicators (KRIs) that should be used for each risk type (however, see Chapters 11 and 12 for some discussion of these). Thus the choice of risk indicators themselves is subjective.

- Given a set of risk indicators, frequency and severity scores are usually assigned by the 'owner' of the operational risk. Careful design of the management process (for example, a 'no blame' culture) is necessary to avoid subjective bias at this stage.

- Not only are the scores themselves subjective, but when scorecard data are used in a loss distribution model, the scores need to be mapped, in a more or less subjective manner, to monetary loss amounts. This is not an easy task (see Section 10.6), particularly for risks that are associated with inadequate or failed people or management processes – these are commonly termed 'human risks'.

To use scorecard data in the AMA, the minimum requirement is to assess both expected frequency and expected severity quantitatively, from scores which may be purely qualitative. For example, the score 'very unlikely' for a loss event might first translate into a probability, depending on the scorecard design. In that case the expected frequency must be quantified by assuming a fixed number N of events that are susceptible to operational loss. In the scorecard below, N = 10 events per month. The scorecard will typically specify a range of expected frequency, and the exact point in this range should be fixed by scenario analysis using comparison with loss experience data. If internal data are not available, then external data should be used to validate the scorecard.

Definition	Probability, p	Expected Frequency, Np
Almost impossible	[0, 0.01]%	Less than once in 10 years
Rare	[0.1, 1]%	Between 1 per year and 1 per 10 years
Very unlikely	[1, 10]%	Between 1 per month and 1 per year
Unlikely	[10, 50]%	Between 1 and 5 per month
Likely	[50, 90]%	Between 5 and 9 per month
Very likely	[90, 100]%	More than 9 per month

The basic IMA requires only expected frequency and expected severity, but for the general IMA formula given in Section 7.5, and the simulation of the total loss distribution explained in Section 7.6, higher moments of the frequency and severity distributions must also be recovered from the scorecard. Uncertainty scores are also needed, i.e. the scorer who forecasts an expected loss severity of £40 000 must also answer the question, 'How certain are you of this forecast?' Although the loss severity standard deviation will be needed in the AMA model, it would be misleading to give a score in these terms. This is because standard deviations are not invariant under monotonic transformations. The standard deviation of log serverity may be only half as large as the mean log severity at the same time as the standard deviation of severity is twice as large as the mean severity. So if standard deviation were used to measure uncertainty, we would conclude from this severity data that we are 'fairly uncertain', but the conclusion from the same data in log form would be that we are 'certain'. However, percentiles are invariant under monotonic transformations, so uncertainty scores should be expressed as upper percentiles, i.e. as 'worst case' frequencies and severities, for example as in the following table.

Definition	Upper 99%-ile – mean (as a multiple of the mean)
Extremely uncertain	5 or more
Very uncertain	2 – 5
Fairly uncertain	1 – 2
Fairly certain	0.5 – 1
Very certain	0.1 – 0.5
Extremely certain	Up to 0.1

Despite the subjectivity of scorecard data there are many advantages in their use, not the least of which is that scores can be forward-looking. Thus they may give a more appropriate view of the future risk than estimates that are based purely on historical loss experience. Moreover, there are well-established quantitative methods that can account for the subjectivity of scorecard data in the proper manner. These are the Bayesian methods that will be introduced in Section 7.3 below.

External data

BCBS (2001b) states:

> The sharing of loss data, based on consistent definitions and metrics, is necessary to arrive at a comprehensive assessment of operational risk. ... For certain event types, banks may need to supplement their internal loss data with external, industry loss data.

However, there are problems when sharing data within a consortium. Suppose a bank joins a data consortium and that Delboy Financial Products Bank (DFPB) is also a member of that consortium. Also suppose that DFPB have just reported a very large operational loss: a rogue trader falsified accounts and incurred losses in the region of $1 billion. If a bank were to use those consortium data as if they were internal data, only scaling the unexpected loss by taking into account its capitalization relative to the total capitalization of the banks in the consortium, the estimated ORR will be rather high, to say the least.

For this reason BCBS (2001b) also states: 'The bank must establish procedures for the use of external data as a supplement to its internal loss data … [it] must specify procedures and methodologies for the scaling of external loss data or internal loss data from other sources.' New methods for combining internal and external data are now being developed (see Sections 8.5 and 13.7). Also, statistical methods that have been established for centuries are now being adapted to the operational loss distribution framework, and these are described in the next section.

7.3 Bayesian estimation

Bayesian estimation is a parameter estimation method that combines 'hard' data that are thought to be more objective, with 'soft' data that can be purely subjective. In operational risk terms, the 'hard' data may be the recent and relevant internal data and the 'soft' data could be from an external consortium, or purely subjective data in the form of risk scores based on opinions from industry experts or the owner of the risk. 'Soft' data could also be past internal data that, following a merger, acquisition or sale of assets, are not so relevant today.[2]

Bayesian estimation methods are based on two sources of information – the 'soft' data are used to estimate a *prior density* for the parameter of interest and the 'hard' data are used to estimate another density for the parameter that is called the *sample likelihood*. These two densities are then multiplied to give the *posterior density* on the model parameter. Figure 7.3 illustrates the effect of different priors on the posterior density. The 'hard' data represented by the likelihood are the same in both cases, but the left-hand figure illustrates the case when 'soft' data are uncertain[3] and the right-hand one the case that 'soft' data are certain.[4]

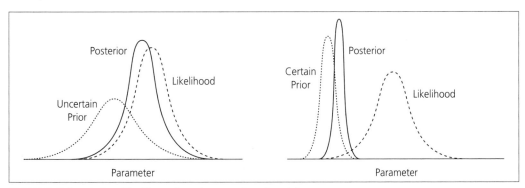

FIGURE 7.3 ■ Prior, likelihood and posterior densities

[2] When a bank's operations undergo a significant change in size, such as would be expected following a merger or acquisition, or a sale of assets, it may not be sufficient simply to rescale the capital charge by the size of its current operations. The internal systems, processes and people are likely to have changed considerably, and in this case the historic loss event data would no longer have the same relevance today.

[3] Uncertain (i.e. vague) priors arise, for example, when: the data in the external data consortium (for this risk type and line of business) are either sparse or very diverse; or when the industry expert or risk owner is uncertain about the scores recorded.

[4] Certain (i.e. precise) priors arise, for example, when there are plenty of quite homogeneous data in the consortium, or when the industry expert or the owner of the risk is fairly certain about their scores.

If desired, a point estimate of the parameter may be obtained from the posterior density, and this is called the Bayesian estimate. The point estimate will be the mean, mode or median of the posterior density, depending on the loss function of the decision-maker.[5] In this section we shall assume that the decision-maker has a quadratic loss function, so that the Bayesian estimate of the parameter will be the mean of the posterior density.

We say that the prior is 'conjugate' with the likelihood if it has the same parametric form as the likelihood and their product (the posterior) is also of this form. For example, if both prior and likelihood are normal, the posterior will also be normal; if both prior and likelihood are beta densities, the posterior will also be a beta density. The concept of conjugate priors allows one to combine data from different sources in a tractable manner. With conjugate priors, posterior densities are easy to compute analytically, otherwise one could use simulation to estimate the posterior density.

We now illustrate the Bayesian method with examples on the estimation of loss frequency and severity distribution parameters using scorecard, internal and external data. When scores for frequency and severity are given as expected values and 'worst case' values, as described in Section 7.2.4 (see also Table 9.4) it is possible to derive prior densities from these scores. We now give examples of such priors and show how internal loss experience data should be used to modify these prior beliefs.

7.3.1 Bayesian estimation of loss severity parameters

Let us first consider how to combine external and internal loss experience data. It is often the case that the uncertainty in the internal sample is less than the uncertainty in the external sample, because of the heterogeneity of members in a data consortium. Thus Bayesian estimates of the expected loss severity will often be nearer the internal mean than the external mean, as in Example 7.1. Note the importance of this for the bank that joins the consortium with Delboy Financial Products Bank: DFPB made a huge operational loss last year, and so, if the bank were to use classical estimation methods (such as maximum likelihood) to estimate μ_L as the average loss in the combined sample, this would be very large indeed. However, the opposite applies if the bank were to use Bayesian estimation! Here, the effect of DFPB's excessive loss will be to increase the standard deviation in the external sample very considerably, and this increased uncertainty will affect the Bayesian estimate so that it will be *closer* to the internal sample mean than the mean in the data consortium.

Another interesting consequence of the Bayesian approach to estimating loss severity distribution parameters when the parameters are normally distributed is that the Bayesian estimate of the standard deviation of the loss severity will be less than *both* the internal estimate and the external estimate of standard deviation. In Example 7.1 the Bayesian estimate of the standard

---

[5] Bayesians view the process of parameter estimation as a *decision* rather than as a statistical objective. That is, parameters are chosen to minimize expected loss, where expected loss is defined by the posterior density and a chosen loss function. Classical statistical estimation, on the other hand, defines a statistical objective such as 'sum of squared errors' or 'sample likelihood' which is minimized (or maximized) and thus the classical estimator is defined.

deviation is $0.83 million, which is less than both the internal estimate ($1 million) and the external estimate ($1.5 million). This reduction in overall variance reflects the value of more information: in simple terms, by adding new information to the internal (or external) density, the uncertainty must be decreased.

Note the importance of this statement for the bank that measures its ORR using an advanced approach. By augmenting the sample with external data, the standard deviation of loss severity will be reduced, and this will tend to decrease the estimate of the ORR. However, the net effect on the ORR is indeterminate for two reasons: firstly, the combined sample estimate of the mean loss severity may be increased, and this will tend to increase the ORR; secondly, the ORR also depends on the combined estimate for the parameters of the loss frequency distribution.

EXAMPLE 7.1

Estimating the mean and standard deviation of a loss severity distribution

Suppose that the internal and external data on losses (over a threshold of $1 million) due to a given type of operational risk are shown in Table 7.3. Based on the internal data only, the mean and standard deviation of loss severity are $2 million and $1 million respectively; based on the external data only, the mean and standard deviation of loss severity are $3 million and $1.5 million respectively. Note that the uncertainty, as measured by the standard deviation, is larger in the external data, and this is probably due to the heterogeneity of banks in the consortium.

TABLE 7.3 ■ Internal and external loss data

	Internal	External
	1.25	3.2
	1.35	1.15
	2.75	6.35
	1.15	1.45
	3.65	4.5
	1.85	2.75
		1.8
		2.3
		3.65
		4.25
		1.3
		4.9
		2.3
		3.2
		1.85
Mean	2.00	3.00
Std Dev.	1.00	1.50

We now show that the Bayesian estimate of the expected loss severity μ_L, based on *both* sources of data, will be closer to the estimate of μ_L that is based only on internal data. The intuition for this is that there is more uncertainty in the external data, so the posterior density will be closer to the density based on the internal data (this is the situation shown on the left in Figure 7.2) and the Bayesian estimate is the mean of the posterior density.

Recall that in Bayesian estimation the parameters are regarded as random variables. Assume that the prior density and the sample likelihood are normal distributions on μ_L (as would be the case if, for example, the loss severity – or log severity – distribution is normal). Therefore the posterior density, being the product of these, will also be normal. From this it follows that the Bayesian estimate of the mean loss severity, or log severity, which combines both internal and external data, will be a weighted average of the external sample mean and the internal sample mean, where the weights will be the reciprocals of the variances of the respective distributions.

In Table 7.3, the Bayesian estimate for the expected loss severity is therefore (in millions of dollars)

$$\frac{2/1^2 + 3/1.5^2}{1/1^2 + 1/1.5^2} = 2.3.$$

This is nearer the internal sample mean ($2 million) than the external sample mean ($3 million) because the internal data have less variability than the external data. Similarly, the Bayesian estimate of the loss severity standard deviation (again in millions of dollars) will be

$$\sqrt{\left(\frac{1}{1^2} + \frac{1}{1.5^2}\right)^{-1}} = 0.83.$$

This is less than both the internal and the external standard deviation estimates because of the additional value of information.

Note that the maximum likelihood estimates that are based on the combined sample with no differentiation of data source, are $2.7 million for the mean and $1.43 million for the standard deviation. This example will be continued below, and in Section 7.5.3, where it will be shown that the estimated capital charges will be significantly different, depending on whether parameter estimates are based on Bayesian or classical estimation.

7.3.2 Bayesian estimation of loss probability

Now let us consider how Bayesian estimation may be used to combine 'hard' and 'soft' data on loss probability. As noted in Section 7.2, an important parameter of the loss frequency distribution is the mean number of loss events over the time period: this is the expected frequency and it may be written as Np, where N is the total number of events that are susceptible to operational losses and p is the probability of a loss event. It is not always possible to estimate N and p separately and, if only a single data source is used, neither is this necessary (see Section 7.5).

However, regulatory capital charges are supposed to be forward-looking, so the value for N used to calculate the ORR should represent a *forecast* over the time period (one year is recommended by the Basel Committee). Thus we should use a target or projected value for N – assuming this can be defined by the management – and this target could be quite different from its historical value. But can N be properly defined – and even if it can be defined, can it be forecast? The answer is yes, but only for some risk types and lines of business. For example, in clients, products and business practices, or in internal fraud in the trading and sales line of business, the value for N should correspond to the target number of ongoing deals during the forthcoming year and p should correspond to the probability of an ongoing deal incurring an operational loss of this type. Assuming one can define a target value for N, the expected frequency will then be determined by the estimate of p, the probability of an operational loss.

Bayesian estimates for probabilities are usually based on beta densities, which take the form

$$f(p) \propto p^a(1-p)^b, \quad 0 < p < 1. \tag{7.1}$$

We use the notation '$\propto$' to express that fact that (7.1) is not a proper density – the integral under that curve is not equal to one because the normalizing constant, which involves the gamma function, has been omitted. However, normalizing constants are not important to carry through at every stage: if both prior and likelihood are beta densities, the posterior will also be a beta density, and we can normalize this at the end. It is easy to show that the beta density $f(p) \propto p^a(1-p)^b$ has mean $(a + 1)/(a + b + 2)$. The mean will be the Bayesian estimate for the loss probability p corresponding to the quadratic loss function, where a and b are the parameters of the posterior density.

EXAMPLE 7.2

Estimating the loss probability using internal data combined with (a) external data and (b) scorecard data

Here are two examples that show how to calculate a Bayesian estimate of loss probability using two sources of data. In each case the 'hard' data will be the internal data given in Table 7.3 of Example 7.1, assuming these data represented a total of 60 deals. Thus, with six loss events, the internal loss probability estimate was 6/60 = 0.1. This is, in fact, the maximum likelihood estimate corresponding to the sample likelihood,

$$f_1(p) \propto p^6(1 - p)^{54}$$

which is a beta density. Now consider two possible sources of 'soft' data: (a) the external data in Table 7.3, which we now suppose represented a total of 300 deals; (b) scorecard data that have assigned an expected loss probability of 5 percent and a 99 percent 'worst case' probability of 10 percent.

In case (a) the external loss probability estimate is 15/300 = 0.05 and the prior is the beta density

$$f_2(p) \propto p^{15}(1-p)^{285}.$$

The posterior density representing the combined data, which is the product of this prior with the likelihood beta density $f_1(p)$, is another beta density,

$$f_3(p) \propto p^{21}(1-p)^{339}$$

The mean of this density gives the Bayesian estimate of p as $\hat{p}$ = 22/362 = 0.061. Note that the classical maximum likelihood estimate that treats all data as the same is 21/360 = 0.058.

In case (b) a prior beta density that has mean 0.05 and upper 99%-ile 0.1 is

$$f_2(p) \propto p^4(1-p)^{94},$$

and this can be verified using the Excel BETA function and the mean formula for a beta density. The posterior becomes

$$f_3(p) \propto p^{10}(1-p)^{148}$$

The mean of this density gives the Bayesian estimate of p as $\hat{p}$ = 11/160 = 0.06875.

The method described in example 7.2 should be used to update scorecard data as new loss experiences come to light. The bank should use its target value for N to compute the expected number of loss events over the next year as $N\hat{p}$ where $\hat{p}$ is the updated score for p. Loss severity should have its scores updated using methods similar to those described in Example 7.1. We shall return to these examples in Section 7.5.3, where the ORR calculations based on a different type of parameter estimates will be compared, using targets for N and classical and Bayesian estimates for p, μ_L and σ_L.

7.4 Introducing the Advanced Measurement Approaches

At first sight, a number of Advanced Measurement Approaches to estimating ORR appear to be proposed in BCBS (2001b). A common phrase used by regulators and supervisors has been 'let a thousand flowers bloom'. However, in this section and the next we show that the Internal Measurement Approach (IMA) of BCBS (2001b) just gives an analytic approximation for the unexpected loss in a typical actuarial loss model. The only difference between the IMA and the Loss Distribution Approach (LDA) is that the latter uses simulation to estimate the whole loss distribution, whereas the former gives an analytic approximation to the unexpected loss. To be more precise, if uncertainty in loss severity is modelled by a standard deviation, but no functional form is imposed on the severity distribution, there is a simple formula for the unexpected annual loss, and that is the general IMA formula. In Section 7.5 we consider a number of generalizations to the 'basic' IMA formula given in BCBS (2001b).

7.4.1 A general framework for the Advanced Measurement Approach

The operational risk capital requirement based on the advanced measurement approach will, under the current proposals, be the unexpected loss in the total loss distribution corresponding to a confidence level of 99.9 percent and a risk horizon of one year.[6] This unexpected loss is illustrated in Figure 7.4: it is the difference between the 99.9th percentile and the expected loss in the total operational loss distribution for the bank. Losses below the expected loss should be covered by general provisions, and losses above the 99.9th percentile could bankrupt the firm, so they will need to be controlled. Capital charges are to cover losses in between these two limits: the common but rather unfortunate term for this is 'unexpected loss'.

Figure 7.5 shows how the annual loss distribution is a compound of the loss frequency distribution and the loss severity distribution. That is, for a given operational risk type in a given line of business, we construct a discrete probability density $h(n)$ of the number of loss events n during one year, and continuous conditional probability densities $g(x|n)$ of the

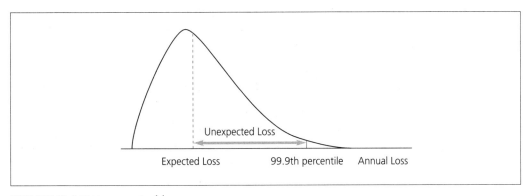

FIGURE 7.4 ▪ Unexpected loss

---

[6] This choice of risk horizon and confidence level by regulators may not be suitable for internal management. Financial institutions may well consider using different parameters for economic capital allocation; for example, a risk horizon of three months and a confidence level of 98 percent.

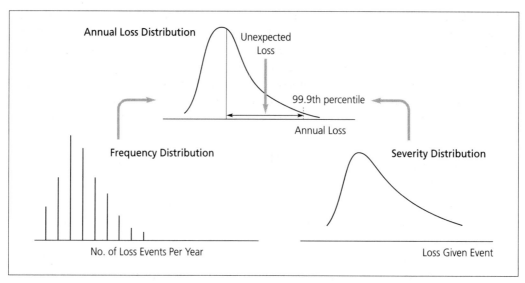

FIGURE 7.5 ■ Compounding frequency and severity distributions

loss severities, x, given there are n loss events during the year.[7] The annual loss then has the compound density

$$f(x) = \sum_{n=0}^{\infty} b(n)\, g(x\,|\,n). \tag{7.2}$$

Following the current Basel II proposals, the bank will construct an annual loss distribution for each line of business and risk type for which it has chosen the AMA. It is free to use different functional forms for the frequency and severity distributions for each risk type/line of business. The aggregation of these loss distributions into a total annual operational loss distribution for the bank will be discussed in Section 7.7.

7.4.2 Functional forms for loss frequency and severity distributions

Consider first the frequency distribution. At the most basic level we can model this by the binomial distribution $B(N, p)$, where N is the total number of events that are susceptible to an operational loss during one year, and p is the probability of a loss event. Assuming independence of events, the density function for the frequency distribution is then given by

$$b(n) = \binom{N}{n} p^n (1-p)^{N-n}, \quad n = 0, 1, \ldots, N. \tag{7.3}$$

---

[7] Appendix 9.2 gives full details of the usual assumptions about these distributions.

The disadvantage of the binomial density (7.3) is that one needs to specify the total number of events, N. However, when p is small the binomial distribution is well approximated by the Poisson distribution, which has a single parameter λ, corresponding to the expected frequency of loss events – that is, Np in the binomial model. Thus low-frequency operational risks may have frequency densities that are well captured by the Poisson distribution, with density function

$$b(n) = \frac{\lambda^n \exp(-\lambda)}{n!}, \qquad n = 0, 1, 2, \dots \tag{7.4}$$

Otherwise a better representation of the loss frequency may be obtained with a more flexible functional form, a two-parameter distribution such as the negative binomial distribution with density function

$$b(n) = \binom{\alpha + n - 1}{n} \left(\frac{1}{1 + \beta}\right)^\alpha \left(\frac{\beta}{1 + \beta}\right)^n, \qquad n = 0, 1, 2, \dots \tag{7.5}$$

Turning now to the loss severity, one does not necessarily wish to choose a functional form for its distribution. In fact when one is content to model uncertainty in the loss severity directly, simply by the loss severity variance, the unexpected annual loss may be approximated by an analytic formula. The precise formula will depend on the functional form for the frequency density, and we shall examine this in Section 7.5.

When setting a functional form for the loss severity distribution, a common simplifying assumption is that loss frequency and loss severity are independent. In this case only one (unconditional) severity distribution $g(x)$ is specified for each risk type and line of business, indeed $g(x|n)$ may be obtained using convolution integrals of $g(x)$. More details about dependence of loss frequencies and severities are given in Chapter 9.

It is clearly not appropriate to assume that aggregate frequency and severity distributions are independent – for example, high-frequency risks tend to have a lower impact than many low-frequency risks. However, within a given risk type and line of business an assumption of independence is not necessarily inappropriate. Clearly the range for severity will not be the same for all risk types (it can be higher for low-frequency risks than for high-frequency risks) and also the functional form chosen for the severity distribution may be different across different risk types.

High-frequency risks can have severity distributions that are relatively lognormal, so that

$$g(x) = \frac{1}{\sqrt{2\pi}\sigma x} \exp\left(-\frac{1}{2}\left(\frac{\ell n x - \mu}{\sigma}\right)^2\right), \qquad x > 0. \tag{7.6}$$

However, some severity distributions may have substantial leptokurtosis and skewness. In that case a better fit is provided by a two-parameter density. Often we use the gamma density

$$g(x) = \frac{x^{\alpha-1} \exp(-x/\beta)}{\beta^\alpha \Gamma(\alpha)}, \qquad x > 0, \tag{7.7}$$

where $\Gamma(\cdot)$ denotes the gamma function, or the two-parameter hyperbolic density

$$g(x) = \frac{\exp\left(-\alpha \sqrt{\beta^2 + x^2}\right)}{2\beta B(\alpha\beta)}, \quad x > 0, \tag{7.8}$$

where $B(\cdot)$ denotes the Bessel function.

Further discussion about the properties of these frequency and severity distributions will be given in Section 7.5, when we shall apply them to estimating the unexpected annual loss.

7.4.3 Comments on parameter estimation

Having chosen the functional forms for the loss frequency and severity densities to represent each cell in the risk type/line of business categorization, the user needs to specify the parameter values for all of these. The parameter values used must represent *forecasts* for the loss frequency and severity distributions, over the risk horizon on the model. If historical data on loss experiences are available, these may provide some indication of the appropriate parameter values. One needs to differentiate between sources of historical data, and if more than one data source is used, or in any case where data have a highly subjective element, a Bayesian approach to parameter estimation should be utilized (see Section 7.3). For example, when combining internal with external data, more weight should be placed on the data with less sampling variation – often the internal data, given that external data consortia may have quite heterogeneous members.

However, the past is not an accurate reflection of the future: not just for market prices, but also for all types of risk, including operational risks. Therefore parameter estimates that are based on historical loss experience data or retrospective operational risk scores can be very misleading. A great advantage of using scorecards, rather than historical loss experience, is that the parameters derived from these can be truly forward-looking. Although more subjective – indeed, they may not even be linked to a historical loss experience – scorecard data may be more appropriate than historical loss event data for predicting the future risk. Moreover, as historical loss experiences are recorded, the scores can be updated and revised using the methods described in Section 7.3.

For internal purposes, a parameterization of the loss severity and frequency distributions is useful for the scenario analysis for operational risks. For example, the management may ask: 'If loss severity uncertainty increases, what is the effect on the unexpected annual loss?' To answer such quantitative questions, one must first specify a functional form for the loss severity and frequency densities, and then perturb their parameters.

7.4.4 Comments on the 99.9th percentile

The data for operational risk models are incomplete, unreliable, and/or have a large subjective element. Thus it is clear that the parameters of the annual loss distribution cannot be estimated very precisely. Consequently, it is not very meaningful to propose the estimation of risk at the 99.9th percentile. Even at the 99th percentile, large changes in the unexpected loss arise from very small changes in parameter estimates. Therefore regulators should ask themselves very seriously whether it is, in fact, sensible to base ORR calculations on this method.

For example, consider the three annual loss distributions shown in Figure 7.6. For the purposes of illustration we suppose that a gamma density (7.7) is fitted to annual loss with slightly different parameters in each of the three cases.[8]

The mean of a gamma distribution (7.7) is $\alpha\beta$. In fact the means, shown in the first column of Table 7.4, are not very different between the three different densities. However, the unexpected losses at the 95th percentile are quite different: the largest difference (between densities 2 and 3) is $20.8 - 18.9 = 1.9$. That is, there is a 10.1 percent increase in the 95 percent unexpected loss from density 2 to density 3. There are even greater differences between the 99.9th percentiles and the associated unexpected loss: even the very small changes in fitted densities shown in Figure 7.6 can lead to a 14 percent increase in the ORR.

It is important to realize that the parameters of an annual operational loss distribution cannot be estimated with precision: a large quantity of objective data is necessary for this, but it is simply not there, and never will be. Operational risks will always be quantified by subjective data, or external data, whose relevance is questionable.

In the example above, we did not even consider the effect on the 99.9th percentile estimate from changing to a different functional form. However, the bank is faced with a plethora of possible distributions to choose from; for severity, in addition to (7.6) – (7.8), the bank could choose to use any of the extreme value distributions (as in Frachot *et al.* 2001) or any mixture distribution that has suitably heavy tails. The effect of moving from one functional form to another is likely to have an even greater impact on the tail behaviour than the effect of small changes in parameter estimates. Furthermore, in Section 7.7.4 we show that, even if there is no uncertainty surrounding the choice for individual functional forms, and no uncertainty about the parameter estimates, the use of slightly different dependence assumptions will have an enormous impact on the 99.9th percentile estimate. It is clear that estimates of the 99.9th percentile of a total

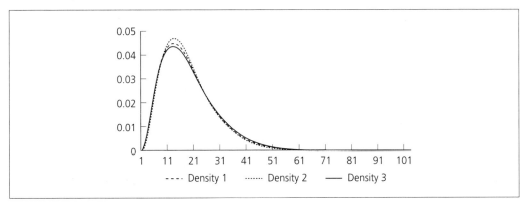

FIGURE 7.6 ■ Three similar densities

---

[8] In density 1 $\alpha = 3$, $\beta = 6$; in density 2 $\alpha = 3.2$, $\beta = 5.5$; in density 3 $\alpha = 2.8$, $\beta = 6.5$.

TABLE 7.4 ■ Comparison of percentiles and unexpected loss

	Mean	Percentile			Unexpected Loss		
		95%	99%	99.9%	95%	99%	99.9%
Density 1	18	38	50.5	67.5	20	32.5	49.5
Density 2	17.6	36.5	48.2	63.5	18.9	30.6	45.9
Density 3	18.2	39	51.5	70.5	20.8	33.3	52.3

annual operational loss distribution will always be very, very imprecise. Nevertheless, regulators propose using the unexpected loss at the 99.9th percentile to estimate the ORR using the AMA.

7.5 Analytic approximations to unexpected annual loss

This section develops some analytic methods for estimating the regulatory capital to cover operational risks (recall that this capital is referred to as the operational risk requirement (ORR) throughout this chapter). All the analytic formulae given here are based on the Internal Measurement Approach that has been recommended by the BCBS (2001b). In the course of this section we will show how to determine the Basel gamma (γ) factor, thus solving a problem that has previously vexed both regulators and risk managers.

The IMA has some advantages:

1   Banks, and other financial institutions, that implement the IMA will gain insight to the most important sources of operational risk. The IMA is not a 'top-down' approach to risk capital, where capital is simply top-sliced from some gross exposure indicator at a percentage that is set by regulators to maintain the aggregate level of regulatory capital in the system. Instead, operational risk estimates are linked to different risk types and lines of business, and to the frequency and severity of operational losses. But the IMA also falls short of being a 'bottom-up' approach, where unexpected losses are linked to causal factors that can be controlled by management. Nevertheless, the implementation of an IMA, or indeed any LDA, is still an important step along the path to operational risk management and control, as demonstrated in Chapter 13.

2   The IMA might produce lower regulatory capital estimates than the Basic Indicator and Standardized approaches, although this will depend very much on the risk type, the data used and the method of estimating parameters, as we shall see in Examples 7.3 and 7.4.

3   The IMA gives rise to several simple analytic formulae for the ORR, all of which are derived from the basic formula given by BCBS (2001b). The basic Basel formula is:

$$\text{ORR} = \text{gamma} \times \text{expected annual loss} = \gamma \times NpL, \tag{7.9}$$

where N is a volume indicator, p is the probability of a loss event and L is the loss given event for each business line/risk type.

It is recognized in the Basel II proposals that NpL corresponds to the expected annual loss when the loss frequency is binomially distributed and the loss severity is L – severity is not regarded as a random variable in the basic form of the IMA. However, no indication of the possible range for gamma has been given. Since gamma is not directly related to observable quantities in the annual loss distribution, it is not surprising that the Basel proposals for calibration of gamma were changed. Initially, in their second consultative document (BCBS 2001a) the committee proposed to provide industry-wide gammas, as it has for the alphas in the Basic Indicator Approach and the betas in the Standardized Approach (see Chapter 3). Currently, it is proposed that individual banks will calibrate their own gammas, subject to regulatory approval.

How should the gammas be calibrated? In this section we show first how (7.9) may be rewritten in a more specific form which, instead of gamma, has a new parameter, denoted phi (ϕ). The advantage of this seemingly innocuous change of notation is that phi has a simple relation to observable quantities in the loss frequency distribution, and therefore phi can be calibrated. In fact, we will show that phi has quite a limited range: it is bounded below by 3.1 (for very high-frequency risks) and is likely to be less than 4, except for some very low-frequency risks with only one loss event every four or more years.

We shall show how to calculate phi from an estimate of the expected loss frequency and that there is a simple relationship between phi and gamma. Table 7.5 gives values for the Basel gamma factors according to the risk frequency. We also consider generalizations of the basic IMA formula (7.9) to use all the standard frequency distributions, not just the binomial distribution, and to include loss severity variability. We show that when loss severity variability is introduced, the gamma (and phi) should be reduced.

7.5.1 A basic formula for the ORR

Operational risk capital is to cover unexpected annual loss, given by the 99.9th percentile of annual loss minus the mean annual loss, as shown in Figure 7.4. Instead of following BCBS (2001b) and writing unexpected loss as a multiple (γ) of expected loss, we write unexpected loss as a multiple (ϕ) of the loss standard deviation. That is,

ORR = $\phi \times$ standard deviation of annual loss.

Since ORR = [99.9th percentile annual loss – mean annual loss], we have

$$\phi = \frac{99.9\text{th percentile} - \text{mean}}{\text{standard deviation}} \tag{7.10}$$

in the annual loss distribution.

The basic IMA formula (7.9) is based on the binomial loss frequency distribution, with no variability in loss severity L. In this case the standard deviation in loss frequency is $\sqrt{(Np(1-p))}$ $\approx \sqrt{(Np)}$ because p is small, and the standard deviation in annual loss is therefore $L\sqrt{(Np)}$. Thus an approximation to (7.9) is:

$$\text{ORR} = \phi \times L \times \sqrt{Np}. \tag{7.11}$$

Some points to note about (7.11) are the following:

1   Equation (7.10) can be used to calibrate ϕ using the 99.9th percentile, mean and standard deviation of the *frequency* distribution, because loss severity is not random. The results are given in Table 7.5.

2   There is a simple relationship between the original parameter (γ) suggested in BCBS (2001b) and ϕ. Indeed, equating (7.9) and (7.11) gives

$$\gamma = \frac{\phi}{\sqrt{(Np)}}$$

We shall see below that ϕ lies in a narrow range, but there is a much larger range for the values of γ.

3   The ORR should increase as the *square root* of the expected frequency: it will not be linearly related to the size of the bank's operations;

4   The ORR is linearly related to loss severity: high severity risks will therefore attract higher capital charges than low severity risks;

5   The ORR also depends on ϕ, which in turn depends on the dispersion in the frequency distribution. Example 7.3 on page 152 illustrates the fact that high-frequency risks will have lower ϕ than low-frequency risks, and therefore they will attract lower capital charges.

7.5.2 Calibration: normal, Poisson and negative binomial frequencies

As mentioned above, the basic IMA formula (7.9) or (7.11) assumes the binomial distribution (7.3) for the loss frequency. But there are some important extensions of this framework to be considered. Consider first the approximation to the binomial model for very high-frequency risks, such as those associated with back office transactions processing. In this case the binomial distribution (7.3) may be approximated by the normal distribution – assuming the loss probability is small enough to warrant this.[9] In the normal distribution, the ratio

$$\phi = \frac{99.9\text{th percentile} - \text{mean}}{\text{standard deviation}} = 3.1,$$

as can be found from standard normal tables. We shall see that this provides a lower bound for ϕ.

Consider another frequency distribution, the Poisson distribution (7.4) with parameter $\lambda = Np$, being the expected number of loss events (per year). The Poisson should be preferred to the binomial frequency distribution if N is difficult to quantify, even as a target. Now (7.11) may be rewritten

$$\text{ORR} = \phi \times L \times \sqrt{\lambda}, \tag{7.12}$$

---

[9] If it were not, the bank would be facing a risk of such high expected frequency that it should be controlling it as a matter of urgency.

and (7.10) becomes ϕ = (99.9th percentile – λ)/$\sqrt{\lambda}$ and note that in this case $\gamma = \phi/\sqrt{\lambda}$. The values of ϕ and γ may be obtained using probability tables of the Poisson distribution.[10] The results are given in Table 7.5. For example, in the Poisson distribution with $\lambda = 5$, the standard deviation is $\sqrt{5}$ and the 99.9th percentile is 12.77, so ϕ = (12.77 – 5)/ $\sqrt{5}$ = 3.475; the Poisson ϕ will be smaller than this for higher-frequency risks, tending to the normal ϕ of 3.1 as λ increases. Lower-frequency risks will have more skewed frequency distributions and therefore greater ϕ; for example, in the Poisson with $\lambda = 1$ the 99.9 percent percentile is 4.868, so ϕ = 3.868. Table 7.5 gives the values of both ϕ and γ for different risk frequencies from 100 loss events per year down to 0.01 (one event in 100 years). If there are more than 200 events per year, the normal value of $\phi = 3.1$ should be used.

The table shows that ϕ must be in a fairly narrow range: from about 3.2 for medium- to high-frequency risks (20 to 100 loss events per year) to about 3.9 for low-frequency risks (one loss event every one or two years) and only above 4 for very rare events that may happen only once every five years or so.[11] However, the Basle Committee's parameter γ ranges from 0.3 (for high frequency risks) to 10, or more, for very low frequency risks.

TABLE 7.5 ■ Gamma and phi values (no loss severity variability)

lamda	100	50	40	30	20	10
99.9th percentile	131.805	72.751	60.452	47.812	34.714	20.662
phi	3.180	3.218	3.234	3.252	3.290	3.372
gamma	0.318	0.455	0.511	0.594	0.736	1.066
lamda	8	6	5	4	3	2
99.9th percentile	17.630	14.449	12.771	10.956	9.127	7.113
phi	3.405	3.449	3.475	3.478	3.537	3.615
gamma	1.204	1.408	1.554	1.739	2.042	2.556
lamda	1	0.9	0.8	0.7	0.6	0.5
99.9th percentile*	4.868	4.551	4.234	3.914	3.584	3.255
phi	3.868	3.848	3.839	3.841	3.853	3.896
gamma	3.868	4.056	4.292	4.591	4.974	5.510
lamda	0.4	0.3	0.2	0.1	0.05	0.01
99.9th percentile*	2.908	2.490	2.072	1.421	1.065	0.904
phi	3.965	3.998	4.187	4.176	4.541	8.940
gamma	6.269	7.300	9.362	13.205	20.306	89.401

* For lamda less than 1, interpolation over both lamda and x has been used to smooth the percentiles; even so, small non-monotonicities arising from the discrete nature of percentiles remain in the estimated values of ϕ.

---

[10] Although all percentiles of the Poisson distribution are by definition integers, we interpolate between integer values to obtain values of ϕ that correspond to 99.9th percentiles in the loss severity distribution on 0, L, $2L$, $3L$, ... (which in this case is a discrete approximation to a continuous distribution). The 99.9th percentiles may be estimated using the formula =POISSON(x, λ, 1) in Excel, where x = 0, 1, 2, ... and interpolating.

[11] When loss severity variability is taken into account, these values should be slightly lower, as we shall see below.

EXAMPLE 7.3

ORR for two risk types

Suppose 25 000 transactions are processed in a year by a back office, the probability of a failed transaction is 0.04 and the expected loss given that a transaction has failed is $1000. Then Np = 1000, the expected annual loss is $1 million, and the standard deviation of annual loss is $1000 × √1000 = $31,622. The loss frequency is binomially distributed with large N and small p, and can therefore be approximated by the normal distribution. In this case we have shown that $\phi \approx 3.1$ so that the ORR $\approx \$(3.1 \times 31,622) \approx \$98,000$.

On the other hand, if 50 investment banking deals are done in one year, the probability of an unauthorized or illegal deal is 0.005 and the expected loss if a deal is unauthorized or illegal is $4 million, then $Np = 0.25$ and the expected annual loss will also be $1 million.

Although the expected loss is the same for both types of risk, the ORR is quite different. The standard deviation of annual loss in investment banking is $4 million × √0.25 = $2 million. If the loss frequency is assumed to be Poisson-distributed with parameter 0.25, the mean and standard deviation of this distribution are 0.25 and 0.5 respectively, and from Poisson tables the 99.9th percentile is approximately 2.28, so the ratio $\phi \approx (2.28 - 0.25)/0.5 \approx 4$.

Thus in investment banking, the unexpected loss (ORR) $\approx \$(4 \times 2$ million$) \approx \$8$ million. This is more than 80 times greater than the unexpected loss in transactions processing, although the expected loss is the same in both!

In the Poisson distribution all moments are closely related because there is only one parameter. For example, the mean is equal to the variance, and the higher moments may be obtained using a recursive formula also depending on λ. In the negative binomial distribution (7.5) there are two parameters, and therefore more flexibility to accommodate difference between the mean and the variance and exceptional skewness or heavy tails.

The negative binomial model also captures the uncertainty in loss probability: it may be viewed as a probability-weighted sum of Poisson distributions, each with a different expected loss frequency. The negative binomial density function is given in (7.5). It has mean $\alpha\beta$ and standard deviation $\beta\sqrt{\alpha}$, so the IMA formula for the ORR (7.10) becomes

$$\text{ORR} = \phi \times \beta\sqrt{\alpha} \times L, \tag{7.13}$$

where

$$\phi = \frac{99.9\text{th percentile} - \alpha\beta}{\beta\sqrt{\alpha}}.$$

Again, values for ϕ and $\gamma = \phi/\sqrt{\alpha}$ may be calculated from statistical tables of the negative binomial density function, for different values of α and β.

7.5.3 The ORR with random severity

Up to this point our discussion of the IMA has assumed that loss severity L was not random. Now suppose that it is random, having mean μ_L and standard deviation σ_L, but that severity is independent of loss frequency. Again denote by p the loss probability in the annual frequency distribution, so that the expected number of loss events during one year is Np, and we assume no uncertainty in loss probability. At each of the N events there is a constant probability p of a loss event, in which case the loss severity is random. The expected annual loss X has moments

$$E(X) = NpE(L) = Np\mu_L,$$

$$E(X^2) = NpE(L^2) = Np(\mu_L^2 + \sigma_L^2).$$

Therefore the annual loss variance is

$$\text{Var}(X) = Np(\mu_L^2 + \sigma_L^2) - (Np\mu_L)^2 \approx Np(\mu_L^2 + \sigma_L^2)$$

because p is small. More generally, writing $\lambda = Np$, the expected loss frequency in the Poisson model, the annual loss X has variance

$$\text{Var}(X) \approx \lambda\,(\mu_L^2 + \sigma_L^2)$$

and the IMA capital charge (7.10) is therefore

$$\text{ORR} = \phi \times \mu_L \times \sqrt{\lambda} \times \sqrt{1 + \left(\frac{\sigma_L}{\mu_L}\right)^2}. \tag{7.14}$$

Note that when the loss severity is random, the calibration parameter ϕ refers to the annual loss distribution, and not just the frequency distribution. With the above notation:

$$\phi = \frac{\text{99.9th percentile of annual loss} - \lambda\mu_L}{\sqrt{[\lambda(\mu_L^2 + \sigma_L^2)]}},$$

and this reduces to the previous formula for ϕ when $\sigma_L = 0$, since in that case the 99.9th percentile of annual loss was equal to the 99.9th percentile of frequency $\times \mu_L$. Note that when $\sigma_L \neq 0$, ϕ should be somewhat *less* than the frequency-based ϕ that has been tabulated in Table 7.5, because the annual distribution will tend to be less skewed than the frequency and severity distribution, but ϕ will still be bounded below by the value of 3.1 which corresponds to the normal annual loss distribution. Recall that in Table 7.5 the value of ϕ ranged from about 3.2 for medium- to high-frequency risks to around 4 for low-frequency risks, and that only for rare events would it be greater than 4. By how much should ϕ be reduced to account for loss severity variability? We address this question by way of an example in Section 7.3.4.

How is the Basel gamma affected by the introduction of loss severity variability? Since now

$$\gamma = \phi \sqrt{\frac{1 + (\sigma_L/\mu_L)^2}{\lambda}},$$

the Basel parameter is likely to be much greater than that given in Table 7.5, particularly if σ_L is large.

Comparison of (7.14) with (7.11) shows that when there is uncertainty in loss severity, an extra term $\sqrt{(1 + (\sigma_L/\mu_L)^2)}$ should be used in the ORR formula. Thus the greater the uncertainty in loss severity, the greater the capital charge. This term is likely to be close to one for high-frequency risks that have little variation in loss severity but it will be greater for low-frequency risks, where loss severity variability may be of a similar order of magnitude to the expected loss severity. In the case that $\sigma_L = \mu_L$ the ORR should be multiplied by $\sqrt{2}$, and if $\sigma_L > \mu_L$ there will be an even greater increase in the ORR.

It is not only the type of risk that determines the magnitude of $\sqrt{(1 + (\sigma_L/\mu_L)^2)}$. The method for estimating the parameters σ_L and μ_L will also play an important role. Recall from Example 7.1 that Bayesian estimation of loss severity parameters can properly recognize subjectivity, and different sources of data. When both 'hard' internal loss experience data and 'soft' data, from an external consortium or a scorecard, are to be combined, it is essential to use Bayesian estimates rather than the maximum likelihood estimates. Example 7.4, which continues Examples 7.1 and 7.2, uses the formulae that we have developed in this section to illustrate the effect on the capital charge when different types of estimators are employed.

EXAMPLE 7.4

Comparison of Bayesian and classical estimates of ORR

In Examples 7.1 and 7.2 the Bayesian and classical estimates of the mean loss severity μ_L, and the standard deviation of loss severity σ_L, and the loss probability p were compared. We used the internal and external data from Table 7.3. Now, using the formulae (7.11) and (7.14), we compute the ORR, with and without loss severity uncertainty, and compare the difference in the ORR when using Bayesian or classical estimation of the parameters.

Without loss severity uncertainty formula (7.11) is used for the ORR, and the calibration of ϕ used the Poisson frequency density with parameter $\lambda = Np \approx 6$, giving $\phi = 3.45$ from Table 7.5. In this case the classical estimate of the ORR is 22.60, which is about 15 percent higher

	Bayesian	Classical
μ_L	2.31	2.71
σ_L	0.83	1.43
p	0.061	0.058
N (target)	100	100
ϕ (7.11)	3.45	3.45
ORR (7.11)	19.61	22.60
ϕ (7.14)	3.2	3.2
ORR (7.14)	19.34	23.70

than the Bayesian estimate. The introduction of severity uncertainty, and consequently the use of (7.14) for the ORR, increases this difference: the classical estimate of the ORR increases to 23.70, which is now 22.5 percent larger than the Bayesian estimate of the ORR.[12]

To conclude, the introduction of loss severity uncertainty, with $\sigma_L > 0$, will always give a larger capital charge than the charge based on the basic IMA formula. This is because the gamma factor increases: even though ϕ is slightly smaller, this reduction is more than offset by the extra factor $\sqrt{1 + (\sigma_L/\mu_L)^2}$.

7.5.4 Inclusion of insurance and the general 'IMA' formula

BCBS (2001b) states that banks will only be permitted to reduce capital charges to allow for insurance cover if they use an advanced measurement approach. Their justification is that 'this reflects the quality of risk identification, measurement, monitoring and control inherent in the AMA and the difficulties in establishing a rigorous mechanism for recognizing insurance where banks use a simpler regulatory capital calculation technique'. Banks that mitigate certain operational risks through insurance will, hopefully, regard this 'carrot' as an extra incentive to invest in the data and technology required by the AMA. They will also need to develop an appropriate formula for recognition of insurance that is 'risk-sensitive but not excessively complex', in the words of the Basel Committee.

A simple formula for including insurance cover in the operational risk charge can be deduced using the binomial model. Insurance reduces the loss amount when the event occurs (an expected amount μ_R is recovered) but introduces a premium C to be paid even if the event does not occur. An expected amount $\mu_L - \mu_R$ is lost with probability p and C is lost with probability 1, so the expected annual loss is now $N[p(\mu_L - \mu_R) + C]$. If we assume that the premium is fairly priced then the introduction of insurance will not affect the expected

---

[12] Note that we used the value $\phi = 3.2$ in (7.14). A slightly lower value is appropriate when $\sigma_L \neq 0$, because the loss distribution becomes less skewed and leptokurtic, so ϕ will be closer to the normal value of 3.1.

loss significantly. Thus the expected loss will be approximately $Np\mu_L$ as it was before the insurance, and this will be the case if the premium is set to be approximately equal to the expected pay-out, that is, $C \approx p\mu_R$. However, insurance will reduce the standard deviation of annual loss and therefore also the capital charge. Assuming p is small, the annual loss standard deviation will now be approximately

$$\sqrt{(Np)} \times (\mu_L - \mu_R) \times \sqrt{(1 + (\sigma_L/\mu_L)^2)}.$$

Denote the expected recovery rate by r, so that $r = \mu_R/\mu_L$, and set $Np = \lambda$ as usual. Then (7.14) becomes

$$\text{ORR} = \phi \times \sqrt{\lambda} \times \mu_L \times \sqrt{1 + (\sigma_L/\mu_L)^2} \times (1 - r).$$

As before, this can be generalized to other types of distributions for loss frequency (in which case $\sqrt{\lambda}$ should be replaced by the standard deviation of the loss frequency distribution). The general result is the same in each case: if risks are insured and the expected recovery rate per claim is r, the capital charge should be reduced by a factor of $1 - r$. The general formula for approximating the ORR is thus

$$\text{ORR} = \phi \times \sigma_F \times \mu_L \times \sqrt{1 + (\sigma_L/\mu_L)^2} \times (1 - r), \tag{7.15}$$

where σ_F is the standard deviation of the frequency distribution. It is stated in BCBS (2001b) that a simple formula, such as (7.15) will be necessary for banks that wish to allow for insurance cover when calculating capital charges.

7.6 Simulating the annual loss distribution

For each risk type/line of business, the annual loss distribution is the compound distribution of the loss frequency and loss severity, as in (7.2) and illustrated in Figure 7.5. A simple simulation algorithm based on (7.2) may be used to generate an annual loss distribution as follows:

1 Take a random draw from the frequency distribution: suppose this simulates n loss events per year.

2 Take n random draws from the severity distribution: denote these simulated losses by L_1, $L_2, \ldots, L_n$.

3 Sum the n simulated losses to obtain an annual loss $X = L_1 + L_2 + \ldots + L_n$.

4 Return to step 1, and repeat several thousand times: thus obtain $X_1, \ldots, X_N$, where N is a very large number.

5 Form the histogram of $X_1, \ldots, X_N$: this represents the simulated annual loss distribution.

6 The ORR for this risk type/line of business is then the difference between the 99.9th percentile and the mean of the simulated annual loss distribution (assuming expected loss is adequately covered by provisions).

Figure 7.7 illustrates the first two steps in the simulation algorithm. The use of empirical frequency and severity distributions is not advised, even if sufficient data are available to generate these distributions empirically. There are two reasons for this. Firstly, the simulated annual loss distribution will not be an accurate representation if the same frequencies and severities are repeatedly sampled. Secondly, there will be no ability for scenario analysis in the model, unless one specifies and fits the parameters of a functional form for the severity and frequency distributions. Some useful functional forms have been listed in Section 7.4.

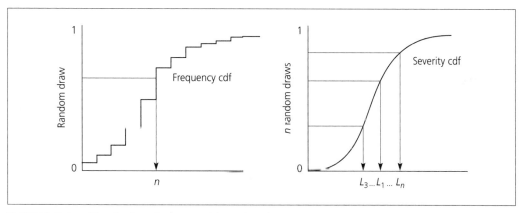

FIGURE 7.7 ■ Simulating the annual loss distribution

Example 7.5 shows that the ORR that is obtained through simulation of the annual loss distribution is approximately the same as that which is estimated through an analytic approximation.

EXAMPLE 7.5

Comparison of ORR from analytic and simulation approximations

Suppose the frequency is Poisson-distributed with parameter $\lambda = 5$, so the expected number of loss events per year is 5. Suppose the severity is gamma-distributed with $\alpha = 4$ and $\beta = 2$, so that the mean severity $\mu_L = \$8$ million and the standard deviation $\sigma_L = \$4$ million. Thus the expected annual loss is $40 million.

We first estimate the ORR using the formula (7.14) with $\lambda = 5$, $\mu_L = 8$, $\sigma_L = 4$. From Table 7.5, when $\lambda = 5$, the upper limit for $\psi = 3.47$ and the lower limit is $\phi = 3.1$. The ORR will be between $64 million ($\phi = 3.2$) and $66 million ($\phi = 3.3$).

Then, using the Poisson frequency with $\lambda = 5$ and gamma severity with $\alpha = 4$ and $\beta = 2$, we performed 5000 frequency simulations, and the requisite number of severity simulations for each. The Excel random number generator function, the Poisson distribution and the formula =(GAMMAINV(RAND(),4,2) according to the compound distribution algorithm described above. In this way, 5000 annual losses were simulated and the ORR was estimated as the difference between the 99.9th percentile and the mean of the simulated distribution. The estimate obtained was $64.3 million.

Note that our previous comments about loss severity uncertainty increasing the 'IMA' capital charge also apply here. We can conclude that, within a risk type/line of business, the LDA capital charge will always be greater than the capital charge·given by (7.12) or (7.13), where there is no loss severity variability assumed.

7.7 Aggregation and the total loss distribution

The aggregation of the ORR over all risk types and lines of business, to obtain a total ORR for the bank, can take into account the likely dependencies between various operational risks. BCBS (2001b) states: 'The bank will be permitted to recognise empirical correlations in operational risk losses across business lines and event types, provided that it can demonstrate that its systems for measuring correlations are sound and implemented with integrity.' In this section we first consider the aggregation to a total unexpected annual loss for the bank when the analytic approximation (the IMA) is used for each unexpected annual loss. We show how to account for correlations in this aggregation. Then we consider the more complex problem of aggregating the individual annual loss distributions into a total annual loss distribution for the bank.

7.7.1 Aggregation of analytic approximations to the ORR

Recall that when unexpected loss is estimated analytically, as described in Section 7.5, for each line of business ($i = 1, 2, ..., n$) and risk type ($j = 1, 2, ..., m$) we have:

$$\text{ORR}_{ij} = \phi_{ij}\, \sigma_{ij},$$

where σ_{ij} is the standard deviation of the annual loss distribution and σ_{ij} can be tabulated as in Table 7.5. Two simple methods for obtaining the total ORR for the bank are:

1 Sum these ORR_{ij} over all lines of business and risk types.
2 Take the square root of the sum of squares of the ORR_{ij} over all lines of business and risk types.

The simple summation (method 1) assumes perfect correlation between the annual losses made in different lines of business and risk types. This remark follows from the observation that the standard deviation of a sum of random variables is only equal to the sum of their standard deviations if their correlations are unity. If all dependency between annual loss distributions were measured by their correlations, we could conclude that the summation of operational risk capital charges assumes that risks are perfectly correlated. This implies that all operational loss events must occur at the same time, which is totally unrealistic.

The summation (in method 2) assumes zero correlation between operational risks, which occurs when they are independent. Again this assumption is not very realistic and it will tend to underestimate the total unexpected loss, as shown by Frachot *et al.* (2001).

More generally, suppose that we have an $(n+m) \times (n+m)$ correlation matrix $\mathbf{V}$ that represents the correlations between different operational risks – this is an heroic assumption, about which we shall say more later on in this section. Nevertheless, suppose that $\mathbf{V}$ is given. We have the $(n+m) \times (n+m)$ diagonal matrix $\mathbf{D}$ of standard deviations σ_{ij}, that is $\mathbf{D} - \mathrm{diag}(\sigma_{11}, \sigma_{12}, \sigma_{13}, ..., \sigma_{21}, \sigma_{22}, \sigma_{23}, ..., \sigma_{nm})$ and the $(n+m)$-vector ϕ of multipliers. Now the total unexpected loss, accounting for the correlations given in $\mathbf{V}$, is $(\phi'\mathbf{DVD}\,\phi)^{1/2}$.

7.7.2 Comments on correlation and dependency

One of the advantages of the simulation approach is that the whole annual loss distribution is estimated for each type of risk, and not just the unexpected loss. In this case it is possible to account for dependencies other than correlations when combining these distributions to obtain the total annual loss distribution. Correlation, which is a standardized form of the first moment of the joint density of two random variables, is not necessarily a good measure of the dependence between two random variables. Correlation only captures linear dependence, and even in liquid financial markets correlations can be very unstable over time. In operational risks is it more meaningful to consider general codependencies, rather than restrict the relationships between losses to simple correlation. An example of a possible dependency structure that may be determined by common risk drivers is given in Table 7.6.

In Appendix 9.2 the dependencies between frequency distributions and between frequency and severity distributions are discussed. Modelling codependency between frequencies is indeed a primary issue, following the observation that operational losses may be grouped in time, rather than by severity. Frachot *et al.* (2001) advocate the use of a multivariate extension of the Poisson distribution to model correlated loss frequencies. However, the approach is only tractable for the aggregation of two frequency distributions. In this section we consider how to model dependency between the annual loss distributions, rather than just the dependency between loss frequencies. It should be noted that loss severities may also be codependent, since operational loss amounts can be affected by the same macroeconomic variable (e.g. an exchange rate).

It should also be noted that the most important dependency is not the dependency between one operational loss and another – it is between the costs and revenues of a particular activity. Operational risks are mostly on the cost side, whereas the revenue side is associated with market and/or credit risks. In fact vertical dependencies, between a given operational risk and the market and/or credit risks associated with that activity, are much the most important dependencies to account for when estimating the total risk of the bank. The effect of accounting for dependencies between different operational risks will be substantial, as shown in Example 7.6 below. However, this effect will be marginal compared to the effect of accounting for dependencies between operational, market and credit risks. Indeed, from the point of view of economic capital within the enterprise-wide framework, Section 4.3 shows that operational risks should be negligible compared with the other two risks, unless one needs to consider extremely rare, large-impact events.

7.7.3 The aggregation algorithm

We now consider how the distribution of the total annual loss is obtained from the distributions of individual annual losses. The method proposed here is to sum losses in pairs where, for each pair, a *copula* is chosen to define a suitable dependency structure. Some details on copulas are given in Appendix 7.1. The algorithm consists of two steps, which are first explained for aggregating two annual losses X and Y. Then we comment on the extension of the algorithm to more than two annual losses.

(a) Find the joint density $h(x, y)$ given the marginal densities $f(x)$ and $g(y)$ and a given dependency structure. If X and Y are independent then $h(x, y) = f(x)g(y)$. When they are not independent, and their dependency is captured by a copula, then

$$h(x,y) = f(x)g(y)c(x,y), \tag{7.16}$$

where $c(x,y)$ is the probability density function of the copula.

(b) Derive the distribution of the sum $X + Y$ from the joint density $h(x, y)$. Let $Z = X + Y$. Then the probability density of Z is the 'convolution sum'

$$k(z) = \sum_x h(x, z - x) = \sum_y h(z - y, y)$$

if $h(x,y)$ is discrete, or the 'convolution integral'

$$k(z) = \int_x h(x, z - x)dx = \int_y h(z - y, y)dy$$

if $h(x, y)$ is continuous.

Now suppose there are three annual losses X, Y and Z, with densities $f_1(x)$, $f_2(y)$ and $f_3(z)$, and suppose that X and Y have a positive dependency but Z is independent of both of these. Then we aggregate in pairs as follows:

1 Using $f_1(x)$ and $f_2(y)$, we obtain the joint density $h_1(x, y)$ of X and Y, and this requires the use of a copula that captures the positive dependency between X and Y.

2 Then we use 'convolution' on $h_1(x, y)$ to calculate the density $k(w)$ of $W = X + Y$.

3 By independence the joint density of W and Z is $h_2(w,z) = k(w)f_3(z)$.

4 Using the convolution on $h_2(w, z)$, we obtain the density of the sum $X + Y + Z$.

The algorithm can be applied to find the sum of any number of random variables: if we denote by X_{ij} the random variable that is the annual loss of business line i and risk type j, the total annual loss has the density of the random variable $X = \Sigma X_{ij}$. The distribution of X is obtained by first using steps (a) and (b) of the algorithm to obtain the distribution of $X_{11} + X_{12} = Y_1$, say, then these steps are repeated to obtain the distribution of $Y_1 + X_{13} = Y_2$, and so on.

7.7.4 Aggregation of annual loss distributions under different dependency assumptions

The above has shown that dependency structures that are more general than correlation may also be used for aggregating distributions, simply by choosing the appropriate copula to generate the joint density in (7.16). A good approximation to the joint density is

$$h(x,y) = f(x)\,g(y)\,c(J_1(x),J_2(y))$$

where the standard normal variables J_1 and J_2 are defined by

$$J_1(x) = \Phi^{-1}(F(x)) \text{ and } J_2(y) = \Phi^{-1}(G(x)),$$

where Φ is the standard normal distribution function, F and G are the distribution functions of X and Y and $c(J_1(x),J_2(y))$ is

$$\exp\{-[J_1(x)^2 + J_2(y)^2 - 2\rho J_1(x)J_2(y)]/2(1-\rho^2)\}\exp\{[J_1(x)^2 + J_2(y)^2]/2\}/\sqrt{(1-\rho^2)}. \quad (7.17)$$

This is the density of the Gaussian copula given in Appendix 7.1.[13] The Gaussian copula can capture positive, negative or zero correlation between X and Y. In the case of zero correlation $c(J_1(x),J_2(y)) = 1$ for all x and y. Note that annual losses do not need to be normally distributed for us to aggregate them using the Gaussian copula. However, a limitation of the Gaussian copula is that dependence is determined by correlation and is therefore symmetric.

Many other copulas are available for dependency structures that are more general than correlation, as described in Appendix 7.1. For example, a useful copula for capturing asymmetric tail dependence is the Gumbel copula, which can be parameterized in two ways: see (v) and (vi) in the Appendix 7.1. For the Gumbel δ copula function we can write $u = F(x)$ and $v = G(y)$ to express the copula density as

$$\exp(-((-\ln u)^\delta + (-\ln v)^\delta)^{1/\delta})(((-\ln u)^\delta + (-\ln v)^\delta)^{1/\delta} + \delta - 1)(\ln u \ln v)^{\delta-1}(uv)^{-1}((-\ln u)^\delta + (-\ln v)^\delta)^{(1/\delta)-2}. \quad (7.18)$$

Similarly, for the Gumbel α copula the density is given by

$$\exp(-\alpha(\ln u \ln v/\ln(uv)))[(1 - \alpha\,(\ln u/\ln(uv))^2)(1 - \alpha\,(\ln v/\ln(uv))^2) - 2\,\alpha \ln u \ln v/(\ln(uv))^3)]. \quad (7.19)$$

Example 7.6 illustrates the aggregation algorithm of Section 7.7.3 using the Gaussian and Gumbel copulas.

[13] This was first shown by Nataf (1962), and Mardia (1970) provides sufficient conditions for $h(x,y)$ to be a joint density function when $c(J_1(x),J_2(y))$ is given by (7.17).

┌─ **EXAMPLE** **7.6**

Aggregation using the Gaussian and Gumbel copulas

Consider the two annual loss distributions with density functions shown in Figure 7.8. For illustrative purposes, the bimodal density has been fitted by a mixture of two normal densities: with probability 0.3 the normal has mean 14 and standard deviation 2.5 and with probability 0.7 the normal has mean 6 and standard deviation 2. The other annual loss is gamma-distributed with $\alpha = 7$ and $\beta = 2$.

Figure 7.9 illustrates step (a) of the aggregation algorithm. The joint densities shown in Figure 7.9(a) have been obtained using the Gaussian copula (7.17), and with $\rho = 0.5, 0, -0.5$, respectively; those in Figure 7.9(b) have been obtained with the Gumbel δ copula (7.18) with $\delta = 2$ and the Gumbel α copula (7.19) with $\alpha = 0.5$.

Figure 7.10 illustrates step (b) of the aggregation algorithm, when convolution is used on the joint densities in Figure 7.9 to obtain the density of the sum of the two random variables. Figure 7.10(a) shows the density of the sum in each of the three cases for the Gaussian copula, according as $\rho = 0.5, 0, -0.5$, and Figure 7.10(b) shows the density of the sum under the Gumbel copulas for $\delta = 2$ and $\alpha = 0.5$, respectively. Note that $\delta = 1$, $\rho = 0$ and $\alpha = 0$ all give the same copula – the independent copula.

The table on page 164 summarizes the densities shown in Figure 7.10. Note that the mean (expected loss) is approximately 22.4 in each case. However, the unexpected loss at the 99.9th percentile[14] is very much affected by the assumption one makes about dependency.

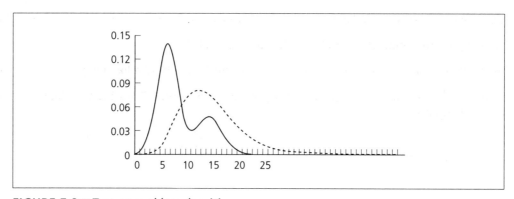

FIGURE 7.8 ■ Two annual loss densities

....

[14] And also at the 99th percentile, though this is not reported.

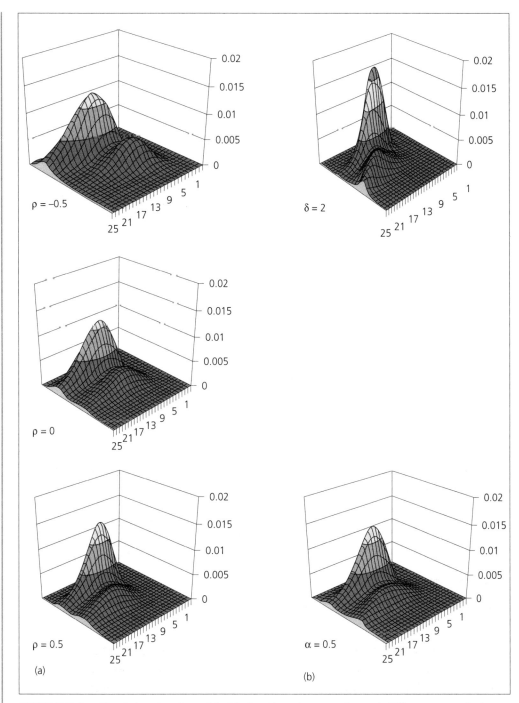

FIGURE 7.9 ■ The joint density with (a) the Gaussian copula and different correlation assumptions; and (b) the Gumbel copula and different dependency assumptions

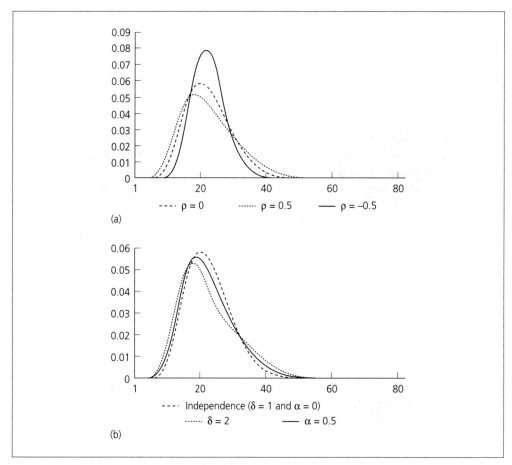

FIGURE 7.10 ■ The total loss distribution with (a) the Gaussian copula and different correlation assumptions; and (b) the Gumbel α and δ copulas

	$\rho = -0.5$	$\rho = 0$	$\rho = 0.5$	$\delta = 2$	$\alpha = 0.5$
Expected loss	22.3909	22.3951	22.3977	22.3959	22.3977
99.9th percentile	41.7658	48.7665	54.1660	54.9715	57.6023
Unexpected loss	**19.3749**	**26.3714**	**31.7683**	**32.5755**	**35.2046**

In this example the total unexpected loss at the 99.9th percentile could be as small as 19.37 (assuming correlation as the dependence measure, with the Gaussian copula and $\rho = -0.5$) or as large as 35.2 (assuming asymmetric upper tail dependence with a Gumbel α copula and $\alpha = 0.5$).

The values of the dependence parameters were chosen arbitrarily in this example. Nevertheless, it has shown that changes in the dependency assumption can produce estimates of unexpected total loss that are doubled – or halved – even when aggregating only two annual loss distributions. Obviously the effect of dependency assumptions on the aggregation of many annual loss distributions to the total annual loss for the firm will be quite enormous.

7.7.5 Specifying dependencies

How should a bank specify the dependence structure between different operational risks? If it seeks to include correlations in the (IMA) analytic approximation to unexpected loss, then it needs a correlation matrix V between all the different operational risks that it faces, over all business lines and risk types. Given the remarks already made about correlations of operational risks, attempting to calibrate such a matrix to any sort of data would be very misleading indeed.

A more realistic exercise is to link the dependencies between operational risks to the likely movements in common attributes. The concept of a 'key risk driver' is introduced in this book as a fundamental tool for operational risk management (see Sections 12.4.4 and 13.9 and Chapter 14). Examples of key risk drivers are volume of transactions processed, product complexity, and staffing (decision) variables such as pay, training and recruitment. Central to the ideas in Chapters 12, 13 and 14, and illustrated in the example below, is the assumption that common risk drivers may be linked to the dependencies between operational risks. Rather than attempting to specify a correlation between each and every operational risk, over all business lines and risk types, a better alternative approach is to examine the impact that likely changes in key risk drivers will have upon the key risk indicators of different categories of operational risks.

Knowing the management policies that are targeted for the next year, a bank should identify the likely changes in key risk drivers resulting from these management decisions. In this way the probable dependence structures across different risk types and lines of business can be identified. For example, suppose two operational risks are thought to be positively dependent because the same risk drivers tend to increase both of these risks and the same risk drivers tend to decrease both of these risks. In that case we should use a copula with positive dependency for aggregating to the total annual loss distribution. We further these ideas by example. Table 7.6 considers the impact of three management policies on the seven risk types that are defined by the Basel Committee, for a fixed line of business. The entries +, 0 , – imply that the policy is likely to increase, have no effect on, or decrease the operational risk.

If a bank were to rationalize the back office with many people being made redundant, this would affect risk drivers such as transactions volume, staff levels, skill levels and so forth. The consequent difficulties with terminations, employee relations and possible discriminatory actions would increase the employment practices and workplace safety risk. The reduction in personnel in the back office could lead to an increased risk of internal and external fraud, since fewer checks would be made on transactions, and there may be

TABLE 7.6 ■ Dependence between operational risks

Risk	Downsizing of back office personnel	Expansion of business in complex products	Outsource and improve systems and IT	Overall effect
1. Internal fraud	+	+	−	+
2. External fraud	+	0	−	0
3. Employment practices and workplace safety	+	0	+	+
4. Clients, products and business practices	0	+	0	+
5. Damage to physical assets	0	0	0	0
6. Business disruption and system failures	0	+	−	0
7. Execution, delivery and process management	+	+	+	+

more errors in execution, delivery and process management. The other risk types are likely to be unaffected.

Suppose the bank expands its business in complex products, perhaps introducing a new team of quantitative analysts. Internal fraud could become more likely and potentially more severe. Model errors, product defects, aggressive selling and other risk indicators in the clients, products and business practices category may increase in both frequency and severity. Business disruption and system failures will become more likely with the new and more complex systems. Finally there are many ways in which execution, delivery and process management risk would increase, including less adequate documentation, more communication errors and collateral management failures.

Finally, suppose the bank decides to outsource its systems and IT, hopefully to improve them. This should have a positive effect on systems downtime, so business disruption and system failures should become less risky. IT skill levels should be increased so internal fraud and external fraud would become more difficult. But this policy could increase risk in execution, delivery and process management, due to communications problems with an external firm having different systems. Also there would be a negative effect on staff levels, and termination of contracts with the present IT and systems personnel may lead to employee relations difficulties and thus increase the employment practices and workplace safety risk.

It may be that these three policies are only some of those under consideration by management, but if they are the only foreseeable changes in management due for implementation during the next year, the likely net effect is shown in the last column of Table 7.6. This would imply that, for aggregating risks 1, 3, 4 and 7, copulas with positive dependence should be used. The weaker the codependency denoted by the + sign in the last column of Table 7.6, the smaller the value of the dependency parameter. Then to aggregate these with the other risks, an independence assumption for the joint densities would be appropriate.

An advantage of this methodology is that operational risk capital and operational risk dependence can be assessed at the scenario level. That is, management may ask 'What would be the net effect on operational risk capital, if a key risk driver (e.g. product complexity) is increased?'. Thus it provides a means whereby the economic capital and the minimum regulatory capital requirement for the bank can be assessed under different management policies.

7.8 Conclusion

The main focus of this chapter has been to give a pedagogical introduction to the statistical/actuarial approach of modelling frequency and severity distributions, with many illustrative examples. From the outset, Bayesian estimation methods are shown to be the natural approach to operational loss parameter estimation, rather than maximum likelihood or other classical techniques such as method-of-moments estimation. This is because of the high level of subjectivity in operational loss data, whether it be from scorecards or from an external data consortium. We have shown how to obtain Bayesian estimates of loss probabilities, and of loss severity means and standard deviations, and we have considered the effect on capital charges of using Bayesian rather than classical estimation.

This chapter has examined the advanced measurement approach that has been suggested by BCBS (2001b) in much detail. In contrast to the impression given by the Basel Committee, there is really only one approach to estimating operational risk, and that is the actuarial approach. That is, the foundation of any advanced measurement model rests on the compounding of frequency and severity distributions. An example is given to show that the analytic approximation to unexpected loss (the IMA formula) is very close to the unexpected loss that is estimated by simulating the annual loss distribution (the LDA method). A useful reference table of the Basel 'gamma' factors has been provided, and various extensions of the basic IMA formula have been derived.

An important consequence of the analysis in Section 7.5 is that the inclusion of loss severity variability will always increase the total unexpected loss for a given risk type and line of business. Therefore, compared with the basic IMA, capital charges will always be greater when based on the general 'IMA' formula, *and* when based on the LDA. The only possibility to obtain a lower overall capital charge with the LDA is to have significant negative dependencies when aggregating.

We have explained how to use copulas for aggregating operational risks and have shown how the correlation – or, more generally, the codependency – between operational risks will have a great impact on the aggregate unexpected loss. Even with just two operational risks, the estimate of unexpected total loss can be doubled when moving from an assumed correlation of –0.5 to an assumed correlation of 0.5! Throughout this chapter we have commented that it is misguided to use the 99.9th percentile to estimate operational risk, given the uncertainty about the form of frequency and severity distributions, the subjectivity of data, the imprecision of parameter estimates and, most of all, the difficulty in capturing their dependencies when aggregating to the total loss distribution.

Appendix 7.1 Some remarks on the use of copulas in operational risk

Copulas have long been recognized as a powerful tool for modelling dependence between random variables. Recently, they have received much attention in finance, with applications to all areas of market and credit risk, including option pricing and portfolio models of defaults. The concept of a copula is not new in statistics, indeed it goes back at least to Schweizer and Sklar (1958).

A copula is just an expression for a multivariate distribution in terms of the marginal distributions. By choosing a copula that has the dependence structure that is thought to be appropriate, two (or more) distributions may be combined to obtain a joint distribution with the required dependence structure.

For example, if two risks X and Y have marginal distribution functions $F(x)$ and $G(y)$ and the copula is $C(\cdot,\cdot)$ then the joint distribution is

$$H(x, y) = C(F(x), G(y)) \tag{7.20}$$

and the joint density $h(x,y) = \partial^2 H(x,y)/\partial x \partial y$ is

$$h(x, y) = f(x)g(y)c(x,y), \tag{7.21}$$

where $f(x)$ and $g(x)$ are the marginal density functions of X and Y and $c(x, y)$ is the probability density function of the copula, given by

$$c(x, y) = \frac{\partial^2 C(F(x), G(y))}{\partial F(x) \partial G(y)}.$$

More generally, a copula is a function of several variables: in fact it is a multivariate uniform distribution function. If $u_1, \dots, u_n$ are values of n univariate distribution functions (so each $u_i \in [0, 1]$) then a copula is a function $C(u_1, \dots, u_n) \rightarrow [0, 1]$. Copulas are unique, so for any given multivariate distribution (with continuous marginal distributions) there is a unique copula that represents it. They are also invariant under strictly increasing transformations of the marginal distributions.

Here are some simple examples of copulas:

(i) $C(u_1, \ldots, u_n) = u_1 u_2 \ldots u_n;$

(ii) $C(u_1, \ldots, u_n) = \min(u_1, \ldots, u_n);$

(iii) $C(u_1, \ldots, u_n) = \max\left(\sum_{i=1}^{n} u_i - (n-1), 0\right).$

Copula (i) corresponds to the case that the random variables are independent: the joint density will be the product of the marginals. Copula (ii) corresponds to counter-monotonic dependency and copula (iii) corresponds to co-monotonic dependency.[15] Note that copulas (i)–(iii) have no parameters and do not allow for much flexibility in the dependence structure. They are useful in so far as they provide upper and lower bounds for the joint distributions that are obtained from more flexible copulas.

The following copulas have many financial applications.[16] They have a single parameter that determines the dependence structure and are stated in bivariate form, with variables u and v rather than $u_1, \ldots, u_n$. The extension to the multivariate case should be obvious:

(iv) Gaussian copula: $C(u, v) = \Phi_\rho(\Phi^{-1}(u), \Phi^{-1}(v))$, where Φ_ρ is the bivariate normal distribution with correlation ρ and Φ is the standard normal distribution function.

(v) Gumbel δ copula with $\delta \in [1, \infty) : C(u, v) = \exp(-((-\ln u)^\delta + (-\ln v)^\delta)^{1/\delta}).$

(vi) Gumbel α copula with $\alpha \in [0,1] : C(u, v) = uv \exp((\alpha \ln u \ln v)/(\ln uv)).$

(vii) Frank copula: $C(u, v) = [\ln\{1 - \exp(\delta) - (1 - \exp(\delta u))(1 - \exp(\delta v))\} - \ln\{1 - \exp(\delta)\}]/\delta.$

Malevergne and Sornette (2001) show that the Gaussian copula can underestimate tail dependencies amongst certain financial assets; this may also be the case for operational losses. The Frank copula would only be appropriate if dependencies were symmetric (positive when δ is negative and negative when δ is positive). However, operational losses are likely to have greater dependency in the upper tail. When tail dependence is asymmetric the Gumbel copula is more appropriate than either the Gaussian or the Frank copulas. In the Gumbel copulas there is greater dependence in the upper tails, and therefore these are likely to be most appropriate for operational risks. In the Gumbel δ copula there is increasing positive dependence as δ increases and less dependence as δ decreases towards 1 (the case $\delta = 1$ corresponds to independence). In the Gumbel α copula there is increasing positive dependence as α increases and less dependence as α decreases towards 0 (the case $\alpha = 0$ corresponds to independence). Many other copulas have been formulated, some of

---

[15] Two random variables X_1 and X_2 are 'counter-monotonic' if there is another random variable X such that X_1 is a decreasing transformation of X and X_2 is an increasing transformation of X. If they are both increasing (or decreasing) transformations of X then X_1 and X_2 are called 'co-monotonic'. (Note that the transformations do not have to be *strictly* increasing or decreasing.)

[16] See, for example, Blum *et al*. (2002); Embrechts *et al*. (2002), Bouyé *et al*. (2000) and http://gro.creditlyonnais.fr/content/rd/home_copulas.htm

which have many parameters to capture more than one type of de pendence. For example, a copula may have one parameter to model the dependency in the tails, and another to model dependency in the centre. More details may be found in Bouyé *et al*. (2000) and Nelsen (1999).

CHAPTER 8

The Loss Distribution Approach

Michael Haubenstock and Lloyd Hardin

8.1 What is the Loss Distribution Approach?

The latest proposals from the Basel Committee on Banking Supervision (BCBS 2001b, 2002b) state that the most advanced approach to quantifying operational risk, the Advanced Measurement Approach, permits institutions to base their capital charge on their own internal models. One of the alternatives is called the Loss Distribution Approach (LDA), where capital calculations are based on a historical database of operational loss events. In this chapter we describe the challenges to using this approach and illustrate a practical solution.

The Basel Committee has defined the LDA as an estimate of the distribution of operational risk losses for each business line/event type, based on assumptions of frequency and severity of events. These assumptions are derived primarily from a history of internal loss events. Calculations assume a future time horizon and level of confidence. The difference between LDA and the Internal Measurement Approach is that LDA estimates unexpected losses directly, without an assumption about the ratio between expected and unexpected losses.

Statistical approaches to quantification of operational risk are clearly the trend among banks that are developing ways of measuring operational risk capital. They can be implemented in two ways: bottom-up or top-down. The bottom-up approach is based on an analysis of loss events in individual business processes and tries to identify and quantify each type of risk at that level. This contrasts with the top-down approach which calculates a capital number at the firm level and then attempts to allocate it down to the businesses, often using a proxy such as expenses or a scorecard approach. Both top-down and bottom-up approaches can rely on historical data as the basis for quantification.

Because of the high degree of subjectivity in the allocation process, and given the lack of a good risk proxy across businesses, bottom-up methods are clearly preferred for capital allocation. Top-down methodologies may be preferable in the short term when there are insufficient data to derive results on a bottom-up basis with a high level of confidence in the results. The two approaches should result in the same amount of total capital, but results at the business line level could vary substantially.

The Basel Committee has proposed that users of the LDA (or other advanced measurement approaches) be eligible for a calculated capital charge with no mandatory floor capital requirement. A key question is whether LDA will result in a lower capital charge. That is a question that cannot be answered generically, since the results will vary by institution. The whole idea of the LDA is that the results are based on historical data, unique to any one institution. Therefore, theoretically, the results can be higher or lower than any specific formula in the Basic Indicator or Standardized Approach. However, our experience in modelling across a range of institutions shows that the results are significantly lower than the Basic or Standardized Approach. Well-managed institutions, and particularly large ones, without a history of repeated large events should find that their investment in data collection and capital methodologies will be well justified with accuracy and a lower regulatory capital charge.

8.2 Basel requirements

The Basel Committee has defined general criteria for institutions to qualify for using any advanced measurement approach, including the LDA. Ultimately, each local regulator will need to approve each model. There are numerous qualitative criteria that need to be satisfied. Most of these qualitative criteria are described and discussed in Chapters 2, 4 and 12. The relevant quantitative criteria that will be discussed in this chapter are:

- *Capturing infrequent but severe events*. The methodology must consider rare events that might not be reflected in the internal loss history of any one institution.

- *Five years of loss data*. Sufficient history must be present to give reasonable confidence of a complete loss distribution. Three years of data may be considered for a transition period.

- *Disciplined override process*. If, for any reason, any of the historical data points are deleted from the data set, there should be a sound reason, documentation and approval process to ensure objectivity in the results.

- *Extensive stress and scenario testing*. This should test the sensitivity to the underlying assumptions and parameters and ensure the adequacy of the overall model results.

- *Disciplined incorporation of external data*. Data from other firms are necessary to understand the full extent of the tails of the distributions. Internal and external data should be combined only in statistically valid ways. Scaling criteria must be defined.

- *99.9 percent level of confidence and one-year holding period*. This implies a statistical framework where the level of confidence and holding period are direct inputs into the approach.

- *Correlations may be taken into account*. Systems for measuring correlations have to be sound and incorporated with integrity.

- *Benefits of insurance may be considered*. The methodology to quantify the benefit of insurance must be well documented and subject to review.

- *Qualitative adjustments are permitted*. The institution would need standards to address the structure, comprehensiveness and rigour of the adjustments.

8.3 Why use historical loss data?

The LDA relies on internal data to capture the unique attributes of each entity. Every business within each institution has its own risk profile. This risk profile is based on inherent risks (e.g. product type, complexity and legal environment) and controls (e.g. culture, systems, internal controls, and policies). Since each institution is unique, the only way to quantify its risk profile is by examining its actual loss experience. Historical loss data represent the net risk between inherent risk and existing controls.

Operational risk capital is driven by the so-called tail events: the low-frequency, high-severity events that can endanger the health of an institution. These events are very rare; therefore, even if an institution were to collect data over a period of years, one could never be sure that there were sufficient losses to accurately measure the shape of the tail of the severity distribution.

For these reasons, external data (events from other institutions) help us understand the tails of the distributions and provide insight into risks where there are insufficient internal data to directly quantify the risk.[1] There are two sources of external data: public loss data and consortium data. Today, the only source that is readily available is public loss data – events extracted from the press. Consortium data rely on institutions compiling their internal data and sharing them through a custodian. Consortium initiatives are still in the formative stages, and comprehensive data sufficient for modelling capital will not be available for some time. We will discuss how internal and external data can be combined in a statistically valid manner. The resulting distributions will reflect the full range of potential results.

Statistical/actuarial approaches create many challenges for the user. The key ones are as follows:

- How large a corpus of internal loss data is necessary in order to develop a risk profile for a business line or an institution?

- How can risks be accurately estimated with external data when sufficient internal data do not exist, even when all publicly available data sets are known to be severely biased? Should external data be scaled?

---

[1] The OpVar external database offered by OpVantage (www.opvantage.com) is one source; another is the ORX consortium (www.orx.org).

- How can you combine internal data and external data in a statistically valid manner, particularly when it is unlikely that any firm whose losses are included in any external data set will have the same risk profile as the institution being modelled?

- How do you fit loss data to a distribution, particularly when the data are not collected from a zero loss level (for practical reasons all loss data are collected above a threshold level, e.g. $5000)?

- How are loss frequencies estimated, especially when data are collected from different sources over different time periods and with different threshold levels?

- How can results be mathematically backtested?

We will provide the insight needed to meet these challenges in the steps and case study that follow.

8.4 Steps to modelling with LDA

There is currently no standard or regulatory approved methodology for the LDA. The steps in a typical approach are summarized in Figure 8.1.

8.4.1 Determining the rules and parameters

One has to set up the parameters for the LDA calculation. The primary variables are as follows:

(a) *Organization chart*. Each organization component for which capital will be estimated will be defined. Typically, these are the profit and loss units of the bank to be assigned capital. An LDA model will usually be limited to one or two levels below the consolidated entity. Further detail tends to dilute the data availability to the point where direct modelling is not feasible. Care should be taken to define organization units for corporate centres and service areas (e.g. information technology and shared back office), as capital might be modelled for these units and the results allocated to the business units. Corporate centres will also benefit from their own data for operational risk analysis purposes.

(b) *Establish categorization*. Events are grouped for the purpose of analysis. For illustration, we will use the Basel event categories. Events are quantified according to specified rules regarding what operational risks are and how to quantify them. The cost of any one loss, or event, is the sum of the various effects that can be measured.

(c) *Modelling parameters*. Input parameters typically include the desired level of confidence, time horizon and correlation assumptions. Basel has proposed a level of confidence of 99.9 percent and a one-year time horizon. Economic capital models often use a level of confidence consistent with the desired debt rating – for example, 99.97 percent.

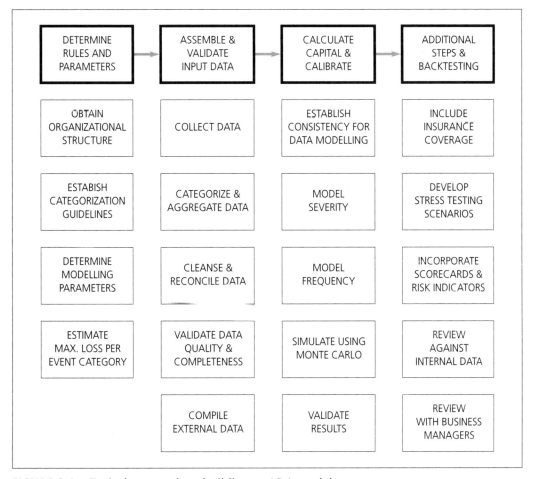

FIGURE 8.1 ■ Typical approach to building an LDA model

(d) *Maximum loss per event category*. Severity distributions have no theoretical maximum, a phenomenon that can lead to some instability in the model. It is helpful to assign a maximum loss that can occur for each type of risk. This is usually set very conservatively based on worst-case losses that have occurred in the industry, and considering a firm's size and country characteristics.

8.4.2 Assemble and validate input data

The basis for the LDA approach is the use of historical operational risk losses from within the target institution and from other firms. There may be many sources throughout the institution where these losses are being collected. For purposes of this chapter, it is assumed that these sources have been identified.

Firstly, the internal data are collected, categorized, aggregated, cleansed and reconciled. This is one of the most important and most frequently underestimated steps in the quantification procedure. In practice, there are typically numerous places in an organization that have procedures for collecting loss events that fall into the operational risk definition. Examples might include legal, human resources, credit card fraud detection and internal audit. Care should be taken to eliminate duplicates, understand the varying thresholds and procedures that were used to accumulate the data at each source and obtain any missing information that is necessary in the loss database and necessary for modelling (e.g. business responsible, date of write-off, event category). Also, steps should be taken to verify that events are truly operational risk events, that they are finalized and that the recoveries are properly quantified.

The next step is to validate the quality of the data. Quantity of data is often cited as the major limiting factor in the calculation of operational risk. A review of the extent of the data capture will provide guidance as to whether more research might be necessary, or what types of qualitative judgement could be required to supplement the data set. An examination of the consistency of number of events by time period, the 'smoothness' of the severity distribution, the lower and upper truncation points in the data, and the relative number of data points by business line and event category is a good start. Also, it is a good idea to look for any noticeable trends, spikes or gaps in the loss data.

External data must also be compiled. It will be assumed in this case that a public database is being used, as described earlier. External data should be organized by risk category within business line, structured similarly to the target organization. It is frequently the case that the standard business lines used in external data do not align with the internal organization structure. In this case the best match can be selected, or alternatively a weighted mixture of the data distributions from two or more standard business lines. The amount of available external data should also be analyzed. There is always a choice of using data from similar business lines, only selected other firms considered as peers, all financial services, or data from across industries. If there is sufficient data, a smaller, more comparable data set is the intuitive choice. Surprisingly, experience shows that for most risks the resulting distributions are not very different in a larger data set, even across industries. The greater the amount of data, the more stable the results. Another consideration arises if for any reason the external data include risks that may not be relevant for any one firm. It is worth the investment in time to consider the underlying legal environment and business characteristics to determine if any events are simply not applicable, or the results should be qualitatively modified.

8.4.3 Calculate capital and calibrate

Once the input into the model has been sufficiently vetted and understood, the severity, frequency and aggregate distributions can be constructed.

(a) *Establish a consistent basis for the data to be modelled*. For a bottom-up approach, it is common to calculate capital at the intersection of a business unit and event category, following internal definitions or those proposed in BCBS (2001b) – see Table 7.2. Automated tools that allow for 'slicing and dicing' aid in this process.

(b) *Model severity*. The purpose of this step is to approximate, given a loss occurs, the probabilities of the potential amount of the loss. In order to estimate the rare but extremely costly losses, one popular technique is to fit a curve to the available data in order to model the entire range of loss amounts that might be incurred. This approach is used to level out the irregularities in the raw experience data, and it successfully provides a means by which to estimate the risk of tail events beyond the largest observed event. In our example, we will use the maximum likelihood estimation (MLE) technique to fit several different types of distributions and use statistical tests to validate how well the different distributions fit the data. Typically, the introduction of a relatively large loss into the data set will not dramatically alter the distribution. A major question that often arises is what can be done if no distribution fits the data well (usually because of insufficient data). This is a complex problem where experience counts. Alternatives include using information about losses that were collected from public sources (i.e. external data), qualitatively estimating potential loss scenarios or distributions, or using data that similar institutions have collected (e.g. loss data consortia).

(c) *Model frequency*. A *de facto* standard is to assume that the frequency of losses follows a Poisson distribution, whose density is given in (7.4). The single parameter of the Poisson distribution is the average frequency of events that have occurred over a particular holding period (e.g. one year). Actual data can be adjusted for any trends that have been discovered and for issues with data capture. A negative binomial distribution, which is defined in (7.5), is also a common and possibly more conservative choice for modelling the frequency of operational risk events.

(d) *Monte Carlo simulation*. The simulation across the frequency and severity distribution will produce a total loss distribution for the selected data (e.g. an event category within a business unit) over the time horizon specified. From the total loss distribution, a mean annual loss and an annual loss at a particular confidence level can be calculated. The difference between these two numbers would be the amount of capital necessary to protect the business unit from the estimated event type. This is repeated for every risk within each business line. In order to calculate diversification and correlation effects, we can include all of the modelled cells into a combined simulation model to obtain an aggregate total loss distribution for the entire firm. Event categories are assumed to be independent of each other; therefore, one simulation per risk category for each business unit will be calculated. The value at risk (VaR) produced for the firm, in total, will incorporate diversification benefits (i.e. the worst loss will not always happen simultaneously in each business unit for every event category). If there is a belief in specific correlation of risks between business units and/or event types, those correlation assumptions can be applied by using copulas, as described in Section 7.7.

(e) *Validating results*. In order to gauge the soundness of this process, each modelled risk should be reviewed for its reasonableness. Does the average loss of the simulation match recent experience? Do various confidence levels match intuition (e.g. worst year out of 10, out of 50, out of 100)? Is the 99.9 percent confidence level of the same order of magnitude as worst-case external losses for similar businesses and risk event types? The firm-wide simulated means and VaR should be compared with actual historical experience in a fashion similar to that of the individual risk validations described above.

8.4.4 Additional steps

(a) *Modelling insurance coverage*. The impact of actual insurance policies in force can be estimated directly by altering the severity distributions and expanding the simulation model. The steps are:

- Obtain insurance policy information. Institutions typically have numerous traditional insurance products whose coverage spans business units and event categories.

- Map insurance policies to those areas for which a capital calculation is feasible and desired. Typically, this would be by major line of business and event or risk category (e.g. investment banking and criminal).

- Record the minimum coverage (attachment point) and maximum coverage.

- Assess the level of risk coverage against the definitions of operational risk. Frequently, many of the risks included in the definition will not be directly covered. The result is a probability of recovery from insurance.

- Rerun the simulation taking the risk transfer into effect. Assess the impact on expected and unexpected loss.

(b) *Develop scenarios for stress testing*. Many assumptions about severity, frequency, insurance and correlations are inherent in the process. Given the quality of internal loss event data and the typically high level of confidence at which capital is being calculated, each one of the major assumptions should be challenged. By varying the assumptions, the boundaries of the potential results can be discovered, thereby leading to further scrutiny of the key drivers of the variability in the calculated numbers.

(c) *Incorporating scorecards and risk indicators*. The above process is an objective statistical process based on historical loss data. An important criterion for any capital model is that the results can change to reflect changes in the control environment. Therefore, we usually include qualitative adjustments to the capital calculations based on some combination of qualitative assessments, risk indicators and audit results. These are weighted and combined into a score that can be used as the basis for modifying the results.

8.5 Case study

In this case study the generic steps discussed in the previous section will be illustrated with actual data. All of the information used in the case study is actual operational loss data from a financial institution, but modified to ensure confidentiality. The case will illustrate how to calculate the operational risk regulatory minimum capital requirement, and internal economic capital, using the LDA approach for a retail banking business.

8.5.1 Determine rules and validate input data

Determine rules and parameters

Following the guidelines given in BCBS (2001b) we use a 99.9 percent level of confidence and a one-year time horizon. We will also assume independence across risk categories. For comparison purposes and internal economic capital, we will also estimate capital at the 99.97 percent level. We will use the Basel event and effect definitions for categorization.

Assemble and validate input data

The collection process covered multiple sources of data across different risk categories. Some events had to be manually input into the database, others were collected in spreadsheets, and some were retrieved as feeds from existing bank systems.

Once the data were collected, they had to be validated. To verify the accuracy of the aggregation process into the central database, the number of data points entered was checked against the number from each source, the total amount in the database was compared to the total amount from each source, and a search was performed to eliminate duplicates. (Note that depending on the type of database used to collect the data, some validation steps can be automated to save considerable time.) In addition to these validation steps, the data were reviewed to ensure accurate categorization. This process is invaluable in understanding the underlying data, and therefore the final results.

Furthermore, a series of histograms was generated to analyze the quality of the data and highlight potential errors. Figure 8.2 shows events by amount bucket on a logarithmic scale, because they are so different. It can be used to assess if data collection was thorough, if it follows expected patterns, and if it contains relevant tail events. Also, this histogram was used to identify the minimum threshold for which the data were collected. It is apparent from the histogram that loss data were not collected below $2000, already a very low truncation point for operational risk data.

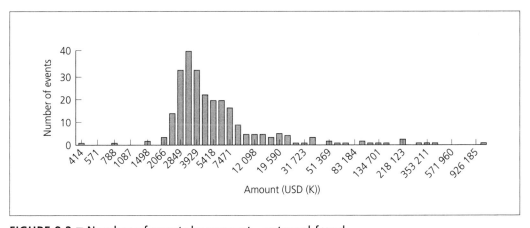

FIGURE 8.2 ■ Number of events by amount – external fraud

Another type of histogram that contributes to understanding the collected data is one that shows the distribution of events over time. Figure 8.3 shows that the collection effort for this category was fairly uniform over time, with a slight increase in recent quarters. Figure 8.4 shows that this might not always be the case and that an adjustment must be made to account for this inconsistency. In this case, only the most recent data may be relevant. These charts are particularly valuable to determine how far back data are available to model severity, as well as what data can provide reliable information to create an average number of events per year, information needed for the frequency distribution.

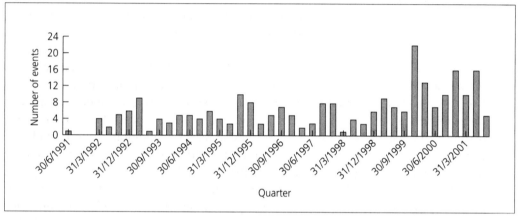

FIGURE 8.3 ■ Number of loss events over time–external fraud

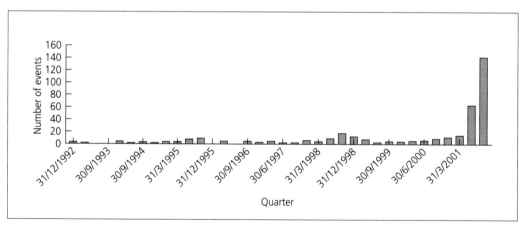

FIGURE 8.4 ■ Number of events over time–clients, products and business practices

8.5.2 Calculate capital and calibrate

In Section 8.5.1 we concentrated on validating and understanding the data. In this section we will detail each step to calculate capital from this data for retail banking. The first step in calculating operational risk capital is to determine the frequency and severity distributions for each of the risk categories within the business unit. As will be seen in the example, the data collected internally are not always sufficient, in which case we will rely on the external data to determine the risk of certain risk categories.

Establishing a consistent basis for the data to be modelled

The first step in the calculation process is to determine where there are sufficient data to model risk using the internal data. Table 8.1 shows summary statistics for the selected business unit by event category. Usually, when there are over 100 events, including some very large events (tail events), there are sufficient data to directly model the risk. The table shows that the external fraud, client and products, and execution categories could potentially have enough data to model. We call these 'anchor cells'.

Model severity

Next, we use the MLE technique to derive the severity distributions that best fit the collected data. Figure 8.5 shows an example using the data from the clients, products and business practices event category. We fit several curves to the data using MLE and statistical tests to determine which curve best fits the data.

For ease of calculation, the loss amounts were converted to natural log terms before the curves were fitted. The bars graph the underlying observations; the superimposed curves are the fitted distributions. The dotted line curve is a normal distribution, and the solid line is a mixture distribution. This mixture distribution is a gamma normal distribution, also referred to as fat-tailed normal (note: since the underlying data were converted to logs, the fitted distributions will be lognormal, and fat-tail lognormal).

TABLE 8.1 ■ Summary statistics for retail banking

	Internal fraud	External fraud	Employment practice	Clients, products and business practices	Damage to physical assets	Business disruption and system failures	Execution, delivery and process	Total
No. of events	45	148	2	295	0	7	146	643
Mean	$178 779	$14 007	$3529	$17 909	NA	$15 202	$19 410	$28 536
Std dev.	$491 771	$45 720	$0	$44 019	NA	$22 676	$100 723	$148 129
Min.	$3021	$353	$3529	$1039	NA	$2787	$1233	$353
Max.	$3 181 479	$366 985	$3529	$478 651	NA	$63 517	$1 199 759	$3 181 479

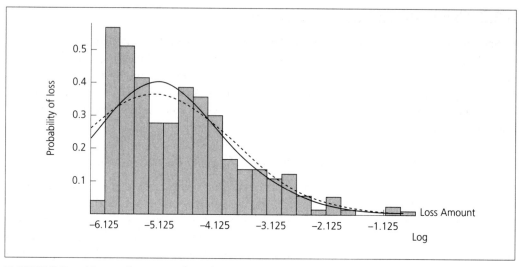

FIGURE 8.5 ■ Alternative curve fits of severity distributions

Remember that the underlying data have a 'natural' lower truncation point. When collecting the data, only those events beyond a specific threshold were collected. In this example the truncation point was $2000 (or –6.21 in log terms). The fitting routine takes into account that the data are truncated and therefore fits a truncated distribution with the same truncation point.

Kolmogorov–Smirnoff (KS) tests indicate whether the theoretical distribution could be a statistically acceptable fit to the empirical data. The KS statistic for the fat-tailed lognormal fit is 0.075 (Table 8.2), which given the number of observations used to fit this curve represents a probability value greater than 20 percent. This is the best fit among the distributions tested. So we cannot reject the hypothesis that this theoretical curve is representative of the empirical data. Therefore, we can move ahead with this anchor cell and use the distribution with the lowest KS statistic, the fat-tailed lognormal distribution, to represent the severity distribution.

Once the process is completed for one event category, the same steps were followed for all other event categories. Some of the other event categories do not have enough data to model the severity. In those cases we used the external data to estimate the parameters for the severity distribution. In this case study we used the relative relationship concept to determine parameters for all the other risk categories.

TABLE 8.2 ■ Results of fitting alternative severity distributions

	Mean	Std dev.	Kurtosis	KS
Lognormal	–5.14	1.34	N/A	0.086
Fat-tail lognormal	–5.10	1.34	4.05	0.075

The relative relationship concept is a method which uses publicly disclosed operational risk events to estimate the severity distribution for event categories for which an institution's internal data are not sufficient. The external data are used to calculate a 'relationship' between risk categories for each business line. Once the relationships have been ascertained, they can be used to determine parameters of a severity distribution for event categories with insufficient loss history. In effect, the relationships observed from the industry are used to scale the internal loss data.

In this case study we used publicly disclosed operational loss events and calculated a relationship for the mean, standard deviation and kurtosis for each of the risk categories for retail banking. Table 8.3 is an illustration of the relationships that were used in this case study (figures are expressed in log terms).

Looking at the institution's loss event database, we determined which risk event categories had sufficient data to model independently using the MLE method previously described. The cell for which the parameters were estimated using the MLE process is referred to as the anchor cell – in this case, clients, products and business practices. All other cells were calculated using Table 8.3. Table 8.4 shows the calculated parameters for all the risk categories. Note that the parameters for the anchor cell are the input to this table and therefore are the same as those calculated using the MLE process. In this example, there were multiple potential anchor cells. In practice, we would do the above calculation for each anchor cell and validate the results of one against each other.

TABLE 8.3 ■ External data statistics

	Damage to physical assets	Business disruption and system failures	Execution, delivery and process management	Internal fraud	External fraud	Employment practices and workplace safety	Clients, products and business practices
Mean	9.55	10.02	8.99	8.90	8.63	8.67	9.18
Std dev.	1.05	1.77	1.70	1.46	1.24	1.23	1.44
Kurtosis	3.62	2.04	3.55	3.48	3.37	2.94	3.38

TABLE 8.4 ■ Final severity distributions for each risk category

	Damage to physical assets	Business disruption and system failures	Execution, delivery and process management	Internal fraud	External fraud	Employment practices and workplace safety	Clients, products and business practices
Mean	−4.74	−4.26	−5.29	−5.38	−5.65	−5.62	−5.10
Std dev.	0.98	1.65	1.58	1.36	1.15	1.14	1.34
Kurtosis	4.34	2.44	4.25	4.17	4.03	3.52	4.05

Model frequency

The frequency of operational risk data is assumed to have a Poisson distribution. The Poisson distribution is characterized by one parameter; therefore, we only need to determine the average number of losses over a certain period of time from the available data. Figure 8.6 shows the 295 losses for retail banking and the clients risk category over time.

Because the collection effort has not been consistent over the period of time that the histogram is displaying, taking the simple yearly average of all the losses would severely underestimate the mean frequency for this data set. By knowing this anomaly, we can adjust the mean frequency to include only the last year (last four bars). Because operational risk occurrences can be cyclical, it is better to use the last four quarters than just the last two. Further adjustments for estimated data capture are possible but have not been included in this example. We assume that the last year's information is complete and representative. Therefore, the mean of the frequency distribution for this data set is 204 events per year.

Monte Carlo simulation

Monte Carlo (MC) simulation is the method used to generate an aggregate loss distribution from the frequency and severity distributions. To start, the MC simulation randomly chooses an annual number of events from the frequency distribution. The most likely choice will always be equal to the mean, and the further a number is away from the mean, the less likely it is that the MC process will chose this number. This randomly selected number is the frequency for that iteration. The frequency is then used as the number of draws that the MC simulation selects from the severity distribution. Each of these draws from the severity distribution represents a loss event. All these drawn loss amounts are summed to create the aggregate annual loss amount. This process is repeated until the desired number of iterations is run. The aggregate loss amounts from each iteration are sorted from low to high. The average of all the results is the mean of the aggregate loss distribution. For example, if

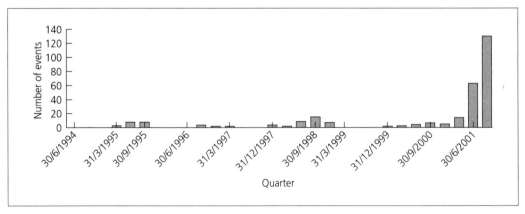

FIGURE 8.6 ■ Client risk events over time

there are 10 000 simulations, take the ten largest losses and the smaller of these is the 99.9th percentile. The amount of capital-at-risk for this business unit and risk category is the difference between the 99.9th percentile and the mean of the aggregate loss distribution. Figure 8.7 illustrates the MC simulation process.

Once the parameters for all the different risk categories are calculated, the combined Monte Carlo simulation is used to generate a total aggregate loss distribution for the business unit. During this process an aggregate loss distribution is calculated for each of the event categories, using the single Monte Carlo simulation. During the simulation process, the loss amounts generated by the iterations are added together to create the amount of the combined distribution. Once all the iterations are complete, the mean of the combined distribution can be calculated by taking the average of the total amounts from the iterations. The amounts at different percentiles are determined using the same method used by the single Monte Carlo simulation process.

Validating results

The numbers generated by the Monte Carlo simulation must be validated against actual observations. An example of this validation process is to compare the mean of the aggregate loss distribution to the recently observed average annual loss amount for this business unit and risk category. Similarly, the annual loss amounts at different confidence levels must be intuitive; for example, the loss amount at the 99th percentile must be equal to the type of loss that could happen once in a hundred years.

Figure 8.8 gives the results for the retail banking line of business. For example, for the simulation for clients, products and business risk, the mean loss is about $6.1 million, and

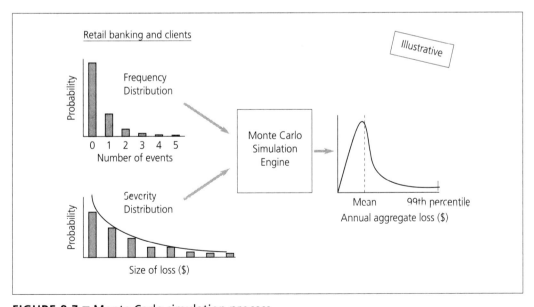

FIGURE 8.7 ■ Monte Carlo simulation process

Retail Banking with Insurance	Assumptions (Million)							
	Damage to Physical Assets	Business Disruption and System Failures	Execution, Delivery and Process Management	Internal Fraud	External Fraud	Employment Practices and Workplace Safety	Clients, Products and Business Practices	Total Diversified
Statistics								
# of Iterations	100,000	100,000	100,000	100,000	100,000	100,000	100,000	100,000
Truncation Point	0.005	0.005	0.005	0.005	N/A	0.005	0.005	N/A
Single Event Cap	12	0.4	74	42	30	3	66	
	Fat-tail LogNormal Distribution Model Parameters							
Avge Annual Freq	2.00	1.70	22.00	14.00	10.00	0.00	204.00	N/A
Mean	-4.74	-4.26	-4.68	-5.38	-5.65	-5.62	-5.10	N/A
Sigma	0.98	1.65	1.16	1.36	1.15	1.14	1.34	N/A
Kurtosis	4.34	2.44	5.35	4.17	4.03	3.52	4.05	N/A
	Simulated OpVar Results (Million)							
Mean	0.018	0.078	0.704	0.378	0.161	0.000	5.975	7.314
Median	0.011	0.027	0.505	0.295	0.137	0.000	5.455	6.724
95.0%	0.053	0.298	1.406	0.774	0.332	0.000	9.227	11.142
99.0%	0.115	0.799	3.785	1.788	0.485	0.000	15.963	19.195
99.9%	0.375	2.639	20.762	8.127	1.116	0.000	41.410	47.069
99.97%	0.677	4.791	40.946	16.770	2.070	0.000	54.773	66.616
VaR 99.9%	**0.357**	**2.561**	**20.058**	**7.749**	**0.955**	**0.000**	**35.434**	**39.756**
VaR 99.97%	**0.659**	**4.713**	**40.243**	**16.392**	**1.909**	**0.000**	**48.798**	**59.303**

Summary & Notes	
Anchor Cell	
Selected Model Distribution	Clients, Products and Business Practices
Mean Annual Loss in $	Fat-Tail Log Normal
	7,313,748
VaR (Diversified) in $	39,755,536

FIGURE 8.8 ■ Retail banking results

the internal experience is $5.6 million, indicating the simulation parameters are about right. The total diversified VaR at 99.9 percent is $42.326 million. The validation process for the output of the combined simulation is the same as the one from the single simulation. The simulated mean of $7.5 million compares favourably to the historical average of $8 million.

Include insurance coverage

The first step in accounting for the mitigating effect of insurance is to map existing insurance coverage for this business unit to each of the risk categories. The goal is to determine the probability of coverage, deductible amount and maximum amount covered for each risk category. Table 8.5 gives an example of this information for this case study.

TABLE 8.5 ■ Insurance coverage ($ millions)

Retail banking	Internal fraud	External fraud	Employment practices and workplace safety	Clients, products and business practices	Damage to physical assets	Business disruption and system failures	Execution, delivery and process management
Probability of coverage	0.26	0.67	0.28	0.07	0.7	0.35	0.02
Deductible	$0.214	$0.240	$0.000	$0.174	$0.003	$0.075	$0.075
Max. limit	$9.741	$9.015	$1.502	$6.642	$37.209	$27.338	$2.554

Retail Banking	Assumptions (Million)							
	Damage to Physical Assets	Business Disruption and System Failures	Execution, Delivery and Process Management	Internal Fraud	External Fraud	Employment Practices and Workplace Safety	Clients, Products and Business Practices	Total Diversified
Statistics								
# of Iterations	1,000,000	1,000,000	1,000,000	1,000,000	1,000,000	1,000,000	1,000,000	1,000,000
Truncation Point	0.002	0.002	0.002	0.002	0.002	0.002	0.002	N/A
Single Event Cap	12	0.4	74	42	30	3	66	
Fat-tail LogNormal Distribution Model Parameters								
Avge Annual Freq	2.00	1.70	22.00	14.00	10.00	0.00	204.00	N/A
Mean	-4.74	-4.26	-4.68	-5.38	-5.65	-5.62	-5.10	N/A
Sigma	0.98	1.65	1.16	1.36	1.15	1.14	1.34	N/A
Kurtosis	4.34	2.44	5.55	4.17	4.08	3.52	4.05	N/A
Simulated OpVar Results (Million)								
Mean	0.038	0.095	0.704	0.389	0.167	0.000	6.083	7.477
Median	0.027	0.027	0.525	0.302	0.141	0.000	5.518	6.853
95.0%	0.118	0.382	1.400	0.883	0.354	0.000	9.459	11.464
99.0%	0.237	1.010	3.544	2.090	0.637	0.000	16.430	19.671
99.9%	0.716	3.222	25.193	8.767	1.924	0.000	43.646	49.803
99.97%	1.405	5.379	44.217	17.556	3.650	0.000	58.167	68.875
VaR 99.9%	**0.677**	**3.127**	**24.489**	**8.378**	**1.757**	**0.000**	**37.563**	**42.326**
VaR 99.97%	**1.366**	**5.284**	**43.513**	**17.167**	**3.483**	**0.000**	**52.084**	**61.398**

Summary & Notes	
Anchor Cell	Clients, Products and Business Practices
Selected Model Distribution	Fat-Tail Log Normal
Mean Annual Loss in $	**7,477,008**
VaR (Diversified) in $	**42,326,453**

FIGURE 8.9 ■ Retail banking results, after insurance

Once the insurance information is gathered, it is input into the Monte Carlo simulation. Figure 8.9 shows the capital-at-risk results from the Monte Carlo simulation for retail banking including insurance.

Note that the effect on insurance in this case study is small: the mean loss declined only 9 percent, and VaR at 99.9 percent declined 5 percent. The impact is small due to the type of coverage. In particular, the main driver for the risk capital figures is the clients, products and business practices category. Looking at the type of coverage for those losses, we see that the probability of coverage when an event does occur is very low (7 percent). Furthermore, the maximum loss amount that is covered is also minimal ($6 million). This type of exercise and review is very useful when trying to determine the level of insurance coverage that should be purchased.

Develop scenarios for stress testing

So far we have described the process used to calculate the 'base case' scenario for one business unit. Given the different assumptions that were made when deriving the frequency and severity distribution and the insurance coverage, it is helpful to understand the sensitivity to each of the assumptions by varying the inputs and identifying the boundaries of the results and then rerunning the simulations.

The types of scenarios that should be run depend on the quality of the internal data and the assumptions that were made. In general, stress testing should be performed to analyze the sensitivity of the results to the following variables:

- Frequency. The frequency was varied up and down by 20 percent.

- Single event cap. This amount was varied up by 100 percent and down by 50 percent. For this parameter, it is important to verify that the cap is not low in relation to the other parameters for the severity curve (mean, standard deviation and kurtosis). If the calculated capital figure for any risk category is too close to the cap, it would indicate that the cap has a large impact on the calculation and therefore might be too low.

- Anchor cell. If multiple anchor cells are available, it is important to see the impact of selecting a different anchor cell. In this case study there were enough data for two anchor cells, clients, products and business practices, and execution, delivery and process management.

- Curve fitting. The truncation point (lower limit) could be varied based on the completeness of the data. Furthermore, stress testing could be done by removing possible outliers and/or adding a high-severity data point to see its impact on the results.

Once the scenarios are finalized, the Monte Carlo simulation processes the information. Table 8.6 displays the results from the Monte Carlo simulation, highlighting the different scenarios and their effects on the final results.

Alternative scenarios might include the sensitivity to alternative distributions or correlation assumptions. With a longer time series and more data points, the range of results should be narrower.

Incorporating scorecards and indicators

Assume for this case study that there is a separate process for self-assessment and risk indicators that can arrive at a 'quality score' for each risk and business line on a scale from 1 to 100. This score indicates the overall quality of the control environment and is updated quarterly to reflect changes in the organization. Given that there is a baseline set of scores

TABLE 8.6 ■ Stress test results

Stress Test Type	VaR @ 99.9 percent (in $ millions)
1. Base case	42.36
2. Frequency up 20 percent	45.72
3. Frequency down 20 percent	40.38
4. Single event cap up 100 percent	44.31
5. Single event cap down 50 percent	35.29
6. Anchor cell: execution	49.12
7. Truncation point: $5000	45.17
8. Adding high-severity loss to anchor cell	48.32

in the organization, changes in the score can drive a change in capital to help provide an incentive for improving controls. Consider Table 8.7 as an example of how to apply these scores.

Depending on the previous (base) score and the level of change, assigned capital can be increased or decreased by up to 20 percent from calculated levels.

8.6 Key assumptions

Similar to insurance techniques, LDA may use either historical loss experience data or scorecard data as the basis for quantification (see Chapters 10 and 11). To incorporate external data, one can use either the relative relationship approach (described in Section 8.5) or a Bayesian approach (described in Section 7.3). The LDA used in the case study of this chapter is but one of many alternative loss distribution approaches, several of which are described in other chapters of this book.

Several important assumptions were made when using historical loss data with the case study LDA of Section 8.5. Each should be fully explored and tested to understand the sensitivities to each assumption.

■ *History is sufficient to profile the risk.* A sufficiently long history is an important assumption. Where there are many data points, a few years' history may be sufficient. Where few events occur, results could be very sensitive to adding only one event, and care must be taken with the results.

■ *History is a proxy for the future.* Organizations, policies and controls can change rapidly, while data change slowly. The usual premise is that although the cause of any one event might have been corrected, and the same thing is unlikely to occur again, the fact that an event of a certain magnitude did occur means that the inherent risk in any business is such that another event of comparable magnitude could occur again. If there are major changes in the control environment, qualitative adjustments to frequency or the resulting capital would have to be made.

TABLE 8.7 ■ Incorporating scores

Base	Base score range	Quality score capital adjustment				
		Significant degradation	Slight degradation	No change	Slight improvement	Significant improvement
Low	0–24	0%	0%	0%	10%	–20%
Low/medium	25–49	8%	4%	0%	–8%	–16%
Medium	50–74	12%	6%	0%	–6%	–12%
Medium/high	75–99	16%	8%	0%	–4%	–8%
High	100	20%	10%	0%	0%	0%

- *Anchor cells contain sufficient tail data to build an accurate severity distribution*. In the case study above, anchor cell severity distributions are derived solely from internal data – no external data are used. In the selection of anchor cells, there must be some of the large but rare tail events, or the resulting risks could be underestimated.

- *Relative relations with external data hold true.* In the case study above, severity distributions for non-anchor cells are extrapolated using external data. This technique assumes that external data points are a random sample of events from each category. *Qualitative adjustments to frequency*. Where there are very few or no events, frequency distributions must be estimated and are often subject to subjective judgements. The frequency estimates are key assumptions that should be subject to review.

8.7 Advantages and limitations of the LDA

Statistically modelling operational risk using the LDA approach has numerous advantages, as follows:

- Results are based on the unique characteristics of each institution instead of relying on a proxy or industry averages. Though many firms operate in any one business line, each firm has its own risk profile. A comprehensive loss history is the best way to capture the unique attributes of each firm.

- Results are based on mathematical principles of term and level of confidence similar to those used to estimate market and credit risk capital. The LDA approach can specify a time horizon and level of confidence. Consequently, the three types of risk capital can be combined in a statistically valid manner.

- Insurance policies can be specifically modelled. The impacts on expected and unexpected losses can be understood for various insurance options.

- Cost and benefits of the change can be measured. Similarly, by estimating the change in frequency or severity for any proposed change to the control environment, the impact on both expected and unexpected losses can be estimated and compared against the costs of implementation.

- Results do evolve over time. Changes in loss experience will result in changes to both the frequency and severity distributions and subsequent changes in the risk calculations.

By the same token, the LDA approach has certain limitations. These can be overcome with a variety of techniques, but they should be clearly understood.

- It is data-intensive. This is perhaps the largest issue with LDA. To apply it consistently across the organization, a comprehensive loss history or set of scorecard data is required. While shorter histories or purely subject scorecard data are feasible for internal analysis, the Basel Committee has specified a minimum of three and preferably five years of historical loss experience data.

It is potentially backward-looking. If all data are historical, many future risks would not be reflected in the data. Upcoming threats to the risk profile (e.g. pending mergers or systems integrations, changing regulation, new product introductions) require qualitative adjustments to be reflected in the results.

Deriving bottom-up data at low levels in the organization is infeasible. Modelling is typically performed for business units one or perhaps two levels below the firm-wide results. While it is theoretically feasible, data are typically too sparse to determine frequency and severity at lower levels. Determining capital to lower organizational levels requires some type of allocation using qualitative and quantitative scorecards.

It does not capture impacts on revenue or margin from operational causes. These risks have been excluded from the Basel definition and are not a regulatory concern. For those organizations wishing to consider these risks for internal purposes, additional methodologies are used for these exposures.

8.8 Issues for further research

This chapter illustrates that the LDA approach is sound and feasible. By the same token, there are some issues where further research will make the results and methodology even more accurate. Some of the areas currently being researched are:

Loss-sharing consortiums. Data are the key to these methodologies. To complement internal data, the only sources available today are external databases researched from public sources. There are several initiatives under way for banks to accumulate and share their internal loss experience through a consortium. This will ultimately provide a more complete data set for all business areas and risk types to better understand the true range of exposures. New approaches will be required to incorporate the consortium results into internal capital models.

Estimating frequencies and severities for missing data. In practice, there is always risk with no or very few data points, resulting in difficulty directly quantifying the required distributions. Once industry consortium data is available, actuarial techniques can be used to estimate risk.

Incorporating internal and external data in the same cell. The anchor cell concept was designed to deal with the data capture biases in external databases. Consequently, it is assumed that anchor cells contain sufficient events to quantify tail risk in severity distributions (external data are not used), and relative relations are used to extrapolate other cells (and internal data are ignored). Valuable information is contained in both internal and external data, and we are researching ways to utilize the two sources together.

Scaling for firm size. The only scaling feasible today is firm-wide data on public databases on public companies. True scaling would be done at the business line level based on financial or volume information. We will have to wait for loss data consortiums to advance before such data will be made available.

- *Linking results to risk indicators*. Linking capital to risk indicators, as in a scorecard approach, is ideal. At the moment there is insufficient history of losses linked to indicators in place at the time to objectively conclude which indicators are truly correlated to losses and to what level.

- *Correlations between event categories and other types of risk*. We currently assume that operational events are either perfectly correlated or independent of each other and other risks. While the mathematics is available to estimate the impact of correlations, the data is not available to derive them.

8.9 Summary

We have demonstrated that the Loss Distribution Approach is a solution that can operate at any level of the organization. It has the ability to reflect the unique risk profile of any organization in an objective and statistically valid manner. LDA obviously is dependent on a history of loss events. Where few or no data are available, scenario analysis or qualitative estimates of risk from a self-assessment process can be used to estimate the required frequency and severity distributions, and all of the firm can be analyzed with a consistent approach.

Sound risk management requires the collection of loss experience independent of the quantification approach. Loss histories help improve risk awareness and act as the basis for empirical analysis. Why not leverage this loss experience and use it for capital as well?

The optimum solution requires a combination of purely quantitative analysis and subjective adjustments. While the data will drive an initial calculation, qualitative adjustments can incorporate the results of self-assessment programmes, audits, changing volumes and risk indicators. Essentially, this means a combination of what Basel refers to as the scorecard approach and the Loss Distribution Approach, applied in a bottom-up fashion.

CHAPTER 9

A general simulation framework for operational loss distributions

Diane Reynolds and Dave Syer

9.1 Introduction

Operational risk managers have the responsibility to preserve shareholder value and meet regulatory requirements. In order to do so, they must achieve three key goals:

- actively measure firm-level regulatory and economic operational risk;
- sustain an internally and externally transparent framework for managing and measuring risk;
- provide decision support methodologies and tools for enterprise-wide operational risk management.

Before any of this is possible, operational risk must be defined. After much debate, the Basel Committee on Banking Supervision (2001b) defined operational risk for regulatory purposes in the international banking industry as 'the risk of loss resulting from inadequate or failed internal processes, people, systems or external events'. Many people extend the definition for non-regulatory purposes to include strategic or business risk – the risk of making a bad business decision.

Once defined, risk cannot be effectively managed without proper risk measures. Tools such as process mapping, control assessment, project management and risk assessment go a long way to identifying and controlling operational risk. It is impossible to determine the appropriateness of such risk-mitigating activities without proper pre- and post-enforcement measures of risk. Furthermore, risk cannot be completely eliminated, making risk measurement the key to effective risk management.

By nature, people use and appreciate what they can understand easily. Transparency in the process, system and methods promotes understanding. This is particularly true in operational risk management because of the strict qualitative requirements of the Basel II Capital Accord and the variety of users who may benefit from the information.

Understanding not only the amount of risk, but also where it resides, what contributes to the risk, and the impact of mitigation strategies is important to the risk manager. Different views of risk are also informative, for example being able to report risk measures across business areas and geographically. Such quantitative decision-support tools are central to advanced operational risk management.

These challenges, however, are not unlike those faced by other sectors of the risk management industry. For example, market and credit risk present many of the same issues. Through the extensive work done in the areas of market and credit risk, it has become clear that no single methodology can stand the test of time. A framework accommodating several different methodologies, over varying periods of time, is required. Several desirable qualities of such an operational risk quantification framework are: flexibility, extensibility, scalability, reliability, performance, and ease of explanation (to non-technical audiences).

In the current environment of rapid change, flexibility and extensibility are clearly desirable: new models, new methodologies and new data sources appear frequently and must be evaluated and adopted. As with any new methods, operational risk measures must be phased in over time. Ease of scaling – adding new businesses or areas – is another key consideration. Reimplementing everything half-way through a roll-out would be expensive. Reliability, performance and ease of explanation all contribute to the ability to sustain the processes served by an operational risk management system. People must believe that the outcomes are correct and accessible before they see them as useful. Without such a framework, operational risk cannot be accurately measured because the necessary data cannot be collected. Without accurate risk measures, risk management becomes near impossible.

This chapter argues that simulation is the best approach to operational risk measurement, and specifically capital calculation. There are many advantages to using a simulation approach. Simulation within the Mark-to-Future framework (Dembo *et al*. 2000) provides:

■ Flexible modelling and the ability to specify arbitrary probability distributions, and relationships (e.g. correlations) between them. In particular, independence of loss processes is not a necessary assumption.

■ Efficient aggregation of risk measures throughout a reporting hierarchy, such as an organization structure.

■ The ability to attribute risks and derive not only a firm-wide capital, but also the marginal contributions of each constituent unit to the whole, facilitating capital allocation.

■ Consistency with existing approaches to market and credit risk calculations. Existing tried and tested tools can be used for calculations, and ultimately will lead to easier integration of market, credit and operational risk.

■ The key concepts, such as that of a 'scenario', are intuitive and easy to understand, and easy to explain to non-technical audiences.

■ Effective use of available data, including the combination of internal and external loss data.

■ A scalable solution where more complex models or hierarchical structures may be added easily.

This chapter aims to elucidate the advantages listed above through a more detailed look at the role of simulation in operational risk management. It begins with a short description of the regulatory proposals on operational risk, and how they relate to capital calculation. Then the problem of operational risk capital measurement and management is discussed in more detail, including a summary of available input data and expected outcomes or measures. The problem is illustrated with a simple hierarchy borrowed from regulatory definitions. Next, the simulation approach is described in the context of the Mark-to Future framework. The simulation methodology for operational risk measurement is illustrated by two examples. The chapter ends with some concluding remarks and directions for future research. A description of loss measurement models and of suitable statistical representations for operational data is provided in Appendices 9.1–9.3.

9.2 The regulatory landscape

Since one of the key concerns of the operational risk manager is regulatory compliance, any risk measurement approach must meet regulatory requirements. An outline of regulatory requirements has been provided in a series of chapters produced by the Basel Committee on Banking Supervision (BCBS 2001a, 2001b, 2001c, 2001d). Specifically, the proposed new Basel Capital Accord (BCBS 2001b) identifies three methods for calculating the operational risk capital charge, each increasing in sophistication: the Basic Indicator Approach, the Standardized Approach and the Advanced Measurement Approaches (AMA). The AMA allow for a range of methods based on banks' internal risk estimates. They include the Internal Measurement Approach (IMA) and the Loss Distribution Approach (LDA), which were introduced in an earlier consultative chapter (BCBS 2001c). In addition to these, a scorecard approach (SCA) was introduced, and the door was left open for other 'best practice' approaches to be considered as time goes on.

Basel II proposes that if banks move from the Basic Indicator along the continuum towards AMA, they will be rewarded with a lower capital charge. Further, it mandates that failure to comply will be addressed by a variety of supervisory actions including increased oversight, senior management changes, and the requirement of additional capital. Many, if not most, internationally active banks now have staff who are dedicated to the quantification of operational risk.

Many banks have indicated that they would prefer to use an advanced measurement approach, and the LDA in particular, for regulatory reporting, because they intend to use it for internal purposes. This is a sign that these banks believe that LDA is more rigorous and more accurate than the simpler approaches. It also indicates a belief that LDA is feasible within the current business practices of their bank.

This chapter is concerned with a simulation approach to operational risk capital, and the application of the Mark-to-Future framework to the quantification of operational risk. In regulatory terms, all the proposed AMA could involve simulation:

- In the IMA the 'gamma' factor relating expected to unexpected losses has to be calibrated (see Table 7.5). Whether or not a bank adopts the IMA, it would be natural to be curious about the corresponding value of gamma. The results could be derived using simulation.

- In the LDA there is scope for direct application of simulation to the calculation of capital, in much the same way that market and credit risk capital are calculated.

- In the SCA, the results of the scorecard can be used to allocate the enterprise-wide capital, or to adjust a capital figure already calculated for each business unit. In either case the initial calculation of the capital must be supported by the same data and methodologies as the LDA, and hence simulation can play an important role.

In all three cases annual loss distributions play a central role, and the regulators insist that the calculations must be underpinned by internal loss data collected over a number of years. This insistence, and the introduction of the AMA, are signs that the distinction between regulatory and economic capital is becoming narrower.

9.3 Setting the stage

Before discussing the simulation framework and identifying its value to operational risk measurement, some key concepts must be introduced. This section provides a discussion of available and applicable input data for simulation models and defines terminology to be adopted in later discussion.

9.3.1 Inputs

The first step in calculating concrete annual loss distributions is to determine and calibrate the most appropriate models. This requires a large amount of input data. Ultimately, the input data must also be used to test the appropriateness and accuracy of the model results. Fortunately, several different types of input data are available for these purposes. Each type of data varies in its quality, quantity, appropriateness and ease of collection. The input data types are summarized in Table 9.1, where they are listed roughly in decreasing order of the ease with which they can be collected.

- Internal loss event data are a list of currency amounts and dates of events experienced by the firm. The regulatory proposals are very clear that these data should form the basis of all capital calculations under the AMA. The proposals also require under Pillar 2 (supervision) that the data are collected and maintained in a robust, systematic way using well-defined and documented internal processes.

- Indicators are a time series of internal or external numeric factors that might influence losses. Indicators can serve as predictors of operational risk. For example, if the volume of transactions increased while the number of staff and availability of new technology

TABLE 9.1 ▦ Summary of input data available for operational risk capital calculation

Data description
Internal loss events
Indicators
Internal near-miss events
Scenarios
External consortium losses
External public domain losses
Detailed classifications of all the above

decreased, the number of losses per period would probably increase. Such intuitive correlations lead many to believe that numerical correlations between indicators and losses can assist in calibrating loss distributions. Indicators are seen as having predictive powers regarding either the frequency or size of loss events. Whether the data bear this out has yet to be determined.

Indicators, both internal and external, also provide static data that are important in developing defensible scaling models. Firms change their business focus, they grow, merge, shrink and operate in inflationary economies. All of these contribute to the need to scale the internal loss data to mark them to the operational market, as it were, of the firm. Both types of external data (public domain and consortium) will also need to be scaled before they can be applied rationally to the calibration of internal loss models. Although the need for scaling is widely accepted, no standards have yet emerged in the finance industry, and no specific methodology has been specified by the regulators.

▪ Near-miss data are comprised of event dates and monetary exposures – sums that might have been lost, although an actual loss was not realized. Near misses have been mentioned in the regulatory proposals (BCBS 2001a), and there are hints that they might be used to augment internal loss data in the calibration of the capital calculation models. In any case they are useful for organizations to learn about the kinds of things that can go wrong, and to help prevent similar mistakes from leading to losses in the future or in other parts of the organization.

▪ Scenarios might consist of a set of estimated frequency and approximate currency amounts of hypothetical events, for example from a risk self-assessment. Many organizations are collecting such data, and scenarios have been mentioned in the regulatory proposals (BCBS 2001a). Scenario data might be more useful as a high-level view of where the most important risks lie than in producing accurate capital calculations. Nevertheless, they could play an important role in areas where there is a lack of other data, such as new business endeavours. They also hold the potential to augment the tails of loss distributions, but such methodologies are currently at best *ad hoc*.

- External public domain loss data are a set of currency amounts and dates of events experienced by other firms, taken from the public domain. An example is the Zurich IC^2 FIRST database.[1] External loss data from a loss data consortium such as $MORE^2$ or the Global Operational Loss Database[3] are similar in form, if not in execution.

Not all of the above data is available in any given situation, and not all will necessarily be used. The decisions about which data to use in what way must be part of the risk management process. It is likely that different procedures will be applicable to different situations, for instance if the required output is regulatory capital the procedure might be different than for internal economic capital. The existing Basel II proposals do not explicitly specify a procedure for making such decisions except in the case of the simpler approaches to capital calculation.

Classification of all of the above data into commonly understood and accepted reporting structures is essential. Such structures are used internally by banks for risk reporting and management purposes. External data often also have hierarchical risk categories, and/or generic organizational units. These might also be categories prescribed by the regulators (BCBS 2001b) or set by a governing body.

The rest of this section formalizes the description of classifications and reporting structures by introducing the concepts of an operational unit and an operational loss process.

9.3.2 Operational units

The goal of operational risk measurement can be stated as the need to calculate consistent operational capital for each operational unit of the firm. An operational unit is any entity (logical or physical) for which a risk manager needs to assess operational risk and possibly allocate capital. Most businesses already break down into such units because of existing structures, such as reporting lines or geographical locations. Operational units are typically defined in a hierarchical fashion.

BCBS (2001b) proposes two such hierarchies: one based on business lines and one based on risk classification. Each node of a classification hierarchy can be interpreted as an operational unit. A hierarchy naturally translates into a portfolio-type view of the operational risk of an organization, breaking it up into categories and sub-categories. A simple example hierarchy is shown in Figure 9.1. The operational units in the figure correspond to a small subsection of the regulatory business line hierarchy from Basel (BCBS 2001b).

Additional operational unit hierarchies include internal, as opposed to regulatory, organization structure and risk categories, which might be desirable for reporting purposes. For instance, there are a number of different risk categorizations in common use, including so-called 'event-based' and 'effect-based' categorizations (BCBS 2001d). Geographical or process-based

[1] www.ic2.zurich.com.
[2] www.moreexchange.org.
[3] www.bba.org.uk.

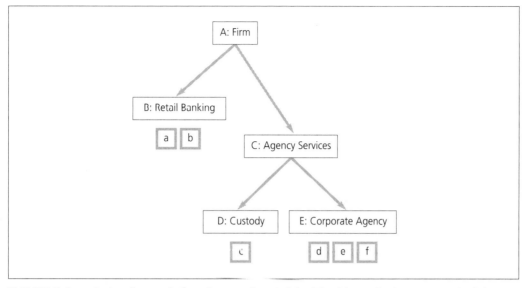

FIGURE 9.1 ■ A simple portfolio of operational risks. The hierarchy is composed of three primary operational units (*B, D, E*), and two aggregate operational units (*A, C*). The primary operational units contain a set of operational loss processes (*a, b, c, d, e, f*). The example is part of the proposed regulatory business line hierarchy (BCBS 2001a, 2001b).

categorizations are also commonly encountered. Some organizations might need to report operational risk measures internally based on more than one of these hierarchies.

Hierarchies can also be combined with each other, as is the case in the IMA, where the business units each have a collection of risk classes for capital reporting purposes. Any pair of hierarchies can be similarly combined: the hierarchies can be viewed as the rows and columns in a table, or as two axes in a plane. Risk measurement takes place at all points in the plane (or cells in the table). This can be extended, in principle, to higher dimensions with more than two hierarchies. In practice, because of insufficient data, it will probably only be possible to obtain accurate measurements when at most two, very shallow, hierarchies are combined (as in the IMA).

9.3.3 Operational loss processes

The constituents of an operational unit for risk measurement purposes are operational loss processes. Each operational loss process can contribute hypothetical losses with a particular set of characteristics (e.g. impact, frequency) to the operational unit it belongs to. It is often useful to be able to assign more than one operational loss process to an operational unit. For instance, if they correspond to actually distinct physical processes (e.g. manual and automatic settlement), then representing the two processes separately is more intuitive, and likely to more accurately reflect reality. Assumptions must be made to create a risk quantification for each operational unit by combining its constituent operational units and operational loss processes, and the range of assumptions that can be made depends on the calculation methodology that is employed. Note that operational loss processes need not be independent of one another in a statistical (or any other) sense.

The same aggregation methods can be used to combine and aggregate operational loss processes as operational units. With this in mind, any operational unit containing only operational loss processes can be referred to as a 'primary' operational unit. Operational units that contain only other operational units can be referred to as 'aggregate'. The distinction is made only to clarify the discussion below; it has no impact on the framework or algorithms employed, and in practice an operational unit might contain both operational loss processes and other operational units.

The simplest hierarchy containing all essential combinations of primary and aggregate operational units is shown in Figure 9.1. Operational units B, D and E are primary operational units. Operational unit C is an aggregate operational unit whose constituents are all primary operational units. Operational unit A is an aggregate operational unit whose constituents are a combination of primary and aggregate operational units.

Once a reporting hierarchy or classification scheme has been defined, many additional issues become easier to articulate. For example, one serious concern is the interrelations between operational units. Codependences between operational units arise in at least two ways. They can arise 'naturally' as a result of internal or external causal influences which affect distinct loss events. For instance, two loss events might be reported in geographically distinct locations, but have a common causative influence, such as an extreme market movement that creates stress and leads to human errors. If the decision has been made to hold capital against such events separately in the two geographical locations, the calculation of the amount of capital to hold will be affected by the correlation between some of the events. Codependences can also arise 'artificially' if a single loss event has effects which are shared through the categorization of operational units. For instance, if the financial impact of a single loss event is shared between two operational units, then that loss is effectively split into two events. But the two events are not independent because they derive from a single underlying loss, so there is an implied correlation. The capital held by the two operational units, and by operational units higher up the hierarchy, depends on this correlation.

Having examined possible data sources, and formalized a language for classifying data into reporting hierarchies, the problem of risk measurement is now more clearly defined. Based on this definition, the following section presents a simulation solution based on the Mark-to-Future framework.

9.4 A simulation approach for operational risk

Operational risk can be seen as the risk of losing money as a result of an event or a chain of events. Many other kinds of risk have this event-driven character. In fact, event risk is a familiar and well-understood concept in a large sector of the financial industry: insurance.

Adapting the experience of the insurance industry to operational risk is a matter of defining the relevant types of events.

Insurance companies underwrite the risk of their clients losing money owing to events that are defined in their policy documents. The key tool for an insurance company in understanding its own risk is an actuarial loss model. The key element of an actuarial model is to say that the annual loss is not a single loss caused by a single event, but the result of the aggregation of a number of loss events.

Based on this property of actuarial models, the elements of a simulation approach to capital calculation can be described as follows. For a risk horizon of one year, the unit of simulation is the sum of losses for the period of one year. (There is nothing special about the period of one year, except that it is commonly used in credit and operational risk. In principle, any time horizon could be applied.) Each scenario represents a set of losses that could hypothetically occur in a single year.

1   The first step is to simulate the number of loss events in each of the scenario years (i.e. the frequency n).

2   The second step is to sample from the distribution of absolute loss amounts. The result is a set of n losses as indicated in the scenario for that year.

3   These losses are summed to form the (simulated) annual loss for each scenario year.

4   The collection of simulated annual losses is analyzed to provide risk measures, for example the largest expected annual loss every 100 years.

The above steps are carried out for each operational loss process. Simulation proceeds by generating scenarios of losses over a large number of scenario years N, according to the model that has been specified. Each year that is simulated is a 'scenario' – a total loss that could hypothetically occur in any given year. Risk measures derive from collecting the scenarios and looking at the statistical properties of the collection (e.g. the largest total loss that can be expected to occur once every 100 years).

Each aggregate operational unit also requires a loss distribution. This distribution is created by aggregation of the constituent operational units. Aggregation consists of identifying all the operational loss processes belonging to the operational unit and all its descendants in the hierarchy. The annual loss in each scenario for the operational unit is simply the sum of all annual losses in the consitituent operational loss processes. In practice, very large savings in calculation time can be achieved simply by caching the values of the annual losses in each scenario for each operational loss process. This is the essential feature of the simulation framework that are now describe.

9.4.1 The Mark-to-Future framework

The purpose of Algorithmics' Mark-to-Future framework (Dembo *et al*. 2000) is to enable a range of simulation approaches to risk management problems. It is an abstraction of the process of scenario generation and the transformation of scenarios into financial results, together with the analysis of those results to produce risk measures. The application of Mark-to-Future to operational risk capital calculation hinges on the generation and analysis of the scenarios. The scenarios in the case of operational risk are realizations of the number of events per year at each primary operational unit. A large degree of flexibility as to how the events are modelled can be accommodated. A simple approach based on directly simulating the number of events per year by drawing from a particular distribution would be an example.

The general simulation framework is designed to enable a new generation of risk quantification and management software, and it has a number of key features that make it an excellent choice for market and credit risk measurement and management purposes:

1 It is efficient for dynamic portfolio measurements, and intra-day calculations such as what-if trades.

2 It allows multiple portfolios to be constructed from the same simulation results.

3 It is efficient for marginal risk calculation within a portfolio. For example, a position can be reset to zero and the risk statistics recalculated without repricing the instruments.

4 It enables integration of market and credit risk through the use of common risk factors.

For operational risk, the most important of these is probably 3, because it provides a natural method for allocating capital. Operational risk managers will also benefit from 2, because capital (and other risk measures) need to be reported in a number of portfolio hierarchies (business units, risk classes, geographical locations, process elements, etc.). There are enormous potential benefits from integration of market, credit and operational risk quantification, so an extension of 4 is also very important. Having market, credit and operational risk quantified within the same framework, on the same platform, and using the same software architecture will promote their eventual integration. The details of the integration are beyond the scope of this chapter.

The advantages of the simulation approach are both its simplicity, and its powerful ability to deal with a variety of frequency and severity distributions with complicated dependencies between loss events.

9.4.2 Codependence structure

A scenario contains information about the frequency of losses and the total annual loss for all the operational loss processes in the firm. Simulation is the best approach to accommodate codependence between those operational loss processes because it places no restrictions on the form of the codependence. If you can imagine it, you can simulate it.

The simplest strategy for including codependence between operational loss processes is to make the *frequency* of losses codependent. The severity then remains conditionally independent of the number of events, consistent with standard actuarial practice. This provides an extremely flexible and powerful framework for measuring loss distributions and related risk measures. The scenarios on the frequency of the different operational loss processes must reflect the fact that an event in one operational loss process might lead to, or be influenced by, an event in another operational loss process.

Specific assumptions related to codependence and independence are explained in more detail in Appendix 9.1, including a discussion of how to break the conditional independence of severity on frequency.

9.5 Example applications

To illustrate the concepts described above, two simple examples have been devised. In both cases, the data are purely hypothetical, and the examples are intended as a proof of concept for the simulation approach framework.

As a simple example of an aggregate loss distribution and derived risk measure, the calculation of operational risk capital at the firm-wide level is considered first. The output is a figure for the annual capital, so in risk management terms there is a one-year horizon. Such a figure could be used (for example) as the starting point for a scorecard allocation of capital amongst business units.

The second example illustrates portfolio aggregation of operational risk using the hierarchy in Figure 9.1. Loss distributions and capital figures for all the operational units in that hierarchy are calculated based on some hypothetical scenario data. The same principles would apply to a calculation using models calibrated from actual loss data (as opposed to scenarios). The steps in the calculation would be the same; only the models of the operational loss processes would be different.

9.5.1 Enterprise-wide capital calculation

In this example, the goal is to calculate firm-wide capital. A list of internal losses including dates and amounts is presumed to be available, and this will be used to calculate capital. Of course, the interpretation of the outcome is limited by the simplicity of the input data. A very different result might be obtained if self-assessment scenarios, external data, near misses or other inputs were included. Also note that the data has been collected for the entire firm. There is no hierarchical structure to which the data are referenced. The assumed input data, consisting of six years of losses totalling 293 observed losses, are summarized in Table 9.2.

A Poisson distribution for the frequency of loss and an empirical distribution for the severity of the loss are selected, requiring estimation of the parameters of the distributions and assessment of the appropriateness of the assumptions based on the (assumed) input data.

The frequency, whose probability distribution function is shown in equation (9.4) in Appendix 9.3, must be calibrated. The only parameter, λ, can be estimated by the average number of events per year over the six years. The result is 52.67. With such a large value of λ, the Poisson distribution is actually barely distinguishable from a normal distribution with mean and variance equal to λ. The Poisson distribution is likely to be appropriate because of the clustering of the number of losses about the mean. This indicates a low variance, much in line with the effects of a Poisson distribution. A more detailed backtesting analysis would have to be carried out to formally determine the appropriateness of the model.

TABLE 9.2 ■ Summary of input data for firm-wide capital calculation. The number of loss events n for each year in the range 2000–2005 is listed, along with the total loss z and the mean $\mu(x)$ and standard deviation $\sigma(x)$ of the severity (individual loss amounts). The data are illustrative only.

Year	n	z ($ million)	$\mu(x)$ ($ thousands)	$\sigma(x)$ ($ thousands)
2000	64	7.55	117.9	109.6
2001	57	6.35	111.3	106.2
2002	52	5.14	98.8	93.7
2003	55	5.29	96.1	88.0
2004	43	3.86	89.7	78.5
2005	45	3.41	75.7	68.5

To construct the severity distribution, use the given 293 individual loss events, with severity $\{x_i\}$, $i = 1, 2, \ldots, 293$. Their broad statistical properties can be deduced from the data in the table: $\mu = \$99\,900$ and standard deviation $\sigma = \$93\,600$. Assuming that all previous losses are equally likely to reappear, sampling, with replacement, can be done directly from the vector of past loss severities. In more formal terms, the implied assumption is that the loss events are conditionally independent, given n (see equation (9.6) in Appendix 9.3).

A choice was made not to fit a smooth parametric model to the data to obtain the severity distribution, but simply to resample the input data, so

$$z = \sum_{i=1}^{n} \hat{x}_i, \tag{9.1}$$

where $\{\hat{x}_i\}$ is a sample (with replacement) of size n from the input data $\{x_i\}$. This choice is purely for the purposes of illustration; in practice one might prefer to fit a parametric distribution, such as lognormal or Weibull.

Having determined and calibrated the distributions, simulation can begin. First, $N = 1000$ scenarios; that is, 1000 simulated years are created. This results in 1000 scenarios for one quantity, the number of events, firm-wide, n.

For every scenario on n an annual loss is generated using equation (9.1), with a different sample of $\{\hat{x}_i\}$. With 1000 scenarios, there will be 1000 samples of annual losses (with different values of n). This is the way that most simulation-based aggregation methods work in market and credit risk.

While in this case, only one sample of z is constructed per frequency scenario, it would also be possible to construct more than one; the results are equivalent for a large enough number of scenarios. The simulated results for one severity sample per frequency scenario are depicted graphically in Figure 9.2 and summarized in Table 9.3.

For comparison, since a large number of events per year are expected, the results of a semi-analytic convolution are also provided. In this case, suppose that the severity distribu-

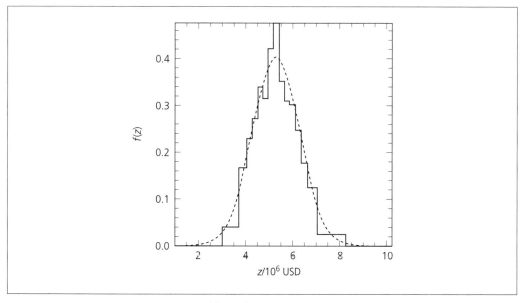

FIGURE 9.2 ■ The firm-wide annual loss distribution calculated using the input data as summarized in Table 9.2. The stepped curve uses a simulation approach with resampling. For comparison, the smooth curve uses the central limit theorem. The expected loss is $5.26 million, and the standard deviation is, from equation (9.7), $0.99 million.

tion does not have an ultra-heavy tail, so that the central limit theorem can be applied to the convolution. With this approximation the frequencies are simulated as before, and the firmwide annual loss distribution can be efficiently calculated to a high degree of accuracy. The result is shown in Figure 9.2 as the smooth curve, and the corresponding risk measures are listed in Table 9.3. Note that 50 events per year is ample to cause the *centre* of the distribution to converge when composed of a single frequency and severity distribution. The tails are perhaps a little on the heavy side (the 99.9 percent VaR is larger in the simulation than the central limit theorem case), but actually the differences in the two results of risk statistics could largely be due to sampling errors owing to the small number of scenarios used.

TABLE 9.3 ■ Firm-wide risk measures using a non-parametric simulation approach (resampling). For comparison the results are also shown after applying the central limit theorem. The expected loss μ is given along with the standard deviation σ. VaR(p) is defined as the difference between the pth percentile and the expected loss. All quantities are in millions of dollars.

Method	μ	σ	VaR(95%)	VaR(99%)	VaR(99.9%)
resampling	5.28	1.00	1.72	2.35	3.47
CLT	5.26	0.99	1.63	2.31	3.07

9.5.2 Capital calculation in a hierarchy

This example looks at calculating capital for each operational unit shown in Figure 9.1. The general approach is to assume or determine distributions for each of the operational loss processes and then to use this information to derive distributions for the operational units. The overall capital is then calculated from the annual loss distribution at operational unit A. Methods for allocating the overall capital figure along the hierarchy are discussed, but not calculated. The basis of the calculation is scenario input data.

To begin, suppose that each of the primary operational units has been through a risk profiling exercise. Business experts (heads of department, risk specialists, internal audit, consultants) have been asked to identify their top risks – the things that make them lose sleep at night. The results are in the form of a list of specific risks, and for each risk there are two scenarios ('typical' and 'worst case') involving hypothetical loss amounts and estimated average frequencies. These are summarized in Table 9.4.

Capital for these risks is not necessarily regulated directly, but economic capital can be held by the firm as a buffer against them. An economic capital figure is also an efficient way of prioritizing the control and mitigation actions. Assume that action plans to control and mitigate the unacceptable risks are to be put into place based on such capital calculations.

The simulation framework is used to calculate the economic capital for the identified risks, and to aggregate it to the firm level. For simplicity, the events in each of the six scenarios are assumed to be independent. This means that operational units (B, D, E) each have two separate operational loss processes ('typical' and 'worst case'), each with its own severity and frequency distribution.

Assume that all the operational loss processes have a Poisson frequency distribution (equation (9.4) in Appendix 9.3) with intensity equal to the estimated average frequency in Table 9.4. All severity distributions are modelled as a simple spike at the value of the estimated loss. Either the frequency or severity distributions could be extended to more complex models without altering the remainder of the example.

TABLE 9.4 ■ Summary of scenario data used in Section 9.5.2. The data relate to a fictional risk profiling of business units from Figure 9.1. Each primary operational unit has provided a 'typical' and a 'worst case' scenario for loss events. Each scenario has a loss amount and an estimated average frequency.

Unit		Scenario	Loss x ($ millions)	Estimated average frequency λ (per year)
B	Retail Banking	typical	0.1	1
		worst case	10	0.01
D	Custody	typical	1	0.1
		worst case	100	0.01
E	Corporate Agency	typical	0.2	5
		worst case	40	0.01

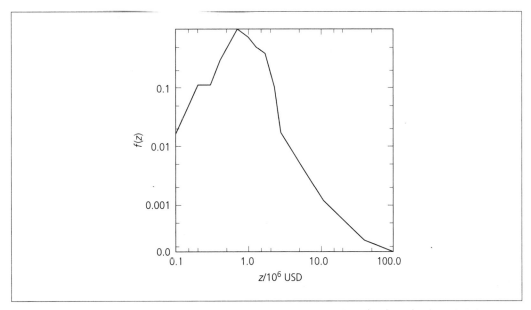

FIGURE 9.3 ■ The firm-wide annual loss distribution calculated using the input data as summarized in Table 9.4. The expected loss is $2.75 million, and the standard deviation is, from equation (9.7) in Appendix 9.3, $10.9 million. The results are summarized in Table 9.5.

Simulating $N = 10\,000$ scenarios over one time-step, with one simulated quantity (frequencies) per operational loss process (six in total), the dimensions of the Mark-to-Future cube (Dembo *et al*. 2000) are $10\,000 \times 1 \times 6$. The results are summarized in Table 9.5 and Figure 9.3. The quantiles were estimated using a kernel method, which improves their stability and reliability (Harrel and Davis 1982). Kernel estimators are essential for applications where the severity distribution is composed of spikes because the cumulative distribution of annual losses is not continuous.

The marginal contributions to VaR are calculated by approximating the partial derivative of the firm-wide VaR with respect to the overall scale of the loss distribution at each operational unit. This is very efficient to calculate within the Mark-to-Future framework because it does not require a resimulation. Most of the VaR for the firm can be traced to operational unit *D* (Custody), so this operational unit would be deemed to be consuming the most capital, and a business decision can now be made as to whether its return on the capital is acceptable to the firm as a whole.

TABLE 9.5 ◼ Summary of risk measurement statistics for the portfolio of scenarios defined by Table 9.4 and Figure 9.1. The expected loss μ is given, along with the standard deviation σ. VaR(p) is defined as the difference between the pth percentile and the expected loss. The last column is the marginal contribution (expressed as a percentage) of each operational unit to the 99.9 percent VaR. All other quantities are in millions of dollars.

Unit	μ	σ	VaR(99%)	VaR(99.9%)	mVaR(99.9%)
A	2.75	10.9	68.7	99.2	100%
C	2.54	10.8	68.7	99.2	94%
B	0.216	1.07	9.14	10.1	6%
D	1.11	10.0	49.9	98.9	91%
E	1.43	4.13	24.9	40.2	3%

Appendix 9.1 Loss models

In terms of the example in Figure 9.1, the goal is to calculate the distribution of losses for each operational unit (A, B, C, D, E) in a consistent manner. The loss distribution $f_k(x)$ is the probability of a loss of magnitude x occurring over a specified period (e.g. one year) in operational unit k.

To illustrate how loss models are used in simulation, operational unit D is first considered in isolation. This operational unit, persuming data collection consistent with BIS II (BCBS 2001b), will have a collection of loss events and a set of indicator time series associated with it. The loss events can be summed year by year to create a series of total annual losses for operational unit D. The events can also be counted year by year to create a series of number of losses per year for the operational unit.

9.1.1 Direct model for losses

To obtain the loss distribution $f(z)$ for an operational unit (e.g. D), the time series of total monthly losses could be used directly. The data could serve as an empirical distribution or to calibrate an assumed distribution. However, even given the regulatory minimum requirement of five years of data (BCBS 2001b), fitting a distribution is difficult because of the limited number of observations in the series (five).

9.1.2 Actuarial models for losses

The key element of an actuarial model is to say that the annual loss z is not a single loss caused by a single event, but the result of the aggregation of a number of losses. A brief mathematical overview of actuarial methods is given below. The literature (e.g. Klugman *et al.* 1998; Frachot *et al.* 2001) provides much more detailed discussions.

Suppose in a particular year there are n events that each cause a loss and that their cash values are given by x_i, $i = 1, \ldots, n$. Then

$$z = \sum_{i=1}^{n} x_i.$$

Understanding of the composition of z is facilitated by viewing both x and n as random variables. Thus x has a distribution g such that

$$dp = g(x)dx$$

is the conditional probability of experiencing a loss with value in the range $[x, z + dx]$ given that an event has ocurred; and n has a distribution h such that

$$p_n = h(n) \tag{9.2}$$

is the probability of experiencing n loss events in a year. Operational risk events are characteristically very rare, so often $p_0 \neq 0$. In actuarial terms, x is the 'severity' of an event, g is the 'severity distribution', n is the 'frequency' and h is the 'frequency distribution' of the operational unit.

The annual loss distribution can now be written as

$$f(z) = \sum_{n=0}^{\infty} h(n)g^{(n)}(z), \tag{9.3}$$

where $g^{(n)}$ is the distribution of annual losses, given that there were precisely n events.

The usual assumption is that the loss events are conditionally independent, given the value of n. Given this assumption, $g^{(n)}$ is equal to g convolved with itself n times (Appendix 9.3.1). The advantage of assuming independence is that there are efficient analytic and numerical techniques for evaluating $g^{(n)}$. The assumption can be relaxed in special cases, at the expense of additional complications. But a simulation approach can overcome most if not all of these (see Appendix 9.3.5).

The great advantage of the actuarial approach to annual loss distributions is efficient use of data. To estimate f accurately by directly sampling z from measured data, one would need many values of z, and hence many years of data. Some insurance contracts have been written for over a hundred years, but these are rare. Operational risk data typically do not span more than a handful of years because their importance has only recently been recognized. Also, if the business environment changes, then data from only a few years ago might no longer be relevant. The actuarial approach allows us to the estimation of g based on a larger number of events than there are years of data.

Having obtained the loss distribution for operational unit D, $f_D(z)$, by the methods outlined above, the other primary operational units can be treated similarly to obtain $f_B(z)$ and $f_E(z)$. Some of the intermediate results might need to be saved for the evaluation of the aggregate operational units, depending on the details of the implementation.

9.1.3 Aggregating loss distributions and overall capital

For operational units A and C, however, different methods are required because no operational loss processes are directly attached to these operational units. For instance, the information available to operational unit C is all the data from its constituent operational units D and E, together with their loss distributions f_D and f_E, and any intermediate results that have been stored. If losses in operational unit D are independent of losses in operational unit E, then $f_C(x)$ may be determined as the convolution of f_D and f_E (see Appendix 9.3.1). (Events within a operational loss process can also be correlated, but this can be taken into account within the actuarial framework; see Appendix 9.2.2.)

However, it is possible that the losses experienced by the operational units D and E are related in some fashion. For example, supposing the hierarchy is based on line of business, then operational units D and E might both experience losses due to the same technology failure event. This illustrates a powerful reason to believe that operational risk will be correlated between operational units. In this case, f_D and f_E are not sufficient; information containing the relations between the two operational units is also required (see Appendix 9.2.2).

Appendix 9.2 Model distributions

Using a simulation approach, no particular model is mandated for either frequency or severity distributions. Simulation provides the flexibility to specify the precise forms and calibration methods of both distributions, and most particularly the severity distribution. This appendix briefly describes some of the common choices.

9.2.1 Severity

The severity distributions are located at the primary operational units. Each primary operational unit has to specify a model, g_k, for itself. In practice there might be a smaller number of elemental distributions which can be shared by two or more operational units, that is to say, some of the g_k might be identical, or related by simple scaling. Also, a primary operational unit might find it convenient to have more than one operational loss process, and hence more than one severity distribution, for different kinds of events. This presents no conceptual problems in the framework, but for simplicity the description assumes that each primary operational unit has exactly one operational loss process.

Candidate models for severity distributions g_k include a variety of parametric and non-parametric distributions. On the parametric side there are the normal, lognormal, tail-adjusted lognormal, beta, Weibull and other standard continuous distributions. Non-parametric choices include various histogram or bucketed representations, or simple resampling of the input data.

9.2.2 Frequency and codependence

A similar range of choices exists for the frequency and models b_k. The simplest and most common parametric model is probably a Poisson distribution (see Appendix 9.3). A homogeneous Poisson distribution (one with a fixed average frequency) will often be used where events in a operational loss process are thought to be independent. Correlations between events in a single operational loss process lead to frequency distributions with characteristically fatter tails (more likelihood of larger number of events per year). An example is the negative binomial distribution.

The relations between the primary operational units (codependences) can be expressed within the actuarial framework in the form of the joint frequency distribution of all m primary operational units. Suppose operational unit k has n_k events per year; then the required distribution is $b^{(m)}(n_1, n_2, \ldots, n_m)$ with

$$p = b^{(m)}(n_1, n_2, \ldots, n_m)$$

equal to the probability of n_1 events at operational unit 1, n_2 events at operational unit 2, etc. The marginal distributions (equation (9.2)) are

$$b_k(n_k) = \sum_{n_j \neq k} b^{(m)}(n_1, n_2, \ldots, n_m).$$

Because the joint distribution must be specified, the frequency and codependence models are linked in the framework.

One example of a method to specify the codependence structure is based on latent variables, in the same way that the Merton model operates in credit risk (see Appendix 9.3.4).

Appendix 9.3 More on actuarial models

The actuarial approach brings large dividends if n is large (not the case for many operational risk applications). The estimation of b is still affected by the small number of years of data, but actuaries are generally more ready to accept assumptions about b. Principal among these is that independent events have a Poisson distribution,

$$b(n) = \frac{\lambda^n e^{-\lambda}}{n!}, \tag{9.4}$$

which has a single parameter λ, the average number of events per year. Another choice is the negative binomial distribution

$$b(n) = \binom{\alpha + n - 1}{n} \left(\frac{1}{1 + \beta}\right)^{\alpha} \left(\frac{\beta}{1 + \beta}\right)^n \tag{9.5}$$

with $\alpha > 0$, $\beta > 0$. It is interesting to note that the negative binomial distribution can be derived as a mixture of Poisson distributions with different frequencies λ. The distribution (9.5) is obtained when λ has a gamma distribution (Klugman *et al.* 1998). Equation (9.5) represents a process where there are expected to be $\bar{\lambda} = \alpha\beta$ loss events per year, but there can be more than this (or less) – the standard deviation of event frequency is $\beta\sqrt{\alpha}$.

9.3.1 Convolution expression for $g^{(n)}$

If loss events at a given operational unit are conditionally independent given the value of n, then $g^{(n)}$ is g convolved with itself n times. It can be written iteratively as

$$g^{(n)}(x) = \int_{-\infty}^{\infty} g^{(n-1)}(y - x)g(y)\, dy$$

$$g^{(0)}(x) = \delta(x), \tag{9.6}$$

where δ is the Dirac delta: $\delta(x) = 0$ for $x \neq 0$.

9.3.2 Statistical properties of $f(z)$

Equation (9.3) has some nice properties which can be exploited to derive the statistical properties of f from the properties of g and h. The expected value and variance of g and h can be written as

$$E(g(x)) = \mu_x, \qquad \text{var}(g(x)) = \sigma_x^2,$$

$$E(h(n)) = \mu_n, \qquad \text{var}(h(n)) = \sigma_n^2.$$

The expected value of x over $g^{(n)}$ is $n\mu_x$, and the variance is $n\sigma_x^2$. Thus the expected value of z over f is

$$E_f(z) = \sum_n h(n)n\mu_x = \mu_n\mu_x$$

and the second moment of z is

$$E_f(z^2) = \sum_n h(n)(n\sigma_x^2 + n^2\mu_x^2),$$

so the variance of z is

$$\text{var}_f(z) = \mu_n\sigma_x^2 + \sigma_n^2\mu_x^2. \tag{9.7}$$

9.3.3 Arrival time modelling

The frequency distribution $h(n)$ can be re-expressed as the distribution of arrival times of an event. For example, the simple Poisson case equation (9.4) can be written in terms of the arrival time t as

$$q(t) = \lambda e^{-\lambda t}$$

where $q(t)\mathrm{d}t$ is the probability of the next event arriving after t years. The arrival time formulation is particularly convenient for some kinds of problem, and can help with the specification of the codependence between different event types.

To write the joint frequency distribution in terms of arrival times requires $q^{(m)}\,(t_1, t_2, \ldots, t_m)$ with

$$dp = q^{(m)}\,(t_1, t_2, \ldots, t_m)\,dt_1, dt_2 \ldots dt_m$$

equal to the probability of the arrival times being in the infinitesimal neighbourhood of $(t_1, t_2, \ldots, t_m)$. The marginal distribution q_k is given by

$$q_k(t_k) = \int_{tj \neq k} q^{(m)}\,(t_1, t_2, \ldots, t_m)\,dt_1, dt_2 \ldots dt_m.$$

Extending the concepts above, arrival time modelling can make it easier to include more complicated ideas in a simulation framework. For instance, instead of $q^{(m)}$ being constant, it could be dependent on the most recent event.

An important and convenient mechanism for specifying joint distributions is through the use of copulas (Frey and McNeil 2001; Embrechts *et al.* 2001). Copulas are a special form of joint distribution of continuous variables, so in this context they would be used to specify $q^{(m)}$. A more detailed treatment of copulas is outside the scope of this chapter, but see Chapter 7.

9.3.4 Latent variable models

There is an important special case of a frequency–codependence structure which is equivalent to specifying the joint frequency distribution but is usually expressed in a different way. That is a latent variable model, based on covariate normal risk factors, and event frequency determined by a threshold model. This is the basis of many portfolio credit risk modelling applications (Merton 1974; Bucay and Rosen 2000; Algorithmics 2000).

There is a set of m risk indexes $\{y_k\}$ at the operational units, which are random variables with a covariate normal joint distribution. An event at operational unit k is deemed to have occurred if y_k crosses a threshold η_k. The marginal distribution of frequencies at each operational unit is a Bernoulli distribution (or binomial of order 1): possible values of n are 0 or 1, with probability

$$p = \int_{\eta_k}^{\infty} N(1, 0)(x)\,\mathrm{d}x.$$

If identical uncorrelated operational units with probability p are grouped together, a binomial marginal frequency distribution is obtained for the group. When the group has v members, the maximum frequency is v, and the probability of a single event is p^v. In the limit that p is very small, but $pv \equiv \lambda$ remains finite, the distribution tends to a Poisson distribution with intensity λ.

Generalizations of the covariate normal approach are possible involving rank correlations and marginal distributions of y_k which are not normal.

9.3.5 Frequency–severity dependence

Intuitively, the independence assumption is hard to believe. Consider a primary operational unit that experiences only loss events of five amounts: critical, very high, high, moderate and low. If a critical loss occurs, the operational unit will cease operations. This means that after a critical loss, the probability of further losses is zero. If a very high loss occurs, the operational unit manager might take out insurance, or enforce a policy change, thus affecting the probability of future losses at each level, or the number of future losses, respectively. The consequence is that $g^{(n)}(z)$ has no explicit functional form.

The simulation framework can accommodate some special forms of dependence between frequency and severity through the process of constructing $g^{(n)}$. For instance, there could be a rule of 'self-correcting behaviour' such that the severity distribution of the first event in a year is different than for subsequent events. Thus the business learning from its mistakes can be simulated – a large loss will often lead to a lesson being learnt that prevents the same magnitude of loss recurring. In the extreme case that a business unit is closed down after a very large loss, subsequent events would be impossible. This could be simulated by assigning zero severity to subsequent events.

Dependencies between different severity modules (basis risks) can in principle also be handled by the simulation framework, given the right implementation.

CHAPTER 10

The path to operational risk economic capital

Ulrich Anders[1]

10.1 Introduction

Operational risk is the risk of a loss resulting from inadequacies or failures in processes, controls or projects due to technology, staff, organization or external factors. Whereas market and credit risks are concerned with external risks, operational risk deals with the risk inherent in the organization, that is, within its operational processes and projects. In order to understand operational risk it is necessary to understand both the size and sources of the risk. Economic capital is the natural measure used to express and summarize the risk facing a company.

This chapter deals with the computation of economic capital for operational risk. Section 10.2 explains what economic capital actually is. Section 10.3 describes how its computation generally works. The computation is based on an economic capital model that requires some input in order to produce an output. Section 10.4 explains how to derive a good economic capital model. Section 10.5 deals with where to find good-quality data for input into the economic capital model. Section 10.6 addresses the question of how to validate the data input. Finally, Section 10.7 explains how to validate the output of the economic capital model – the economic capital number itself.

10.2 What is economic capital?

Economic capital is the amount of capital that a company (or organizational unit) needs in order to protect itself with a chosen level of certainty against insolvency due to unexpected losses over a given time period (e.g. one year). Consequently, *operational risk*

[1] The author extends his thanks to Dr. Gerrit Jan van den Brink for overall very knowledgeable comments, Dr. Peter Neu for initial, very valuable thoughts on this subject, Dr. Markus Klomfass for researching some of the statistical groundwork for this chapter, and the employees of Goetzfried AG (www.goetzfried-ag.com) for programming the Operational Risk Economic Capital (OREC) engine.

economic capital protects the company against insolvency due to unexpected operational losses. To determine the amount of economic capital, the company (or organizational unit) must decide upon the level of certainty with which it wishes to protect itself against insolvency: the higher the chosen level of certainty, the greater the amount of economic capital needed. The same is true for the time period: the longer the time period in which losses could accumulate, the greater the amount of economic capital needed. In order to be compatible with the financial year, the most sensible choice for the time period is also one year.

Economic capital is a number which summarizes the current (market, credit, operational or overall) risk profile of the company in a single figure. This figure serves as a measure for understanding the absolute size of risk, as well as the change in risk over time. It also helps to compare the risk across different risk types or business lines. Furthermore, it is the basis used to calculate whether the company has earned a sufficient return given the size of the risk that it is taking. Concepts such as economic value added and risk-adjusted return on economic capital help to compute the risk–return relationship.

10.3 How to compute economic capital

The computation of economic capital is not a trivial task. It is based on an economic capital model which transforms the model input (i.e. parameter values) into the model output (i.e. the economic capital number).

Given a poor model or poor input data, a reliable output cannot be expected. Therefore, both the design of the economic capital model and the quality assurance of the input data must be carefully exercised.

The model itself must fulfil four basic conditions:

■ It must be *consistent*, so that the relative change in economic capital adequately reflects the change in the underlying risk profile over time and across business lines.

■ It must be *reliable*, so that the absolute size of the economic capital gives an adequate picture of the level of economic risk. Only then can the number be compared across risk types and used for steering purposes of the company.

■ It must be *robust*, so that small changes in the risk profile do not lead to big erratic jumps in the output.

■ It must be *stable*, so that economic capital numbers can be compared over time on the basis of the underlying model.

The data input into the economic capital model must be of good quality in order to represent the risk profile of the company or business line for which the economic capital is to be computed. This usually requires: an input data validation which is a check on size, frequency, consistency and representativity; and an input data cleansing process which leaves only data that adequately represent the risk profile of the company or business line.

We are thus left with two basic questions: how to derive a good economic capital model; and where to obtain good-quality input data. The answer to the first question will be given in Section 10.4, and the answer to the second question will be given in Section 10.5.

10.4 How to derive a good economic capital model

A good model is a simplified yet fair representation of reality. We have already established that economic capital tries to protect a company against insolvency resulting from unexpected losses that a company could in a worse case experience over the course of one year. That means the model should give us some idea of the size of the potential loss experiences which could accumulate over one year, together with their corresponding likelihoods.

In order to achieve this, it is necessary to simulate a potential loss distribution from which it is possible to see what potential loss experience (i.e. sum of individual potential

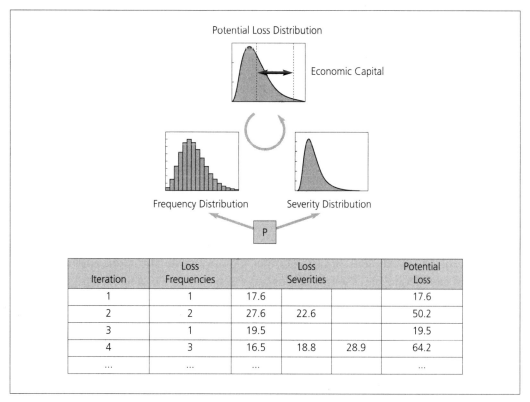

Iteration	Loss Frequencies	Loss Severities			Potential Loss
1	1	17.6			17.6
2	2	27.6	22.6		50.2
3	1	19.5			19.5
4	3	16.5	18.8	28.9	64.2
...	...	...			...

Figure 10.1 ■ Given a parameter set *P* of parameter values, loss frequencies and loss severities are generated randomly via Monte Carlo simulation. The compound potential loss distribution reflects the total loss incurred per annum. The economic capital is given by the unexpected loss at a certain percentile, typically 99 percent or 99.9 percent.

losses) has what likelihood. The simulation requires two types of distribution as input: a frequency distribution which models how frequently potential losses are occurring; and a severity distribution which models how severe potential losses are if they are occurring. These two types of distribution are compounded into one potential loss distribution. Probably the best technique used for this purpose is called Monte Carlo simulation. Basically, a Monte Carlo simulation is a big dice-rolling exercise where the dice are shaped so that their different sides fall with different likelihoods (given by the corresponding distributions). One die is for the likelihood, the other for the severity of potential losses. Each iteration starts with a roll of the frequency die. The number that falls determines how often the severity die is rolled. Say, for instance, the frequency die shows 3. This means that we roll the severity die three times. The severities are added up to make the potential loss for this iteration. This procedure is carried out hundreds of thousands of times, resulting in the corresponding number of potential losses (see Figure 10.1).

The 99th percentile of the histogram of these potential losses corresponds to the quantity that is greater than 99 percent and smaller than 1 percent of all potential losses. The difference between this quantile and the mean of the distribution is the *economic capital* for the percentile. The mean is sometimes called *expected (potential) loss* and the economic capital *unexpected (potential) loss*.

When we talk about a distribution, we are usually referring to two things at the same time: the general family of distributions (e.g. normal distribution) with its parameters (e.g. mean and variance); and concrete parameter values of the distribution. The choice of family is a fundamental part of any economic capital model; the choice of concrete parameter values of the distribution depends on the input data (see Figure 10.2).

Some approaches to economic capital modelling for operational risk disregard the distinction between the general family and the concrete parameter values of a distribution, and both are chosen at the same time. For example, simply generating a histogram – that is, an empirical probability density function (pdf) – of historic data or fitting a theoretical pdf to a histogram has nothing to do with building a model, since each time the data change so too do the empirical or theoretical pdfs.[2] In such approaches, no explicit assumptions are made about the underlying families of distributions. Consequently, the model does not exist explicitly or stand alone, and therefore does not meet the criteria of Section 10.3. A model implicitly given through one particular set of data cannot be consistent, reliable, robust and stable as a different set of data might change not only the parameter values of the model (which is necessary), but also the model itself (which is most definitely not desired).

To come back to explicit modelling, we will now concentrate on the fundamental choice of distribution families. For the frequency, the choice is fairly obvious. Statistics offers us a Poisson distribution which models the occurrence of rare events. The Poisson distribution

---

[2] The same is true for the extreme value theory, and its application in specifying economic capital for operational risk is therefore at the very least questionable.

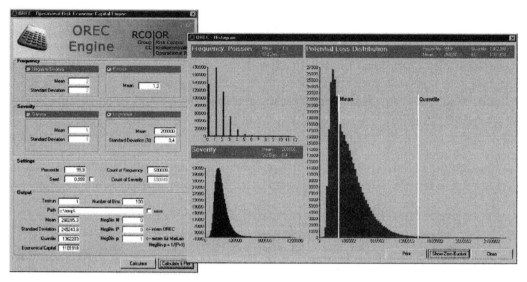

Figure 10.2 ▪ The picture shows a Monte Carlo tool (OREC engine) that compounds a frequency distribution, Poisson or (negative) binomial, and a severity distribution, lognormal or gamma, into a potential loss distribution. The parameters of the chosen distributions can be entered on the left-hand side. Similarly, the percentile for the economic capital as well as the number of Monte Carlo rounds can be selected. The tool computes the quantile, the expected loss and the economic capital.

only has one parameter, since mean and variance are equal. If they are unequal, the alternative is the binomial or negative binomial distribution which serves the same purpose.[3]

As to the severity, there are a variety of distributions which make sense, such as the log normal or gamma. These distributions are fat-tailed and asymmetrical in nature. A fat tail means that high-impact losses occur with a much higher likelihood than a normal distribution would suggest (i.e. the tail is fatter than that of the normal distribution), while the asymmetry refers to the fact that high-impact, low-frequency losses are not symmetrical to low-impact, high-frequency losses. Which severity distribution is the best choice depends on which distribution best reflects reality. This question can be answered in part on the basis of experience, and in part by means of model validation using historic loss data.[4]

We have started to build a model for economic capital for operational risk using one frequency and one severity distribution for any kind of potential operational loss. However,

---

[3] The Poisson distribution is a special form of the (negative) binomial distribution where mean and variance are equal. The negative binomial distribution only allows for variances that are greater than the mean. In the alternative case, the binomial distribution should be chosen.

[4] Current research at Dresdner Bank would suggest that the lognormal distribution is very well suited to internal historic operational loss data.

operational risk is usually broken down into so-called operational risk categories, such as technology, personnel, organization and external factors, or even further into operational risk sub-categories. Instead of using one frequency and one severity for all kinds of potential operational losses, it would be possible to choose an individual pair of frequency and loss distributions for each operational risk (sub-)category. This would allow a more granular model of reality, as different families of distributions could be chosen across risk

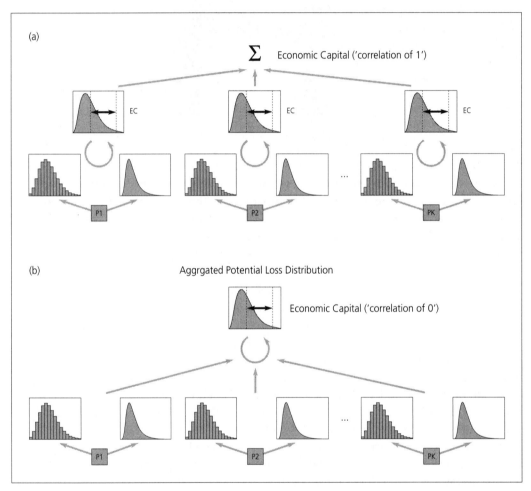

Figure 10.3 ▪ (a) For each parameter set P1 ... Pn, potential loss distributions are generated via Monte Carlo simulation. An economic capital is calculated for each potential loss distribution separately. The overall economic capital is given by sum of the indiviual contributions. This corresponds to fully correlated compound loss amounts. (b) For each parameter set P1 ... Pn, potential loss distributions are generated via Monte Carlo simulation. For each Monte Carlo iteration, the aggregated loss potential is calculated, resulting in an aggregated potential loss distribution upon which the diversified economic capital is based.

(sub-)categories and – much more importantly – different parameters for those distributions across risk (sub-)categories.[5]

The Monte Carlo technique for several risk (sub-)categories works similarly to Figure 10.1. The only difference is that the computer needs to handle not just one frequency and one severity distribution, but a number of paired frequency and severity distributions for each risk (sub-)category. There is, however, an additional decision to be taken: (a) do we calculate an individual economic capital number for each risk (sub-)category and add these up; or (b) do we compound all distribution pairs into a single potential loss distribution and take the economic capital from that? The alternatives are shown in Figure 10.3. Alternative (a) is very conservative and may overestimate the economic capital needed for operational risk, because it is assumed that severe operational losses are dependent on each other, and therefore always occur at the same time ('correlation of 1'). Alternative (b) is less conservative and probably more realistic in so far as it assumes that severe operational risks occur independently of each other and do not have to occur at the same time ('correlation of 0'). There is actually a further alternative which allows for the explicit modelling of correlations between the occurrence of severe events. However, this is very technical and is beyond the scope of this chapter.

10.5 Where to obtain good-quality input data

There is no simple answer to the question of where to get good-quality input data. From the previous discussion, we know that we need to parameterize the severity and frequency distributions of our economic capital model. These parameter values are at least the estimates of the mean frequency and mean severity. Further estimates of the variances of the frequency and severity of losses may also be required. These parameter values may differ if we have chosen to distinguish between risk (sub-)categories.

Two data sources have been suggested for the estimation of these parameters: historical loss data; and evaluations from experts from within the organization.

Historical loss data are a valuable data source for analyzing the weaknesses of the organization. They are also invaluable for validating forecasts of potential future losses in an *ex-post* comparison. However, historic loss data only represent the past, and the extent to which they can be used to predict the future is doubtful at the very least. Furthermore, loss data are not always complete, and a history of no losses does not mean that one is not running any risk (successfully climbing Mount Everest three times does not mean that a fourth attempt is risk-free). The use of external loss data for this purpose has also been suggested. Again, external loss scenarios are very valuable as a source for scenario analysis. However, it is unclear how external loss amounts can accurately represent an internal risk situation.

For these reasons, historic loss data alone do not seem to be an adequate choice for determining the parameters of loss and severity distributions. The better choice seems to be

---

[5] Note that the same family of distributions must be chosen within each risk (sub-)category to ensure consistency of results.

to make the experts of the organization responsible for evaluating the internal risk based on the loss history, the insurance cover, their understanding of the processes, their banking and industry experience, and their knowledge of the embedded controls (see Figure 10.4). This is not an easy task, as a lot of effort needs to go into debriefing the experts so that their

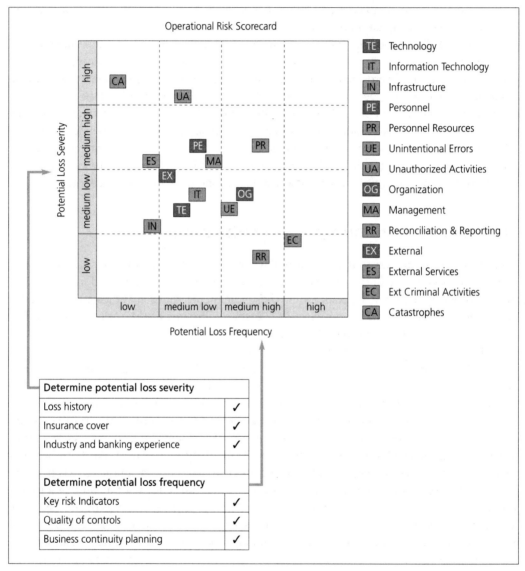

Figure 10.4 ■ Before the self-assessment for a particular set of processes and projects is performed it is useful for the experts who assess to know for this set of processes and projects the loss history, the insurance cover, and the past development of key risk indicators over time.

evaluations are consistent and comparable, can be validated, and are truthful to the highest possible degree. The expert evaluations will then be translated into the parameter values of the severity and frequency distributions.[6] Once the exercise has been successfully completed, the economic capital and the cost of economic capital will be based on a real and forward-looking evaluation of the risk profile of the organization.

Approaches which base the risk profile on organizational information other than historic loss data are usually called *scorecard approaches*. The name is derived from the fact that the results of the evaluations are reported in scorecards. Operational risk scorecards usually show scores for operational risk in euros for potential loss severities, in the number of times per year for potential loss frequencies, and in the form of ratings (e.g. excellent, good, fair, weak, poor) for operational qualities. A typical visualization of a scorecard is shown in Figure 10.4. The scores usually relate to a particular part of the organization, that is, to particular processes specified by an organizational unit, location or product. In addition, the scorecard may be supplemented by an operational risk management information system to show the corresponding loss history or the past development of the so-called key risk indicators that are used to monitor the processes under consideration.

The scorecard approach usually provides the right incentive, since it is risk-sensitive: a change in the risk profile due to an increase in quality, an improvement in controls or the introduction of new insurance cover will be reflected in the scorecard, and will then also lead to a reduction of economic capital. To base the economic capital on the expert evaluations is a transparent and comprehensive approach for the organization or business lines.

We have now explained *why* it seems sensible to base the economic capital calculation on expert evaluations. The following paragraphs will explain *how* to perform such expert evaluations. Basically, the expert evaluations are carried out by means of a self-assessment exercise. The self-assessment comes in the form of a questionnaire which needs to be well designed and which relates to the dimensions of operational risk and quality.

It is common sense that if you want good answers then you must ask good questions. Unfortunately, simply creating a number of good questions does not make a good and valid questionnaire. On the contrary, the creation of a valid and reliable questionnaire is a difficult task. A questionnaire is designed to gather information, and this information must be complete, consistent and representative in order for the questionnaire to measure what it is supposed to. The design of a questionnaire should therefore follow a scientific, well-defined and proven methodology. This design must also allow for a statistical evaluation of the reliability and validity of the questionnaire. The validity tells us whether the questionnaire is in fact measuring what it claims to measure. The reliability tells us whether the questionnaire is collecting data in a consistent and accurate way.

Before the self-assessment exercise can be performed, the experts need to be chosen and it needs to be defined who is evaluating which part of the organization, i.e. which

---

[6] The methodology for transferring the estimates of the scorecard into the parameter values of the distribution is very technical but straightforward. It is based on the aggregation of scorecards and on some parameter transformations for the asymmetric distributions.

processes of which location, organizational unit or product should be assessed. Each expert then performs an evaluation by filling in the questionnaire, resulting in an individual score-card for the corresponding processes. All scorecards can then be compared to each other or aggregated across location, organizational unit or product.

10.6 How to validate input data

Once the experts have completed the questionnaire and the corresponding scorecard reports have been produced, we face the question of how to validate the data. The valida-tion of the input data is based on organizational information, financial information, measurable monitoring information and psychometric analysis of the completed question-naires themselves.

The organizational validation works in three independent stages. Firstly, in order to ensure quality of input, each expert's evaluation needs to be approved by a different person. Secondly, the internal audit function reviews the expert's evaluation. Wherever they per-form an audit of processes, they review whether the self-assessment reveals a good reflection of riskiness and quality. Thirdly, the independent oversight function has the task of ensuring consistency across different questionnaires as well as the quality of the answers. This is achieved by supporting the completion of the questionnaires in person or by means of a call centre, by comparing similar processes which have been evaluated by different experts, and by examining questionnaires in detail.

The scorecard provides estimates of potential loss severity and potential loss frequency for operational risk categories. The product of the two estimates is called *standard risk cost*. Standard risk costs are used for provisioning against individual operational losses. Standard risk costs are usually applied to products or business lines, and are booked into a standard risk cost account. They are called *cost* because they add to the costs of doing business. If they are used in the company, they are shown in the internal management accounts. Individual actual operational losses are then covered from the standard risk cost account. The way to validate the expert evaluations is to compare the sum of the actual losses against the total standard risk costs. Over a sequence of years, the standard risk costs should be suf-ficient to provide cover for all sorts of expected operational losses.

Key operational risk indicators are used to indicate operational risks or a change in the operational risk profile. They need to be set up individually if they are to be meaningful, since different processes may require different indicators, and even the same indicator may need a different interpretation in different situations. An analysis of a particular set of key risk indicators for a particular process or project will reveal whether their past development is consistent with the expert's risk evaluation of this process or project.

The science of psychometrics provides a number of well-proven statistical methodolo-gies for the purpose of evaluation of completed questionnaires. Such methodologies are principal components analysis, dependency analysis, correlation test and consistency statis-tics. They help to derive quite a lot of knowledge about both individual questionnaires and the set of questionnaires as a whole. The methodologies also allow for filtering out deviating questionnaires for a more detailed analysis and subsequent quality assurance.

If these validation techniques are applied prudently, the overall result of the questionnaire exercise will be of very good quality and its data will serve as a valid basis for further economic capital calculations.

10.7 How to validate the economic capital number

The best proof of any economic capital number is if it is applied in an organization. An economic capital number will only be accepted by the organization if it matches the risk profiles of the organization. If the number is too low, the board of directors will not believe it and will not base its steering decisions on it. If the number is too high, the business lines in the organization will not accept it, since they have to bear the cost of economic capital.

The second means of proof is that the ordinal ranking of the economic capital numbers across business lines and risk categories must be plausible. If the ranking does not reflect the managerial experience in the company, then the economic capital number is probably not good either.

As a third means of proof, the absolute size of the economic capital number can be compared with that of other companies or business lines of similar size. Furthermore, the absolute economic capital number must also relate in a reasonable manner to the economic capital numbers computed for market or credit risk.

The fourth means of proof is to perform a statistical hypothesis test on the economic capital number. This technique is often called *backtesting*. However, the higher the chosen percentile, the weaker the power (reliability) of the test becomes and the longer it takes to have the data available to perform the test. It therefore makes sense to carry out hypothesis testing on economic capital numbers with a much lower percentile than, say, 99.9 percent or 99 percent. If such tests fail, a test on the higher percentile is also prone to fail. If such tests hold, then it is reasonable to assume that a test on a higher percentile will also hold.

10.8 Summary

Economic capital is a number which summarizes the risk profile of the company in one single figure. This figure serves as a measure for understanding the change in risk over time, across different risk types or business lines, and as a basis for risk–return computations. In order to fulfil this goal, the economic capital model must be consistent, reliable, robust and stable. It is therefore essential to distinguish between the actual economic capital model that should not change and the model input that must change. To derive such a model is a straightforward task. The difficulty lies in the input to the model – its parameters. Loss data do not appear to be a good basis for this task as they only represent the past. A better approach seems to be the scorecard approach which relies on expert evaluations from within the company. In order for this approach to be reliable, a lot of effort has to go into the validation of the input and output data. But this effort pays off as an economic capital calculation based on an expert analysis of the actual risk profile provides the right incentives within the company and combines the perspectives of local business line management with global top management.

PART III

Management

CHAPTER 11

Scorecard approaches

Tony Blunden

11.1 Introduction

It is as likely to bring a company to its knees as a market collapse, and in many cases it is clearly within management control, but it is still not fully understood or exploited. Operational risk is as important to financial services organizations as market or credit risk but, as a comparatively new discipline, how can business use it to gain substantial competitive advantage? Most managers agree that understanding, managing and mitigating risk is fundamentally more important than merely quantifying it. The management of an organization should be looking to improve both its risk and control knowledge in order to reduce its risk capital needs and, more importantly, to reap the benefits that a robust operational risk management capability can deliver.

It is now clear that a publicly listed company's share price will reflect the market's perception of its governance structure and process in comparison with competitors. Many countries have issued either mandatory or guideline requirements on corporate governance. In the UK, for example, boards are now required to ensure that appropriate systems of internal control exist and to review those systems at least annually. This global trend to increased corporate transparency has forced business to consider the risks to shareholder value and to develop explicit processes to identify, monitor and manage those risks.

In fact, many financial institutions, whether listed or not, have already undertaken, or are undertaking, risk and control self-assessments as essential prerequisites to the identification and design of appropriate key indicators of risk, control and performance. Although self-assessment may not have the sophistication of risk indicator and loss database models, the process demands a greater step-change in awareness of risk and control that, in itself, is extremely valuable in advancing the risk management capability and culture.

The way that the management team anticipates and responds to risk is key to the level of risk in an organization. If a capital framework is to create an incentive to manage operational risk, the numeric quantification must measure management's capability to identify, manage and mitigate that risk. It is the way that an individual risk is controlled and managed that is fundamental in understanding its potential impact.

An organization's own review of its existing risk and control processes will generate information that focuses specifically on that individual organization – its unique risk profile and its control responses to those risks – producing a potentially far more sensitive valuation of operational risk if the results of the review are used as the primary data in a capital model.

11.2 Why use a scorecard model?

Building on a risk and control assessment can give great value to an organization. Using a model that quantifies the risks faced by an organization and that also quantifies the controls used to mitigate those risks enables a far greater understanding of the interaction of risks and controls. Compared to collecting loss data for a model, it also gives much earlier experience of quantifying risks. This can be valuable in challenging the efficiency of the mitigation of the risks much sooner and therefore identifying poorly performing controls and, as a corollary, the most efficient way to focus the use of resources to improve poor controls. This is particularly helpful if an organization has identified the controls that mitigate several risks, because the effect of such multiple controls is sometimes counter-intuitive. With a quantified risk inventory it is also easy to stress-test the risks and controls using 'what if' analysis. From this, it is possible to see, through clear monetary values, the sensitivities of the risks to an increasing level of exposure and of the controls to either downgrading or enhancing the design and/or performance.

11.3 Risks and controls

Before quantifying and managing the operational risk of an institution, its management must first identify the elements from which the institution is most at risk and then find a method of monitoring and controlling the risks. Only when an institution's risk profile has been identified and is being monitored can its senior management hope to begin serious efforts to manage and then mitigate the risks. Examples of typical risks with associated controls are given in Table 11.1.

11.3.1 Risk identification

The identification of the operational risks facing an institution can be carried out in a variety of ways. The objectives of the institution and the possible causes that will prevent the institution from reaching those objectives are typically explored in interview and/or senior management workshops. Alternatively, processes may be identified and the risks to those processes considered by the managers and supervisors most familiar with the process. Both the objectives and the process can be high-level strategic ones that affect the entire institu-

TABLE 11.1 ■ Examples of risks and their associated controls

Risk	*Controls*
Loss of reputation	Brand survey Complaints procedure Quality of staff Public relations firm retained
Loss of key staff	Mentoring schemes Long-term incentives Annual reward surveys
Loss of information technology infrastructure	Uninterruptible power supply Preventative maintenance Hot-standby system Physical security

tion or, equally, they can be part of a detailed procedure specific to a department. The identification of the objectives (or the process) is a necessary first step without which the risks subsequently explored will have no context. Without boundaries it is very difficult to determine at what level the risks should properly be analyzed and the development of an appropriate risk profile becomes much more problematic.

The monitoring of risks is assisted by an analysis of each risk in terms of the owner of the risk, the risk's impact on an organization and the likelihood that it will happen. The identification of a risk owner is to ensure that a specific person (or sometimes a committee) takes responsibility for the risk and therefore for its management and mitigation, where possible. Risk owners are not identified in order to generate (or perpetuate) a blame culture and the institution's senior management must be fully committed to the responsibility approach in order for the institution to benefit from the management and mitigation of its risk. Without a commitment to the responsibility approach for risk ownership (rather than the blame approach) there will be many fewer risks identified and much less enthusiasm on the part of management and supervisors to be conscious of the risks faced by an organization (and the reduction of those risks).

Typically the impact of a risk on an organization is initially evaluated as high, medium or low. However, this often rapidly becomes a monetary value and is generally viewed from a value perspective once the management of risk has been embedded in an organization. Similarly, the likelihood that a risk will happen to an organization is also often initially evaluated as high, medium or low. This also tends to transform into a percentage likelihood or a time value (such as once every three months) as the managers become more familiar with risk management.

Many of the previously manual approaches to self-assessment are increasingly being automated to provide a more proactive method of monitoring operational risk. The implementation and operation of an effective control and risk self-assessment process can provide valuable management information on both the level of operational risk and the adequacy of the control responses to those risks. There are several critical factors that can be used to guide the success of a self-assessment process, including senior management sponsorship for the process, a focus on the development of action plans to address key operational weaknesses rather than a focus on the existence of the weakness, and the willingness of senior and middle management to own and drive risk and control accountability through the organization.

11.3.2 Control identification

The same process applied to each control yields the beginnings of a tool to manage (and mitigate) operation risk. The control owner should be identified as the person who is responsible for the control operating effectively. The control's importance and effectiveness are also assessed in either interviews or workshops. The importance of a control tells management whether the control is fundamental or important to mitigating the inherent risk or is one of perhaps a suite of controls no single one of which by itself will prevent a risk from occurring. The effectiveness of a control is its ability to mitigate the risk based on the control's design and on how the control is carried out in practice. In practice, the effectiveness is broken down into separate assessments of the design of a control (i.e. the inherent ability of the control to mitigate the risk) and the performance (or how the control is actually carried out in practice). Such separate assessments allow clearer action plans to be drawn up. Defective control design will often be due to poor systems or processes, whereas poor performance is frequently down to people.

11.3.3 The risk–control relationship

An approach to the modelling of operational risk using the results of a risk and control assessment, which is then simulated to give a wide variety of scenarios, enables an organization to utilize its view of its risks both before and after the effects of the identified controls. An organization's view of its risks will inevitably be based on future expectations of the effectiveness of the control environment and the likely risks that will be encountered in the future. Although risks that have previously occurred will be taken into account when preparing a risk profile, most organizations evaluate their risks with respect to the future and not the past. This is only natural as control mechanisms are likely to be in place to mitigate previous risks but future risks are unknown and therefore more feared.

In order to embed risk awareness in the organization, managers often use key indicators that are linked back to the risks and controls identified. Such indicators are useful to assess how an organization is currently performing its risk management processes and should be used when available to review the severity and frequency of the identified risks and the effectiveness of the controls. Similarly, internal data on loss occurrences should also be used to review and, if necessary, reassess the risks and adequacy of the controls.

In reality, businesses do not fit into a simple and neat model. Some controls are designed to mitigate a number of risks (usually with varying degrees of success) and sometimes those controls are human. A single manager may be responsible for a number of risks or controls, and his or her competency (or, at the very least, the collective responsibility in which he or she shares) is an important variable in the risk likelihood. Each individual organization will experience trends in risk, both in its own enterprise and in its broader industry sector. What an organization needs is not a snapshot of its response to risk at any one time but an ability to look forward at the whole range of potential impacts of these risks at any point in the future.

11.4 The scorecard approach

Given the above organizational and shareholder needs, it is encouraging to see one regulator (in the form of the Basel Committee for Banking Supervision) recognizing a scorecard approach as one of the Advanced Measurement Approaches for operational risk Pillar 1 capital calculations (BCBS 2001b, pp. 34–35; 2001c, p. 20, paras 84–85).

A scorecard approach to operational risk capital calculation is inherently flexible as it automatically fits in with an organization's identified risks and controls and does not require an external view of the risk categories faced by a firm. Additionally, an organization has the ability to gain skills and knowledge from starting operational risk capital calculation early and not waiting to build up a database of internal data or to use external data that may not be relevant to the organization. Together these provide a powerful incentive to use a scorecard approach and to obtain extra value from existing risk and control data.

A scorecard is simply a list of a firm's own assessment of its risks and controls containing the elements mentioned above – typically the risk event, risk owner, risk likelihood, risk impact, control(s) that mitigate the risk event, control owner, control design and control impact. Although the list is a matter of judgement, it is nevertheless based on what the business believes may occur in the future rather than historical risk occurrences where controls are likely to have been tightened already.

At a minimum, the scorecard must contain the risk event, risk likelihood and risk impact. However, if it only contains these three elements a great deal of useful information will not be available to the organization as the risk will inevitably have been reviewed only at a net (or residual) risk level. Information on the control contribution to the risk reduction will, therefore, clearly not be calculated by the model and not be available for resource allocation and cost-efficiency checking (see below).

A risk scorecard may also contain commentary and/or values for action plans to enhance controls or reduce (and sometimes, optimize) risks. Furthermore, key indicators for the risk events (and controls, if included in the scorecard) also sometimes appear in a scorecard and can be used in a model to sensitize the risk assessment to what is actually happening.

As organizations become more familiar with (and indeed capture) loss data, scorecards will also record the losses incurred from each risk event. The loss may be incurred by the organization and therefore directly relevant to it. However, the loss may also have been incurred by another organization, which either is part of a group of organizations sharing loss information or has made the loss public and therefore available for use in others' scorecards.

Actual losses from risk events are valuable for two reasons. Firstly, the losses can be used for education and training purposes to challenge the existing scorecard in terms of impact and likelihood. Additionally, the losses can be used within a scorecard again to sensitize the risk assessment. It is, however, unnecessary for there to be a direct fit with standard loss types in order for a scorecard approach to yield valuable management information about the organization's risks and controls, assuming that the losses do fit the scorecard risks.

In order to measure the operation risk capital from the collected data, the occurrence of the risks and the failure of controls is simulated a considerable number of times and the resulting distribution collected and analyzed. This is a very similar process to that used for market risk modelling. A scorecard is also sometimes called a risk map or a risk inventory.

In order to use a scorecard list of risks to run a model that produces a capital figure, it is necessary to give values to the elements of the scorecard such as percentages of occurrence for the risk likelihood, a monetary value for the risk impact and percentages of control failure (or success) for the control design and performance. Owners (of risk and controls) can be given a correlation value between −1.0 and +1.0, where −1.0 represents perfect inverse correlation, 0.0 represents no correlation at all and +1.0 represents perfect correlation (see also Section 11.5.2).

11.5 Model simulations

Having collected data on risks and controls, as noted above, it is possible to run simulations on the risk and control profile. There are three possibilities for such simulations, and the choice depends on the efficiency of the simulation, the capability of the technology used and the completeness of the risk and control data:

1   Simulate the controls first and, if a control fails, then simulate the risks. The advantage of this method is that it focuses on the control dimensions. The risks only need to be considered if a control has failed. However, there are usually considerably more controls than risks, although controls often have a narrower range of values.

2   Simulate the risks first and, if a risk happens, then simulate the controls. The advantage of this method is that it focuses on the risk likelihood. Only if the risk happens, in the risk simulation, is it then necessary to check to see if the control has failed. Clearly a risk can only have an impact if it has happened and if its control has failed. This leads to an efficient simulation process although at the expense of a complete set of data for risks and controls. The simulation is more efficient than possibility 1 as the number of risks is generally much smaller than the number of controls and therefore fewer simulations will be required in total than in possibility 1 for a similar size set of results.

3   Simulate both the risks and controls. This enables a full set of data to be simulated for both risks and controls, although a very efficient simulation model is required as ideally all four variables (likelihood, impact, design and performance) should be simulated. A check is then made as to whether or not the control has failed (due to design or

performance reasons) and whether or not the risk has occurred (from the likelihood simulation) and what the impact has been (from the impact simulation results).

11.5.1 Distributions

In the previous chapters of this book there has been considerable discussion on which mathematical distribution to use for a particular type of data and/or data set. Some risks appear naturally to have distributions that are complex. However, given the degree of judgement already exercised over the likelihood and impact of the identified risks and the identified variables of the controls, it can be argued that to introduce a further level of estimation (in the type of distribution to simulate) is unnecessary and does not add significantly to the quality of the results. For these reasons, it is suggested that a normal distribution is used for all simulations. If an efficient simulation model is used it is easily possible to generate, say, a hundred thousand simulations in only a few hours. These results will yield more useful data than layering mathematical approximations of complex distributions on top of business judgements of the identified risks and mitigating controls.

11.5.2 Correlations

Risks often correlate to other risks, and this should be reflected in a scorecard model. There are various indicators for correlations of risks such as risk owners, geographic location of risks or risks evolving from the same (or similar) causes. Controls also correlate with each other and indicators can be the same control owner, the same system or the same group of staff carrying out a control.

Again, care should be taken not to become too granular in setting correlations. Firstly, there is the danger of building estimates upon judgements and making the model less robust. Secondly, it is very easy to end up with an illogical set of correlations (mathematically, a matrix which is not positive definite). Although the mathematical test for this is beyond the scope of this chapter, it is difficult to take all possible correlations into account when constructing a correlation matrix and therefore it is easy to end up with a mathematically impossible set of correlations. A scorecard model that takes risk and control correlations into account will check the correlations for consistency.

By correlating risks (or controls) the model simulation comes closer to reality and reflects the interdependency of the risks (and controls). Further details are given in Section 7.7.

11.5.3 Murphy's law

Murphy's law ('if anything can go wrong, it will') was born at a US Air Force Flight Test Centre in 1949. It was named after Captain Edward A. Murphy, an engineer working on an Air Force project designed to see how much sudden deceleration a person can stand in a crash. One day, after finding that a technician had incorrectly wired a transducer, he said: 'If there is any way to do it wrong, he'll find it.' Shortly afterwards, the Air Force doctor gave a press conference at which he said that the project's good safety record was due to a firm belief in Murphy's law and in the necessity of trying to circumvent it.[1]

In the world of risk management, Murphy's law is well known and commonly regarded as an occupational hazard. In the modelling of a risk and control scorecard, Murphy's law can be regarded as a risk occurring (and having an impact) even when all of the controls mitigating the risk have worked. In other words, something happened (or did not happen) that allowed the risk to occur even though management had identified the appropriate controls and ensured that the controls were well designed and performed adequately. Most risk people know of such circumstances. In a model, Murphy's law can be easily simulated although the impact from such occurrences should be identified in the results so that they can be reviewed if necessary.

11.6 Quantification of gross and net risks

The ability to quantify, at an early opportunity, the gross risk and the value of a control enables an institution to benefit by allocating control resources more efficiently. By knowing the gross value of the risk, an organization can start to rank risks by likely monetary impact rather than by simple high, medium or low scores. Additionally, by knowing the reduction of risk gained by using a control it is possible to assess both the monetary value of the control and the percentage improvement in the risk exposure that the control gives. These two figures together, the gross risk and the control value, enable a far more efficient method of resource allocation than has previously been possible.

For example, most available additional resources will intuitively be allocated to the most significant risk that an institution faces. However, if the biggest risk is already well controlled (which is generally likely) it will be more efficient to use the additional control resources to improve the controls over some of the smaller risks.

The quantification of gross risk and control values enables the management to see which risk is most susceptible to reduction by focusing on the control improvement already achieved and still possible. In Figure 11.1, using more control resources on risk 2 (which is currently only 50 percent effectively controlled) rather that risk 3, which is the biggest risk (but effectively controlled), will give better value for money. Similarly, risk 8 (although small) will reduce significantly as a net risk if only a little more additional control attention is paid to it. Only the detailed values for the first four risks are shown, although the values for risk 8 can be deduced from the histogram. The monetary values in Figure 11.1 are obtained from the simulation and the values shown are the mean values for the overall risk and each composite risk both before and after controls (i.e. gross (or inherent) risk and net (or residual) risk).

Figures 11.2 and 11.3 show different ways of recording this information, and give further clarity to it. For instance, Figure 11.2 shows that risks 12 and 8 have the highest potential

---

[1] See http://www.edwards.af.mil/history/docs_html/tidbits/murphy's_law.html.

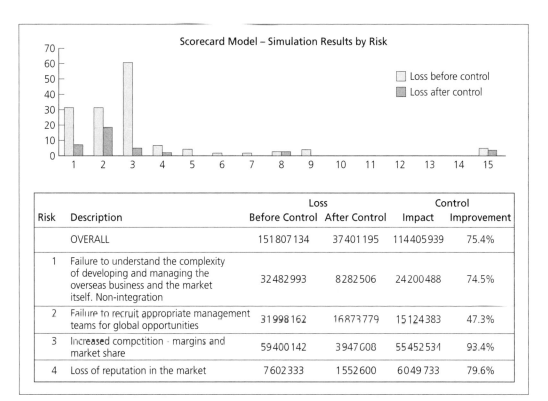

Risk	Description	Loss		Control	
		Before Control	After Control	Impact	Improvement
	OVERALL	151807134	37401195	114405939	75.4%
1	Failure to understand the complexity of developing and managing the overseas business and the market itself. Non-integration	32482993	8282506	24200488	74.5%
2	Failure to recruit appropriate management teams for global opportunities	31998162	16873779	15124383	47.3%
3	Increased competition - margins and market share	59400142	3947608	55452534	93.4%
4	Loss of reputation in the market	7602333	1552600	6049733	79.6%

FIGURE 11.1 ■ Mean loss and control values

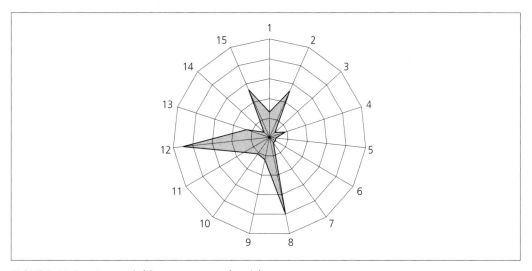

FIGURE 11.2 ■ Potential improvement by risk

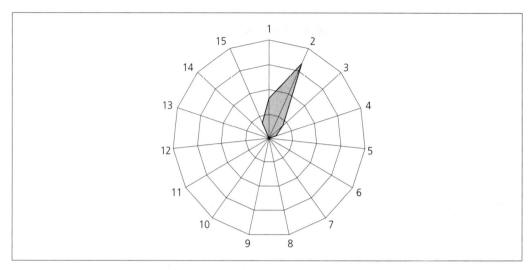

FIGURE 11.3 ■ Potential loss by risk

improvement, followed by risks 15, 2 and 13. If the histogram in Figure 11.1 had been used for an improvement programme, risks 12 and 13 would not have been selected. Similarly, Figure 11.3 focuses attention more clearly on the net (residual) risk values.

11.7 Risk appetite

An organization's operational risk appetite is frequently discussed but it has previously been very difficult to develop a method of giving actual monetary values to the risk appetite. Previously, organizations have only been able to make qualitative comments on their risk appetite, such as 'conservative' or 'aggressive'. Such comments describe only the organization's reaction to the likely occurrence of the perils to which it is vulnerable.

Quantitative risk appetite can be described as a measure of the risks that an organization chooses to accept, whether as a monetary measure for the possible loss suffered and/or as a frequency measure for the likelihood of the risk occurring. One of the benefits of a scorecard approach is the quantification of net risk and therefore the ability to look at an organization's aggregate loss exposure after controls. The question then arises as to which possible loss figure to take: a value at a confidence level or an expected shortfall value.

The advantage of using a value at a confidence level is that it is easily understood. This method is used for market risk value-at-risk figures in the financial services sector. However, it takes no account of possible losses beyond the confidence level and is simply the aggregate loss at one point on the risk distribution. This means that the loss event on which the organization is basing its risk appetite will only take into account controls that have failed in this particular loss event and that, conversely, no account will be taken of controls that have not failed at this point.

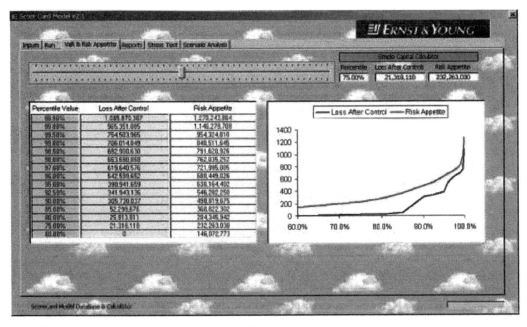

FIGURE 11.4 ■ Value-at-risk and risk appetite

From a management perspective for operational risk it would seem worth considering the losses in the distribution tail, that is, losses after the loss event relating directly to the chosen confidence level, as well as the loss event at the chosen confidence level. This leads to an expected shortfall value derived from the simulation. This is the average of all values that may be incurred by an organization and that have resulted from the simulation at and beyond the required confidence level. The expected shortfall figure is larger than the confidence level figure for the same percentage value but gives a more realistic figure for management purposes precisely because it takes into account more extreme values than a simple 'value-at-risk' figure. A comprehensive scorecard model will produce a significant number of possible risk appetite figures (see Figure 11.4) for the institution's management to consider.

11.8 Stress testing and scenario analysis

One of the benefits of quantifying risks and controls is that an organization can then perform analyses on its risk inventory. This crucially allows the organization to see, in monetary terms, the likely increase in risk exposure of removing a control or the likely reduction in risk exposure of increasing the quality of controls. Performing a scenario analysis over a number of risks and controls enables the management to conduct extensive 'what if' analysis without putting the organization at risk by increasing various risks or removing a swathe of controls. An example of a scenario analysis screen in a scorecard model is shown

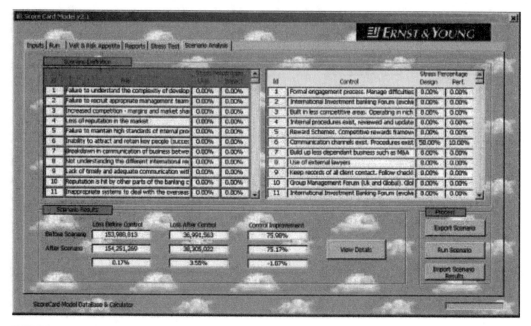

FIGURE 11.5 ■ Scenario analysis

in Figure 11.5. Such a screen will show all risks and controls and allow as many or as few as are required to be amended.

11.9 Conclusion

By including risk and control data, key indicator data, internal loss data and externally supplied loss data, it is possible to build a complex and comprehensive view of the entire range of risk, controls and impacts in any organization. The benefits of this approach go well beyond an accurate (and most likely reduced) capital requirement for operational risk. This sophisticated model can be used to inform both strategic and process execution, giving management and investors alike the confidence that strategic objectives can be met. Equally, it can be used to challenge management's assumptions around priorities as well as giving a valuable sense check around the organization's risk appetite.

The acceptance by the Basel Committee on Banking Supervision that a scorecard approach is a recognized methodology for calculating operational risk capital means that this approach is now in the mainstream of risk calculations. The management benefits that can be derived by using a scorecard approach to quantify a risk inventory go far beyond those that may be gained for regulatory purposes.

CHAPTER 12

The operational risk management framework

Michael Haubenstock[1]

12.1 Introduction

The terrorist attacks on the United States immediately changed the risk profile of all institutions. Certain risks suddenly jumped in magnitude: those related to business continuity, diversification and human resources, among others. These are operational risks, and managing them requires a framework to identify, assess, control, monitor and mitigate exposures.

In the past five to ten years operational risk management in financial institutions has evolved into a discipline in its own right, with specialized staff, policies, measurement, reporting and related technology. This was reported extensively in Robert Morris Associates *et al.* (1999). Since that study appeared the underlying components have basically remained the same, but their content has continued to evolve and become more widely accepted as well as more sophisticated.

In addition, the Basel Committee (BCBS) is now proposing an operational risk capital charge. The proposed new Capital Accord outlines three alternative methodologies to quantify capital, each with increasing levels of sophistication and the potential for a lower capital charge. These alternatives and the relevant criteria for using them are described in the first part of this book. Related to the operational risk management framework, ten qualitative principles have been outlined by the Committee. These principles will have to be implemented for a firm to be eligible to use the more advanced models (BCBS 2002b). To be eligible for a lower capital charge, institutions must demonstrate they have implemented both the principles and a sound quantitative model. The principles are summarized as follows:

1 The board of directors should be aware of the major aspects of operational risk, approve and periodically review the operational risk management framework.

---

[1] Parts of this chapter have been extracted from 'OR', a series of articles on operational risk published by the *RMA Journal* in 2002 and co-authored by Michael Haubenstock.

2   The board of directors should ensure that the framework is subject to effective internal audit.

3   Senior management has responsibility for implementing the framework, and all levels of staff should understand their responsibilities.

4   Banks should identify the operational risk in all products, activities, processes and systems for both existing operations and new products.

5   Banks should establish the processes to regularly monitor operational risk profiles and material exposure to losses.

6   Banks should have policies, processes and procedures to control or mitigate operational risk. They should assess the feasibility of alternative strategies and adjust their exposures appropriately.

7   Banks should have in place contingency and business continuity plans to ensure their ability to operate as going concerns in the event of business disruption.

8   Bank supervisors should require banks to have an effective operational risk management strategy as part of an overall approach to risk management.

9   Supervisors should conduct regular independent evaluations of the related bank operational risk management strategies.

10 Banks should make sufficient public disclosure to allow market participants to assess their approach to operational risk management.

The implementation of the above principles can be called an operational risk management framework. Banks will also have to pass a 'use test' – that is, is the framework implemented as part of the day-to-day management processes in the organization used effectively to manage risk? This chapter describes how to construct this framework and integrate it into the management processes of the bank.

An operational risk framework has four components: strategy, process, infrastructure and environment (see Figure 12.1). Strategy sets the overall tone of and approach to risk management. It includes the statement of business objectives and risk appetite, the organizational approach to managing risk and the expression of related policy that is the approach to operational risk management. Process describes the day-to-day activities and decisions used to manage risk within the chosen strategy. Infrastructure identifies the systems, data and other tools used in the management process. Environment describes the culture and external factors. Culture refers to the involvement and support of senior management and the related values and communication that set the tone for decision-making. Each institution should define the degree of top-down versus bottom-up approach used in the qualitative and quantitative analysis.

This chapter is organized around the four components of the framework and their related components.

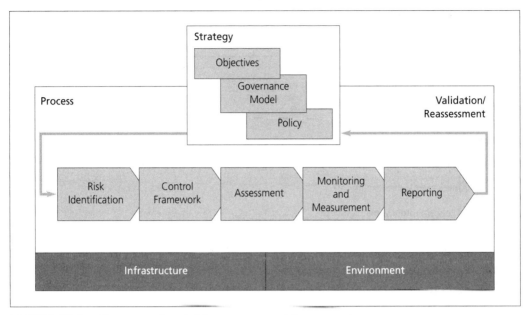

FIGURE 12.1 ■ The operational risk management framework

12.2 Defining operational risk

A definition of operational risk is central to any operational risk framework. The most common definition, first published in Robert Morris Associates *et al*. (1999), is: 'Operational risk is the direct or indirect loss resulting from inadequate or failed internal processes, people and systems, or from external events.' The Basel Committee adopted the same definition but eliminated the reference to indirect losses for the purposes of quantification of regulatory capital, since these risks are so difficult to measure. But for internal purposes, indirect exposures such as service, reputation, and business interruption should be considered within the scope.

This definition is a good overall statement, but further refinement is necessary to build an operational risk framework. A comprehensive set of risk categories helps organize the process and create a common language across the organization. While there is no industry standard, many firms have adopted definitions with categories of operational risk *events*, complemented by a list of *effects* that are the types of financial consequences. The definitions proposed by the Basel Committee are shown in Table 12.1.

Many organizations supplement event and effect categories with a third category, causes. The causes refer to the underlying cause or control that failed related to an event. Examples include training, segregation of duties, management oversight, turnover and reconciliations. There are often multiple causes that contribute to any one event. The important point to remember regarding these risk categories is that the institution must use the same categories throughout all the components of the framework, such as the self-assessment

TABLE 12.1 ■ Event and effect definitions

Events	Effects
Internal fraud	Legal cost/settlement
External fraud	Regulatory/compliance
Employment practices/workplace safety	Restitution
Clients, products and business practices	Loss of recourse
Damage to physical assets	Write-downs
Business disruption and system failures	Loss of physical asset
Execution, delivery and process management	

process, risk indicators, capital quantification and management reporting. This approach will help to facilitate the aggregation of risk and permit common reporting formats across the organization.

12.3 Strategy

Strategy is the place for senior management involvement to start. As indicated in the ten principles from the Basel Committee, we expect directors' involvement in and approval of the risk management approach, and we expect senior management involvement as well. This applies to all aspects of the strategy portion of the framework.

12.3.1 Business objectives

Risk management should be focused to help achieve a goal that is defined by business objectives. Objectives can include business strategy, such as gaining a certain percentage of market share or introducing a new product or technology. Objectives are also stated for internal units, where, for example, a finance organization might have the objective of closing the books each month within five days, or identifying a certain amount of cost reduction. These objectives also determine the types of risks that an organization faces.

Objectives should also include an expression of risk appetite – the level of acceptable risk and what types of risks are not acceptable. In operational risk, quantifiable measures of risk appetite include what combinations of frequency and severity in a risk map create unacceptable risks, the level of operational losses and escalation criteria on various risk indicators. Examples of qualitative expressions of risk appetite include expectations of compliance with policy and law; transacting only in products with appropriate levels of control and automation; openness, transparency and sharing of control issues and loss events; and prompt completion of assessment programmes. Risk management objectives often revolve around reducing uncertainty and avoiding surprises.

12.3.2 Governance model

Traditionally, operational risk was part of everyone's job; line and staff people had to manage their respective operational risks. While the responsibility for risk still rests with line management, there is a new governance model evolving in financial institutions. This model and its resultant roles and responsibilities will define the approach to operational risk management. It is characterized by having a central operational risk manager, most often reporting to the chief risk officer. The role is one of policy setting, development of tools, co-ordination, independent analysis and benchmarking, and integration and aggregation of the risk profile. For example, the operational risk manager would set out the common definitions for operational risk, develop and facilitate the implementation of common risk management tools such as risk maps, self-assessment programmes and loss event databases, and develop measurement models, such as the economic capital model, that cross organizational boundaries and functions.

Line management remains responsible for the day-to-day risk management activities, since it is the business areas that face the customer, introduce products, manage the majority of people, operate processes and technologies and deal with other external exposures. In addition, staff organizations like human resources, information technology, security, legal and finance develop specific policies and procedures, monitor emerging risks and advise the organization on risk as applicable to their areas of expertise.

The differentiation between line and corporate responsibilities is important. Risks really occur in the line, and detailed risk analysis and monitoring can be very different across business lines. The corporate function has to focus on standards and activities that cross business lines. The value that the corporate function can add includes analysis of risks and trends across business lines, sharing of experience and best practices, benchmarking, participation in external databases, capital measurement and consolidated reporting to senior management.

Operational risk units are often complemented by risk committees. The role of the risk committee is to understand the risk profile, ensure that resources are properly allocated and risk issues are addressed, and approve policies, including capital allocation.

The definition of this governance model includes the roles, authority levels and accountabilities of each organizational component. Any organizational model requires the right people. The right skills base, combined with a training programme for both operational risk staff and other affected people in the organization, becomes an important consideration for success.

12.3.3 Policy

Corporate policy sets the overall strategy for operational risk management. Organizations should have an operational risk policy statement that describes their overall approach. This policy statement can be made specific to each business area as applicable.

Policies often start with the objectives of operational risk management. Some alternate objectives include increased awareness, reduced operational losses, capital measurement and quality of service. This statement of objectives can be complemented by a description of how the organization goes about the process and the agreed-upon definition of operational risk. The approach is often a description of the framework itself, and this chapter is an illustration of the contents. One can also touch on how business and strategic planning and performance measurement should include risk management as a component.

Next, a policy statement might discuss the governance model and related roles and responsibilities. This would include any committees that have operational risk as part of their scope, the roles of any central operational risk group, responsibilities of the business lines, and involvement with other staff groups such as compliance, legal, insurance, information technology and human resources.

Some general statements of risk management principles can help define the cultural aspects of the process. These principles set the standard for expected behaviour for both management and staff. For example, one principle could reinforce the expectation that loss events will be collected and shared in an open and transparent manner. Another potential principle is that measurement of capital will be used as a key focus in the process for risk analysis and to create behavioural incentives. It is also valuable to reinforce the expectation that business areas are responsible for their own controls and bear the profit and loss consequences of any errors. These are just three examples. In the process of developing the framework, many more underlying rules will become evident as the basis for decision-making around the design. These decisions often form the basis for underlying principles that can be communicated to the organization.

Lastly, the policy might describe the expectations for the use of tools and reporting. For example, if there is a common self-assessment or database tool, the policy might state that every business area should implement it and maintain the information in an up-to-date manner. The policy could also describe what information each business area is expected to report to the group level.

12.4 The operational risk process

Process steps are the day-to-day activities required to understand and manage operational risks. The risk process can be interpreted to apply enterprise-wide to a transaction or an initiative, to operations such as a back office, or to a periodic, more formal process, such as risk and control self-assessment. As applicable, the related tools to support the process will also be described.

12.4.1 Risk identification

In the context of business objectives, what are the risks incurred? What can prevent the accomplishment of those objectives? The definition of operational risk provides a broad context for potential threats. In addition, a history of events, open issues and risk indicators provides additional information on potential sources of risk. The result of risk identification is a risk map detailing which of these risks applies to any one business, process or organizational unit and to what degree. Degree is often defined as frequency and severity, rated either qualitatively (high, medium, low) or on a quantitative scale.

Risks are first assessed based on the inherent exposure – that is, before the applicable controls or insurance are applied. Although it is difficult to determine the cost of risk before the current controls are present, it is important to consider the costs and benefits of alternative approaches to control.

Some organizations find it valuable to expand the standard definitions of operational risk to identify more specifically risks that are applicable to any given business line. For example, fiduciary risk is not specifically identified in the definition above but would be a large operational risk exposure for a private banking business. In this example, fiduciary risk could be an additional major category or sub-category. For purposes of self-assessment processes, risk factors other than the event categories should be considered. Cause and effect categories might be major categories by themselves. Some organizations use risks such as governance, reporting, legal, compliance and level of management support in their risk identification and self-assessment processes.

Risk identification should also include monitoring of the external environment and industry trends. New risks emerge every day. Even if not new, existing risks may take on a new dimension. For example, Internet security, privacy, patent risk and discrimination are a few examples of exposures that have increased dramatically over the past few years.

12.4.2 Control framework

How do we control or mitigate operational risks? The definition of controls is broad. For example, typical controls include management oversight, information processing, activity monitoring, automation, process controls, segregation of duties, performance indicators and policies and procedures. Other types of risk mitigators include training, insurance programmes, diversification and outsourcing. The control framework defines the appropriate approach to controlling each identified risk. Costs of alternative approaches should be considered, and if the potential costs are high, it is possible to make the explicit decision to take the risk or apply a less than optimal control.

Many risk management programmes define the 'best practice' controls applicable to any one process, and these will be documented in the risk management process or policies and procedures. This list of controls will form the basis of the risk assessment that is described in Section 12.4.3, where businesses assess if and how well those controls are operating.

Insurance is a risk control/mitigation strategy in itself. Insurance is typically applied against the large exposures where a loss would cause a charge to earnings greater than that acceptable in the risk appetite. There are numerous strategies for insurance coverage that go beyond the scope of this chapter.

After controls are defined, we should be sure they are aligned with the original business objectives. Alignment may occur up and down the organization or across business units, processes and geographies. Sometimes controls may be designed so tightly as to prevent accomplishment of objectives. All components should be working together toward a common risk–reward profile.

12.4.3 Assessment

Assessment processes provide the organization with an objective process by which to determine how it is doing – that is, what the exposures are, how well the organization is controlling and monitoring them, what the potential weaknesses are, what the organization should be doing to improve, who is responsible for these actions, and how the organization plans to accomplish them. Assessment is a qualitative process, and it complements the measurement processes described below because not all risks can be individually measured. Many require fundamental analysis and thinking to understand their implications.

One of the key objectives of any self-assessment programme is to create accountability in the line organizations. Line business areas are the 'risk takers' for operational risk and bear the profit and loss impact of any problems. A self-assessment process makes the risk analysis explicit, and line managers are therefore accountable for the results. At the same time, the process helps to reinforce a culture of openness and transparency. Risk requires an open discussion to improve awareness and allocate appropriate resources. Self-assessment creates a common language for risk, a commitment to disclosure and the forum to discuss the issues that arise.

Self-assessment helps break down the silos to discuss risk across the organization and discuss interdependencies. It also helps to ensure that all risks are considered. Operational risks cannot be specifically measured at a detailed level. While many risk indicators exist, they are not comprehensive, and capital measures operate at too high a level to provide detailed insight into individual exposures. The qualitative analysis of self-assessment complements other, more quantitative measures to ensure that the full scope of operational risk is analyzed.

Regardless of the source, the self-assessment process should result in the identification of control gaps, and consequently the appropriate action should be taken. Self-assessment consolidates the information from all sources into specific plans for improvement, accountability and target dates. The process ensures oversight by senior management, so it should improve the decision-making and subsequent allocation of resources.

Approaches to self-assessment tend to evolve over time and often change purposefully to maintain interest in the process and bring new insights into the risk profile. The alternative self-assessment approaches include checklists, narratives and facilitated workshops.

Checklists are probably the most common approach. There are structured questionnaires that are distributed to business areas to help them identify their level of risk and the related controls. Some checklists are very short, containing only the broad categories of risk (e.g. governance, compliance, processing, people, technology), while others provide a more detailed list of the controls that are expected to be in place. The manager's response would (typically) indicate the degree to which the given risk affects their process. It would also give some indication of the frequency and severity or impact of the risk, and the level of risk control that is already in place. Some organizations attempt to indicate the level of inherent risk (prior to control) and the level of risk after current controls are in effect. Any control weaknesses demand some type of corrective action (or a specific statement to accept the exposure) with a clear indication of the lines of responsibility for implementing this action and a planned completion date.

The starting point of narratives is different from the checklist approach, but the end result is similar. Narratives usually start with business areas defining their own objectives and the resulting risks. In place of checking off expected controls, they have to defend the way they control these risks. Gaps are addressed in a similar way. This approach requires more effort but also results in more original thinking about the business and the framework that defines risks and controls.

The workshop approach tries to skip the paperwork and get people to talk about their risks, controls and required improvements. Workshops are typically facilitated by an independent person and contain a cross-section of line and staff people that are familiar with the selected topic. Alternative points of view are debated in the hope of improving the consensus and validating the decisions that are implemented. Initially, in order to bring the key issues into focus, workshops may be used in conjunction with checklists and narratives.

Automated tools that support the assessment process, record the results and provide reporting are becoming more widely implemented. Typically these tools include a representation of the organizational structure of the institution, contain definitions of the operational processes and the inherent risks, and document the controls that are in place. These tools should also record the results of the assessment of controls and the appropriate action items.

A key element in self-assessment is to keep the process and results objective. Any self-assessment process must be independently verified, since, if an organization assesses itself, the results will be dependent on the reporting individuals. Typically some central group, often risk management, plays a central co-ordinating role, reviewing, discussing and challenging the results to ensure that everyone is responding in a consistent fashion. Similarly, central staff groups can play an important verifying role. Groups like information technology, human resources, compliance, audit, insurance and finance have a cross-enterprise perspective and can validate the results from the business areas related to their specific functions.

12.4.4 Measurement and monitoring

As risks and controls are identified, risk measurement provides insight into the magnitude of exposure, how well controls are operating, and whether exposures are changing and consequently require attention. Six types of measures are commonly applied to operational risk management.

Risk drivers

These are measures that drive the inherent risk profile of the organization. Changes in these measures would usually indicate that the risk profile is changing. Examples of risk drivers include transaction volumes, staff levels, skill levels, customer satisfaction, market volatility, product maturity, number of locations, level of change, product complexity and level of automation. The measure might be qualitative, but it can have value when analyzed as a relative measure across business areas. Risk drivers are more forward-looking, or *ex ante*, and therefore predictive of future issues. Significant changes in risk drivers could imply significant changes in the overall level of quality or indicate a potential increase in operational losses or other types of risk.

Risk indicators

In an operational risk management framework, risk indicators are among the key tools used to support risk assessment and risk monitoring. Risk indicators are a broad category of measures used to monitor the activities and status of the control environment of a particular business area for a given operational risk category. While typical control assessment processes occur only periodically, risk indicators can be measured as often as daily. Risk indicators help keep the operational risk management process dynamic and risk profiles current. As the use of risk indicators becomes integrated into a risk management process, indicator levels or measures must have a frame of reference, commonly referred to as escalation criteria or trigger levels. These levels represent thresholds of an indicator or a tolerance that, when passed, will require management to step up its actions.

When indicator programmes are established, there are a few primary objectives. Above all, indicators must be risk-sensitive, that is, must give insight into changes in the resulting loss profile. This is easier said than done. The indicator should be directionally consistent with changes in losses suffered and should ideally give insight into the relative risk of one business area or process to another. However, this falls a long way short of being a true predictor of loss.

By the same token, indicators have certain limitations. For example, many indicators are specific to an individual risk and often specific to a business or process. It is difficult to design a set of indicators that is consistent across business lines and locations, as well as logically consistent across risks. Without this as an objective, the value of the framework may be undermined. Some risk categories are much more difficult to create indicators for than others. While all this effort is designed to predict problems or losses, there is little proven correlation between the risk indicators and actual events. We do not really know which are predictive and for what types of losses.

Before embarking on the design of the specific indicators, or even the overall framework, it is worth summarizing the groups of users involved and the uses to which they will put this information. There are generally two groups of users. First, the *business unit* operational risk managers are responsible for managing specific operational risks and events and managing the overall status of the environment. They work with the business unit managers to define appropriate measures, accept them, and work within the risk indicator framework. This is where the operational risk framework defines risk indicators as tools used to provide transparency and communicate risk appetite.

Second are the *group level* risk managers, who set the risk appetite and translate it into the thresholds or escalation triggers for each business area. They are also responsible for the aggregation of risk information across business areas and risk categories. Risk managers may use risk indicators for causal analysis and/or to overlay the observed changes in the control environment on the historical observed losses to generate more forward-looking measures. The risk indicator framework should be a common data set that meets the requirements of both groups. Both groups should be consulted in the design phase.

Indicators help monitor the quality of operations for all different risk types. The most common measures are *ex-post*, or lagging, measures, which inform us of what has happened but may not provide insight about where to focus resources today. One challenge is to transform these measures into leading indicators that can be more predictive of future problems. Common process measures for processing operations include profit and loss breaks, open confirmations and failed trades and settlements. These can be transformed into more leading measures by making them more exception-oriented – for example, by focusing on issues open after some specified time period (e.g. 24 hours). Other common measures address issues outstanding, error rates, systems reliability or service levels.

Escalation criteria can be set for most indicators. These define the acceptable levels of performance, related to risk appetite or target quality levels. Escalation criteria are not limits in the strict sense of market or credit limits. Escalation criteria set the level at which a higher layer of management should be informed. They may also be used to set the standard for quality expectations. Managers should expect to explain what is happening, why, what they are doing to gain better control and if more resources are required. Some firms establish multiple bands of escalation criteria defining what level should be informed under what criteria.

Loss history

Institutions develop databases to accumulate a history of operational risk losses. They may also record the near misses and pending issues.

There are three basic reasons to collect a history of loss data. The first is to create or enhance awareness at multiple levels of the organization. A basic understanding of exposure and loss experience is a prerequisite for comprehensive and effective operational risk management. A record of losses accumulating into an aggregated picture of the losses per year by risk and business provides the baseline for analysis and the value proposition for improvement. The second is that the data can be used for empirical analysis. What is happening, what events are repeating, for which products, at what control point, for what causes? This analysis can help to direct corrective action to improve the control environment. It also lets experience confirm the qualitative analysis of inherent and actual exposure. Lastly, the data form the basis for quantification. The latest thinking in capital models, as verified by the new Basel recommendations, uses loss data and actuarial techniques as the basis to quantify operational risk capital. This is equally applicable for top-down and bottom-up approaches. A three- to five-year loss history will be required for institutions to be eligible to use advanced models for the new Basel Accord.

A loss history provides at least some information on the 'expected loss' that is necessary for pricing and provisioning. Analysis of these data forms one element of the value proposition for risk management and is an important source of information when determining possible risk mitigating actions.

Causal models

Everyone's goal in operational risk management is to be able to predict potential losses and act on them before it is too late. Causal models provide the mathematical framework for this type of analysis. Usually based on Bayesian networks or discriminate analysis, these models take a history of risk drivers, risk indicators and loss events (or just errors or some other result) and develop the associated multivariate distributions. The models can determine which factor or factors have the highest associations with losses (risk). As the causal factors change, the model can help predict potential losses. The model can then be used to assess root causes and perform scenario analysis relating to potential future environments.

A word of caution is worthwhile here. Causal models require many data points, preferably collected over a period of years, to be useful. High-frequency data are applicable to only some categories of risk, often in operations departments. Experience to date has shown mixed success in causal models, with correlations between losses and underlying variables very low, or even contrary to intuition. More details on causal models are given in Chapter 14.

Capital models

Quantifying economic capital is the expression for 'unexpected losses'. Capital for operational risk is necessary for complete pricing models and risk-adjusted performance measures. Capital models are used in internal economic models and will be applied for regulatory capital under the new Basel rules. The Basel Committee has proposed three alternate approaches. The Basic Indicator Approach and Standardized Approach use multipliers times gross revenue, at the bank level or the business line level, respectively. The Advanced Measurement Approaches are more open, leaving it up to the bank to develop a model, with Basel mentioning three industry methodologies. These three approaches are a multiplier of expected losses, a statistical/actuarial approach based on a loss history, and a more qualitative scorecard approach. Investing in advanced models provides the best insight into the risk profile and may entitle banks to a lower capital charge. Another key benefit of using Advanced Measurement Approaches is that the models can create a behavioural incentive by being responsive to the changing risk profile of the institution. Details of the various approaches to capital models are discussed in the chapters in Part II of this book.

Performance measures

In comparison to other types of measures, performance measures are typically more global and historically focused and are tied into a balanced scorecard used to evaluate performance and ultimately influence compensation. The measures described above help managers understand and manage the risk profile on a continual basis. Performance measures are the measures used at the beginning of the year to set goals and at the end of the year to measure performance. Examples of performance measures in operational risk include the coverage of the self-assessment process, issues resolved on time and percentage of issues discovered as a result of the self-assessment process. The point of this last measure is to encourage issue identification by the businesses in the self-assessment process as opposed to by audit or other sources. The level of losses is often a common goal and consideration for a performance measure. Care must be taken, since this can be a volatile number, and one large incident out of everyone's control can cause poor performance.

The monitoring process helps management understand the current risk profile, how it is changing and which risks warrant attention. An important aspect of the process is to monitor the risk measures and analyze trends. Risk monitoring should also follow the results of the risk assessment processes. Assessments will identify the exposure areas and gaps. The level of participation in the assessment process itself is an indication of risk. Are assessments being performed in a timely manner? Are the right people participating, and what do the results indicate? Also, are the corrective action measures being executed and completed according to plan?

12.4.5 Reporting

Reporting and validation/reassessment are the final components of the process framework. Figure 12.2 illustrates the overall framework and related roles. Business lines perform the majority of data collection and reporting as part of their normal responsibilities. The central operational risk groups add value through benchmarking, analysis and capital quantification.

Typical contents of a reporting package are listed in Figure 12.2. Reporting is necessary for all levels of the organization, but the exact content and frequency of the information must be tailored to each business area. Reporting should satisfy the requirements of individual business managers as well as offering a consolidated view for senior management. A key objective is to communicate the overall profile of operational risk across all business areas and types of risk. Returning to the principles from the Basel Committee, this is where we inform senior management of major risks in the organization. Reporting communicates the overall level of risk and highlights key trends or exceptions that may require particular attention. Examples of the types of reports in a senior management reporting package are described below.

Self-assessments are performed by the business areas, and results are aggregated to provide a qualitative profile of risk across the organization and related action items. The results are communicated with a combination of risk maps, graphic results, issues and initiatives.

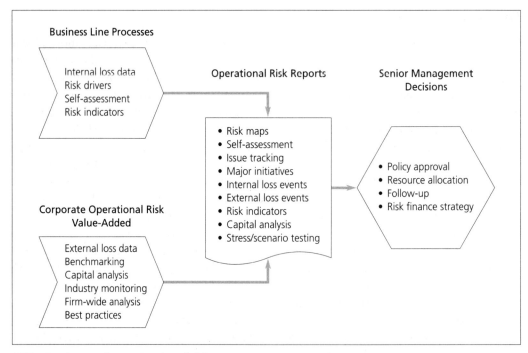

FIGURE 12.2 ■ The operational risk management reporting process

Risk maps are typically graphs in which risks are plotted against axes of frequency and severity. The source can be the self-assessment process or the results of the loss event data-base. Risk maps can be designed either to show inherent risks or to show the risks after control. Figure 12.3 shows an example. The plotted points are categorized by line of business, and within each line of business each point represents a different risk category. If we divide the analysis into generic quadrants, risks in the upper right are very serious and should be transformed out of that category. High-frequency, low-severity risks create the basis for expected losses and are often subject to detailed analysis focused on reducing the level of losses, receiving the highest level of management attention. The low-frequency, high-severity events are what keep us awake at night and also require attention. These are the subject of detailed analysis, contingency plans and insurance policies. Low-frequency, low-severity events can be managed down, but they are often accepted as a cost of doing business if a substantial investment is required to reduce them.

Self-assessment results often are summarized as red/yellow/green indicators for each business and major risk category. Figure 12.4 shows one way to communicate the results (where red/yellow/green are shown as dark grey/white/light grey respectively). Arrows in select cells communicate the trend in the risk profile. Another effective tool is to summarize findings into a 'top ten' list of risks facing the institution. These summary results are accompanied by descriptions of the significant gaps and trends. The list is complemented by a summary of the issue and the action plan.

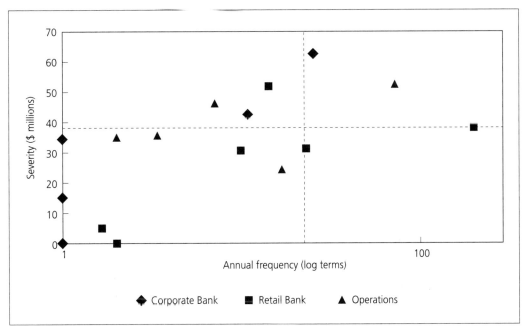

FIGURE 12.3 ▩ A sample risk map

Issues can surface from the internal self-assessment process, audit or regulators. A key result of the self-assessment process is an action plan with assigned responsibilities. This report can contain a recap of major issues, status of the action plan and ageing of overdue tasks.

Major initiatives are always a concern. Another section of any reporting package can contain an update on the status of any major initiatives related to operational risk – for example, systems projects, process improvement or merger integration.

Event Category	Retail	Mortgage	Investment Bank	Asset Mgt	Brokerage	Other
People	●	●	● ➡	●	●	●
Processsing	●	● ⬇	●	●	●	●
System	● ⬇	●	●	● ⬆	● ⬇	● ⬇
External	● ⬇	●	● ⬆	●	●	●

FIGURE 12.4 ▩ Summary of self-assessment

Events are the operational losses, both internal and external, that provide the historical base for risk analysis and quantification. The primary report is summary statistics from the loss event database, showing trends of total losses and mean average loss, with analysis by type of loss and business line. Any significant changes are described. A sample format is depicted in Figure 12.5. Comprehensive event databases can be linked to insurance claims management processes and can illustrate loss history before and after insurance coverage. If there are any significant internal losses, incidents or threats, these are reported for discussion with a description of what happened, what permitted it to occur, whether there are any other potential incidences and what action steps are in place to prevent future occurrence. By the same token, reporting often includes any relevant external losses, industry trends or news related to regulation, competitors or other risk factors that might be of interest.

Key indicators may also be reported, including related escalation criteria, explanations of any excesses and identified trends. Many indicators are customized at the business unit or process level, but some may be common and reported in a consolidated fashion.

Capital levels are reported with breakdowns by risk category and business line and with related trends over time. The trends and relative explanations are important to the communication of the changing risk profile of the organization. Along with capital, there are the related stress/scenario tests around the capital model. Tests may stress operational capacity, model assumptions and their sensitivity, and capital coverage of major events. One way to

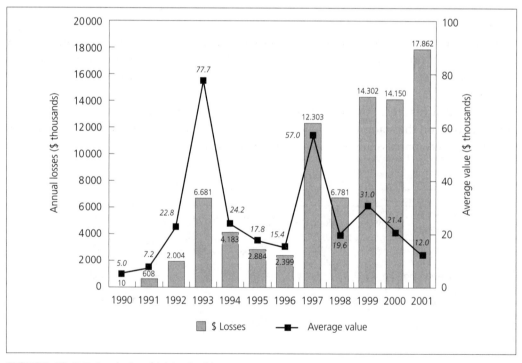

FIGURE 12.5 ■ Analysis of historical losses

report the results is to rank the tests from high to low, graph them and illustrate them in comparison to the related capital coverage to show which might push or exceed the level of assigned capital.

These reports are oriented towards communicating an enterprise-wide perspective of the operational risk profile. Most of this information would be equally applicable to the group and individual business lines. Business line reporting is typically in detail, with additional information tailored to each area, such as business-specific risk indicators.

12.5 Infrastructure

Infrastructure refers to the tools used to facilitate the entire risk management process. Infrastructure is the tangible components that are used to support decision-making in the process. Typical components of the infrastructure include systems, data, methodologies, and policies and procedures.

Technology is a necessary enabler. In operational risk, the common systems are tools to support the self-assessment process, loss database, risk indicator collection and reporting, insurance claims management and capital models. Each is its own application but should work from a common database and definitions whenever possible.

Data are the core for objective measurement and decision-making. Internally, we collect loss event data and risk drivers and indicators. Firms also subscribe to external databases of loss information, whether for publicly disclosed events or in consortiums to share internal experience.

Any of the quantification approaches require a fully documented methodology. Methodologies are required for scoring, capital and causal modelling.

The actual policy documents and related procedures around the control policies are also part of the infrastructure. While an operational risk policy document may be fairly thin, there are numerous other policies and detailed procedures describing specific topics – for example, money laundering, security, privacy, compliance and information technology.

Each of these components of the infrastructure has been described previously.

12.6 Environment

The environment refers to the surroundings that set the tone and behaviour of the organization. The primary component is the culture that supports the risk management objectives. We can define culture as the set of shared attitudes, values, goals and practices that characterize how a company considers risk in its day-to-day activities. Culture can either be explicitly formulated or be allowed to evolve over time. The definition of the entire risk management framework is an explicit communication of the desired culture.

Risk culture often is viewed as the soft side of risk management and is taken for granted. It is much harder to describe and work on than the quantitative methods we learn about.

However, the culture will define the balance between quantitative and qualitative approaches, top-down versus bottom-up analysis, and the level of involvement of senior management. Culture is about capturing the hearts and minds of people and setting common values.

Risk management must have the support and involvement of senior management. They can send the message that operational risks are important, that they deserve attention, and management will allocate resources accordingly. Individuals should be open to communicating issues to senior managers.

The institution should communicate and embody a high degree of ethics. This can be demonstrated through a code of conduct and by management setting the example of following it, as well as in other ethical and legal ways.

Environment is also about communications. The institution's mission and strategy are clearly communicated, are understood, and individuals understand the overall mission and their individual organization's role in its achievement. Consideration of risk is an explicit part of business planning. Policies are also a type of communication. Comprehensive policies should exist, individuals should understand them and feel they provide constructive guidance, and the level of risk appetite must be understood and communicated. Individuals must receive timely, relevant and sufficient information to do their jobs.

Another component is accountability and reinforcement. Roles should be clearly communicated and understood. Risk is to be considered a part of everyone's job, and people should have an adequate level of authority to carry out their responsibilities. By the same token, performance incentives must include consideration of risk management. Performance is to be regularly tracked, and individuals are to be responsible for certain performance targets. Good performance is rewarded, and misconduct is disciplined. Design of performance incentives should not provide incentives to people to operate contrary to the desired risk management values.

People are another component. There should be adequate and trained people to do the job; morale must be good and turnover low. Individuals ought to receive training on risk management and on how to do their jobs, and they must find the training effective.

A successful operational risk management framework requires some cultural characteristics that are contrary to the way that some organizations have historically operated. One principle, for example, is openness and transparency. We have to create an environment in which people can share their concerns and operational weaknesses without fear of repercussions. The same is true for pending or actual loss events. Events become opportunities to improve, rather than to shoot the messenger.

There is also an external component of the environment. We operate in a business faced by competitors, serving customers, overseen by regulators, and subject to the economy, workforce and law. These external factors must be monitored and assessed to ensure the internal processes are aligned to meet or exceed expectations.

12.7 The role of internal audit

As operational risk management processes become more explicit, the role of internal audit should change. In traditional models, audit was responsible for assessing controls, but now the primary responsibility for assessment is shifting to the business areas under the coordination of the operational risk management department. The role of audit should refocus on evaluating how well the overall risk management framework is functioning and on the testing of controls. Audit should remain active in the risk management process, participating in assessments and key decisions. Audit should ensure that a comprehensive view is taken of risk management, and that risk analysis crosses the traditional silos of risk (i.e. market, credit and operational) as well as organizational lines.

Audit should be assessing the risk management framework (strategy, process, infrastructure, environment) and how well the framework has been developed and implemented across the businesses. It can test to see if risk taking and controls are in compliance with policy. For example, are new-product approval policies being followed with appropriate sign offs, and have business areas promptly recorded loss events in the applicable databases?

Audit may also perform model testing for capital methodologies and valuations. Similarly, it might evaluate loss reserves. Audit would typically independently value the models to verify calculations. This review includes testing inputs, approach, actual calculations and comparison to industry practice.

Another role is the investigation of incidents such as frauds. It is usually valuable to have incident investigations and any recommendation for disciplinary action, if appropriate, performed by a group outside the risk management function. This fosters the partnership between risk management and business areas and helps maintain open communications.

12.8 Tying risk management into the business process

Risk management should be integrated into business planning and operational processes. Just like market and credit risks, operational risks should be proactively considered, managed and evaluated. As illustrated in Figure 12.6, management processes can be divided into three steps: business strategy and planning, execution and evaluation.

Business strategy and planning refers to setting overall strategy, capital allocation, business budgeting and risk analysis, and the setting of performance targets. From an operational risk management perspective, each business carries operational risk capital, identifies potential exposures and mitigation programmes, and sets target performance measures and risk indicator escalation criteria.

Execution refers to the running of the business. Operational risk management refers to the activities and controls related to all risks, from sales practices to reconciliations. It is in this process that institutions operate within defined controls, perform self-assessments, analyze and improve controls, measure risks, report events outside escalation criteria, track incidents and indicators, and mitigate risks.

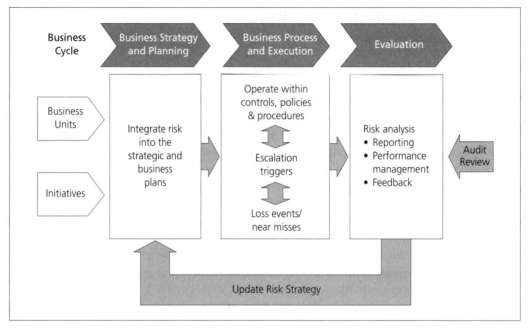

FIGURE 12.6 ■ Operational risk in the business process

Evaluation refers to the monitoring and evaluation of performance against goals. The management reporting process accumulates information from all aspects of the organization for review of the risk profile and initiation of change. Performance is evaluated, and recommendations for change in the coming cycle are made.

12.9 Success factors

The operational risk management framework covers many components and touches nearly everyone in the organization. Given the experience of implementing risk management frameworks, there are several recurring themes that will be helpful for any firm to keep in mind.

First, there is senior management support. In many respects, operational risk has always existed, many firms manage it well, and an explicit framework may appear to be extra work. It is the support by senior management and their belief that this process adds value to the organization in improved quality, lower volatility and reduced capital that will make the difference to those who execute it. The clear expression of the value proposition helps articulate the impetus for the programme.

Along these lines, the framework must be implemented to provide direct value to the line organizations. Any central process designed primarily to aggregate information and support senior management is destined to fail. Business units must believe they are benefiting, and if the same information provides some value to any central function, then they can have it.

Incentives should be built into the system. One of the primary incentives is in the capital process. But the methodology has to be responsive to changes in the organization so that improvements in controls provide immediate benefits in reductions in capital. A cost–benefit approach to risk mitigation that is linked to performance measures will capture attention.

Care should be taken to ensure consistency in the process. The risk definitions play a key role here. A common risk language across business areas and tools is critical. The actual implementation of approaches and tools may differ across the business areas, but if the results can be aggregated and compared, the process will be much more successful.

The right people should be brought into the process. At all levels, individuals should have the right training, motivation and cultural fit. Staffing should include a combination of quantitative, audit, process improvement, technology and risk analysis skills. A sufficient budget for both people and technology is necessary. While the majority of the cost is typically borne by the business areas, some central staff group is required.

The process must always be dynamic. Risk management is a process, constantly searching for new exposures and improvements in measures and controls. The assessment process should be varied, processes constantly reviewed and new measures researched for greater effectiveness.

The results must be shared with all business areas. One of the key roles of any operational risk function is benchmarking, both internal and external. There are common data and measures across businesses, and there are best practices that can be applied. Good practice in one area might have value in many other parts of the organization.

12.10 Summary

The risk management framework incorporates strategy, process, infrastructure and environment. It utilizes tools and technology to facilitate the process. It is reinforced by a common culture and language and the performance measures and rewards that influence behaviour.

Institutions committed to implementation of an operational risk framework are convinced they are receiving value from the process. From a shareholder value standpoint, they are helping reduce surprises and volatility. In addition, management can often point to a direct reduction in operational losses with consequent contribution to profit and loss, as well as improved quality of service to customers.

The regulatory community is also convinced that operational risk is good practice. They are expecting banks to implement a framework using the components described here. The Basel Committee has also proposed an operational risk capital charge in recognition of the high level of exposure to these risks. The approaches used to quantify the capital charge are still under debate. Regardless of the outcome, the implementation and use of a framework will be not only expected, but mandatory to qualify for the lowest possible capital charge.

CHAPTER 13

Using operational risk models to manage operational risk

Anthony Peccia

13.1 Introduction

Why is modelling necessary? After all, banks have been successfully managing operational risk from the start, and those that did not either disappeared or were acquired. The very survival of the remaining firms would argue that they have all the necessary skills and procedures for managing operational risk, without ever having measured it, let alone modelled it. So why should they do anything different?

They must change because the environment in which banks operate has changed dramatically, and to remain fit banks must adapt to the new reality. The new environment is much more complex, in terms of product offerings, delivery channels and jurisdictions. New complexities are emerging in relationships with suppliers, employees, clients and regulators. Whereas a detailed road map (the policies, operating procedures and controls) was sufficient in the past, banks now need a telescope and compass to help them navigate in a rapidly shifting environment. A model is simply a telescope with a compass.

The only purpose of an operational risk model is to give business leaders a tool for making better operational decisions. This exclusive purpose should guide and constrain each decision along the model construction process. Focusing on the decisional output of the model also avoids introducing tangential elements, which may be mathematically rigorous but less managerially useful.

Over the past few years, there has been a regulatory push to determine the amount of capital that is required to support operational risk. The regulators have proposed three alternative approaches to determining the amount of regulatory capital. These are the Basic Indicator Approach, the Standardized Approach and the Advanced Measurement Approaches (AMA). The Basic Indicator Approach and the Standardized Approach relate the amount of capital to the size of the bank, and size is measured by gross income. The AMA will permit the use of qualifying internal models to arrive at regulatory capital. The attractiveness of the AMA alternative is that it is generally believed that it will result in lower capital than either the Basic Indicator Approach or the Standardized Approach. More importantly, even if the AMA initially required higher capital, as banks reduce their risk, the AMA will result in lower capital. By contrast, there is no such opportunity under either the Basic Indicator Approach or the Standardized Approach. This has led to quite an interest in developing operational risk measurement and capital models. One might even say that there is now a proliferation of operational risk models, where none existed a few years ago.

The rest of this chapter will focus on the construction and applications of an operational risk model based on the actuarial approach described in Part II of this book. This model borrows heavily from concepts and techniques that have been developed and used in the insurance industry for well over a century. As will be demonstrated, the model, by design, gives management the information to make better operational risk decisions and almost as a by-product satisfies the AMA regulatory requirements.

13.2 Operational risk and reward

The purpose of the operational risk model is to provide management with a tool for making better decisions about the level of operational risk to take. At this point, some would argue that a model is not necessary to answer that question. They would say that the appropriate level of operational risk is zero and therefore should always be minimized given technical and human constraints. No model is required to do that.

That is certainly one way to manage a bank, but it leaves too much value on the table. To extract that value, banks need to make the appropriate risk–reward trade-off for operational risk, as they are now accustomed to doing for credit and market risk.

In some instances, such as payments systems, asset management, trading and other advisory businesses, a risk tolerance of zero would require the bank to shut down these businesses. For example, a bank may choose to implement so many controls around trading that it will be certain that rogue trading will not happen. In achieving this zero level of operational risk, the bank will have made it so prohibitory expensive to trade that it is no longer worthwhile.

At present, most banks put in a level of controls that allows for some level of rogue trading risk, but most cannot tell if the level is acceptable or the amount of rogue trading risk that they are implicitly accepting. The same may be said of information security, identity theft, aggressive selling and a myriad of other operational risks. The fact is that most banks operate these businesses and therefore operate within certain implicit operational risk tolerances.

Operational risk models make risk tolerances explicit and transparent. The models allow one to determine whether the risks are commensurate with the potential reward. After all, the bank should allocate capital to support the risks that yield the most return for a given unit of risk, regardless of whether the risk is market, credit or operational.

In the case of market and credit risk, the rewards are well understood. In the case of operational risk, they are perhaps not well understood. This is not surprising. The traditional approach to operational risk management has focused attention primarily on the risk. The reward comes in the form of either extra revenue from engaging in more operationally risky activities than otherwise, or from reduced costs from implementing a lower level of operational controls. These are real bottom-line issues that should interest any business executive, not only risk management.

The point is, that with respect to operational risk, risk–reward trade-offs have been and are being made all the time, albeit implicitly and with no assurance of consistency. Operational risk modelling will make this trade-off explicit, transparent and consistent.

How does one go about creating an operational risk model? We start at the end of the modelling process and work backwards. From various conversations with business executives at several banks, six questions were distilled from their ideas of what they wanted to know about the operational risk within their business:

- What are my biggest operational risks?
- What hits can I expect my profit and loss to take from my biggest operational risk?
- How bad can those hits get?
- How bad can those hits get under stress conditions?
- How will changes to my business strategy or control environment affect those hits?
- How do my potential hits compare internally or externally?

Let us consider each one in detail.

Firstly, business managers want to understand the operational risks embedded in their business activities. In other words, operational risk exposures should be identified. Once the risks have been identified and understood, business managers want to know the financial impact of these risks. This means that reasonable estimates of the potential hits (charges) to the profit and loss statement should be provided. Those potential hits come in three types: expected, unexpected and stress hits.

So far we have addressed 'what is', but business management is also interested in 'what will be'. Businesses are constantly changing their strategies, product offering, distribution channels and operating environment. These changes will change the business's exposure to the operational risk and therefore the potential hits. If the operational risk model is to be of any use it should supply answers to these questions. The model results should also allow for easy comparison between the operational risk profile of similar businesses, and identify what contributes to the similarities and the differences. In addition to providing answers to these specific questions for each business line, the model must also allow for the results to be easily aggregated at each level of the organization.

This is indeed a tall order. And if one attempted to build a model that provided answers to all these six questions and met all the above-specified conditions, it would take a long, long time to build the model and therefore a long, long time before any answers could be obtained. Common practice shows that it is better to build a working model that provides reasonable estimates for answers to some of the questions, and provides indications for some of the others. This gives immediate benefits and allows for continuous improvement. So which should be answered first? To answer this question it is useful first to examine the operational risk management framework.

13.3 The integrated operational risk framework

Operational risk management, like credit and market risk management, goes through a well-defined cycle, beginning with risk identification and followed by risk measurement, risk analysis and monitoring, obtaining sufficient capital and finally loss management. Figure 13.1 illustrates the framework and embodies the practice of continuous improvement since, as was said earlier in the context of the operational risk model, not all steps can be achieved with the same degree of quality at the same time. But each step should be of sufficient quality to render the operational risk management process of use to the business management, sooner rather than later.

Let us now review each step of the operational risk management process and how it influences the development of the model. In the case of operational risk, risk identification usually begins with a rigorous self-assessment of the exposures, the control environment and risk metrics, referred to here as key risk drivers (KRDs). For example, in asset manage-

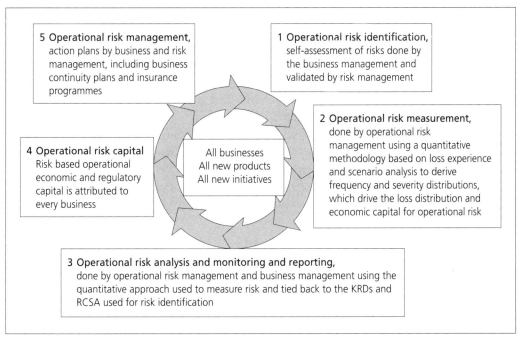

FIGURE 13.1 ■ Operational risk framework

ment, risk identification consists of identifying such risks as client claims arising from excessive account churning, the quality of the controls that are in place to reduce the likelihood that this happens and the related KRDs such as daily account turnover rates.

Once the risks have been identified, the financial impact of these risks needs to be measured – by which is meant the quantification of the expected and unexpected losses. However, before turning to risk measurement, let us examine some of the requirements of risk identification. Firstly, risk identification has to be done according to a well-defined and consistent classification of operational risk, otherwise similar risks within different business lines or at different times may be identified differently and different risks may be identified as similar. The importance of a consistent and useful classification of operational risk is therefore of paramount importance. Let us, however, recognize that although there is no unique way to classify things there are many right ways and many wrong ways. So, too, with operational risk.

Operational risks may be classified, for example, according to cause, according to the event giving rise to the loss, according to financial effect, according to who benefits, or according to who is harmed. Any consistent set of rules will do for ensuring that the classification scheme is coherent and self-consistent. However, since our interest goes beyond risk identification, and extends to the measurement of the financial impact of the risk, the classification of operational risk must, in addition to being coherent and self-consistent, be determined by the operational risk model itself. In other words, risks that have the same patterns of loss (i.e. financial impact) should be put into the same class.[1]

Let us now return to the output of the model. The expected and unexpected losses cannot be measured directly. Instead, first the frequency with which an individual loss can happen and the severity (the actual financial loss suffered when the loss occurs) are measured. Since the frequency and severity tend to be stochastic what is generally measured are the frequency and severity parameters that define the respective distributions. The loss distribution is obtained by combining, through Monte Carlo simulation, the frequency and severity distributions. Once the loss distribution is so obtained, reasonable estimates[2] of the expected loss and the unexpected loss can be determined. Many examples of this methodology have been presented in Chapters 7–10. The remaining three important elements of the operational risk management framework are concerned with the actual management of the risk. Since what gets measured most often gets managed, the operational risk measurement model is of critical importance.

[1] Market risk faced a similar situation in the early 1990s. Eventually the most useful classification scheme for measuring the financial impact was found to involve breaking market risks down into interest rate risk, foreign exchange risk, equity risk and commodity price risk.
[2] We say 'reasonable estimates' because, as will be shown later, the frequency and severity are themselves reasonable estimates and therefore any model that relies on them can at best only give reasonable estimates.

13.4 Risk and control self-assessment

A risk and control self-assessment (RCSA) programme is one on the most utilized operational risk tools and one of the most misunderstood, as shown in Robert Morris Associates *et al.* (1999). Many institutions that have implemented one are quite satisfied with it for risk management purposes and, apart for some operational capital requirements (regulatory or economic), see no need to go beyond it. Why does one need an operational risk model, if one is already doing an RCSA? Let us evaluate RCSAs against each of the five elements of the operational risk framework – risk identification, risk measurement, risk analysis and monitoring, risk capital, and loss management – and see if more is needed.

Some take RCSAs as the primary means for identifying risks. It is argued that business managers are closest to the risks and therefore it is concluded that they are in the best position to identify them. The premiss is, of course, true not only for operational risks but also for market and credit risk. The traders had better be fully aware of the risks they are taking, or the bank is in very serious trouble. And yet in market risk we do not ask the traders to self-assess their risk even though they are fully knowledgeable about the market risks they are taking. The reason for not doing so is just good common sense. A trader will tell you the market risk of his position if the position is under control, meaning that he is comfortable in taking the risk and has a reasonable expectation of making money from persisting with it. However, it would be very naïve to expect the trader to tell you the actual level of risk if the position is out of control. This is because the trader, even an honest one, would reason that it is best to try to bring the position under control first and then tell management about the risk. Self-assessment of operational risks works fine when they are under control and fails when needed most, that is, when risks are out of control.

Sound risk management requires that risks be independently identified and monitored. The counter-argument against the potential failure of self-assessment is that the business units are audited and therefore if business management is hiding risks, audit will find them. If this is so, RCSAs are a superfluous step. They cannot be a prudent mechanism for bring transparency to the actual risks. For that an independent mechanism is required. That mechanism is usually an independently designed, maintained and operated model. This is not to say that RCSAs are without merit. In fact they are a very important identification tool. But before discussing what RCSAs actually identify, let us analyze another commonly misunderstood aspect of them.

RCSAs also contain an element of operational risk measurement. Most ask management to rank the risks as high, medium or low. Some go further and break down the components of frequency and severity; these usually give numeric ranges for frequency (e.g. one in five years or one in ten years) and for severity (e.g. less than $1 million, $1 million to 5 million and so on). To the extent that managers are asked about expected losses, accurate estimates can be obtained. But to the extent that they are asked about unexpected losses, the answers are at best a very crude measure of the risk and at worst very misleading. With the exception of everyday occurrences, such as credit card fraud, most operational risk events rarely happen and therefore management has fortunately little experience in anticipating and dealing with them. So how are they to gain the experience to be able to distil any meaningful estimates about frequency or severity? Their estimates of frequency and severity for unexpected events are little more than pure guesses, and to use them for any measurement purposes is very imprudent indeed. What management can be relied upon to estimate is the expected losses. These happen with regularity (even if the regular occurrence is no loss at all) and therefore management has sufficient experience to provide reasonably accurate estimates of them.

Models, as in other disciplines such as engineering and science, are the only way to extend the valuable business judgement about expected losses into the unknown territory of unexpected losses. Models are used not to replace business management judgement, but to supplement it.

So what do RCSAs do if they do not identify or measure operational risk? They identify control gaps, that is, the things that can go wrong, and that if left unattended will lead to some operational failure. The control gaps, once the appropriate risk–reward trade-off has been made, can be used to develop action plans to close the gaps. Operational risk managers then monitor progress against those plans. In this respect RCSAs are a form of analysis and monitoring of the things that can affect operational risk. They have often been misused in practice; however, they are very valuable and effective when they are used in the way they were designed to be used. That is, they are a systematic means to identify control gaps, and to monitor what management is doing to close the gaps. Only indirectly are they a monitor of the level of operational risk. The gaps, if not closed, contribute in some way to the risk, but are not the risk. Often, the word 'risk' is loosely used to refer to anything that is uncertain, but it has a very precise meaning. It means the volatility around an expected loss. This embodies a measurement of some kind, which RCSAs were never designed to do. Models do that.

Some have suggested that RCSAs could be used to determine the amount of required economic or regulatory capital. As has been demonstrated, they cannot provide a measure of the risk, and therefore cannot be used to determine the level of capital. However, they can be used in combination with KRDs to determine the change in risk and therefore the change in capital. The usual approach (see Chapter 11) is to convert the RCSA into some score and use the change in the score to determine the change in the amount of capital. An example that illustrates how this can be done is given in Section 13.8.

Having evaluated the uses of RCSAs against the first four of the five steps of the operational risk management framework, there remains the evaluation against the final step, that is, the requirement of business loss management. It is here that RCSAs have a very useful role to play.

The familar situation of driving a car can be used to illustrate the uses and misuses of an RCSA. If one were to apply an RCSA to driving a car, one would ask the driver to enumerate all the associated risks. Things like failing brakes or inadequate driver training would be identified. But the risk of driving a car is not the risk that the brakes will fail or the risks that the tail light will not function or that the driver is not qualified to drive in slippery conditions, or a myriad of other things that can go wrong. These are things that can go wrong, that is, control gaps. The risk is simply that there will be a car accident in which there may result some damage to the car, to other cars or property, or bodily injury.[3] Any one of the control gaps could have contributed to both the accident happening and to the severity of the accident, depending on other circumstances such as speed, weather or traffic conditions. However, the same control gaps under different circumstances may not affect either the frequency or the severity of the potential accident. The risk is the uncertainty in the distribution of outcomes.

Next, the driver is asked to estimate the frequency and severity of the potential accident that may result from the control gaps. But to ask the driver, no matter how experienced and talented, what is the frequency and the severity of the damage as a result of improper functioning of the brakes or a broken tail light is to invite him to take pure guesses and mask them with spurious mathematical precision. In any event, having arrived at these so-called estimates, what possible use could they be put to? To say that they could be used to rank which control gaps needs to be closed first is to complicate a simple process beyond recognition. Any driver will tell you that brakes are more important than tail lights. How does he know? He knows through intuition gained through knowledge of driving, the experience of driving and near-miss experiences.

So does that mean that RCSAs are useless for driving? Absolutely not! They are the essence of safe driving. Every driver does either a formal or informal, comprehensive or cursory RCSA before and while driving a car. For Sunday driving in the country a cursory and informal RCSA is adequate, while for a Formula One race a very comprehensive and formal RCSA is done.

RCSAs are effective for ensuring the control gaps, which can bring the risk beyond an acceptable level, are closed. However, knowing what is the acceptable level of risk from driving is a completely different matter. The risk is measured by relying on statistical relationships that relate the risk class of the driver, the car and the external conditions[4] to certain observed patterns of frequency of accident and severity of accident to arrive at a potential loss distribution. This process should not only take into account the existence and effectiveness of controls but also recognize that, depending on the combination of circumstances, accidents happen even if effective controls are in place. Of course if the controls are lacking then the frequency and severity are even higher, and this is usually taken into account by placing the combination of driver, car and conditions in a higher risk class. This measurement provides the basis for the financial coverage for the driver, should an accident happen. This shows why measurement is very important. Measuring the risk does not make driving less risky, but the very fact that the risk can be measured, and therefore the right amount of financial coverage can be put in place, makes driving possible in the first place. So as we can see, in the case of driving, that the RCSA is not a qualitative substitute for

---

[3] It is important to distinguish these three types of effect, each arising from one car accident event, since each will have possibly different frequency and most definitely different severity distributions.

[4] External conditions refer to such things as driving on Sunday in the country as opposed to driving in a Formula One race.

measurement of the risk, nor is measurement of the risk a quantitative substitute for the RCSA. Both are indispensable for good driving.

In the same way, RCSAs are an essential component of good business risk management. All businesses should engage in an comprehensive review of what can go wrong and the effectiveness of the controls, and develop action plans to close cost-effectively[5] those control gaps that need closing. Business management should also demand that the risk of being in business be accurately measured so that the proper level of financial coverage, through either capital or insurance, is in place. Without this appropriate level of coverage, when the inevitable failure happens, losses are suffered, and if the losses are sufficiently large, the business will have to close. If too much coverage is in place then the business may not earn an adequate return, and will eventually also have to close. Therefore it is important to obtain the right amount of coverage, which can only be achieved through a proper and reasonable measurement of the risk.

Let us now return to the measurement of operational risk.

13.5 Exposures and losses

The operational risk measurement model relies on the measurement of both frequency and severity of the potential individual losses. Before addressing how to measure these, let us recall that the model is designed to provide business management with useful answers to the six operational risk questions in Section 13.2. The answers should improve the management of operational risk. The model must, therefore, not only provide the expected and unexpected losses, but also allow for comparison of those amounts with other similar businesses and over time. This immediately suggests that, in addition to absolute loss amounts, the model should produce loss rates. This is an important consideration, since it forces the introduction of exposures in the context of operational risk. An exposure is a relatively new concept for operational risk, but well established in market and credit risk.

For example, in credit risk, the exposure is the amount of the loan (for loans) and a percentage of the notional amount for derivatives (see Das 1993, Chapter 37). The exposure is simply a measure of the size of the amount at risk. For example, a $100 million loan is twice as risky as a $50 million loan to the same borrower with the same covenants and loan terms; but it is important to note that the linear relationship only holds if all other things are kept the same. In the case of operational risk it is usually impossible to keep all other things the same. So instead of the direct relationship that holds for loans, in the case of operational risk, we seek a measure of the amount at risk which has a high correlation with the actual risk.

Let us consider some examples to illustrate what is meant. What could be used to measure exposure in transactions processing risk? The financial volume of transactions (number of transactions times the average amount per transaction) is one such measure of size and

---

[5] Cost-effectiveness, in this case, refers to the trade-off between the cost of closing the gap and thereby reducing the risk and the savings from having lower capital to support the lower risk.

therefore a useful exposure base for this risk. For client claims, it might be number of clients times the average claim per client. Note that the exposure base is a product of a frequency exposure (number of transactions or number of clients) and a severity exposure (average amount per transaction or claim per client). Similar exposure bases can be found for the remaining operational risk types. Note that the emphasis is on a 'useful' exposure base, not a perfect one. There may be other exposure bases, which may even have a higher correlation with the actual risk, but these may be impractical or too costly to obtain. In such cases the less costly and less risk-sensitive exposure base is used as a proxy. This practice of using proxies is well established in the insurance industry. For example, ideally car insurance premia should be related to the number of miles driven in a year, but in practice the number of miles driven is substituted by a much cruder measure such as the extent to which the vehicle is used for pleasure or for business.

EXAMPLE 13.1

Transactions processing risk

Let us look into transaction processing risk to illustrate more concretely what is meant. Transactions are run through a string of processes involving people, procedures and systems. The process string begins with a negotiation, such as a purchase or sale of securities in trading or taking a deposit in retail banking, and ends with the settlement. Added to this string are the processes and systems that make the negotiations possible, such as the telephone system in trading and the branch network in retail banking. After settlement, processes include such activities as generating and issuing statements to clients.

This description of the processes and systems involved is by no means intended to be exhaustive, but only to make the point that there is a defined string of processes for initiating and completing a transaction. The string of processes is not perfect and is subject to failure, which will give rise to transaction errors such as wrong currency amount, buy versus sell, or delayed settlement. The string of processes will have a certain failure rate, which can be expressed as the number of failed transactions per 10 000 processed. The failure rate may even depend on the type of transaction processed, but for simplicity let us assume that all the transactions processed by a given string are the same.

As a first approximation, the number of failed transactions, and therefore the number of losses is directly proportional to the number of transactions processed. In other words, the number of transactions is a good exposure base for the frequency of losses. Likewise, it is reasonable to conclude that for each failed transaction, the size of the loss is proportional to the size of the transaction. This argues that the severity exposure should be the average size of the transactions. Note that the selected exposure base may be too costly to obtain, in which

▶

case a proxy is chosen. For example, the number of transactions may not be tracked and therefore the number of accounts can be used instead, with its corresponding average account size.

In order to compare the evolution of losses over time, it is useful to measure the loss probability rather than the absolute number of losses. This is a good starting point, although refinements such as different loss probabilities for different types of transactions can be introduced later. Some would argue that the loss probability is proportional to the number of transaction processed since the greater the number of transactions, the greater the strain of the string of processes and therefore the greater the propensity for failure. This may very well be the case.

Denoting by N the frequency exposure, p the probability of a loss event, E the severity exposure and r the loss rate, given that a loss event occurs, the above discussion can be summarized as follows. The expected number of losses is given by

$$\lambda = Np.$$

The expected loss severity is

$$\mu_{L} = Er.$$

The expected total losses are then given by $\lambda\mu_{L}$.

The relationship between an exposure measure and the number of losses is a great deal more complex than the linear or the proportional relationship. This (and other) refinements are valid and should be incorporated into the model. Yet they remain refinements and enhancements. It is better to begin with a linear approximation, develop a satisfactorily accurate model, start using the model and add those enhancements as usage demands. Repeating this process ensures continuous improvement, while having an adequate model each step of the way.

Having introduced loss probabilities and exposure bases, the expected losses can now be compared across businesses and across time for the same business, without the comparison being distorted by different sizes of different businesses or by the change in size as the business grows.

Knowing the expected losses is very important but not sufficient to manage operational risk. Risk is a measure of volatility around the expected loss. The bigger the volatility, the bigger the risk. In other words, a business with a much larger expected loss rate than another business may have a much lower risk, if the possible losses are confined to a narrow range around the expected losses. Credit card fraud and rogue trading offer specific examples of this. Credit card fraud unfortunately happens routinely, whereas trading fraud (rogue trading) fortunately happens rarely. The expected fraud loss rate for credit cards is therefore much higher than for trading. However, credit card losses tend to be at most five times the expected losses, whereas rogue-trading losses can be hundreds of times the expected loss.

Let us now see how the operational risk model can give us a measure of the loss volatility.

13.6 Gamma and the measure of operational risk

Operational risk is the unexpected total loss to some confidence level, which is related to the standard deviation of the total loss distribution. We will use statistics to arrive at the answers, but represent the answers in such a way that a detailed knowledge of statistics is not necessary.

Let us see how this can be done. The unexpected loss is the potential loss, from all possible losses contained in the total loss distribution, at some confidence level. This means that for a confidence level of, say, 99 percent there is a 99 percent probability that all losses will be less than the expected loss plus the unexpected loss or that there is only a 1 percent probability that losses will be more than the expected loss plus the unexpected loss. To arrive at the unexpected loss, the loss distribution must be constructed, and this requires knowledge of statistics in order to apply rigorous mathematical techniques, such as the Monte Carlo simulation for combining frequency and severity distributions into a loss distribution. Some of the previous chapters of this book, and many other books such as Klugman *et al.* (1998), provide details of these techniques, so there is no need to go into them here.

However, whatever this unexpected amount actually is, it can be expressed as a multiple of the expected loss. It is important to emphasize that this only simplifies the way to talk about and illustrate the operational risk, not the calculation of that risk. The calculation of the unexpected loss may still be done using sophisticated mathematical techniques involving the Monte Carlo simulation. And, as Example 7.5 in Section 7.6 shows, the result should be approximately the same whether we use a formula based on an expression of unexpected loss as a multiple of expected loss, or whether we use the full simulation approach.

It is necessary to distinguish between the simplification of the results of the calculation and the simplification of the calculation, because there have been many debates challenging the mathematical validity of the simplification.[6] Most car drivers make do with a simplified understanding of the engineering that makes a car work, while engineers need to know the workings in full detail. The same is true in risk management. Financial engineers need to use the actual and rigorous mathematical relationships to develop the loss distributions. Risk and business management can make do with the simplified version, and concentrate on what the calculations tells them about the risk, rather than how the calculation is done.

Unexpected loss can be expressed as a multiple of the expected total loss which, following the regulatory nomenclature, is referred to as the gamma. Gamma is an easy way to represent the different levels of riskiness. For example, credit card fraud losses may have a

[6] The Basel Committee on Banking Supervision (2001a) proposed several methodologies for determining the operational risk capital charge, and these are discussed in Chapter 7. One, known, as the Internal Measurement Approach, is similar to the representational simplification discussed in the above. That is, the capital charge was determined by multiplying the expected loss by a 'gamma factor'. In reaction to this proposal some quants nearly had a heart attack. They could have spared themselves much agitation, if they had realized that since the paper did not specify how the gamma would be calculated, the approach could accommodate the cherished pristine mathematical rigour, as demonstrated in Section 7.5.

gamma of 5, rogue trading may have a gamma of 100, and client claims in asset management a gamma of 25. As can be seen, this gives us a common and easy language to express the relative riskiness of different types of risks in different businesses. For financial engineers, a detailed description of how to calibrate the gamma for different types of risk is given in Section 7.5.

13.7 Sufficiency, relevancy and completeness of loss data

We have talked about the frequency and severity distributions and how they can be combined to yield the loss distribution. But where are the frequency and severity distributions to come from?

The first place to look, of course, is the historical internal loss experience. The time period over which the historical record needs to be analyzed to extract the historical distributions, is dependent on two competing factors: sufficient data points to make the statistical parameters such as expected values and standard deviations meaningful; and relevance of the data points. The further back into history one searches, provided that the loss data have been collected, the more data points will be obtained and the more confidence can be placed in the calculated parameters. However, businesses do not remain static and therefore the further back one goes the less relevant are the loss data to businesses' current risk and control environment. The historical loss experience is the starting point, not the end point.

In addition to the problem of obtaining enough relevant loss data, there is the very practical problem of completeness of the historical loss experience record. Most banks have not collected operational loss information with sufficient granularity for it to be useful. With the exceptions of fraud losses, most losses would have been aggregated in either certain expense items or as contra revenue items, and therefore it is next to impossible to extract the actual individual loss from the aggregate accounts. Nothing much can be done about what was done in the past; however, the completeness problem can be solved going forward. Many banks have begun to implement robust data collection initiatives, which will collect individual operational losses[7] with sufficient granularity to provide a complete set after some years of collecting the data.

Low-frequency losses, namely the large losses, and therefore the most relevant for determining the risk, will happen so rarely that the problem of sufficiency and relevancy still remains going forward. Many industry practitioners believe that supplementing the internal loss experience with industry loss data can solve these problems. This has given rise to the establishment of various operational loss collecting consortia.

---

[7] Not all individual losses are collected. Thresholds such as $10 000 are often established, with losses below the threshold collected in aggregate. This introduces some statistical complications, and without compensating techniques will distort the actual distributions.

Of course, industry loss data will solve the sufficiency problem, but will replace the problem of relevancy in time within the bank with the problem of relevancy across banks. Since banks have different business strategies, operate in different external environments and have different internal operating and control environments, taking in too much industry information may mask the actual risk of the bank, to the point that it is no longer useful to managing the bank's operational risk.

So what to do? A common way to obtain sufficient relevant loss data is to create the data synthetically through a well-defined process of scenario analysis.

13.8 Scenario analysis

For low-frequency events, such as client lawsuits in corporate finance, a very long observation period (greater than ten years) may be required to estimate the expected frequency, let alone other parameters such as the severity mean or its standard deviation. This means that in practice the required parameters cannot be directly determined.

One way to fill the data gap is to create synthetic data through scenario analysis. Scenario analysis often means different things to different people. What is meant here is a rigorous process carried out by risk management with the active participation of business management, involving estimates of the expected and the unexpected for both the frequency and severity distributions, selecting distributions to fit these estimates and simulating the loss distribution. It is important to realize that this approach to scenario analysis is identical to the actuarial loss model approach used when there are sufficient loss experience data. Only the inputs are different. In scenario analysis the inputs are derived from expert opinions, all available internal loss data, and relevant examples from industry: they do not rely on internal loss data alone. Nor do they rely only upon formalized scorecards, as do the actuarial loss models that are described in Chapters 10 and 11.

In this type of scenario analysis the parameters of the frequency and severity distributions are 'guestimated' using all available quantitative and qualitative data, including the subjective judgements of business line and senior management. Once the simulated loss distribution is obtained, the expected and unexpected loss should be compared against similar businesses, and evaluated for reasonableness by risk management and business management. If adjustments are required to the initial 'guestimates', the whole process should be repeated at the level of the frequency and severity distribution.

Unfortunately, the usefulness of scenario analysis may be very limited. Business and risk management have intuition about expected losses but may lack the necessary experience to develop any intuition about unexpected losses, because these events are rare (recall the discussion on RCSAs).

Another approach is to follow the example of the insurance industry and create operational risk classes from the industry data. Let us consider the case of the risk of driving a car. Fortunately, the loss experience of most car drivers is so sparse that there are insufficient data to create a loss distribution for them individually. However, there are sufficient data if the loss experience of all drivers is used. This collective loss experience is used to create the population loss distribution. However, recognizing that not all car drivers pose the same risk, the population loss distribution is decomposed into several loss distributions and each is associated with a particular class of driver. The risk of an individual driver is then determined not solely by his loss experience but the risk class to which he is assigned.

The population loss distribution is equivalent to the industry loss distribution in the case of operational risk. How risk classes are determined and assigned is discussed next.

13.9 Operational risk classes and key risk drivers

As mentioned above, borrowing from techniques developed by the insurance industry can solve the problems of sufficient and relevant data. It is common practice in the insurance industry to create risk classes, that is, a group of individuals or entities sharing the same loss distribution. For example, the individual loss history for a car driver is one component in determining the expected losses from insuring that driver, but it is not sufficient. Instead the insurance industry has developed a set of risk characteristics, including the age and marital status of the driver, the condition of the car and the accident record (i.e. the loss experience) of the driver. These risk characteristics put the driver in a particular class of drivers that have a common expected loss. The same is true for life insurance where, by definition, the historical loss experience for the insured is non-existent. So mortality rates are assigned to individuals based on certain mortality risk indicators, such as age, parental history, occupation and lifestyle.

Let us now apply the same concepts to operational risks. Suppose that for each operational risk type the industry loss data can be grouped into several distinct loss distributions, each uniquely characterized by the operational risk parameters p (probability of a loss event), μ_L (expected loss given event) and γ (gamma). Each distinct loss distribution, or set of parameters, defines a particular risk class. This is more than a mere supposition. Banks share some of the same risk characteristics, since they offer similar products and use the same consultants for selecting and implementing systems. However, banks also differ in their quality of people, processes and systems. So it is reasonable to believe, even without sufficient data, that within the general population of all banks, clusters of banks that share the same risk characteristics will emerge. These clusters are the risk classes.

These risk characteristics are called key risk drivers. Since the KRDs determine the risk class, obtaining the KRDs for a bank will allow a risk class to be assigned to the bank. Figure 13.2 shows how the KRDs are used to assign a risk class (i.e. a set of operational risk parameters or loss distribution) to a particular bank.

The above has illustrated how KRDs can, in concept, be used to assign a risk class to a particular bank, which in turn determines its loss distribution and therefore its expected and unexpected loss. It is easy to extrapolate the process and see how a change in the business and control environment of the bank, as measured by the change in KRDs, can be used to reclassify the risk classes and thereby determine the new expected and unexpected losses in the bank.

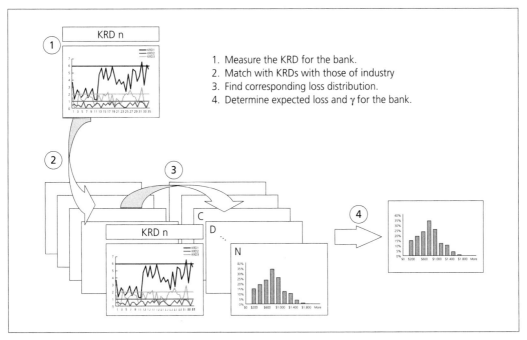

1. Measure the KRD for the bank.
2. Match with KRDs with those of industry
3. Find corresponding loss distribution.
4. Determine expected loss and γ for the bank.

FIGURE 13.2 ▥ How a risk class is chosen for each risk type

How are risk classes used in practice? Using a combination of historical loss experience, industry loss experience and scenario analysis,[8] a table can be constructed as illustrated in Table 13.1. This shows ten different operational risk classes, and to each operational risk type and class associates a gamma. Recall that gamma is the ratio of the unexpected total loss to the expected total loss and therefore a measure of risk. Note that the range of gamma varies with the operational risk type. For example, in theft/fraud/unauthorized activities the gamma ranges from 2 to 125. This reflects the wide range of different types of theft and fraud included in this risk type. It includes routine fraud such as occurs daily in credit card fraud (high-frequency, low-severity events, with low gamma), and rarer frauds such as rogue trading (low-frequency, high-severity events, with high gamma). The range of gamma for transaction errors is much smaller. This risk type includes routine high-frequency, low-severity errors, and medium-frequency, medium-severity errors associated with high-ticket transactions such as derivatives or corporate loans, but errors comparable to the effects of rogue trading are extremely rare, if at all possible.[9]

Note that Table 13.1 shows the gamma for each of the loss types in a given risk class. This is only for the purpose of simplifying the illustration. In practice, it is possible for a business

---

[8] For reasons mentioned above, scenario analysis is not very reliable, it is a good starting point where no data exist, but should be replaced by industry data as they become available.

[9] The only way such large errors could occur is through concentration, that is, millions of transactions processed through the same flawed systems.

TABLE 13.1 ■ Volatility (gamma) by operational risk class

Theft/fraud unauthorized activities	Loss or damage to assets	Client claims	Employee claims	Regulatory claims	Transaction errors
125					
100	100				
80	80	60			
40	40	40	40		
30	30	30	30		
20	20	20	20	20	
12	12	12	12	12	12
8	8	8	8	8	8
5	5	5	5	5	5
2	2	2	2	2	2

to be in a low risk class for, say, fraud and in a high risk class for, say, employee claims. This would apply if fraud prevention relied primarily on technology, and the business was under-taking massive layoffs due to, say, automation.

Where do these gammas come from? Firstly, they are for illustration purposes only and are not to be taken as actual gammas. However, they are representative of the values and relative relationships between gammas derived from an actual internal loss data set and scenario analysis applicable to an actual bank. Section 7.5 describes how to calibrate gammas, in terms of the corresponding parameter (phi) for the standard deviation. Once constructed, the table is then used to determine the unexpected loss. Example 13.2 shows how.

EXAMPLE 13.2

Credit card fraud

Suppose a credit card operation has KRDs which result in assigning it to the risk class 3 for theft and fraud. Then, from Table 13.1, the gamma associated with this credit card operation is 8. Now suppose that this card operation has 10 million accounts, and each account has an average balance of $3000. The exposure for this credit card operation, as discussed in Section 13.6, is $30 billion. If the theft and fraud losses are expected to average 12 basis points (bps), the expected loss is $36 million, and the unexpected loss is $288 million ($36 million × 8).

But what does this mean for the business manager? This credit card operation has been assigned to risk class 3, based on the values of its KRDs. An important KRD is the number of 'priority one' gaps identified through the RCSAs. Priority one gaps are those open issues that are judged to have an important and significant effect on the frequency of theft and fraud. Further, suppose that in this instance it is the number of priority one gaps that has the most impact on the assignment of the risk class. The credit card business manager realizes that the number of priority one gaps largely determines the riskiness of his operation and therefore chooses to invest in closing these gaps. Having successfully done so, the risk class now falls to, say, 2. In this case, the expected loss may fall to 9 bps (based on experience or judgement) or to $27 million, and the unexpected loss falls to $135 million ($27 million × 5). Since economic capital is most often set equal to the unexpected loss less expected loss, the capital drops from $252 million to $108 million, a saving of $144 million in capital which can then be employed elsewhere. At a cost of capital of, say, 20 percent this reduction is worth about $29 million in savings per year. As long as closing those gaps and their maintenance costs is less than this saving, the gaps should be closed. The manager now has a rigorous decision process for determining whether to close the identified gaps or leave them open and live with the higher risk. Of course, the approach outlined here for theft and fraud can be applied to other operational risk types.

The above illustrates how risk–reward trade-offs can be made explicitly for operational risk. For the first time, business management has a tool for managing operational risk based on the same rigour that is commonly applied to credit, market risk and to other type of financial decisions. And it is this that makes operational risk models valuable to business management.

What are key risk drivers? They are risk characteristics that distinguish the level of operational risk in one business unit[10] from another similar unit or for the same unit across time. As already mentioned, one KRD is the number of priority one gaps identified in the RCSA. Others are the complexity of the products, the complexity of the delivery system, the growth rate of the business unit, the frequency of systems downtime, capacity usage and the skill level of staff. KRDs are most often obtained from existing performance measures and from intuition, based on a deep knowledge of the business activity.

Much time and money can be wasted researching and arguing which are the best KRDs. A more practical approach is to start by implementing a set that both business management and risk management agree to be useful. As experience is gained with this set, it can be modified. Certain initial KRDs will inevitably be found not to be very risk-sensitive, while new ones will be discovered. Note that size or volume type performance indicators are not used as these are already incorporated into the measure of risk, through exposures. A scoring mechanism may be developed to slot the business unit into a particular risk class, using the weighted average score from each KRD. Again, a simple average may be used until evidence is obtained that indicates that certain KRDs should be more heavily weighted than others.

---

[10] A business unit in this context is a homogeneous set of activities, such as trading, consumer lending and credit cards.

It is important to emphasize that the association of the weighted average KRD score with a risk class is done by analyzing internal loss experience, industry loss experience and scenario analysis. At first the association may be crude, but with use it will get better and better.

13.10 Management applications of an operational risk model

Having described the elements of an actuarial operational risk model and how it can help with the management of operational risk, let us now see how it can help with general business management of which (operational) risk management is but one, albeit important, component.

Figure 13.3 represents the traditional approach, where senior managers, including the board of directors, receive many reports dealing with operational risk issues from various business and support units within the organization. However, this leaves senior management with the task of taking these various reports and constructing a coherent picture of the operational risks facing the institution. And since there is no commonality in the various reports, the construction of the coherent picture is next to impossible. This means that there can be no assurance that the risks are being managed within the tolerance level that senior management requires. Instead, the approach is to let every business unit manager

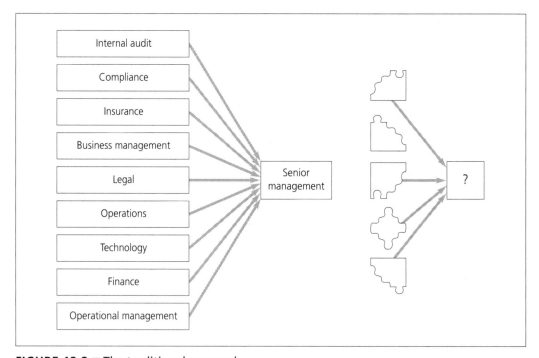

FIGURE 13.3 ■ The traditional approach

manage his own risk as he sees fit and hope for the best. We know from experience[11] that this will lead at best to some very unpleasant surprises and at worst to bankruptcy.

The operational risk framework that has been outlined in this chapter, with its five inter-related components, creates a coherent picture for senior management. The operational risk model (which through risk classes makes heavy use of loss experience, RCSAs and KRDs) creates the common language of value-at-risk for operational risk. This common language in turn allows the board of directors and senior managers to set consistent operational risk tolerances and to consistently guide business managers in their management of operational risk throughout the institution.

Figure 13.4 shows a sample report of an operational risk profile (i.e. the coherent picture) by business unit and by operational risk type. The operational risk profile can be viewed either by the risk class as shown here or by the capital at risk, which takes volume or size into account. It is clear that this provides a bird's-eye view of the operational risk taken by each business unit and for each business unit the exposure by operational risk type. This type of reports can be used retrospectively to examine the risk that has been taken and prospectively to examine the potential risk embodied in a business plan. It also allows for the explicit setting of risk tolerances. For example, the board of directors may set a certain amount of capital at risk for each operational risk type and for each business. Alternatively, tolerances can be set by risk class, just as in credit risk where a risk tolerance limits the amount of loans that can be made to counterparties of lower credit quality.

13.11 Modelling and the new regulatory requirements

The discussion up to now has focused on how business and risk management can use the actuarial operational risk model to improve the quality of its operational risk management. Let us now turn our attention to how the model can be used to meet the proposed regulatory requirements.

The Basel Committee on Banking Supervision (2001a, 2001b) has set out the regularity framework for a capital charge for operational risk. This capital charge is based on three approaches: the Basic Indicator, the Standardized Approach and Advanced Measurement Approaches (AMA). The Basic Indicator Approach sets the regulatory capital as a percentage of some size indicator. The proposed indicator is gross income. The Standardized Approach recognizes that most banks are not homogenous entities, but rather composed of several distinct business lines, and that each business line has its own particular operational risks. Therefore capital is set similarly to the Basic Indicator Approach except that the percentage of gross income varies from business line to business line. These two approaches are size-dependent

---

[11] Consider the case of Baring's. After the fact, many outsiders created, from the various internal reports issued to management prior to the collapse, a coherent picture that indicated the potential for a serious problem at the Singapore futures trading desk. Management had the pieces but not the entire picture. Baring's may have still been around had that picture been available to management before instead of after the fact.

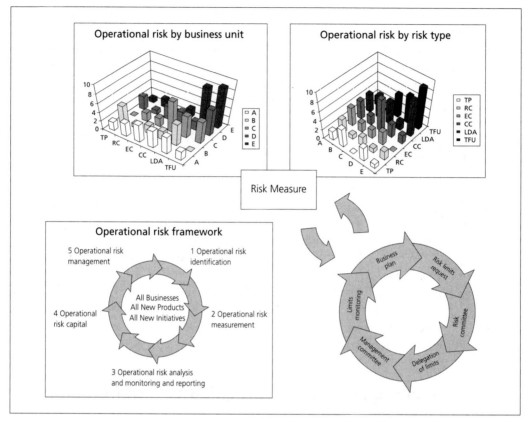

FIGURE 13.4 ■ A coherent picture of the operational risk enterprise-wide, through measurement

and reflect the risks of the average bank rather than the bank's own level of operational risk. The AMA allow for the use of a bank's own internal operational risk measurement model and therefore can be more reflective of the actual operational risk taken by the bank. Unlike the other two approaches where regulatory capital increases as the business grows, the AMA recognize that a business which keeps the level of controls consistent with its growth has kept its risk constant, and therefore there is no automatic increase in regulatory operational risk capital.

There are clear regulatory advantages for a bank to implement the AMA. However, to achieve these benefits, the bank must ensure that it meets some stringent criteria. These criteria address not only the requirements of the operational internal measurement model, but also prudent practices, such as reporting, monitoring and tolerances, around the management of operational risk. The operational risk model as outlined in this chapter is an example of a measurement model that is designed to meet the requirements of the AMA.

In addition, the Basel Committee (2001c, 2002b) has also issued proposed *Sound Practices* for operational risk management. These are meant to be minimum requirements for all banks, whereas more stringent requirements are imposed for those banks seeking to use the AMA. They contain ten principles: eight deal with bank management and two with the supervisory role. More details are given in Chapter 2. As can be seen from Figure 13.5, the eight management principles fit neatly into the operational risk framework described in this chapter.

Once again it is important to stress that the operational risk framework and the associated measurement model were designed exclusively to provide business management with the tools necessary to improve their management of operational risk. Regulatory requirements were taken into account throughout the model construction process. So the tool is Basel compliant, but remains first and foremost a business management tool.

13.12 Summary

This chapter has described why a new and integrated approach to operational risk management is required. It has described in detail an operational risk management framework which has five interrelated and interdependent elements: risk identification, risk measure-

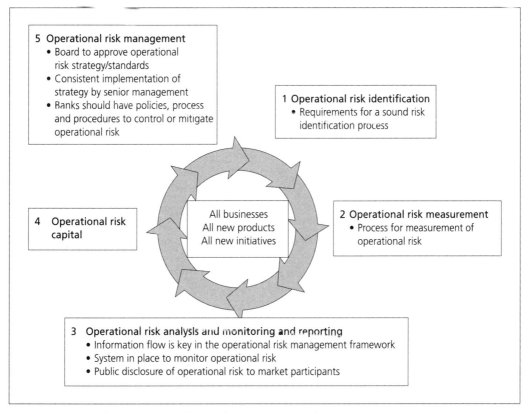

FIGURE 13.5 ■ The principles of sound operational risk management practice

ment, risk analysis and monitoring, risk capital, and loss management. An actuarial operational risk measurement model was presented which takes into account internal loss
experience, external loss experience, scenario analysis and key risk drivers to arrive at operational risk classes. These classes are then used to determine the capital at risk for each line
of business and operational risk type.

The framework and the measurement model provide management with a powerful tool
for analyzing, monitoring and managing operational risk. The actuarial measurement model
can be used to provide answers to the six fundamental management questions about operational risk: What are the largest operational risk exposures? What hits can the profit and loss
statement expect to take from these exposures? How bad can the hits get? How bad can the
hits really get under stress conditions? How do changes in the control and business environment affect the potential hits? How do my potential hits compare to those of other business
units and other banks? In addition, the framework and the measurement model meet the
proposed regulatory requirement for both the capital model using the risk-sensitive and
capital-advantaged Advanced Measurement Approaches and sound operational risk management practices. These sound practices can be further enhanced using the same framework,
but at a higher and deeper degree of application and sophistication to meet the qualifying
criteria of the Advanced Measurement Approaches.

CHAPTER 14

Managing operational risks with Bayesian networks

Carol Alexander

14.1 Introduction

This chapter introduces Bayesian belief and decision networks as quantitative management tools for operational risks. Bayesian networks are already well established for use in the risk management of large corporations, and the aim of this chapter is to describe how these powerful statistical tools may be applied to operational risk management in banks and other financial institutions.

In order to manage operational risks effectively, the factors that are thought to influence the risk must be identified. These can be the 'key risk drivers' of the firm's operations (see Sections 12.4.4. and 13.8) or they can be classified into a separate category of their own (see Section 12.2). Ideally, by exerting some control over these factors, operational risks will be reduced. Before attempting this, some important questions should be addressed:

1 *Effectiveness*. What effect will the controls have on the risk? It is one thing to identify the factors that contribute to the risk, but quite another to actually quantify the effect that changes in a factor will have upon the risk. For this one needs a quantitative model that relates the risk to the factors. This is precisely what a Bayesian network is.

2 *Dependency*. Is it possible that by reducing one risk, another risk will be increased? How can one quantify the dependency between risks, and can this dependency also be controlled? Managing the dependency between risks is one of the main strengths of a Bayesian network. In scenario analysis, where many possible scenarios are examined by risk control, the risk dependency structure is explored in a very systematic way. An example of this will be given in Section 14.4.

3 *Cost*. What will be the cost of the controls, and is the likely reduction in risk worth the expense? The answer to this question will depend on the risk attitude of the firm – and this risk attitude is usually modelled by a utility function over costs and benefits of a

decision (see Appendix 15.1). In Section 14.5 we shall explain how to incorporate a utility function into the management decision process, using an influence diagram called a Bayesian 'decision' network.

The outline of this chapter is as follows. Section 14.2 provides references and website links for further information on Bayesian networks and their applications. Section 14.3 introduces the reader to Bayesian networks: their architecture (parent and child nodes, initial and terminal nodes, the edges that imply risk attribution and so forth) and their propagation – that is, how the parameters are estimated using Bayes' rule. Section 14.4 gives an example of the design of a Bayesian network for the management of operational risks in banks. It highlights the major advantage of Bayesian networks, which is the scenario analysis of operational risks. Section 14.5 explains how Bayesian networks can be augmented to include decision nodes, and thereby facilitate a cost–benefit analysis of a management decision. Bayesian decision networks enable management decisions to be more informed because the choice of management action can be evaluated in terms of different scenarios on the important attributes of the operational risk. Section 14.6 concludes.

14.2 Bayesian networks: useful references and web links

The extensive literature on Bayesian networks goes back over a decade: see Pearl (1988), Neapolitan (1990) and Jensen (1996). For many years Bayesian belief and decision networks have been used very successfully in the management and decision sciences: see Geoffrion (1987), Morgan and Henrion (1990), Heckerman *et al.* (1995) and Henrion *et al.* (1986). Other important applications of Bayesian networks and influence diagrams include reliability analysis (see Fenton and Littlewood 1991) and the design of expert systems (see Henrion *et al.* 1991; Neapolitan 1990). Applications of Bayesian networks to modelling operational risks in banking and finance have been described in Alexander (2000, 2001) and King (2001).

Characteristically, one of the first risk management software vendors in the financial industry to offer a Bayesian network product was Algorithmics: see www.algorithmics.com. For an example of commercial software that uses Bayesian networks to manage operational risk, see www.lumina.com. There are several software packages for Bayesian networks that are freely downloadable from the Internet. The examples in this chapter have been generated using an excellent package called 'Hugin lite' (downloadable free for research purposes from www.hugin.com). Microsoft provides a free package for personal research only that is Excel compatible at www.research.microsoft.com/dtas/msbn/default.htm. On David Heckerman's home page at www.research.microsoft.com/~heckerman there is a useful collection of working papers on Bayesian networks. An up-to-date list of free (and other) Bayesian network software to download from the web is at http.cs.berkeley.edu/~murphyk/Bayes/bnsoft.html.

An interesting new initiative from www.inferspace.com is to provide free, open-source software for Bayesian networks. Intel has initiated the 'OpenBayes' system, a translation of the Bayes Net Toolbox (BNT) Matlab package. The APIs are written in C++, but functions can be written to enable the functionality of the APIs to be accessed from within mathematical and statistical software packages, such as S-Plus and Mathematica.

14.3 Introducing Bayesian networks

A Bayesian network is a statistical model that relates the marginal distributions of 'causal' factors, or 'attributes' of a risk to its multivariate distribution. The basic structure or 'architecture' of a Bayesian network is a directed acyclic graph where nodes represent random variables and links represent relationships between the variables. Figure 14.1 illustrates on the right the architecture of a simple Bayesian network with a single target or 'terminal' node Z having two 'parent' nodes X and Y; on the left the distributions associated with each node are displayed. The initial nodes are nodes with no parents (X and Y in this example). They each have univariate distributions that must be specified by the modeller: in Figure 14.1 the probability that X is in state 0 is 20 percent, and so forth. The terminal node Z has a multivariate distribution that is determined by the initial node's distributions and conditional distributions (the probability that Z is in state a given that X is in state 2 and Y is in state 1, and so forth). These conditional probabilities are not shown in Figure 14.1, and only the joint distribution of the target node is shown in the left-hand frame.

A network uses Bayes' rule to 'propagate' through the network, and thus the distributions at all nodes can be quantified, given the initial node probabilities and the conditional probabilities for all nodes. For two events Y and Z, Bayes' rule is

$$P(Z|Y) = \frac{P(Y|Z)\,P(Z)}{P(Y)}$$

(see Bernardo and Smith 1994). Moreover, if the states of any nodes are fixed, the network can use Bayes' rule to propagate backwards and forwards through the network and hence calculate the posterior probabilities of every node in the network. This is the basis of scenario analysis in Bayesian networks, and it is one of their most attractive features. The ability to perform scenario analysis in this rigorous, but also tractable and visual manner should be viewed as the overriding reason for their use.

Figure 14.2 illustrates how a scenario analysis is implemented in the simple Bayesian network of Figure 14.1. The initial state of the network is as shown in Figure 14.1. But suppose that we design a risk control so that X will be in state 0 – what then would be the distribution of Z?

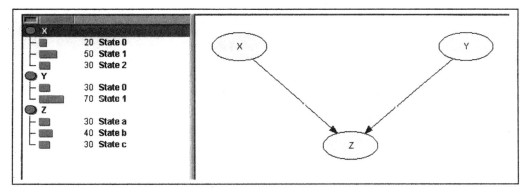

FIGURE 14.1 ■ Architecture and node probabilities of a simple Bayesian network

Alternatively, we might ask, what are the conditions that lead to a given state of the terminal node: for example, suppose we target Z to be in state a, then what are the posterior probabilities associated with X and Y, given this information? Questions like this, which form the basis of an operational risk scenario analysis, are very easy to answer with a Bayesian network.

Figure 14.2 shows the results of applying Bayes' rule to the two scenarios that have just been described. Given the risk control, our prior belief is that X will be in state 0, and then the posterior density of Z is shown at the foot of the left-hand frame; compared with the base scenario in Figure 14.1 the probability that it will be in state b is reduced, but the probabilities that Z will be in state a or state c have increased. We may then ask whether the control is likely to produce the desired results. For the second scenario, given the target that Z is in state c, the posterior probabilities of X and Y are shown above it, in the right-hand frame. Initially the probability that Y is in state 0 is 30 percent. But if we want Z to be in state a, then we know that we shall have to increase the probability that Y is in state 0, in fact the probability of Y being in state 0 rises to 56 percent.

In Figures 14.1 and 14.2, very simple discrete random variables have been used, but a Bayesian network has the flexibility to model discrete random variables with many states, and discrete or continuous random variables from some family of distributions where parameter values themselves have distributions that are conditional on the states of the parent nodes. We shall see an example of this in the next section, when scenario analysis in a Bayesian network that targets a 'key risk indicator' (KRI) of an operational loss will be developed.

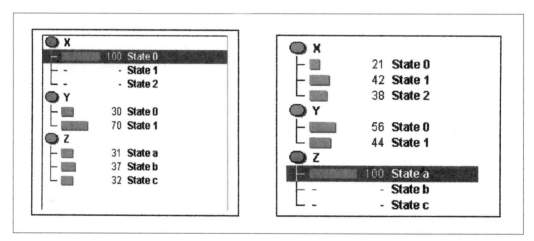

FIGURE 14.2 ■ Propagation of a Bayesian network

14.4 Applications of Bayesian networks in banking and finance

There is no unique Bayesian network to represent any situation, unless it is extremely simple. Rather, a Bayesian network should be regarded as the analyst's own particular view of a process. Many different Bayesian networks could be used to depict the same process.[1]

When designing Bayesian networks for scenario analysis of operational risks in bank, terminal nodes can be the KRIs that have been identified, and agreed upon, as targets for control. Examples of KRIs include the number of failed trades, staff turnover rates, or the frequency and/or severity of errors. The 'causal' factors or 'attributes' of the risk will be identified with 'key risk drivers' (KRDs) over which management has some control. Examples of KRDs and KRIs are given in Table 14.1. See Chapters 12 and 13 for further discussion of risk drivers and risk indicators.

For a fully integrated view of management and capital allocation, a Bayesian network could have terminal nodes corresponding to the number of loss events and the loss given event. Thus the Bayesian network will model the frequency and severity distributions, and therefore their composite (the annual loss distribution), as functions of the key risk drivers in the firm. In this way, the management and control of operational risks can be linked to the economic capital of a firm, or the regulatory capital of a bank. Furthermore, the Bayesian network will allow management decisions to be supported by scenario analysis, and to be integrated with the risk capital and budgeting of the firm.

TABLE 14.1 ■ Examples of key risk drivers and key risk indicators

Risk	KRD	KRI
Internal fraud	Management and supervision Recruitment policy (vetting) Pay structure (bonus schemes)	Time stamp delays (front running)
External fraud	Systems quality (authentification processes)	Number of unauthorized credit card transactions
Clients, products and business practices	Product complexity Training of sales staff	Number of client complaints Fines for improper practices
Employment practices and workplace safety	Recruitment policy (discrimination) Pay structure Safety measures	Number of employee complaints Staff turnover Time off work
Damage to physical assets	Location of buildings	Insurance premiums
Business disruption and systems failures	Systems quality Back-up policies Business continuity plans	System downtime
Execution, delivery and process management	Management and supervision Recruitment policy (qualifications) Volume of transactions Training of back office staff Pay structure	Number of failed trades Settlement delay Errors in transactions processing

[1] If a node has many parent nodes, these conditional probabilities can be difficult to determine because they correspond to high-dimensional multivariate distributions. An alternative approach is to define a Bayesian network so that every node has no more than two parent nodes. In this way the conditional probabilities correspond to bivariate distributions, which are easier for the analyst to visualize.

Bayesian networks can also be used to determine the 'trigger levels' associated with a KRI. The trigger levels are bounds that determine various actions that must be taken by management if the risk indicator crosses that level. All nodes in a Bayesian network (with more than one state) are random variables. So when a KRI is used as a target node in a Bayesian network, the network will determine its distribution, under any given scenario. This includes the mean, the standard deviation and the upper percentiles of the KRI. From the initial state of the network, trigger levels can be set at either some multiples of the standard deviation or, if the distribution is skewed or fat-tailed, the upper percentiles. The precise trigger levels set will, of course, depend on the risk aversion (the more risk-averse, the lower the percentile). A variety of trigger levels may be set, for example at increasing percentiles, and the trigger levels at higher percentiles should prompt more drastic actions than those at lower percentiles.

Having determined the trigger levels, the Bayesian network can then be used to decide on the most appropriate risk controls when trigger levels are exceeded. Through scenario analysis, the Bayesian network can answer questions such as:

- Suppose the KRI staff turnover enters the 'red flag' zone. What then would be the probability that the pay scale is too low, and is this more likely to be a result of bad management, or poor training for our employees?

- If the number of failed trades has entered the 'red flag' zone will increasing staff levels be the best course of action that is most likely bring failures down to acceptable levels again?

Answers to this type of question will help management to decide on the best course of action when trigger levels are exceeded. More details may be found in Alexander (2000, 2001). Only one Bayesian network for operational risk in banking will be presented in this chapter. The network shown in Figure 14.3 represents the number of failed trades in, for example, the interest rate swaps desks of the bank.

The nodes in the network are as follows:

Instrument. The initial node 'Instrument' represents all the over-the-counter (OTC) trades in interest swaps, including their hedging with other swaps and listed instruments such as futures and bonds. The probabilities in the left-hand panel of Figure 14.3 means that 50 percent of the number of trades during a particular time interval (say, one week) are in OTC swaps, and 50 percent are in the listed instruments for hedging.

Agreement. Although the terms and conditions are likely to have been agreed before the swap, the master agreement may not have been finalized before the deal is made, and this is represented by the node 'Agreement'. The node probabilities shown represent a 5 percent chance that the master agreement has not been finalized before the deal. This has been calculated (using Bayes' rule) assuming that only 90 percent of the OTC trades have finalized master agreements, and recalling that 50 percent of the trades are OTC.

Valuation and booking. The failure may occur on the internal side of the deal, over which the bank has some control, or on the external side. The number of fails on both sides are represented by continuous nodes that are conditional on both the valuation and the booking of the trade. The distributions of the internal and external valuation and booking nodes are given on the left-hand side of Figure 14.3.

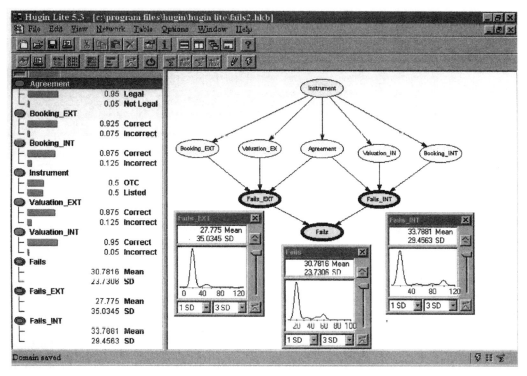

FIGURE 14.3 ■ A Bayesian network for the number of failed trades

Internal and external number of fails. The conditional probabilities that a deal fails, given that it is incorrectly or correctly booked, and incorrectly or correctly valued, and given that a legal master agreement has or has not been finalized, will determine the distributions of these nodes. Figure 14.4 shows the conditional densities as those of normal variates, with a mean and variance representing the number of fails in a given time frame, for example one week. Thus the number of failed trades per week, arising on the external side, given that both valuation and booking are correct but when no legal master agreement has been finalized before the deal, is normally distributed with mean 50 and variance 50. The numbers of fails per week on the external and internal side are therefore mixtures of normal densities, with the distributions shown in the monitor windows next to these nodes in Figure 14.3.

Number of fails. The distribution of the target node, the number of failed trades per week, is assumed to be a mixture of these two densities, with probability 0.5 on each. That is, we assume that it is equally likely that a fail will arise from either side of the trade.

Valuation_EX	Correct				Incorrect			
Booking_EXT	Correct		Incorrect		Correct		Incorrect	
Agreement	Legal	Not Legal	Legal	Not Legal	Legal	Not Legal	Legal	Not Legal
Mean	0	50	50	200	20	250	300	350
Variance	0	50	50	100	20	50	100	30

Agreement	Legal				Not Legal			
Valuation_INT	Correct		Incorrect		Correct		Incorrect	
Booking_INT	Correct	Incorrect	Correct	Incorrect	Correct	Incorrect	Correct	Incorrect
Mean	0	100	80	120	50	55	100	400
Variance	0	20	30	20	50	55	50	100

FIGURE 14.4 ■ Conditional distributions for Fails_EXT and Fails_INT

For reasons of space we do not list all the conditional probabilities of every node in the network; but below we shall consider the conditional distribution of the internal booking node, so we need to know that 85 percent of OTC trades and 90 percent of listed trades are correctly booked internally.

The initial state of the network may be used to set trigger levels for the KRI 'number of fails'. In this case, with a mean number of failed trades per week of 30.78, with standard deviation 23.73, a trigger level might be set at [mean + 2 standard deviations] ≈ 80. Another trigger level, prompting more drastic action if it is exceeded, might be set at [mean + 3 standard deviations] ≈ 100 failed trades per week. If a risk indicator such as number of failed trades exceeds a trigger level, the management will be prompted into some sort of action. But which is the most efficient action to take (we shall leave aside the question of costs to the next section): for example, is it better to have a review of the internal booking procedure, or to ensure that no trades commence until the master agreement has been finalized? Which action will be most efficient in reducing the number of failed trades?

The Bayesian network will allow the manager to simulate what can happen if one of these controls is put in place. For example, Figure 14.5 shows the effect on the number of failed trades if the internal booking of a deal is always correct. The network propagates forwards and backwards through each node, using Bayes' rule, and we shall now go through this in some detail.

Let us derive the posterior probabilities of the 'Instrument' node, given that the internal booking is correct. Let Y be the event 'the instrument is listed' and Z be the event 'the internal booking is correct', so the posterior probability $P(Z|Y) = 0.514286$ in Figure 14.5. Without any information on the booking, in the initial state of the network we assumed that 50 percent of the instruments are listed and that 85 percent of OTC instruments and 90 percent of listed instruments are correctly booked internally. Now, using Bayes' rule, we have the posterior probability that the instrument is listed, given that it has been correctly booked, as

$$P(Y|Z) = \frac{P(Z|Y)\,P(Y)}{P(Z)} = \frac{0.9 \times 0.5}{0.9 \times 0.5 + 0.85 \times 0.5} = 0.514286.$$

In this scenario, the network shows that if the management were able to ensure correct internal booking, the mean number of fails should reduce from about 31 trades to about 26 trades per week, and the standard deviation would be reduced from about 24 to about 20.

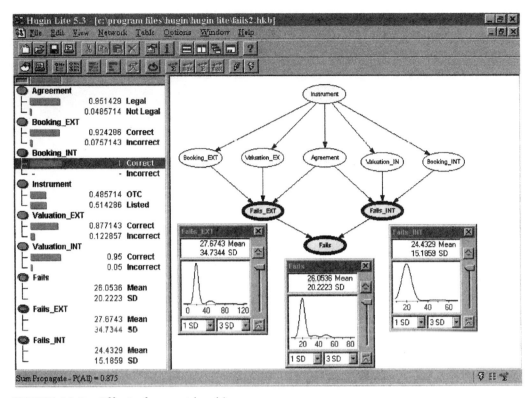

FIGURE 14.5 ▓ Effect of correct booking

So, if the KRI 'number of fails' exceeds a trigger level, should management attempt to improve the booking procedures? What is the likely effect of other risk controls – are they more efficient? The Bayesian network can be used with other scenarios, in exactly the same manner as we have just illustrated, to evaluate the effect of possible risk controls on the distribution of the risk indicator.

14.5 Bayesian decision networks

So far, so good, but there is another important question, and that is whether it will be cost-effective to implement a risk control. Having identified the most efficient risk control, through scenario analysis on the Bayesian network as described above, we now have to ask: will the cost of the control exceed the benefit? To answer this question, the Bayesian network must be augmented with decision and utility nodes, in which case it becomes a particular type of influence diagram called a Bayesian decision network.

The decision network in Figure 14.6 models the probability of a failed trade due to internal valuation or booking errors, or a dispute arising with the counterparty when the master agreement had not been finalized before the trade. The boxed decision node labelled 'Control'

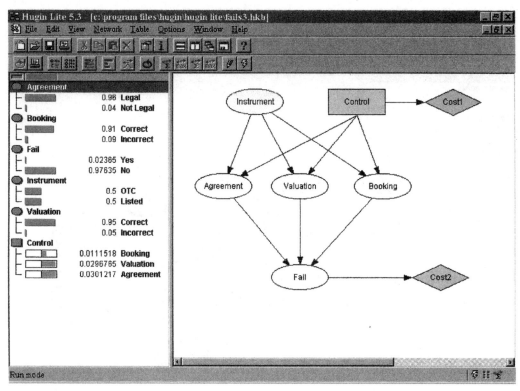

FIGURE 14.6 ■ A Bayesian decision network

represents three possible risk controls, each aiming to reduce the probability of a failed trade. This will be by reducing either the number of valuation errors, or the number of booking errors, or the probability that legal agreements have not been finalized before the trade.

In the initial state shown in Figure 14.6, all three controls are in place, but although a risk control cost node 'Cost1' is depicted in the network, for the initial state of the network no costs have been assumed. The other cost node, 'Cost2', represents the cost of a failed trade. For the initial state this is fixed at unity, and in this case the values in the left-hand frame associated with the 'Control' node are just proportional to the conditional probabilities of a failed trade, given that the fail occurred in booking, valuation and agreements, respectively. That is, three causes of a failed trade have been identified: with probability 11.1518 percent it will fail because it has been incorrectly booked, with probability 29.6765 percent it will fail because of incorrect valuation, with probability 30.1217 percent it will fail because of a dispute over an unfinalized master agreement, and with probability 29.05 percent none of these will be the cause of the failure.

When costs are associated with the controls in 'Cost1', and the cost of a failed trade is not unity, the values associated with the 'Control' node represent the relative cost of implementing each control, assuming a linear utility function. For example, if a cost of 10 is associated with a failed trade and a cost of 20 is associated with each control, the costs associated with the 'Control' node would be 20.1115, 20.2968 and 20.3012. The least cost control in this case is to reduce the number of errors in the booking process. On the other hand, if a cost of 1000 were associated with a failed trade and costs of 30, 5 and 10 are allocated to the booking, valuation and agreement controls respectively, then the net costs are 41.15 for controls on the booking process, 34.68 for controls on the instrument valuation process and 40.12 for controls on the finalization of the master agreement. The least cost control in this case would be to improve the valuation process.

This example has just illustrated the cost–benefit analysis of risk control using a linear utility function – more general utility functions that reflect the risk aversion of the firm may also be employed in the Bayesian network framework. More details on utility functions and their crucial role in operational risk management are given in the next chapter.

Finally, the decision network may be used in scenario analysis in just the same way as in Section 14.4. With scenario analysis, management decisions can be based on a cost–benefit analysis of such questions as: 'What is the most cost-effective risk control in the interest rate swaps desk to bring the number of failed trades down to my target of no more than 15 fails per week?'.

14.6 Conclusion

When all is said and done, a Bayesian network is simply a model for a multivariate distribution. As with every model, it is not unique; it is a picture of the mind of the modeller. There is no universal Bayesian network that models an operational risk; the network must be specific not only to the institution, but also to the management role.

Bayesian networks have been applied for many years in large corporations. Advantages of using Bayesian networks for operational risk management in banking and finance include the following:

- Bayesian networks have applications to a wide variety of operational risks. Conditional probabilities may be based on scorecard and/or historical data from the trading book or balance sheet. They can be used to model loss distributions, or the distributions of key risk indicators.

- A Bayesian belief network relates the factors that are thought to influence operational risk (the key risk drivers) to the risk measures or key risk indicators of the firm. This type of process model of risk can provide explicit incentives for behavioural modifications. Also, when a key risk indicator is the target node, the Bayesian network can be used to set the trigger levels and to evaluate the effectiveness of risk control.

- Bayesian decision networks provide a cost–benefit analysis of risk controls, where the optimal controls are determined within a scenario analysis framework.

This chapter has provided some examples where Bayesian networks are designed to answer specific questions, and in each case this is achieved through scenario analysis in the network. In my opinion, the ability to perform scenario analysis in a quantitatively rigorous, but also tractable and visually intuitive manner, is the overriding reason for choosing Bayesian network modelling as the key operational risk management tool.

CHAPTER 15

Operational risk management

Jacques Pézier

15.1 Introduction

We view risk management as an integral part of good management. Risk management should take a balanced view of decision problems encompassing all significant risks and rewards. Operational risks are only one type of risk and therefore are only one piece in the jigsaw puzzle that only makes sense when all pieces are assembled. All risk analyses are based on the same general principles – generation of alternatives, quantification of uncertainties and preferences, modelling of consequences – but factors deserving the most attention vary from problem to problem. We distinguish three broad types of operational risks according to the frequencies of loss events: *nominal, ordinary* and *exceptional*. Depending on the type, uncertainties are negligible, similar or very large compared to expected losses. Nominal risks are the province of total quality management, a well-developed discipline, but perhaps better known in manufacturing than in financial services. The analysis of ordinary and exceptional risks is illustrated by case studies from which we draw general lessons. With ordinary risks, it is crucial to understand the interaction among risks and with costs and rewards; risks do not add up, indeed operational risks may sometimes reduce other uncertainties. With exceptional risks, we show the importance of quantifying the risk attitude of a financial institution in order to arrive at rational decisions such as mitigation or transfer of risks.

15.2 Risk management – an integral part of good management

The debate between regulators and bankers over the past 15 years or so has been a powerful driver for the development of better risk management and consequently greater efficiency in the use of capital resources in the banking industry. It matters more to see new initiatives in this growing field than to argue where they should come from, as long as the two sides can agree and keep up with each other. But do they really agree or are they just pretending to agree? Are the objectives of the regulator and those of the banker sufficiently in line to ensure frank and open co-operation?

What is good risk management for a banker and why is it so important? Personally, I do not see any distinction between good management and good risk management in a world where most important decisions have uncertain outcomes. If we knew precisely the consequences of our actions, good management would reduce to (i) generating attractive alternatives and (ii) agreeing on preferences among various possible outcomes. A good decision – the rational choice – would simply be the choice of the alternative leading to the preferred outcome; one may dispute the limits of rationality, yet no manager would favour 'irrationality'. But when do we know precisely the consequences of our actions except in trivial cases? Significant management decisions are taken in the context of complex systems where outcomes result from the interaction of many factors not known with certainty, including decisions from other economic agents. Thus management must also be good at (iii) identifying and framing the problems to be addressed, (iv) translating limited information into quantitative probability assessments, and (v) expressing preferences not only among various outcomes but also between various combinations of outcomes with different probabilities, what is called risk preference. In an uncertain world, good decisions no longer equate to good outcomes and good management becomes synonymous with good risk management. Risk management is much more than assessing, reporting and controlling risks.[1]

It would be a tragedy if, somehow, risk management were seen as a discipline divorced from that of management when it should be an integral part of it. Alas, there are already signs of separation. True, risk management requires that certain specific tasks be carried out by qualified staff supervised by independent managers with wide rights of access to information, but the support functions, including model building, monitoring and reporting, should not be confused with risk management itself. In too many banks, risk management is now seen as the task of one department alongside other departments fulfilling other support functions such as human resources management and information systems. Whether it is seen as a luxury or a mere necessity (to satisfy regulators) is questionable. It is certainly regarded as a cost centre for, perhaps, a not so crucial service; witness crises when the risk management department is often among the first to be pared down.

The separation is encouraged by supervisors as well as by internal forces. Banking supervisors are more concerned with protecting depositors, investors and other creditors than with maximizing returns to shareholders or providing better performance for customers. So supervisors take a prudent, one-sided view: limit the probability of insolvency and ensure that risks are assessed as objectively as possible. It follows that risk assessments should be carried out by staff not reporting to front office managers and not directly and immediately interested in the results of the bank. It follows also that supervisors prefer to focus on

---

[1] For a primer on decision analysis see Howard (2000), and for further developments and applications see Howard and Matheson (1984).

'measures' (their word) of risk that, they hope, can be obtained objectively and independently of wider performance measures.

Tradition and internal politics conspire with supervisors to isolate the risk management function. In a bygone age of credit controls and rationing rather than pricing, credit risks were first assessed as acceptable or not. Not so long ago (perhaps even now), many banking supervisors wanted the chief credit officer of a bank to have the ultimate responsibility for such decisions. Paradoxically, senior management often agrees with this division of responsibilities and even welcomes it for the screening of all sorts of risks. At first, one may wonder why senior management would want to delegate such important decisions. On second thoughts, one realizes that senior managers may find two advantages in this approach. If a prospect is not rejected, they have a freer hand as they no longer have to worry about risks; should a bad outcome ensue, it is the prime responsibility of the risk manager who failed to reject the prospect. If a prospect is rejected as too risky, they do not have to consider difficult trade-offs between risks and rewards. Of course, this approach would fail if credit officers and other risk managers, having no incentive to accept risky prospects but only fearing potential blame, rejected them all. But that is not realistic; risk managers would rapidly lose their credibility and suffer the general opprobrium of their colleagues in profit centres. They have to accept a decent proportion of all opportunities submitted for their review. Unfortunately, they must decide without having all the elements necessary to make a rational choice. Their decisions have to be arbitrary to some degree.

The reluctance to make trade-offs between risks and rewards is not specific to managers in the financial industry. It is a pervasive modern-day pathology; in fact, it is probably less pronounced in the financial industry where outcomes are readily measured in cash flows than it is in other fields where, say, moral values or human lives may be at stake.[2] There is even reluctance in some firms to be seen as making decisions at all. Business decisions are irreversible allocations of resources; small or large, they shape the future of a company. But instead of focusing on decisions, many 'managers' prefer to talk about management 'framework' and 'processes' for 'monitoring' and 'control'.

This disease has two root causes. One is judging people on results – because some senior managers do not know any better – rather than on the quality of their decisions; then survival instincts will naturally lead managers to avoid making decisions or to be over-conservative. The other is fragmentation of responsibilities, leaving decision-makers not only with partial information but also with limited objectives. Banking supervisors should avoid reinforcing these regrettable tendencies.

---

[2] Can we put a price on freedom or human life? Many find the question preposterous, so it remains unanswered. But medical doctors and politicians, among others, face situations requiring such value judgements. Unable to rely on reasoned and publicly agreed views, they must rely on their own judgement. Politicians even find it advantageous at times to play on public emotions (e.g. following a major accident) by declaring proudly that they refuse to put a price on human life (e.g. 'We shall not compromise safety' or 'Safety is our only priority, regardless of costs') or that the preservation of freedom is invaluable. An intelligent public should ask the exponents of such glaring abdications of responsibility to resign.

15.3 Nominal, ordinary and exceptional operational risks

The starting point of good management is to focus attention on critical issues, by which I mean situations where good ideas and good decisions can make a difference. There is no point in worrying about things that cannot be controlled nor any commercial value in gathering information unless it may affect some decisions (learning for pleasure is a different matter). Events may command attention to particular problems, but many opportunities may be missed or alternatives become unavailable unless one tries to think ahead about critical issues. At any rate, rarely do problems come well defined and neatly framed as in textbooks. An open, attentive, inquisitive and creative mind and broad experience are prime qualities for a good decision-maker.

But good individuals cannot succeed in bad organizations. Some types of internal organization and company culture foster forward thinking, whereas others stifle it. An organization where functions and responsibilities are highly fragmented, where internal communications are limited and codified, where individualism is encouraged more than co-operation, where objectives are not clearly defined and shared, where staff and managers are too busy with immediate tasks to look at what is happening around them, where blame is more readily attributed than rewards, where there is no service ethics, where some key executives have an unquestionable authority … is an organization prone to running blindly into operational accidents.

If, on the other hand, a firm's global objectives and values are understood, managers are encouraged to look beyond their desks, to communicate and to co-operate, if there are checks and balances in the decision-making process, if there are individuals (from non-executive board members to junior employees) who are given time to think about the future and alternative ways of doing business and proper forums to discuss new ideas, then such a firm is less likely to be caught by surprise and more likely to develop efficient ways of doing business.

Thus the collection, analysis and reporting of operational loss data is not the be-all and end-all of operational risk management. At best, it may stimulate reflection about operational problems but it is by no means the only or even the privileged starting point. Consider, for example, the operational loss data assembled in the Basel Committee's Second Quantitative Impact Study (BCBS 2001d); there is nothing there to suggest that the responding banks are not properly controlling their operational risks nor any suggestions about what they should do better. Should they pay more attention to operational loss categories[3] where the largest total losses have been recorded? These would be: 'Clients, products and business services in corporate finance and in retail banking'; 'Execution, delivery and process management in trading and sales, and in payment and settlement'; and 'External fraud in commercial bank-

[3] QIS2 operational loss data contain 90 bank-years of experience (30 banks over the years 1998–2000) arrayed according to the eight business lines and seven loss types defined by Basel for the proposed Advanced Management Approaches. For the 56 resulting loss categories, total number of loss events with severities above €10 000 and total losses have been recorded.

ing'. Or should they pay more attention to categories creating the largest uncertainties because of the presence of few but relatively large losses? The main categories would be: 'Clients, products and business services in corporate finance and retail banking'; 'Internal fraud in trading and sales, and external fraud in corporate finance'. In both cases the figures are not particularly impressive. For an average bank in the sample, the largest loss categories account each for about 0.1 percent of capital and the largest uncertainties (in standard deviations) about 0.2 percent of capital. Small numbers indeed compared to expected earnings and earnings variability that are more like 15 percent and 5 percent of capital, respectively.

The debate fuelled by the Basel proposals about operational risks will be fruitful if it leads some banks to realize that they have not paid enough attention to risks of this type and the industry to develop appropriate methods to analyze them. An interesting subject, then, is to explore whether there are generic methodologies to address situations where operational losses play a role. My own view is that it would be useful to distinguish three types of operational risks according to loss frequencies because they reveal different salient features: (i) *nominal operational risks*; (ii) *ordinary operational risks*, both encompassing the vast majority of all operational risks, typically illustrated by QIS2 loss data; and (iii) *exceptional operational risks*, absent from QIS2, a few instances appearing in much larger databases, but mostly lurking out in the future.

I call 'nominal operational risk' the risk of repetitive losses (say, losses that may occur on average once a week or more frequently) associated with an ongoing activity, for example, settlement risk, minor external fraud (one credit card lost or stolen every 8 seconds, my bank reminds me!), or human error in transaction processing. Such losses must be taken into consideration in the optimization of processes but they hardly deserve to be called risks for only the expected losses are significant (many times larger than the standard deviation of losses) and should be compared to the cost of controls. We shall not discuss them here, not because the subject is unimportant, but because it has been addressed well elsewhere. There is an excellent literature on the subject of quality management, a concept first developed by the late Edward Demmings who revolutionized the Japanese industry after the Second World War. Only later were Demmings' ideas accepted in his home country, the USA. They are now applied successfully in most industrialized countries and most industries (see your local total quality management group and the *TQM Magazine*). A frequent conclusion after studying nominal risks is that they are excessively costly; improved procedures and a better quality culture often prove not only to be less expensive immediately but also to have beneficial long-term effects on client relationships and reputation. Many of the methods currently proposed to tackle operational risks in banking are designed to cope with nominal risks, that is, with expected operational losses. It would not be surprising if many financial institutions came to realize that nominal operational losses are very costly and business could be conducted more efficiently with greater emphasis on quality of services (in banking, as compared to manufacturing, it is often the quality of the service rather than the quality of the product that counts, something that may have been overlooked in early applications of Quality Management to banking).

'Ordinary operational risks' I define as the risk of less frequent (say, between once a week and once every generation) but larger losses, yet not life-threatening for financial institutions. They are usually one among several important consequences of a strategic choice and should be analyzed within the wider context of that choice; in particular, the relationships between these risks and other risks associated with the same strategic choice need to be understood. We give an illustration in the first case study below.

Of the 'exceptional operational risks' (say, losses that have no more than a few percent chance of occurrence over a year) only those that may be life-threatening to financial institutions matter. These risks deserve specific attention. We discuss them later and use a second case study to illustrate the importance of quantifying a firm's risk appetite to make rational decisions.

On a graph of log-frequency against log-severity,[4] the three main types of operational risks we have just defined could be mapped approximately as in Figure 15.1. We have also separated out in the lower left-hand corner the loss categories that are too small to be material; these are categories where both the expected loss and the standard deviation of losses are less than 0.01 percent of the current minimum regulatory capital.[5] Obviously, the boundaries we have drawn are only approximate limits between zones where attention should be given either to expected losses or to risks (i.e. uncertainties), or where these features are negligible. To summarize: for immaterial losses, both expected losses and risks are negligible; for nominal operational risks, expected losses are much more important than risks; for ordinary operational risks, both risks and expected losses are significant; and for exceptional operational risks, risks are much more important than expected losses.

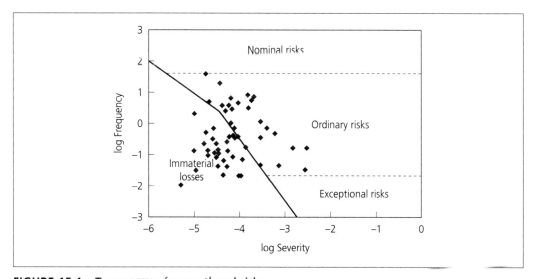

FIGURE 15.1 ■ Taxonomy of operational risks

---

[4] The graph displays loss categories on decimal logarithm scales for frequency (vertically) and relative severity (horizontally). The frequencies are calculated by dividing the number of loss events recorded in QIS2 by 90 (the number of bank-years in the database); the relative severities are calculated by dividing the average loss per loss event by €3 billion, a low estimate of the average capital of the banks in the sample.

[5] Minimum regulatory capital (MRC) is defined as the capital requirement for credit and market risks under the Basel I rules to meet the minimum 8 percent solvency ratio.

More than half the operational losses reported in QIS2 fall into the immaterial zone. Not surprisingly, the rest would be classified as ordinary operational risks. The only category near the nominal operational risks boundary is 'External fraud in retail banking' although there would have been many nominal risks reported in QIS2 data if it had not been for the cut-off reporting level of €10 000 per loss. The few reported rare risks have low impact and are therefore immaterial. As expected, no truly exceptional operational risks show up in QIS2 data. The category that would come closest is 'External fraud in corporate finance'.

15.4 An ordinary operational risk case study

We choose an example from the category 'Client, products and services in corporate finance', which appears in both lists of top expected losses and risks.[6] Suppose that within corporate finance, the bond origination department is forecast to win about two mandates per month and that each successful deal brings an average of €4 million in fees. However, a few deals have turned sour over the years because of poor preparation, incorrect pricing, erroneous disclosures, etc. Most of these errors resulted in the bank being unable to place its entire share of the issue at the expected price and losing money on the rump, having to pay additional fees to other managers or occasionally being sued by investors. The best guess of managers in the debt origination department is that, given the current organization and market conditions, there may be about one bad case per year with an average loss of €10 million. The bond origination function employs 100 people and has an expense budget of €30 million. History shows that it has also generated market losses of about 10 percent of fees on average.

The departmental budget for next year is summarized in Table 15.1. Note that the case study has been designed to exaggerate operational losses reported in QIS2 for the corresponding category; the frequency of losses has been increased sixfold and the average severity by 20 percent. At first sight this is a good business, good enough for employees to

TABLE 15.1 ■ Debt origination – base case budget

Expected number of mandates	25	
Expected fee per mandate	€4m	
Expected revenue		€100m
Operational loss probability per mandate	4%	
Expected operational loss per loss event	€10m	
Expected operational loss		€10m
Expected market losses (percentage of gross revenue)	10%	
Expected market loss		€10m
Operating expenses		€30m
Expected operating income		€50m

---

[6] This example is hypothetical; the figures are purely illustrative and are not meant to reflect the economics of any particular firm.

expect bonuses at year-end. Of course, it is not without uncertainties, so we call the budget above the *base case* budget (we cannot pretend at this stage that it is the most likely case or the expected case or anything more significant than a starting point in our analysis).

Which uncertainties could have the greatest impact on operating income? It is laborious to translate views into probabilities and it is costly to gather additional information to narrow down uncertainties, so we proceed step by step, starting with a simple, 'back-of-an-envelope' sensitivity analysis to discover the most influential factors. For each of the entries in Table 15.1, we ask the relevant managers to state a range of possible variations that would not unduly surprise them, say a range that, in their mind, would have about two chances in three of capturing the correct figure. The answers are given in Table 15.2, together with their marginal impact on operating income.

The sensitivity table calls for a few remarks:

(i) There is an intrinsic uncertainty in the origination activity. While we may expect and be prepared for 25 mandates per year, each opportunity for a deal and each mandate won is the result of not only hard work but also luck. We could describe the process as a succession of independent mandates won at an average rate of 25 per year. The most general mathematical description of this process is the Poisson process;[7] it implies that for a given average rate, one standard deviation for the actual number of mandates is the square root of the rate of arrival, here 5, which leads to a range of uncertainty on operating income of ± €16 million.[8] But, in addition, management is uncertain about the rate of arrival of mandates. Suppose they give the rate of arrival a range from 20 to 31.

TABLE 15.2 ■ Debt origination – sensitivities

Key factors	Base case	Range		Gross income	
		Low	High	Variations	(€m)
Number of mandates p.a.	25	18	33	23	81
Average fee per mandate	€4m	€3m	€5m	25	75
Number of operational loss events p.a.	1	0	3	60	30
Average operational loss per loss event	€10m	€5m	€20m	55	40
Average market losses (% fee)	10%	5%	20%	55	40
Operating expenses	€30m	€27m	€35m	53	45

---

[7] The Poisson assumption is probably a slight exaggeration of the uncertainty because the team is likely to work harder and have more time available if few mandates are won, and vice versa.

[8] Revenue per mandate, net of operational and market losses, is $4 - 0.04 \times 10 - 0.10 \times 4 = €3.2$ million or €16 million for five mandates.

The figures appearing in the range for the number of mandates show approximately the combined effect of these two uncertainties.[9]

(ii) Likewise an operational loss rate of 4 percent on an average of 25 deals, or one loss per year, would also create an intrinsic uncertainty of almost ± 1 loss or ± €10 million. The figures shown in the range combine this intrinsic statistical uncertainty with an uncertainty about the operational loss event probability. Note also that the probability of an operational loss may be related to the total number of deals; we shall come back to this point later.

(iii) The sensitivities have been calculated one by one, holding all factors at their base-case values except for the one being tested. In reality, factors may move together and, as a result, the relative importance of each factor may be different than it appears to be in the sensitivity table. For example, uncertainties about 'average market losses' and about 'average operational loss per loss event' appear to have similar impacts. In reality the uncertainty on market losses may be more significant because it is probably related to the rate of generation of mandates: in lean times, there are not only fewer mandates but also greater placement difficulties, leading to potentially greater market losses. An opposite relationship may hold for operational losses: the busier the team the greater the chance of a major error, and vice versa. It should also be noted that operating income is not a linear function of all risk factors and therefore the combined effect of several factors may be greater or smaller than the sum of their marginal effects.

Keeping in mind the limitations of the sensitivity analysis, it is still fair to say that the first two factors 'number of mandates per annum' and 'average fee per mandate' have the greatest impact on operating income, and management's time would be well spent finding alternative strategies that could influence these two factors to reduce risks and/or to increase operating income. Alternative strategies could be: a general increase in departmental resources; new ways of seeking profitable mandates, such as concentration of efforts on large deals; strengthening of experience in some country/sector; and adjustment of fee/pricing policies. Other factors are less important but, because 'number of operational loss events per annum' comes third on the list and we are discussing operational risks, let us suppose that a keen operational risk manager has convinced senior management that it seems ridiculous to lose perhaps €10 million to €30 million per year because of flawed deals. After all, €30 million is equal to the expense budget of the department. It would seem that, with a little more resources and care, such operational losses could be greatly reduced.

To formulate a simple decision, suppose a 20 percent increase in personnel and other resources is considered at an additional cost of €5 million per year. The operational risk manager proposes that the extra resources be used to do a more thorough and professional job and avoid operational losses rather than to try to increase the volume of business – that

[9] A 66 percent range is about 2 standard deviations, but this one is not quite symmetrical around the mean (25–5, 25+6). Combining two independent uncertainties with standard deviations of 5 and 5.5 yields a total standard deviation of 7.4 but, due to the asymmetry around the mean, we choose 25–7 and 25+8 as a range.

is alternative A. The head of department proposes to explore also the consequences of using these extra resources to try to capture more business, keeping the working practices unchanged – that is alternative B. We summarize the expected impacts of the two alternatives compared to the status quo in Table 15.3.

Under strategy A, the 20 percent increase in resources is expected to decrease the probability of making a significant error from 4 percent down to 1 percent per deal (it is very hard to eliminate all possibilities of error). Under strategy B, the number of mandates is expected to increase by only 12 percent because of stiff competition and limited markets. All other factors except for the €5 million increase in expenses remain the same as in the status quo.

A quick reckoning shows that alternative A achieves an expected operational loss saving of $0.03 \times 25 \times 10 = $ €7.5 million for an extra cost of €5 million, whereas alternative B is expected to increase revenues by $0.12(100 - 10 - 10) = $ €9.6 million for the same extra cost. Prima facie, the two alternatives appear favourable compared to the status quo, but B is not a clear winner as A has been designed to be less risky than the status quo whereas B will amplify the risks.

Again we try a 'back-of-an-envelope' calculation to determine whether the relative riskiness of the three alternatives might influence our choice. We assume Poisson arrivals of mandates, and, given a mandate, an independent binomial process for the occurrence of a foul-up. For each mandate, we assume a fee distribution with standard deviation equal to its expected value and, likewise, for each operational loss, a standard deviation equal to the expected loss. On this basis, and including uncertainties for other factors in line with the sensitivity ranges shown in Table 15.2, we calculate some summary characteristics of the three alternatives to help decide among them.[10]

TABLE 15.3 ■ Debt origination – alternative strategies

Strategy	Status quo	Alternative A	Alternative B
Arrival rate of mandates	25	25	28
Operational loss probability per mandate	4 percent	1 percent	4 percent
Operating expenses	€30m	€35m	€35m

TABLE 15.4 ■ Debt origination – evaluation of alternative strategies

Strategy	Status quo	Alternative A	Alternative B
Expected operating income	€50m	€52.5m	€54.6m
Standard deviation of operating income	€37.8m	€36.6m	€40.0m
Probability of negative operating income	9.3 percent	7.6 percent	8.6 percent

---

[10] The specific parameters used in our calculations (other than those already described) are: standard deviation of rate of arrival of mandates: 20 percent and standard deviation of expense budget: 8.33 percent.

No great surprise here, except perhaps that the risk reduction achieved by the 'safe' alternative A is only nominal. Indeed, a complete elimination of operational losses, if it were feasible, could be shown to result in a standard deviation of €36.2 million, a very small risk reduction compared to €37.8 million standard deviation with the status quo. Both alternatives A and B appear more favourable than the status quo but there is not much to choose between them. A more refined analysis would be necessary (including a better description of objectives, such as return on capital and risk attitude) to arrive at a definitive conclusion.[11] Perhaps more importantly, it would be useful to imagine better alternative strategies or turn management's attention towards more critical problems – all the analysis in the world cannot make up for the lack of one good idea!

This case study is only meant as an illustration, but it reveals two general reasons why ordinary operational risks are unlikely to play a significant role in risk management (even when grossly exaggerated compared to recorded loss experience). Firstly, ordinary operational risks are only one type among the many types of risks faced by a firm, including large risks that are not recognized in current and proposed regulations. As we see in our case study, the predominant risks found in the bond origination activity are number of mandates won and profitability of each mandate; such risks are classified as business risks by Basel and simply ignored under Pillar 1. The second reason is that ordinary operational risks will often be negatively correlated with the main risks. An increase in activity, leading to increasing revenues, is often linked with an increase in operational risk exposure, be it human error, client fraud, or even system failure. Thus, paradoxically, operational risks could even reduce total risks.[12]

The main lesson is that risk management, as part of good management, should be concerned with all aspects of risks and revenues. Ignoring some aspects is likely to lead to poor decisions. Thus the emphasis put by Basel on operational risk could be useful if that aspect was previously overlooked – although there is no evidence that it was. Conversely, it could be dangerous if it focused attention too much on operational risks and away from other risks and costs, for example by requesting a narrowly defined monitoring of operational losses and providing incentives targeted to reduce operational losses without regard to other economic factors. Alas, this is what Pillar 1 does.

This case study also illustrates the arbitrariness of the capital charges currently proposed. Under the 'Basic Approach', the capital charge would be 15 percent of gross income, or €12 million. Under the 'Standard Approach', the charge would be for the 'Corporate Finance' business line, that is 18 percent of gross income, or €14.4 million. Under an 'Advanced Measurement Approach' based on loss experience, the target of a 99.9 percent confidence level over one year would require taking into consideration at least five potential errors.

---

[11] It would be improper to say that the choice between A and B is *difficult*; *indifferent* or *not material* would be more apposite.

[12] For the sake of curiosity, the reader could modify the parameters of the case study to create an increase in total risks when reducing operational risk. One way is to choose an expected operational loss equal to the expected fee and a standard deviation of operational loss smaller than the expected fee. Another way is to develop a more realistic model showing that the probability of error, for a given department size, increases with the amount of work to be done, that is, with the number of contracts won.

Including the uncertainty on loss severity, the operational risk capital charge would be in excess of €70 million. This could possibly be reduced by claiming that the €10 million expected loss should be covered by sufficient profits (although not at the 99.9 percent confidence level).

Thus, depending on the calculation method, the capital charge ranges from small to large and, contrary to intended incentives, it increases with the degree of sophistication of the chosen calculation method.

15.5 Understanding exceptional operational risks

Are there common features among what we called exceptional operational risks beyond their defining characteristics of rarity and severe consequences? Table 15.5 lists a dozen cases of banking, broking and asset management institutions that have been greatly affected by operational losses since 1991. Ten of these went bankrupt, were taken over or were forced to merge as a consequence of their losses. One could not say that these are the most significant operational losses recorded over the period without entering into a debate on ranking criteria (e.g. how to account for the impact of the loss, the size of the company, or the strength of the operational causality). Let us say simply that these are representative exceptional operational losses.

It is striking that the cases listed were consequences of deliberate actions and not mere accidents. In ten cases these actions were unethical, illegal or criminal.[13] They were not necessarily initiated by senior management, but they were at least allowed to endure by management incompetence or negligence. The root cause, not surprisingly, is individual and corporate greed.

A second feature of the observed exceptional operational risks is the diversity in their manifestations. The ingenuity of an unscrupulous human mind is unbounded when it comes to devising new ways to profit from an insufficiently controlled environment. Firms are less likely to fall victim to the same scheme than to fall into new traps. With globalization, new products, new technologies, increased competition and pressure to perform, one may expect new forms of operational risks in the future. The observed heterogeneity of circumstances in which exceptional operational losses have occurred should help exorcise a few ghosts before sketching an appropriate methodology to tackle exceptional operational risks.

The first ghost is the belief that 'industry-wide' operational loss databases will provide the basis to assess exceptional risks. Some companies have launched into the collection of operational losses across financial institutions and continents in the vain hope that an exceptional loss incurred by, say, a broker in Bombay could help 'fatten the tail' of an operational loss distribution for an asset manager in Manhattan. Of course, there are always things to learn from the past – one might even argue that there is nowhere else to learn from – but the mere recording of a loss amount in one firm cannot be translated mechanically into a probability and severity of loss in another firm. On the other hand, the anecdotal evidence about the way

---

[13] The two special cases are: (i) The 11 September terrorist strike – although it had been planned for years by its perpetrators, it still came as a total surprise to the victims; (ii) The reduced final bonus policy put in place by the Equitable Life Assurance Society to offset the benefits of guaranteed annuity rates given to some policyholders was, in the end, judged illegal by the UK House of Lords but this ruling was difficult to foresee.

TABLE 15.5 ▪ Exceptional operational risks illustrations

Company	Cause of loss
1991 Salomon Brothers (USA)	US T-Bond primary market manipulation
1993 Bank of Commerce and Credit International (BCCI) (Luxembourg)	Illegal activities (drugs, arms)
1994 Kidder Peabody (USA)	Management incompetence
1995 Baring's (UK)	Rogue trader and management incompetence
1995 Daiwa Securities (Japan)	Involvement with gangsters
1996 Bankers Trust (USA)	Selling products clients did not fully understand
1997 Morgan Grenfell (UK)	Unauthorized investments in illiquid assets
1997 NatWest Markets (UK)	Mispricing of derivatives
2000 Equitable Life Assurance Society (UK)	Non-respect of guaranteed annuity contracts
2001 Cantor Fitzgerald and others (USA)	Terrorist attack on World Trade Center
2002 Allied Irish Bank (USA)	Rogue trader
2002 Merrill Lynch (USA)	Biased analyst recommendations

disasters occurred (or were avoided – there must be more near disasters than actual disasters and therefore more to learn from them) and the way they were handled may be very informative; it may stimulate thought and help discover vulnerabilities in one's organization and therefore identify potential problems to be examined; that is all, but it is a lot.

The second ghost is the belief that extreme value theory (EVT), a branch of probability theory and statistics, can make an important contribution to the assessment of exceptional operational risks. EVT was developed many years ago to describe the distribution of extreme values in repetitive processes (see Gumbel 1958; Embrechts *et al.* 1997). In mathematical terms, it is possible to describe the probability distribution of the maximum value (or the distribution of excess over threshold) in a set of observations of identically and independently distributed (i.i.d.) random variables, based on a few assumptions about the underlying distribution (about its tail in particular). Thus, Gumbel produced estimates of the floods of the Colorado River based on many years of observations of river flows at Black Canyon. In general, EVT has been successful at describing extremes of physical processes where a theory gives some indication about the underlying distribution and the observations are i.i.d. More recently, EVT has been applied with some success in finance (maximum variations of the stock market) and insurance (estimation of extreme losses of a given type) under similar circumstances. But the attempt to apply EVT to a small set of unrelated operational losses in different firms around the globe is another triumph of wishful thinking over reason. At best, it could be used to study the extreme severities in one category of what we called ordinary operational risks, provided losses have been observed many times and may be assumed (perhaps after recalibration) to follow the same distribution.

A poor cousin of the EVT ghost has also been spotted around financial institutions, often in the company of management consultants; we shall call him the extreme value simulation (EVS) ghost. The EVS ghost proceeds like this. Start with a large external operational losses database that contains all sorts of loss events. Screen out the events that obviously could not occur in the firm under review; for example, no rogue trader losses in a firm not involved in trading. Somehow scale the severities of the remaining events to the relative size of the firm (perhaps by looking at relative size and number of transactions). Also scale the number of loss events to one year for the relevant firm. For example, if there are N loss events remaining in the revised database contributed over Y years by banks with an adjusted total capital[14] C, and if the capital of the target firm is c, the expected equivalent number of loss events during one year for the target firm could be assessed as $E(n) = Nc/CY$. The penultimate step is now to pick at random n loss events among the N events in the database, where n is a random variable (perhaps Poisson-distributed) with mean $E(n)$. The sum of all n losses gives a realization of what could be operational losses for the target firm over one year. The final step is to repeat the sampling exercise 10 000 or perhaps 100 000 or 1 million times (computers are fast and cheap) to create a histogram of losses with about 10 (or 100 or 1000) occurrences beyond the 99.9 percent quantile, thus yielding an estimate of losses at that confidence level. The whole process can be obfuscated with enough technical jargon to make it look scientific and justify a high fee.

What is wrong with EVS? Aside from all the difficulties in trying to make external data relevant to a specific firm, the main problem is confusing the observation of a few rare loss events with a model for extreme losses. As we have discussed, the extreme tail, or 99.9 percent quantile, of an operational loss distribution is dominated by the possibility of a few very large impact but very improbable losses. The largest industry-wide databases will still contain just a few examples of these exceptional losses and therefore can only lead to highly unreliable estimates of their probabilities. For example, if five loss events of a certain type are observed in a 5000 firm-year database, should the probability of occurrence of such events in one firm over the next year be estimated at one in a thousand? Statistics tell us that the probability of occurrence could very well be twice as small or twice as big. And what about the probability of several of these events happening in one year? How small? We do not have much of an idea unless we examine these events in detail. Perhaps if one happens now it cannot happen again for several years or precludes others from happening. Or, at the other extreme, the occurrence of one may greatly increase that of others as in a chain reaction.[15] All that, which is crucial, is overlooked by EVS. It is a blind approach.

---

[14] Capital corresponding only to relevant activities of the target bank.

[15] I heard Prof R Howard of Stanford University, whom many regard as the father of modern decision analysis, give this vivid illustration of a combination of rare events. Suppose your company has invested in the biggest, most luxurious, most state-of-the-art and safest ocean liner in history and you want to assess the main risks for this ship that will cruise the North Atlantic route. Historical records will show ships damaged or completely lost due to heavy seas, collisions with other ships or icebergs, fires, mechanical problems, etc. Loss severities depend on the preparedness of the crew, the availability of lifeboats, communications, proximity to other ships, etc. A consultant might well have used these data and, after scaling and numerous simulations, come up with a loss distribution and an estimate of the 99.9 percent quantile. The ship was the *Titanic* and we know what happened during her maiden voyage. The unique combination of rare circumstances during this fateful crossing – wanting to regain the blue ribbon and therefore progressing at maximum speed along the shortest route, further north than normal; ship

15.6 An exceptional operational risk case study

Is there a general methodology that can be devised to analyze rare but important operational risks? I do not think that there is a single approach or mathematical technique, but there are a couple of features that must be recognized and addressed in any meaningful approach. The first is the need for models to assess low probabilities; the second is the need for a quantitative trade-off between profit (or cost) and uncertainty, that is to say, an expression of risk attitude, to enable a rational choice among alternative courses of action to deal with exceptional risks. Courses of action span a range from risk retention, perhaps combined with additional safety measures, to partial or total risk transfer (insurance, outsourcing). In the spirit of the previous comments about the nature of exceptional risks we illustrate a general approach by looking at a new type of man-made threat – a computer super-virus that could affect an e-banking venture.

15.6.1 An e-banking venture

A leading bank plans to gain market share through an e-banking subsidiary. Considerable effort has been put into ensuring the reliability and client safety of the systems: multi-key authentication, encrypted communications, transmission firewalls, systems redundancy including distributed processing and multiple data storage centres, disaster recovery sites, etc. But is there any protection against a mad individual bent on creating havoc for whatever reason? Alas, brilliant but twisted minds are not rare.

We know how rapidly a known organic virus can spread and how difficult it may be to control; witness the recent foot-and-mouth epidemic in Great Britain. The consequences of more potent, perhaps yet unknown, viruses could be devastating. Computer viruses can also be very potent. Designed by man, they can be very infectious;[16] they can have a very long 'incubation' period during which they spread undetected. They can be designed to break down safety mechanisms, to reveal confidential information that will permit fraud, to wipe out critical information on a broad scale and to render systems unusable for a time. Like meteorites, they are not uncommon but few are catastrophic. Thousands have been detected and dealt with by specialist companies before they could spread too far and create huge damage. Yet, one day, a single one could have devastating consequences.

To assess the probability of a computer virus infection and the damage it could potentially cause, a detailed map of the systems hardware and software will be studied by experts looking at possible entry points for the virus, deciding where to put the main firewalls, which tests, where and at what frequencies should be carried out, what recovery strategy

---

more than full with passengers, many festivities on board, minimum watch, incredulity at first about the scale of the accident and slow reaction time, lack of life-saving equipment and unavailability of some because of heavy listing, etc. – makes the historical data largely irrelevant. Furthermore, much more can be learned about this disaster for future safety management than from the mere recording of one major loss event.

[16] Viruses have been transmitted by simple e-mails without the recipient having to open any file or simply by accessing an Internet service.

should be put in place depending on the extent and severity of the infection. Many decisions will require trade-offs between safety and costs or convenience. For example, should a time-consuming virus check be carried out every time a connection is established with a client? Should backups of all communications and transactions be kept in various remote places? What resources should be arranged on a standby basis to recreate lost or corrupted records? In the terms and conditions for opening accounts, which liabilities will the bank be prepared to accept and which will they decline? Should a guarantee on client moneys be provided by the parent bank? Could part or nearly all the operations be outsourced to a major information technology company that would bear the main responsibility in case of a virus attack? Could the bank purchase insurance to cover at least some of the risks?

It would be all too easy to lose sight of the essentials when studying such complex situations. A team of experts without management guidance would be no better than a patrol of ants trying to make sense of a Pollock painting by running all over it. Good managers and decision analysts have found from experience two semi-universal laws:

1   Experts will often get lost in details and be overconfident about their state of knowledge; after all, they are being paid to know. Thus systems analyses will include a vast number of variables, but scenarios about what may happen will be confined to rather narrow, uninventive ranges.

2   Decision situations, no matter how complex at first sight, are generally dominated by just a few critical factors, be they dominant sources of uncertainty or key decision variables. The art of decision-making is to identify these factors and focus the analysis on them.

Critical factors are identified step by step by refining a model and assessing consequences iteratively. The decision situation can be depicted with the help of an influence diagram (see Section 7.4.4): some nodes represent choices between alternatives (decision variables), others sources of uncertainty (state variables); terminal nodes reflect states of the systems to which values can be attributed. The connections leading to terminal nodes represent the interactions between decisions and external factors leading to various terminal states of the systems with corresponding probabilities. One starts with a simple representation and conducts sensitivity analyses. Unimportant state variables are set at fixed values; unimportant decision variables are simplified or predetermined. But the most influential factors are subjected to further investigations: additional information is sought where economically justified; large uncertainties are described with full probability distributions; major alternatives are refined. This type of approach has been used in a number of industries to analyze complex systems and assess reliability and safety standards where the probabilities of failure or accidents are extremely small.[17]

Proceeding along these lines but without further details, suppose the e-banking venture has been reduced to a choice between two main strategies:

[17] Probabilities of failure with ensuing fatalities can typically be set at between one in a million and one in 100 million per year or per mission.

(i) *Standard Safety*. All measures are put in place to protect against known strains of computer viruses and new strains as they are discovered. The business plan, taking into account the initial investment and projections of revenues and operating costs over the effective life of the venture, indicates an €800 million expected net present value in the absence of any super-virus attack but a loss of €400 million if a super-virus strikes. The probability of the latter event is perceived at around 5 percent. Of course there are enormous uncertainties around all of these figures. These are indicated in Table 15.6.

(ii) *Enhanced Safety*. Extra precautions are taken which will not only increase the initial investment and the operating costs but are also expected to reduce market share because the services will be less user-friendly. Consequently, the net present value of the venture is lower than under the Standard Safety plan but the probability of a super-virus attack is reduced to about 0.5 percent and the consequences (e.g. reputational effects) are also mitigated. The key figures for the two alternatives are reported in Table 15.6.

A few comments are in order:

1   There is no hiding the difficulty of reducing a choice of strategies to simple terms. All outcomes must be reduced to monetary values. Future cash flows must be expressed at a present value using some discount factor (normally the minimum return on capital required by the parent bank). Uncertainties must be assessed and aggregated. The relative importance of various choices must be ascertained to identify the few most critical.

2   The probabilities of a super-virus strike during the effective life of the venture (i.e. many years) would be most difficult to assess. The views of experts could span wide ranges; for example, 5 percent for the Standard Safety strategy could mean somewhere between 2 percent and 10 percent. But, interestingly, we shall see that uncertainty about such probabilities should not be a major concern; that is why no uncertainty range for the probability of a strike has been shown in Table 15.6.

3   The losses in the event of a strike are larger for the Standard Safety than for the Enhanced Safety strategy for several reasons. Firstly, the venture being a limited liability company, direct losses to the parent company cannot be larger than the capital they have invested in the venture, which capital may be larger for the Standard Safety strategy because of greater operational risk capital requirements. Secondly, whatever the legal limitations to the liability of the parent bank, there will be reputational damages and these will be more limited if the parent bank can show that exceptional precautions had been taken. Thirdly, the Enhanced Safety strategy can be thought as having additional mechanisms in place to contain the severity of the damages. The results we show in case of a super-virus attack mean that the initial investment of the parent bank would be wiped out and there are additional but uncertain reputational losses. In other words, the losses to the parent bank attributable to the super-virus are perceived as €(1200 ± 200) million under the Standard Safety strategy and €(850 ± 150) million under the Enhanced Safety strategy.

TABLE 15.6 ■ E-banking alternative strategies

Strategy	Standard Safety	Enhanced Safety
Probability of super-virus strike	5 percent	0.5 percent
Net present value if no strike	€(800 ± 200) million	€(500 ± 200) million
Net present value if strike	−€(400 ± 200) million	−€(350 ± 150) million

Now let us compare the two alternatives. On an expected value basis, the Standard Safety strategy is a clear winner with an expected value of $0.95 \times 800 - 0.05 \times 400 = €740$ million, against $0.995 \times 500 - 0.05 \times 350 = €495.75$ million, for the Enhanced Safety strategy. But that ignores the risks, and the directors of the parent bank may have different opinions about the right choice, indeed they are all entitled and expected to defend their own views; still, a decision must be reached.

15.6.2 Quantification of risk attitude

Each situation where risks play a determinant role could be decided on its own merits, perhaps on a majority vote of the board, and that is indeed how many important business decisions are taken. At the same time, there should be some feeling of uneasiness about the subjective nature of this decision process. One should like to ensure a minimum degree of consistency across successive decisions. It would not make sense if, depending on the mood of the moment, the decisions were wildly fluctuating over time from risk-averse to risk-taking. Likewise, it would not make sense if some opportunities were deemed to be too risky for one division but desirable for another. The firm could be arbitraged, that is, one could imagine a hypothetical third party being paid to take away opportunities that are too risky from one division only to sell them at a profit to another less risk-averse division.

It would be much more satisfactory if risky opportunities could be summarized in a systematic way by just one number, something like a minimum selling price, that would encapsulate the degree of risk aversion of a firm. Intuitively, the degree of risk aversion or trade-off between risks and rewards ought to be relatively stable. It should evolve over time with the accumulated results of the firm but only progressively and, at any point in time, there should be only one trade-off otherwise, as we mentioned earlier, the firm could be vulnerable to internal arbitrage.

Fortunately, the methodology exists; it was developed more than 50 years ago and is known as utility theory.[18] The fact that it is not widely used has more to do with conflicts between personal interests of decision-makers and the good of a company – a subject far beyond the scope of this chapter – than with any flaw in the theory. The concept is simple and based on just a few basic rules of behaviour that no businessman would knowingly want to violate. A utility theory primer is given in Appendix 15.1. We shall assume for the rest of this discussion that the parent bank, as part of its risk management framework, has chosen to describe its risk attitude with the utility function represented in Figure 15.2.

---

[18] Utility theory was developed in 1947 by the mathematician John von Neumann and the economist Oskar Morgenstern.

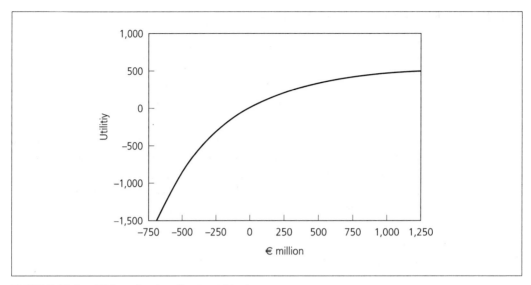

FIGURE 15.2 ■ Risk attitude of parent bank

Firms that have gone through the effort of drawing a utility function may be satisfied with an exponential fit, that is, a function of the form

$$u(x) = \lambda(1 - \exp(-x/\lambda)),$$

where the parameter λ, called the coefficient of risk tolerance, often lies between 10 percent and 20 percent of the capital of the firm. To clarify the evaluations in our case study, we shall assume that the parent bank has capital of the order of €3 billion, and adopts an exponential utility function with a coefficient of risk tolerance of €500 million. That is the utility curve actually plotted in Figure 15.2.

15.6.3 Choice of strategy, value of information and value of insurance

The best strategic choice as a function of risk attitude

The two alternative strategies, Standard and Enhanced Safety, are far from yielding normally distributed outcomes, so it would be inaccurate to use the mean–variance approximation of the certain equivalent. We therefore carry out exact calculations of the certain equivalent for each strategy but we assume, for simplicity, that the main risks of the e-banking venture are independent of the existing risks of the parent bank. The results, together with the expected values, are shown in Table 15.7.

With the €500 million level of risk tolerance the decision should be clearly in favour of the Standard Safety alternative; it is worth €108 million more than the Enhanced Safety alternative.

TABLE 15.7 ■ Choice criteria for e-banking strategies

Strategy	Standard Safety	Enhanced Safety
Expected value	€740 million	€496 million
Certain equivalent (λ – €500 million)	€557 million	€449 million

But given that the €500 million level of risk tolerance is rather an order of magnitude than a precise figure, it would be interesting to know at what level of risk tolerance the decision could shift in favour of the Enhanced Safety alternative or perhaps even in favour of abandoning both alternatives because they would be deemed too risky. To that end we calculate the certain equivalent of both alternatives over a wide range of risk tolerance coefficients. The results are plotted in Figure 15.3. The evaluations show that as long as the coefficient of risk tolerance is above €350 million, the Standard Safety strategy is the preferred option. For a risk tolerance between €350 million and €90 million, the Enhanced Safety strategy is better. But if the risk tolerance of the parent bank were below €90 million, neither of the e-banking proposals would be acceptable, even the Enhanced Safety strategy would be perceived as too risky.

The value of additional information/analysis

There is a great simplifying virtue in focusing an analysis on decisions that matter. A situation like the choice of e-banking strategies that we have just considered is fraught with complexities and uncertainties but it is not necessary to study every detail to reach rational decisions. For example, we have just seen that it is not necessary to pin down very precisely the risk attitude

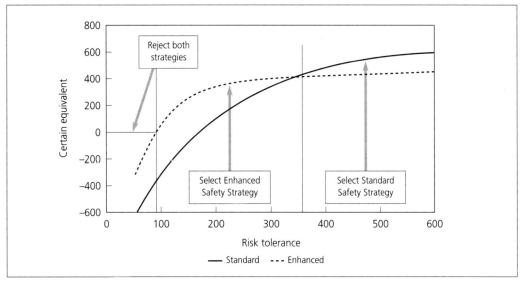

FIGURE 15.3 ■ Certain equivalent of e-banking strategies

of the parent bank to choose between the two key safety strategies. Having made this key choice, one can proceed to refine the chosen strategy and worry less about risk tolerance.

Another example would be the value of ascertaining with greater confidence the probability of a super-virus strike during the effective life of the venture. We commented earlier that such probabilities are difficult to assess; given half a chance, experts will disagree! But we also said that uncertainty about a low probability event is not so important. The reason should be clear now – the expected utility criterion is nearly linear in the probability of rare events, therefore an average probability will do. Of course it may matter whether the average, or best guess, is, say for the Standard Safety strategy, 5 percent as we have assumed, or 3 percent, or 7 percent; that can be tested.

By recalculating the certain equivalent with higher probabilities of super-virus strikes, we would find that, at the €500 million risk tolerance level, the probability of a strike would have to be greater than 8.5 percent under the Standard Safety strategy to justify switching to the Enhanced Safety strategy. Refining the analysis of the probability of a strike to improve its accuracy would add costs and delays. It would not be worthwhile, because it would not affect the key strategic decision, unless there is a chance that the findings could lead to a probability estimate larger than 8.5 percent. Thus the value of refining the analysis depends on the uncertainty shrouding the initial estimate, the improvement in accuracy expected from further studies and, of course, the risk attitude of the company. In the current situation, with a coefficient of risk tolerance of €500 million, further studies of the strike probability would not be worth very much as they would be unlikely to lead to an improved decision. By contrast, if the coefficient of risk tolerance were only €350 million, we would not be sure which of the two strategies is best and better information on the probability of a strike would help select the best alternative; better information would be quite valuable.[19]

Displaying the domains of parameter values over which one strategy is better than another requires more calculations but helps identify critical parameters and reduces the task of assessing their values to judging in which ranges they are. This approach is often referred to as the extensive form of decision analysis.

[19] By way of a 'back-of-the-envelope' calculation, suppose that the initial estimate of 5 percent strike probability has an uncertainty represented by a normal distribution with standard deviation σ_1; a refined analysis could reduce the uncertainty to σ_2 ($\sigma_2 < \sigma_1$). With a €350 million risk tolerance both strategies have about the same value (certain equivalent) of €425 million. But the value of the Standard Safety strategy decreases by €38 million per percentage point increase in the probability of a strike. Perfect information would lead us to choose the Enhanced Safety strategy if the probability of a strike turned out to be greater than 5 percent, a saving of €38 million per percentage point above 5 percent, that is, an expected saving equal to the value of a call at 5 percent on the probability of a strike at €38m per point. Perfect information would be worth about $0.4 \times 38\sigma_1$; e.g. €22.8 million if σ_1 were equal to 1.5 percent. But perfect information may remain a dream; if the residual uncertainty is $\sigma_2 > 0$, the information would still be worth $0.4 \times 38(\sigma_1 - \sigma_2)$; e.g. €7.6 million if $\sigma_2 = 1$ percent and $\sigma_1 = 1.5$ percent.

The value of insurance and risk sharing

Finally, armed with a quantitative statement of risk attitude, we can address in the same consistent way a number of other decisions where uncertainty matters. The process of encoding risk attitude into a utility function would be hardly worthwhile if only one critical decision had to be analyzed, but it is likely that a firm would wish to examine a number of problems, be they exceptional operational or business risks, with the same tool. To illustrate, consider the general problem of sharing or totally transferring some risks through insurance.

There are many reasons why firms, like individuals, buy insurance – force of habit, convenience, sometimes legal requirements – but fundamentally it should be based on economic reasons. The value of the insured risk net of insurance premium should be greater than the value of the uninsured risk. Within our valuation framework, for 'value', read 'certain equivalent'. We complete our case study of e-banking by estimating what would be the value of insuring the venture against a super-virus.

For the sake of simplicity, we confine our analysis to the maximum value of an insurance policy that would provide 100 percent cover against all economic consequences related to a super-virus strike and nothing else.[20] This is the maximum value we would be prepared to pay for a single, front-end premium; knowing this value would help decide whether various insurance proposals could be attractive. The calculation of the maximum insurance premium P would in general be iterative, that is, we would have to solve the equation

Certain Equivalent (insured strategy $- P$) = Certain Equivalent (non-insured strategy)

by searching over P. With the exponential utility function we have chosen, the solution for P can be directly obtained since

Certain Equivalent (insured strategy $- P$) = Certain Equivalent (insured strategy) $- P$.

The maximum economic insurance premium for both strategies is shown in Figure 15.4 over a wide range of risk tolerance. Not surprisingly, it is much higher for the Standard Safety strategy, which is more vulnerable to a super-virus, than for the Enhanced Safety strategy. For both strategies, the maximum economic premium decreases with increasing levels of risk tolerance but remains always larger than the expected loss being covered. The expected losses due to a super-virus are easy to calculate: for the Standard Safety strategy it is $0.05(800 - (-400)) = €60$ million and for the Enhanced Safety strategy only $0.005(500 - (-350)) = €4.25$ million. For example, at the €500 million risk tolerance level the maximum economic insurance premia

---

[20] Note that we do not address here the possible effect that the existence of an insurance contract could have on the potential claim amount. We alluded earlier to the fact that the total capital invested in the company would put a limit on the maximum amount of losses to the parent. The existence of an insurance contract could raise this limit unless an equivalent maximum loss amount were stated in the contract. But then the venture, and therefore the parent company, could still make excess losses and that would make the cover less valuable. On the other hand, the existence of an insurance contract could justify a reduction of the regulatory capital of the e-banking venture, thus making the insurance contract more valuable. Without pretending that the two effects would cancel each other, we shall ignore these thorny issues for the sake of simplicity. In a real-life situation, the proposed methodology could be readily extended to cover such issues.

would be €203 million for the Standard Safety strategy and €11 million for the Enhanced Safety strategy. These figures are markedly larger than the respective expected losses, leaving room for a profit margin and a risk premium for the would-be insurer.

But is it likely indeed that insurance could be obtained at a lower cost than its maximum value? Why should an insurance company be in a better position than the parent bank to absorb the potential losses? We can apply the same methodology to calculate the minimum premium that an insurance company would be willing to accept.

Covering the e-banking venture designed under the Standard Safety strategy against the risk of a super-virus attack could cost an insurance company a net present value of €1200 million with an uncertainty of €283 million if a strike took place; at least, that is what the parent company would think based on its analysis. The €283 million uncertainty is the uncertainty between the gains without the virus and the losses with the virus, two independent uncertainties of €200 million each for the insurance company.[21] The corresponding figures for the Enhanced Safety strategy would be €850 million with an uncertainty of €250 million (combining independent uncertainties of €200 million and €150 million). Of course, the insurer could carry out a different analysis with different estimates and parameters, but for the time being let us assume that the insurer and the parent bank agree on the risks.

As compensation the insurer would receive a front-end premium Q. What should be the minimum economic value of Q? If we pursue a similar analysis of the certain equivalent of the insurance contract for the insurer, the minimum premium value would solve:

Certain Equivalent $(Q - \text{Liabilities}) = 0$.

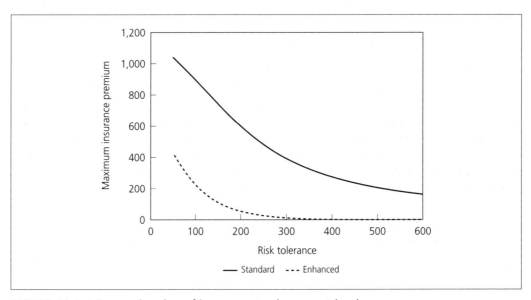

FIGURE 15.4 ■ Economic value of insurance to the parent bank

[21] For the parent company these two uncertainties are not independent. The losses in the event of a virus attack that would bankrupt the venture are larger if the profits before the attack were larger themselves.

Given that the liabilities for the insurer have the same expected value but a greater uncertainty than the corresponding risk reduction for the parent bank, for equal levels of risk attitude, it is clear that there would be no possible insurance deal. The minimum premium requested by the insurer would exceed the maximum premium that the parent bank would be willing to pay. Figure 15.5 confirms this point by comparing the maximum value of the insurance cover (as in Figure 15.4) with the minimum cost of the cover to the insurer for various levels of risk tolerance. For example, the figures for the base case €500 million risk tolerance level are as shown in Table 15.8.

Under what circumstances would insurance become economically viable (leaving aside patent errors or accounting and regulatory distortions)? Our analysis reveals three situations that could justify insurance cover:

1   The transferred risk provides more diversification (or hedging) to the insurer than to the insured.

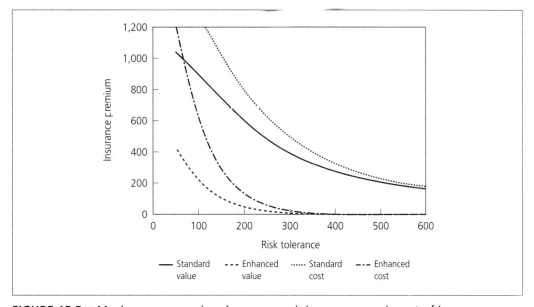

FIGURE 15.5 ■ Maximum economic value versus minimum economic cost of insurance

TABLE 15.8 ■ Comparison of acceptable insurance premia for insurer and insured with the same €500 million risk tolerance coefficient

Insurance premium	Standard Safety	Enhanced Safety
Maximum value to the bank	€203 million	€11 million
Minimum cost to the insurer	€234 million	€13 million

2   The insurance company has a greater coefficient of risk tolerance than the insured, possibly because it has a much larger capital.

3   Partial insurance cover is considered.

The first situation is the reverse of what we observed in our case study and which caused the excess of cost over value. It may occur if a bank wishes to insure some of several positively correlated risks and, on the other hand, the insurance company seeks to diversify its risks.[22]

The second situation can be found either when large insurance companies insure small clients or when the risk of a large client is shared among large reinsurers. Otherwise, if insurer and insured are similarly capitalized there is no obvious reason why the insurer should adopt a more risk taking attitude than the insured. For large risks the insured would simply exchange a business risk against a credit risk on the insurer, a factor that should be taken into account in the analysis of the value of the insurance contract.

The third situation is particularly interesting because of its general applicability. One should note that any risky opportunity with a positive expected value is worth sharing in, no matter how risk-averse one may be.[23] In the case of exponential utility functions it can be shown that the optimal sharing in a risky opportunity (independent from existing risks) among various interested parties, that is, the allocation that maximizes total expected utility, is in proportion to the coefficient of risk tolerance of each party. Even small insurers can therefore insure big banks provided they cover only a small fraction of the risks.

15.7 Conclusions

We live more and more in a culture of caution where the 'ownership' of risks is assigned to individuals who may have a limited understanding of global objectives or, at any rate, are given limited responsibilities and personal incentives. Thus, in some schools, little girls are no longer allowed to have skipping ropes or make daisy chains because they might get hurt or transmit diseases.

We should have a similar concern that by institutionalizing a risk management function in financial firms and creating separate departments with responsibilities restricted to specific types of risks – as if these risks could be treated separately and independently of the economics of the main business activities – we may be creating an environment that is not conducive to good management.

---

[22] Major insurance disasters have been caused more often by small but highly correlated losses (e.g. asbestos or collapse in residual value of leased computers) than by major single losses which are normally shared through reinsurance.

[23] In footnote 25 we show that the risk discount D varies proportionally to the variance of a risky project and therefore proportionally to the square of the share in that project, whereas the expected value varies proportionally to the share itself. Therefore, when the share is decreased, at some point the risk discount is bound to become smaller than the expected value of the small share.

A balance has to be found between the need, on the one hand, to develop specific risk analysis skills and to have independent reviews of the risk management process and, on the other hand, to integrate all the elements that are necessary to reach intelligent decisions balancing risks and rewards.

Finding the right balance is particularly relevant when considering operational risks. It would be naïve to assume that operational risks must be minimized – that unlike credit and market risks, which must be accepted to some degree in order to generate a profit, operational risks should be eliminated as far as possible.[24] The main difference between operational, credit and market risks is that the last two can be manipulated by adding or taking away risks at market price, that is, without affecting the current fair value of the activity (except for transaction costs), whereas operational risks can only be altered at a cost, hence the importance of taking expenses and revenues into account.

We have argued that the framework for operational risk management should be focused on improving decision-making, that is, on evaluating alternatives to the status quo, taking into account all major consequences rather than just the impact on operational risks. It is all very well to collect operational loss data and to monitor so-called key risk indicators and key risk drivers, but unless key risk drivers are clearly defined as decision variables and all consequences of these decisions, not only their effects on key risk indicators, or even on operational losses, are taken into account, no progress towards better management will be made.

To carry out a decision-focused approach, we found that it would be useful to distinguish various types of operational risks based on the relative importance of uncertainties compared to expected losses.

Routine risks, that is, operational loss events that may occur once a week or more frequently, are at the very low end of the uncertainty scale; it is expected losses, both direct and indirect (reputation) and impact on costs and revenues that count. Some techniques from total quality management that have been used very successfully in other industries could be adapted to the management of *nominal operational risks* in banking.

We called *ordinary risks* those operational loss events that would happen less frequently than once a week and could be as rare as once every few years. Both the uncertainties and the expected losses generated by ordinary risks are significant. It is crucial to assess the relationships between these risks and other risks to obtain a comprehensive picture of risks and rewards.

We singled out as *extraordinary risks* operational loss events that are very unlikely (say, 2 percent or less probability of occurrence per year) but would have devastating effects if they occurred. There again it is important to establish how these risks would interact with others, but one new ingredient, the risk attitude of the firm, becomes paramount for choosing the best risk control method (risk mitigation, insurance, outsourcing, etc.). Many

---

[24] It is interesting to note that in the revised draft on *Sound Practices* (BCBS 2002b, p.4), Basel kept the statement that 'it is clear that operational risk differ from other banking risks in that it is typically not taken in return for an expected reward', but adds in a footnote: 'However, the Committee recognises that in some business lines … the decision to incur operational risk, or compete based on the ability to manage and effectively price this risk, is an integral part of a bank's risk/reward calculus.'

financial institutions and, indeed, regulators talk about risk appetite or use similar expressions, but very few have gone as far as quantifying this concept to make it useful for decision-making. Perhaps banks should be urged to do so.

Appendix 15.1 A primer on utility theory

Utility theory, as developed by J. von Neumann and O. Morgenstern, rests on only three behavioural assumptions:

1 All outcomes of the decisions under examination can be ranked in order of preference; that is, if among three outcomes A, B and C, we strictly prefer A to B and B to C, then we ought strictly to prefer A to C.

2 If, as in (1), we strictly preferred A to B and B to C, then for some probability p, we should be indifferent between receiving B for sure and having a probability p of receiving A and $(1-p)$ of receiving C.

3 Among two risky opportunities offering the same two possible outcomes, we ought to prefer the opportunity presenting the larger probability of obtaining the preferred outcome

Few decision-makers would refuse to accept these rules. Indeed, if they were shown to violate any of these rules, they would probably want to modify their behaviour to conform to them.

The powerful consequence of these simple rules is that matters of choice between risky alternatives can be resolved by attributing a utility value to each outcome and calculating the expected utility of each alternative. The alternative with the maximum expected utility ought to be preferred over the others.

The reasoning is as follows. We wish to identify the best among a set of risky alternatives. From the first assumption, we should be able to identify among all possible outcomes a least desirable outcome, m, and a most desirable income, M. From the second assumption, we can replace every possible outcome, x_i, with a gamble between M with probability u_i and m with probability $(1 - u_i)$. Each alternative is now equivalent to a gamble between the same two outcomes, m and M. The third assumption tells us that we ought to prefer the alternative with the largest probability of winning the most desirable outcome M. For each alternative, the probability of winning M is the expected value for that alternative of the relevant u_i; in other words, if we call the u_i's utilities, the expected utility of that alternative. Note that the description of the outcomes should be comprehensive, i.e. reflective of ultimate results and not limited to a particular concern such as operational losses.

Assigning utilities to possible outcomes is the critical step to which we will come back shortly. But let us remark first that, for financial decisions, outcomes will already be measured on a monetary scale. Utilities will therefore form a continuous, non-decreasing function (because we can be trusted always to prefer more money to less) over a range of possible monetary outcomes as illustrated in Figure 15.6.

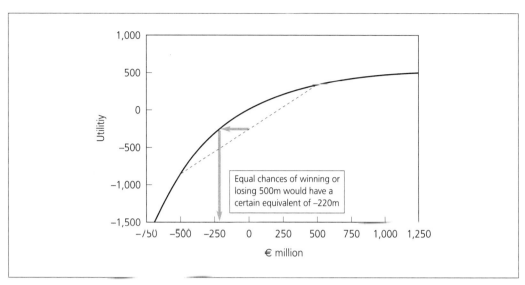

FIGURE 15.6 ■ Describing risk attitude with a utility function

It is the curvature of this function that captures the degree of risk attitude of the firm. A downward curvature expresses a certain degree of risk aversion;[25] the minimum selling price of a risky opportunity shall be less than its expected value. For example, faced with a risk of winning or losing €500 million with equal probability, the firm with the utility function plotted above would perceive an expected utility of about −270; that has the same utility as a sure loss of €220 million. In other words, the firm would be willing to pay someone €220 million to take the risk away. The sure quantity equivalent to a risky opportunity, its minimum selling price, is often referred to as its *certain equivalent*. Choosing the alternative with the maximum expected utility amounts to choosing the alternative with the maximum certain equivalent.

Drawing a utility function for a firm is a tricky exercise best conducted by an experienced outsider. A few points along the curve can be inferred from choices directors and executives would agree to make among simple risky prospects. The results would probably form an elongated cluster of points rather than a smooth monotonic function, but precision is not all that important and a freehand curve drawn through a first set of points would be a good start for further debates

---

[25] Consider a risky prospect X with expected value $E(X)$ and variance $Var(X)$, and a utility curve $u(x)$. From the first couple of terms of a Taylor series expansion of $u(x)$ at the expected value $E(X)$ we obtain: $E(u(x)) = u(E(X)) + \frac{1}{2}u''((E(X))Var(X)$. Equating this to the utility of $E(X) - D$, where D stands for the risk discount, which we approximate with $u(E(X)) - D\,u'(E(X))$, we obtain the approximate risk discount value $D = -\frac{1}{2}(u''/u')\,Var(X)$ which shows that the risk discount is proportional to both the local curvature of the utility curve u''/u' at $E(X)$ and the variance of the risky prospect.

To ensure a smooth function (i.e. without sharp kinks, as often happens on first assessment) one can try to fit a known functional form, for example, an exponential, a logarithmic or a power curve. An ancillary benefit is that a simple functional form (defined within a positive linear transformation[26]) can be summarized by one curvature parameter.

For example, a firm could adopt an exponential utility curve. Parameterized as

$$u(x) = \lambda(1 - \exp(-x/\lambda),$$

utilities are nearly equal to monetary values for small amounts ($x \ll \lambda$); parameter λ is directly related to the curvature[27] and describes the degree of risk tolerance of the firm. For large λ the utility function becomes almost linear, that is, the firm would be risk-neutral, whereas for small positive λ the firm would be risk-averse. The exponential utility curve has a few interesting properties that may appeal. For example, if a sure quantity (positive or negative) is added to all outcomes, the certain equivalent is modified by that quantity. Therefore there is no need to define an absolute zero on the outcome scale; the same exponential utility function can be used for different decisions simultaneously or over time (provided that correlations between risks are taken into account).

If the outcome variable X is normally distributed with expected value E(X) and variance Var(X), the certain equivalent with an exponential utility is simply

$$CE = E(X) - \frac{1}{2\lambda} \, Var(X),$$

that is, the maximum expected utility (or maximum certain equivalent) criterion reduces to a mean–variance criterion in which the trade-off between expected value and risk (measured by a variance) is directly related to the coefficient of risk tolerance λ.

This property can be used to obtain an approximate but quick estimation of the risk tolerance of a firm. Suppose a firm is presented with a 50–50 chance of gaining x or losing $x/2$ immediately. The opportunity has a positive expected value of $x/4$; it is therefore attractive for small values of x when the risk is negligible. It is easy to see, using the mean–variance criterion above, that it will become unattractive at some point when x becomes large; there is indifference between accepting and rejecting the opportunity when x is close to the coefficient of risk tolerance λ.

The expression for the certain equivalent of an exponential utility curve also shows that certain equivalents of independent projects can be added (both expected values and variances of independent risks are additive). In particular, new projects can be analyzed without referring to the risks inherent in the status quo situation, provided the new risks are independent of the existing risks.

---

[26] Mathematical expectation being a linear operator, maximum expected utility choices are invariant under any positive linear transformation of the utility scale.

[27] The curvature defined as u''/u' is equal to $-1/\lambda$ and is therefore constant. The exponential utility function is said to show constant absolute risk aversion (CARA). By comparison, a logarithmic utility function would show constant relative risk aversion (CRRA).

References

All publications issued by the Basel Committee on Banking Supervision are available from www.bis.org.

Alexander, C. (2000) Bayesian methods for measuring operational risks. *Derivatives, Use Trading and Regulation*, 6(2), 166–186.

Alexander, C. (2001) The Bayesian approach to measuring operational risks, in C. Alexander (ed.), *Mastering Risk, Volume 2*. London: Financial Times Prentice Hall.

Algorithmics (2000) *PCRE 3.1 User's Guide*. Toronto: Algorithmics.

Anthony, R.N. (1960) *Management Accounting*. Homewood, IL: Irwin.

Basel Committee on Banking Supervision (1988) *International Convergence of Capital Measurement and Capital Standards*, July.

Basle Committee on Banking Supervision (1998) *Enhancing Bank Transparency*, Publication No. 41, September.

Basle Committee on Banking Supervision (1999) *Sound Practices for Loan Accounting and Disclosure*, Publication No. 55, July.

Basle Committee on Banking Supervision (2000), *Best Practices for Credit Risk Disclosure*, Publication No. 74, September.

Basel Committee on Banking Supervision (2001a) *Operational Risk*, Consultative Paper 2, January.

Basel Committee on Banking Supervision (2001b) *Working Paper on the Regulatory Treatment of Operational Risk*, September.

Basel Committee on Banking Supervision (2001c) *Sound Practices for the Management and Supervision of Operational Risk*, Publication No. 86, December.

Basel Committee on Banking Supervision (2001d) *QIS 2: Operational Risk Data*, May.

Basel Committee on Banking Supervision (2001e) *Results of the Second Quantitative Information Survey*, November.

Basel Committee on Banking Supervision (2002a) *The Quantitative Impact Study for Operational Risk: Overview of Individual Loss Data and Lessons Learned*, January.

Basel Committee on Banking Supervision (2002b) *Sound Practices for the Management and Supervision of Operational Risk*, Publication No. 91, July.

Basel Committee on Banking Supervision (2002c) *Qualitative Impact Study 3 – Technical Guidance*. October.

Basle Committee on Banking Supervision and Technical Committee of the International Organisation of Securities Commissions (1995) *Public Disclosure of the Trading and Derivatives Activities of Banks and Securities Firms*, Publication No. 21, November.

Bernardo, J.M. and Smith, A.F.M. (1994) *Bayesian Theory*. Chichester: Wiley.

Blum, P., Dias, A. and Embrechts, P. (2002) The ART of dependence modelling: the latest advances in correlation analysis, in M. Lane (ed.), *Alternative Risk Strategies*. London: Risk Books, pp. 339–356.

Bouyé, E., Durrleman, V., Nikeghbali, A., Riboulet, G. and Roncalli, T. (2000) Copulas for finance: a reading guide and some applications. Available from www.business.city.ac.uk/ferc/eric.

Bucay, N. and Rosen, D. (2000) Applying portfolio credit risk models to retail portfolios. *Algo Research Quarterly*, 3(1), 45–73.

Clarke, C.J. and Varma, S. (1999) Strategic risk measurement: the new competitive edge. *Long Range Planning*, 32, 414–424.

Das, S. (1993) *Swap and Derivative Financing: The Global Reference to Products, Pricing, Applications and Markets*, 2nd edn. New York: McGraw-Hill Trade.

Dembo, R., Aziz, A., Rosen, D. and Zerbs, M. (2000) *Mark-to-Future*. Algorithmics: Toronto.

Embrechts, P., Klüppelberg C. and Mikosch, T. (1997) *Modelling Extremal Events for Insurance and Finance*. Berlin: Springer-Verlag.

Embrechts, P., McNeil, A. and Straumann, D. (2002) Correlation and dependence in risk management: properties and pitfalls, in M.A.H. Dempster (ed.), *Risk Management: Value at Risk and Beyond*. Cambridge: Cambridge University Press, pp. 176–223.

Federal Reserve System (1997) *Framework for Risk-Focused Supervision of Large Complex Institutions*. Washington, DC: Federal Reserve System, 8 August.

Fenton, N.E. and B. Littlewood (eds) (1991) *Software Reliability and Metrics*, Elsevier.

Frachot, A., Georges, P. and Roncalli, T. (2001) Loss distribution approach for operational risk. Available from http://gro.creditlyonnais.fr/content/rd/home_copulas.htm.

Frey, R. and McNeil, A.J. (2001) Modelling dependent defaults. Preprint, ETH, Zurich. Available from www.math.ethz.ch/~mcneil.

Geoffrion, A.M. (1987) An introduction to structured modelling. *Management Science*, 33, 547–588.

Gumbel, E.J (1958) *Statistics of Extremes*. New York: Columbia University Press.

Harrell, F.E. and Davis, C.E. (1982) A new distribution-free quantile estimator. *Biometrika*, 69, 635–640.

Haubenstock, M. (2000) Loss data. *Operational Risk*, December.

Heckerman, D., Mamdani, A. and Wellman, M. (1995) Real-world applications of Bayesian networks. *Communications of the ACM*, 38(3), 25–26.

Henrion, M., Breese, J.S. and Horvitz, E.J. (1991) Decision analysis and expert systems. *Artificial Intelligence Magazine*, 12(4), 64–91.

Henrion, M., Morgan, M.G., Nair, I. and Wiecha, C. (1986) Evaluating an information system for policy modelling and uncertainty analysis. *Journal of the American Society for Information Science*, 37(5), 319–330.

Howard, R. (2000) Decisions in the face of uncertainty, in C. Alexander (ed.),. *Visions of Risk*. London: Financial Times Prentice Hall.

Howard, R. and Matheson, J. (eds) (1984) *The Principles and Applications of Decision Analysis*, Vols 1 and 2. Menlo Park, CA: Strategic Decisions Group.

IFCI Financial Risk Institute (2000) *Sources of Risk*, May. Available from http://risk.ifci.ch/00007127.htm.

Instefjord, N., Jackson, P. and Perraudin, W. (1998) Securities fraud. *Economic Policy*, 27, 585–623.

International Swaps and Derivatives Association (2002) Response to Basel Committee discussion paper of September 2001, March.

Jensen, F.V. (1996) *Introduction to Bayesian Networks*. New York: Springer-Verlag.

King, J. (2001) *Operational Risk: Measurement and Modelling*. Chichester: Wiley.

Kirk, D. (2000) Serious fraud – a banker's perspective, in Joseph J. Norton and George A. Walker (eds), *Banks: Fraud and Crime* (2nd edn). London and Hong Kong: LLP, pp. 13–28.

Klugman, S.A., Panjer, H. H. and Willmot, G.E. (1998) *Loss Models: From Data to Decisions*. New York: Wiley.

Legal Risk Review Committee (1992a) *Reducing Uncertainty: the Way Forward*, February.

Legal Risk Review Committee (1992b) *Final Report of the Legal Risk Review Committee*, October.

Mardia, K.V. (1970) Some problems of fitting for contingency-type bivariate distributions. *Journal of the Royal Statistical Society B*, 32, 254–264.

Malevergne, Y. and Sornette, D. (2001) Testing the Gaussian copula hypothesis for financial assets dependences. Available from www.ssrn.com.

Merton, R. (1974) On the pricing of corporate debt: the risk structure of interest rates. *Journal of Finance*, 29, 449–470.

Morgan, M.G. and M. Henrion (1990) *Uncertainty: A Guide to Dealing with Uncertainty in Quantitative Risk and Policy Analysis*. Cambridge: Cambridge University Press. (Reprinted in 1998.)

Nataf, A. (1962) Détermination des distributions dont les marges sont données. *Comptes Rendus de l'Académie des Sciences*, 255, 42–43.

Neapolitan, R. (1990) *Probabilistic Reasoning in Expert Systems: Theory and Algorithms*. New York: Wiley.

Nelsen, R.B. (1999) *An Introduction to Copulas*, Lecture Notes in Statistics 139. New York: Springer-Verlag.

Olson, G.N. (2000) Financial fraud and crime and lessons from the American bank and thrift crisis, in Joseph J. Norton and George A. Walker (eds), *Banks: Fraud and Crime* (2nd edn). London and Hong Kong: LLP, pp. 303–343.

Pearl, J. (1988) *Probabilistic Reasoning in Intelligent Systems*. San Francisco: Morgan Kaufmann.

RAFT International (2002) *Emerging Trends in Operational Risk within the Financial Services Industry*. Available from www.raft.co.uk.

Robert Morris Associates, British Bankers' Association and International Swaps and Derivatives Association (1999) *Operational Risk, The Next Frontier*. Philadelphia: RMA. Available from www.isda.org.

Schweizer, B. and Sklar, A. (1958) Espaces métriques aléatoires. *Comptes Rendues de l'Académie des Sciences de Paris*, 247, 2092–2094.

Shih, J., Samad-Khan, A. and Medapa, P. (2000) Is the size of an operational loss related to firm size? *Operational Risk*, January.

Tribus, M. (1969) *Rational Descriptions, Decisions and Designs*. New York: Pergamon Press.

Walden, I. (2000) Internet payment services and crime in cyberspace, in Joseph J. Norton and George A. Walker (eds), *Banks: Fraud and Crime* (2nd edn). London and Hong Kong: LLP, pp. 391–404.

Index